PUBLICATIONS OF THE
STATE HISTORICAL SOCIETY OF WISCONSIN

EDITED BY
JOSEPH SCHAFER
SUPERINTENDENT OF THE SOCIETY

THE FRENCH RÉGIME IN WISCONSIN
AND THE NORTHWEST

THE FRENCH RÉGIME IN WISCONSIN
AND THE NORTHWEST

The French Regime in Wisconsin and the Northwest

Louise Phelps Kellogg
Research Associate of
State Historical Society of Wisconsin

HERITAGE BOOKS
2007

HERITAGE BOOKS
AN IMPRINT OF HERITAGE BOOKS, INC.

Books, CDs, and more—Worldwide

For our listing of thousands of titles see our website
at
www.HeritageBooks.com

A Facsimile Reprint
Published 2007 by
HERITAGE BOOKS, INC.
Publishing Division
65 East Main Street
Westminster, Maryland 21157-5026

Copyright © 1925 State Historical Society of Wisconsin

Other books by Louise Phelps Kellogg:

Early Narratives Of The Northwest: 1634-1699

Frontier Advance on the Upper Ohio, 1778-1779

Frontier Retreat on the Upper Ohio, 1779-1781

The French Regime in Wisconsin and the Northwest

Documentary History of Dunmore's War, 1774
Reuben Gold Thwaites, LL.D. and Louise Phelps Kellogg, Ph.D

The Revolution on the Upper Ohio, 1775-1777
Reuben Gold Thwaites, LL.D. and Louise Phelps Kellogg, Ph.D

— Publisher's Notice —
In reprints such as this, it is often not possible to remove blemishes from the original. We feel the contents of this book warrant its reissue despite these blemishes and hope you will agree and read it with pleasure.

International Standard Book Number: 978-0-7884-1766-5

DEDICATED TO THE MEMORY
OF
REUBEN GOLD THWAITES
HISTORIAN OF NEW FRANCE AND WISCONSIN
MENTOR AND FRIEND

PREFACE

When so much has been written about the activities of the French in North America, the question arises: why another volume on this subject; why attempt to repeat Parkman, Winsor, and Thwaites? Most of what has been written, however, has centralized in the East, has made the St. Lawrence valley the standpoint of departure. In this volume the attempt has been made to write from the standpoint of the West, to make the Northwest the unit of consideration and to relate first the approach to the West, then its occupation and its economic development, then its external relations with other portions of New France, and lastly its share in the downfall of French power in America. In this study the sources have been consulted anew, and evaluated as though no one had ever done this before. The result has been to overthrow some accepted traditions of the French régime in Wisconsin, and to place a different perspective upon many accepted interpretations. The eighteenth century, which has been largely ignored by historians, although it was the period of greatest activity of the French in our region, has been accorded nearly one-half of the present volume. While due value has been given, we hope, to the motives of the French travelers, missionaries, and traders that appear on these pages, we have attempted no glorification, and no distortion of the results of their efforts.

It may be thought that the first chapters go too far afield in describing the earliest explorations on the coast lines and great rivers of the North American continent. The author desired to show the difficulties encountered in the approach to our region, and the progressive discovery of the Great Lakes. These large fresh-water seas were a geographical phenomenon beyond the ex-

PREFACE

perience of Old-World scientists and map makers, and only by the study of their misconceptions of them and their slow progress in finding their true nature, can we understand the first discoveries in our upper lakes region.

It will be noticed that, unlike most historical works of this kind, there is no chapter on the Indians. Since the entire history is concerned with the relations of the intruding white men with the tribesmen, and since French occupation was conditioned upon peace or war with the Indians, it has been thought unnecessary to attempt a separate description of the red men. Their history before the coming of the whites can only be known by archeological remains, and by such descriptions as have been written by the first traders and missionaries. Tribal migrations were influenced by relations with civilized men or with other tribes who had obtained power through the use of the superior weapons of the white men. He who wishes can find in this volume a history of Wisconsin Indians for one hundred and fifty years, since that forms the warp of the story, of which the coming of the French forms the woof.

The history of the French missions in the West has been narrated in a single chapter, because the period of their activity was relatively brief and covered only a small portion of the history we have attempted to write. Less than fifteen years of the missions in the West are detailed in the *Jesuit Relations*, and the years 1660 to 1675 were not the years of the greatest progress in the French occupation of our region. The mission sources are voluminous, but very limited in time and space. They are confined to small areas, as well as to a limited period. It seems to us that too much stress has been placed on the share of the missionaries in developing

PREFACE

the West, and that what they accomplished has been overemphasized. We have endeavored to give them their proper place as a small, highly specialized group, the reports of whose activities have assigned them an undue share in the opening of the West to civilization.

In conclusion, I wish to acknowledge my indebtedness to those who have aided me in the preparation of this book. The librarians of the New York Public Library, the John Carter Brown Library at Providence, the Widener Library at Harvard, and the Chicago Historical Society have been most courteous in affording me access to their treasures; while Waldo G. Leland, of the Carnegie Institution of Washington, allowed me to see portions of his forthcoming report on the Archives of Paris. Thanks are due to Deborah B. Martin and Arthur Neville, of Green Bay, who have given me the benefit of their broad knowledge of the French inhabitants of that place. I especially wish to acknowledge my obligations to Charles E. Brown, secretary of the Wisconsin Archeological Society, for his approval of such portions of this work as deal with his subject; to Dr. Joseph Schafer, superintendent of the State Historical Society of Wisconsin, for his constant interest and for reading the entire manuscript and giving it the value of his historical judgment; and to Edna Louise Jacobson, of the Society's staff, for her editorial criticism and her keen sense of form. All my colleagues on the staff of our Society have helped me by their active interest in the progress of this book. It is offered to the public and to all Westerners interested in our earliest history, with the hope that it may increase that interest and stimulate it anew.

LOUISE PHELPS KELLOGG

Madison, November, 1924.

CONTENTS

CHAPTER		PAGE
I	The North American Continent	1
II	The Great Rivers	15
III	Conjectures concerning the Great Lakes	31
IV	The Discovery of the Great Lakes, 1598-1632	44
V	The Voyage of Jean Nicolet, 1634-1635	65
VI	Tribal Wars and Dispersion, 1635-1654	84
VII	The First Traders, 1654-1670	101
VIII	The Missions, 1660-1675	139
IX	Annexation, 1671	179
X	Exploration of the Mississippi Valley, 1671-1682	191
XI	Iroquois War and the West, 1682-1689	221
XII	The West Evacuated, 1689-1701	243
XIII	The First Fox War, 1701-1716	268
XIV	The Reoccupation of the Posts, 1714-1727	290
XV	The Second Fox War, 1727-1738	314
XVI	Early Mining in the Northwest	341
XVII	Changes in Fur Trade Methods, 1738-1759	364
XVIII	The French Residents of Wisconsin	386
XIX	Intercolonial Rivalry for the Western Trade, 1741-1752	406
XX	The End of the French Régime in the Northwest, 1752-1761	423

ILLUSTRATIONS

	FACING PAGE
A Portion of Franquelin's Map of 1688	*Frontispiece*
Western Hemisphere of Lenox Globe, 1510-1512	2
Franciscus Monachus, *De Orbis*, 1524	6
French Ship of Sixteenth Century	20
The Fountain of the Great Lakes	32
Hakluyt-Wright-Molineaux Map of Great Lakes	42
Portion of Champlain's Manuscript Describing His West Indian Voyage	46
Map of North America, 1610	52
Champlain's Map of New France, 1632	62
A Winnebago Village	74
Wisconsin Landfall of Jean Nicolet, 1634	80
Amérique Septentrionale par N. Sanson d'Abbeville, 1650	92
Perrot's Contract for Western Trade, 1667	124
Map of the Great Lakes about 1680—Parkman No. 4	150
French Ship of Seventeenth Century	176
Jolliet and Marquette at Portage, 1673	194
Signature of Duluth, 1681	202
Hennepin's Map, 1683, Showing Royal Arms Fastened to a Tree	210
The Perrot Ostensorium	232
Site of Fort St. Antoine	242
Signature of Le Sueur, 1695	252
The West, 1650-1700	266
Signatures of Montigny and Marin, 1719	296
La Pointe Region	299
Carte du Pays des Sauvages Renards par Léry	314
The French Post near Trempealeau	328
The West, 1700-1760	364
The Tank Cottage, Green Bay, in 1906	392
Joseph Jourdain	400
Braddock's Defeat, July 9, 1755	428

xv

I. THE NORTH AMERICAN CONTINENT

IT IS well known that Columbus and his fellow discoverers of the fifteenth century sought not a new continent, but a new route to the eastern edge of the Old-World continent. America was a barrier, and so loath were the explorers to believe it was a continent, that for over fifty years geographers represented it either as a series of islands or as a projection of the eastern continent. Even the term "Novus Mundus," when applied to the new-found lands, was indicative only of land beyond the previous range of European knowledge. This mistake with reference to the western continent arose from a misconception of the size of the earth, which Columbus and his contemporaries estimated at about two-thirds of its real circumference. Columbus himself named the islands found upon his first voyage the West Indies, because he believed they lay not far from the East Indies he had sought. Even after he had found and explored the coast of South America, Columbus still believed in a passage through the West Indies to Japan and the coast of Cathay. This misconception is strikingly shown on the Lenox Globe, made between 1510 and 1512. South America appears as "Mundus Novus," Cuba as "Isabel," San Domingo as "Spagnola"; while just to the west is "Zipancri" (Japan) on the borders of the continent of Asia.[1]

The voyage of Magellan and his vessels around the world in 1519 to 1522 disproved the nearness of

[1] This tiny bronze globe, beautifully executed, is now in the New York Public Library. We reproduce it from a proof print made by Mr. Bierstadt in 1901, furnished by Victor H. Paltsits, chief of the American History Division.

America to Asia. Balboa before this had seen the South Sea on the farther side of South America. The coast line of South America was rapidly outlined by Spanish and Portuguese navigators. The discovery of North America proceeded more slowly, and with less precision. Historians do not know who first set foot upon our northern shores, nor where nor by what nation the landfall was made. Both the English and the Portuguese sent out expeditions to the northward before the fifteenth century ended. The Cortereals of Portugal sailed very far north. Many of the maps of the early sixteenth century show in the eastern part of the Atlantic Ocean a separate land mass marked "Terra Cortereal,"[2] over which waves the Portuguese flag.

The documentary sources for the English expeditions of the Cabots are few and contain but little information. A vessel under the pilot John Cabot set sail and returned to Bristol in 1497. The extent or the range of the voyage has never been definitely ascertained. A second expedition may have been undertaken the following year. The evidence for this is still more inconclusive than that for the first voyage. The English based their claim to North America upon these two voyages of discovery; while the earliest authentic chart of the Americas, made by Juan de la Cosa, companion of Columbus and pilot for the Spanish in South American waters, places English flags along a coast line northwest of Cuba for many degrees, with the legend

[2] The reason this land discovered by the Cortereals was placed so far east was to bring it east of the line of demarcation between the Spanish and Portuguese dominions as defined by the papal bull of 1493.

WESTERN HEMISPHERE OF LENOX GLOBE, 1510-1512
From the New York Public Library

THE NORTH AMERICAN CONTINENT 3

"mar descubierta por inglese" ("sea discovered by the English").[3]

The earliest Spanish voyage to the North American mainland was that undertaken by Columbus in 1502, when he touched the shore of Honduras and sailed southward to the isthmus, proving the continuity of the coast line from sixteen degrees north to eight degrees south of the equator. Anonymous and unauthorized expeditions seem to have been made about this same time to the Florida coast and some distance north. These are known only by the maps of the period—that of Alberto Cantino in the Modena library, and a marine chart of Nicolay de Canerio discovered in 1890 at Paris. Both these maps were executed within the first five years of the sixteenth century, and both show a land mass northwest of the West Indies with circumstantial names and exact delineation.[4] These maps make it "very certain that more of the geography of the New World was known in 1502 than can now be gathered from the records of the few official expeditions made under the flags of Spain, of England, and of Portugal."[5]

Only five years later, the Gulf of Mexico and the entire peninsula of Florida were charted by pilots of whose expeditions we have no account except that recorded by the scientific geographers of the day. In 1507 Martin Waldseemüller issued a *Universal Cos-*

[3] A reproduction of this famous chart of 1500, now in the Royal Library at Madrid, is in E. M. Avery, *History of the United States* (Cleveland, 1904), i, 208.
[4] The Cantino map is reproduced in E. L. Stevenson, *Maps Illustrating the Early Discovery and Exploration in America 1502-1530*, Facsimile No. I. The Canerio marine chart is issued by the same author under the joint auspices of the American Geographical Society and the Hispanic Society of America (New York, 1907-1908).
[5] Stevenson, *op. cit.*, p. 35.

mography, upon which the name "America" appeared for the first time. This word was placed upon the southern continent about the region of Argentine. The North American continent was separated from the southern by a wide strait in the latitude of Honduras.[6] The Gulf of Mexico was distinctly marked, and into its northern coast several rivers ran. The peninsula of Florida on this map swung too far east, but was drawn with considerable skill, while the whole length of the Atlantic coast appeared to about sixty degrees of north latitude, where it was cut off sharply with the words "terra ultra incognita" (land beyond this unknown). Both ends of this northern continent bore the royal flag of Spain. Upon the marine chart issued by the same geographer in 1516, found at the same time and place with the *Cosmography* of 1507, the name "America" was dropped and North America was distinctly declared to be a part of Asia.[7] Waldseemüller, on this marine chart, represented a strait ten degrees in width between North and South America. Evidently he was not informed of Balboa's expedition in 1513 across the

[6] The discovery in 1901 of this long-sought map by Professor Fischer in the library of Prince Waldburg at Wolfegg Castle, caused a great sensation among Americanists, and decided several disputed points in early cartography. The great map, showing the American continent with a strait through in the vicinity of Honduras, is supplemented by a small hemisphere at the top giving the same continent without a passage. A facsimile of this map is in the Wisconsin Historical Library.

[7] Marked "Terra de Cuba, Asie Partis." Professor Edward Channing thinks that Waldseemüller hesitated between the two ideas of North America as a separate continent or as a projection of Asia, and finally decided for the latter. Other early maps showing North America as a projection of Asia are: the Bartholomew Columbus map of 1506; an anonymous *Globus Mundi* of 1509, apparently of German origin, in the John Carter Brown Library; a manuscript map in the same library, in Glareanus, *De principiis*, of 1516.

Isthmus of Panama. Nor did he indicate on this chart any of the Ponce de Leon expedition of 1512 or 1513 to Florida, since the Gulf of Mexico, the peninsula of Florida, and the continental coast of North America merely duplicated those of the map of 1507.

The enterprise of the Spaniards in exploration was unceasing. With a settled base in the West Indies, they had by the quarter-century after their first discovery, explored and annexed all the adjacent mainland. Cortes from 1519 to 1522 conquered and explored Mexico. Pineda in 1519 was authorized to continue the work of Ponce de Leon. He sailed around the entire gulf from Florida to Vera Cruz. Somewhere about the middle of the northern shore of the gulf he entered the Rio del Espíritu Santo, long supposed to be the mouth of the Mississippi. This first appears upon a Spanish map, now in the Royal Library at Turin, supposed to have been drawn about 1523.[8]

The eastern coast of North America was followed by a caravel sent in 1521 by Lucas Vasques de Ayllon, of San Domingo, that went as far north as the Carolinas. Two years later the same adventurer received a patent from the government for exploration and settlement. His advance exploration in 1525 is said to have been carried as high as Delaware Bay. He himself settled in 1526 a colony at San Miguel, variously supposed to have been in Virginia or on one of the rivers of the Carolinas. The commandant himself perished of malarial fever, and the survivors of the colony hastened to return to San Domingo.[9]

In 1524 a grand council of pilots was held at Badajos,

[8] Stevenson, *Facsimile* No. VI.
[9] E. G. Bourne, *Spain in America*, in American Nation Series (New York, 1904), 138-140; Justin Winsor, *Narrative and Critical History of America* (New York, 1886), ii, 238-241.

6   THE FRENCH RÉGIME

to determine the demarcation between the claims of
Spain and Portugal. One of the experts in attendance
was Estévan Gómez, who had deserted from Magellan's
expedition on the coast of South America and had
returned to Spain. Gómez insisted that somewhere in
north latitude a strait could be found through the
American land mass, and the Spanish king gave him a
caravel with which to test his theory. Gómez sailed
northwest and made land somewhere on our coast
between Maine and Newfoundland; then sailed slowly
south, entering every bay and inlet in search of the
desired channel.[10] He finally reached the land familiar
to the Spanish by their exploration of Florida, and
returned to Spain convinced of the continental character of the American world.

Spain had now explored all the North American
coast from Labrador to Panama. The results of these
explorations quickly appeared upon the globes, maps,
and charts of the period. One of the earliest to depict
the continuous coast line of North America is a small
hemisphere found in the work of Franciscus Monachus.
This is patterned after Waldseemüller's maps and shows
a channel through the land mass of America, by which
North America is made a part of Asia; but the coast line
assumes a definite outline that approximates the true
projection.[11] A manuscript world map in the Laurentian
Library at Florence, prepared between 1525 and 1527,
is probably the earliest map to show a continuous coast
line for the two continents from Labrador to the Straits

[10] See the notice of a Spanish fort on the Hudson, in *Journal
of Jasper Danckaerts*, Original Narratives Series (New York, 1913),
215.

[11] *De Orbis Situ ac Descriptione. . . Francisci Monachi*
(1524). We reproduce this map by special permission from the
John Carter Brown Library at Providence.

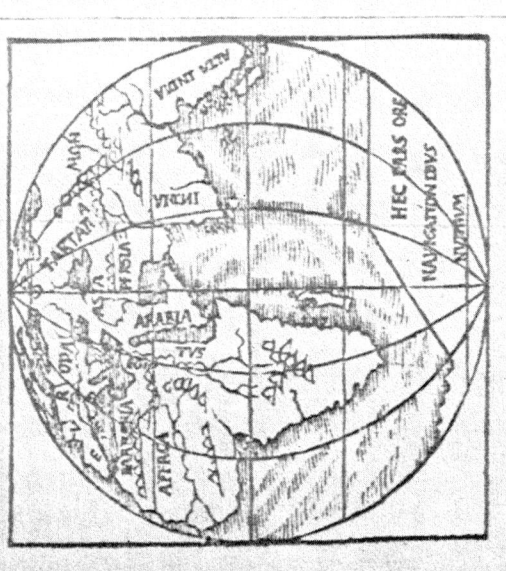

FRANCISCUS MONACHUS, *De Orbis*, 1524

of Magellan.[12] Upon this the coast line of North America trends too far east, as it does upon most of the Spanish maps of this period; the outlines, however, of the east coast of Newfoundland, of the coast of Maine, of Florida, and of the Gulf of Mexico are very distinct. Trees, indicating forests, cover the entire North American interior, among which range strange wild animals difficult to identify. The nomenclature of all the northern portion is that of Gómez. In the Gulf of Mexico the names are those of Ponce de Leon and Pineda. A large lake contains the legend "City of Mexico." A small portion of the Pacific coast appears stretching south from Mexico to Colombia.

A dated Spanish map (1527) now in the library at Weimar, formerly ascribed to Ferdinand Columbus, became the prototype of most of the later Spanish maps. Like the one just described, it outlines the entire continent of America. A large inlet appears on the New England coast, into which a great river flows, called "Juan Baptista."[13] Another Sevillian map of the same date was sent to the English ambassador to Spain by the merchant Robert Thorne. This is less well-developed than the Weimar map. It has long been known, since it first appeared in Richard Hakluyt's *Divers Voyages Touching the Discovery of America*.[14]

Another famous map of Spanish origin appeared two years later under the name of the pilot Diego Ribero. It is similar to the Weimar map of 1527, but contains more coast names and certain interesting legends. The

[12] Stevenson, Facsimile No. VII.
[13] This map is reproduced in Stevenson, Facsimile No. IX. Harrisse thinks the bay and river intended for the Bay of Fundy. We think it the Penobscot, as the "Bay of Many Islands" on other Spanish maps with Gómez names has been so identified.
[14] Published in London in 1582. In the Glasgow edition of Hakluyt's works (1903-1905), the Thorne map is in vol. ii, p. 176.

interior of what became New France is called "the land of Estévan Gómez, which he discovered in 1525." This map, or one from which it was drawn, became the prototype of the Spanish maps for a generation.[15]

Of the three great monarchs that ruled Europe during the first half of the sixteenth century, only Charles V of Spain seriously concerned himself with the exploitation of the New World. Henry VIII of England, following the example of his father, who patronized the Cabots, made several unsuccessful attempts to set on foot expeditions to North America.[16] Francis I of France, immersed in his Italian wars, seemed for some time oblivious of the rich prizes in the New World which were falling to his rival. The French, however, were not unrepresented on the North American shores. Some writers claim that French fisher folk preceded the Cabots and Cortereals to the shores of Newfoundland. By 1508 their commerce was well established, and the island now known as Cape Breton had received its name.[17] In 1509 a Norman navigator from Dieppe brought seven savages to France, whose appearance was the wonder of the day. When in 1511 the queen of Spain was making plans to send a voyage of exploration to Newfoundland, claimed to be within the sphere of Spanish influence, she directed that pilots should be sought in Brittany.[18] The markets of Rouen were supplied with fish from the Banks as early as 1506, and the annual fishing fleets brought back to all the French

[15] Stevenson, Facsimile No. XI.
[16] H. P. Biggar, "The Precursors of Jacques Cartier," *Publications of the Canadian Archives*, No. 5, p. xxix-xxx.
[17] Biggar, *op. cit.*, p. xxii-xxiii; Henry Harrisse, *Découverte et Evolution Cartographique de Terre Neuve* (Paris, 1900), p. xxx-xlix. See also the Ruysch map in Ptolemy for 1508.
[18] Biggar, *op. cit.*, 107-108. The expedition was never undertaken.

seaports great stores of cod. A beginning had also been made in the barter with the Indians for furs. All these commercial enterprises, however, were private concerns, and made but slight impression on the scientific knowledge of the New World.[19]

Francis I became interested in geographical discovery when the one remaining caravel of Magellan's fleet of circumnavigation appeared in 1522 at the port of San Lucar. The sensation paralleled that occasioned by Columbus' arrival thirty years before. Magellan himself had been killed in the Philippines; among the survivors of the expedition, however, was the Italian, Antonio Pigafetta, who became its historian. On his way to his home in Lombardy Pigafetta passed through France, where the queen mother, Louise of Savoy, was regent for Francis during his absence on a war expedition. The returned mariner was the hero of the court, which was thronged with Italians of every type, for Francis I was then the most renowned patron of Renaissance talent in Christendom. Pigafetta, in return for his cordial entertainment, presented to the regent a copy of his journal of the voyage.[20] The interest of the king was at once aroused, and he consulted the admiral of France—an Italian whom he called Bonnivet—with regard to an official French voyage of exploration. Bonnivet enthusiastically embraced the plan, and assured the king that an Italian navigator then living at Dieppe had long desired to undertake such a voyage.

Giovanni Verrazano was born at Florence and was a member of one of its prominent families of merchant

---

[19] Such legends as "Terra de los Bretones" and "land discovered by the Bretons" appear on many of the early maps, notably the Wolfenbüttel map, Stevenson, Facsimile No. VIII.

[20] James A. Robertson, *Magellan's Voyage around the World by Antonio Pigafetta* (Cleveland, 1906), ii, 189.

princes. He was both a scholar and a man of affairs, and had long cherished the desire to reach the East by sailing west. Whether he had had practical experience in navigation is not known; but theoretically he was well equipped to conduct such an expedition. At Dieppe he had come in contact with the pilots of the fishing boats, and learned of their routes across the ocean. Summoned to court, five months after Pigafetta's visit, Verrazano made a favorable impression upon the king, who gave orders that four ships should be fitted out for the intended voyage of discovery.

The preparations for this undertaking were made with great secrecy; nevertheless the Portuguese ambassador learned of them and informed his master that "Maestro Giovanni Verrazano goes to discover Cathay."[21] By the middle of 1523 the ships were ready, but from storms and other vicissitudes all were abandoned but one, *La Dauphine*, which set sail from Madeira in January, 1524. March 7 land was sighted in what Verrazano calculated to be north latitude thirty-four.[22] Thence he coasted south for a short distance, but recognizing that the French were approaching too near to the lands of their Spanish rivals, he turned his

[21] The long controversy which has been waged over the authenticity of Verrazano's report of his voyage was determined in his favor by the discovery in 1909, in a library at Rome, of a hitherto unknown manuscript of his report to the king. This account is annotated by Verrazano's own hand, and its discovery explains the inconsistencies in the previously-known accounts. It is also fuller than these, and adds to our knowledge of this first careful survey of the eastern coast of the United States. It is published in American Scenic and Historic Society of New York, *Fifteenth Annual Proceedings* (Albany, 1910), 137-226. All our citations are taken from this edition. For the reports of the Portuguese, see page 153.

[22] Verrazano's calculations were some degrees out of the way. His landfall seems to have been on the coast of North Carolina, but probably south of Cape Fear.

prow northward and by March 25 had reached his first landfall. By this time the southern spring was in full flower, and Verrazano was enchanted with the beauty of the virgin land, which he called Annunziata, from the Florentine feast of the date of his return. Passing north along the coast of Annunziata the explorer found an "isthmus a mile in width and about 200 long, in which, from the ship was seen the oriental sea between the west and north. This is the one, without doubt, which goes about the extremity of India, China, and Cathay. We navigated along the said isthmus with the continual hope of finding some strait or true promontory at which the land would end towards the north in order to be able to penetrate to those blessed shores of Cathay. To which isthmus was given by the discoverer [the name] Verrazanio: as all the land found was named Francesco for our Francis."[23] This was the origin of the famous "Verrazano's Sea," whose non-appearance in the known copies of the letter of the discoverer had puzzled scholars for nearly four centuries. It is not difficult with this passage before one to believe that Verrazano, coasting Pamlico Sound and seeing the waters dashing beyond the barrier islands, thought of the strait portrayed by Waldseemüller and supposed he had found it, barred only by a narrow isthmus.

Thence Verrazano continued north, noting the large forests of Virginia and Delaware, which region he termed Arcadia, for "the beauty of the trees." He also mentions the wild grape vines, roses, violets, and lilies. Farther along the coast he placed the names of his friends and patrons, Cardinal di Lorena, Admiral Bonnivet, and the Count de St. Pol. For New York

[23] Verrazano's narrative, 185. All this citation appears for the first time in the recently found manuscript.

harbor he reserved the name of the king's sister Marguerite, "who vanquishes the other matrons of modesty and art." Block Island was named "Louise" for the queen mother. At Newport *La Dauphine* tarried fifteen days, when the bay received the title of "Refugio." Maine, with its islands, was to the explorer the "Dalmatia of the New World." At last, after "six hundred leagues and more of new land," he arrived near the shores with which he was already familiar from the descriptions and charts of the Breton and Norman fishers. Then, since provisions and stores were growing scanty, the captain turned homeward, and in July entered the harbor of Dieppe.

Verrazano's voyage of 1524 accomplished several results. It convinced the explorer himself that the globe was much larger than had previously been held by mathematicians and geographers, and that America was a continent standing midway between East and West. He calculated that the coast line of the New World stretched from fifty-four degrees south latitude to more than seventy degrees north latitude, longer than Asia or Europe.[24] These conclusions, and the names given on his voyage, soon appeared on world maps. The well-known parchment map of Vesconte de Maggiolo, dated 1527, which is preserved in the library at Milan, is one of the earliest to show Verrazano's discoveries. Upon this map the name "Francesca" appears across North America; Portuguese and Spanish names jostle the new names of Verrazano along its coast; the western ocean comes to the edge of Carolina with only an isthmus between.[25] Still more illustrative is the map of Gerolamo Verrazano, brother of the explorer, found in the archives at Rome. This gives the

[24] See Verrazano's conclusions in his narrative, 200-202.
[25] Stevenson, Facsimile No. X.

family name "Verrazana" to the newly found land, shows Verrazano's Sea on the west, and on the coast of the United States places the names taken from his brother's journal, differing widely from those of the Spanish maps of the time.[26] Verrazano's Sea also appears upon the Ulpius Globe of 1542, but the explorer's conclusion concerning a separate continent is thereon ignored, since the North American coast line is but a projection of Asia.[27]

Verrazano's welcome upon his return was diminished by the evil days upon which France had fallen during his absence. The struggle between the great monarchs for power had grown apace. Francis was at the lowest ebb of his fortunes. His kingdom had been invaded from Picardy, when the enemy had approached within thirty miles of Paris. This enemy having been repulsed by heroic efforts, Francis had sent an army into Italy, where Bonnivet was seriously wounded at the battle of Sestia. The next year he was killed at Pavia, where the king himself fell a prisoner into the hands of his archenemy Charles V. The voyage which placed New France upon the map of America was forgotten, and its discoverer ignored. Verrazano's personal fate is not certain; he is thought to have undertaken a voyage on his own account in 1527, and to have perished at sea.

His fame has been even more the sport of fortune.

[26] Stevenson, Facsimile No. XII. An account of this map was published in the *American Magazine of History*, August, 1878, by B. F. de Costa. This map, or one similar, may have been the one presented to Henry VIII, referred to by Hakluyt in 1582, who says it was then in the custody of Michael Lok. Lok's map published by Hakluyt shows "Mare de Verrazana 1524" upon the North American interior.

[27] This globe is in New York Historical Society; with the exception of the legend "Verrazana sivi Nova Gallia a Verrazano Florentino Comperta Anno Sal M D [blank]," the names are not those given by the French explorer.

A man of culture and refined appreciation, he prepared a beautiful description of his voyage, which was garbled and mutilated before publication, and not until four centuries passed was it recovered in its original form. Not only so, but the discrepancies and mistakes of the published journal led competent scholars to doubt the authenticity of the voyage itself. No such expedition was undertaken, it was claimed; the account was forged in order to give glory to France and to Florence. Worse than all, Verrazano's character was assailed; his identity was confounded with that of a notorious French pirate who was hanged at the yard-arm.[28] Thus the gentle Italian merchant, man of letters, friend of Paolo Giovio (Jovius) and Pallavicino, business partner of the Florentine Rucellai, scholar, gentleman, and dreamer, was defamed and his accomplishment denied. At last, after the lapse of centuries, his true fame is restored, and he is placed among his compeers, the great Italian navigators who gave to Spain, to England, and to France their claims to the New World. After 1525 the name "Francesca" appears across the continent of North America between Florida of the Spaniards and Baccalos (Newfoundland) and Labrador of the Portuguese and English. Upon the most fertile and most temperate region of the New World Verrazano placed the French flag. Thereafter France had but to colonize and occupy. Verrazano also announced the continental character of America, its true position between the East and the West. He completed the work of Columbus, the Cabots, and Magellan; and in a narrative of surpassing beauty gave us the earliest description of the eastern coast of the United States.

[28] For a summary of the controversy, see Winsor, *America*, iv, 16-28. Even Harrisse, who maintained the reality of Verrazano's voyage, identified him with the pirate Jean Florin of La Rochelle.

II. THE GREAT RIVERS

AMERICA, within forty years after Columbus' discovery, was by most cosmographers believed to be a continent. Its South American coasts had early been made known.[1] North America, however, more gradually emerged upon the globes and maps of the sixteenth century. The northward discoveries of the Spaniards and Verrazano's French voyage of 1524 outlined the Atlantic coast. The Gulf of Mexico was explored by 1520. The Pacific shore of Mexico was known by 1525. Thence the Spanish navigators continued northward, until in 1542-43 Cabrillo had sailed along the entire length of the California coast.[2] The interior of North America was as yet an unknown region. Hidden away in its wilderness fastness, at the head of its two greatest water systems, lay the region we now know as Wisconsin. Before this could be explored the great rivers of the continent must be discovered.

To France belongs the honor of finding the St. Lawrence, and of planting upon its banks the first colony. After the death of Verrazano, Francis I began to emerge from his difficulties; the Ladies' Peace of Cambrai, arranged in 1529 by Francis' mother and Charles V's aunt, gave France a breathing space after its long wars. Bonnivet had been succeeded in the

---

[1] The outline of South America with its west coast appears roughly upon maps as early as 1507. The Franciscus Monachus hemisphere of 1524 shows the outline of South America very well.

[2] For Cabrillo's expedition, see a good description in Woodbury Lowery, *Spanish Settlements within the Present Limits of the United States* (New York, 1911), 340-350. See also on early Pacific exploration, Joseph Schafer, *History of the Pacific Northwest* (New York, 1918), 1-6.

admiralty by Philippe Chabot, who urged the continued exploration of the New World. Chabot secured for the second French official voyage of exploration the services of Jacques Cartier, an experienced pilot of St. Malo. Of Cartier's early life little is known. He had been at sea for several years, is thought to have visited Brazil, and is known to have accompanied the Breton and Norman fishing fleets to the Banks of Newfoundland. Now, at the age of forty-three, a bronzed and experienced navigator, Cartier was eager to attempt to find a northwest passage through America. His little fleet of two small ships, outfitted by the king, left St. Malo April 20, 1534. On this first voyage Cartier went around Newfoundland and explored the entire St. Lawrence Gulf. Fogs withheld from his view the mouth of the great river which empties into it. Twice he thought he had found the entrance to a strait leading to the South Sea, and twice he was doomed to disappointment—once when pushing through Belle Isle Strait on the north shore of Newfoundland; once when exploring Chaleur Bay. July 24, upon the shore of this latter bay, the explorer erected a cross carrying a royal shield, and took possession of all the country for the king of France. He then determined to postpone further exploration until another year, and turned his prow homeward, bearing with him in token of his discovery two Indians enticed aboard ship at Gaspé Bay.[3]

[3] The narratives of Cartier's first and second voyages first appeared in Giovanni Battista Ramusio, *Delle Navigationi et Viaggi* (Venice, 1556); the University of Wisconsin Library has an edition of Ramusio of 1606. There are several modern editions of Cartier's voyages, the latest of which is H. P. Biggar, *The Voyages of Jacques Cartier, Publications of the Canadian Archives*, No. 11 (Ottawa, 1924). This chapter was written before the appearance of this edition; therefore our references are to that of James P. Baxter, *A Memoir of Jacques Cartier* (New York, 1906).

THE GREAT RIVERS 17

Cartier's little ships arrived at St. Malo on September 5; their arrival created an intense interest, and the populace crowded the roads as Cartier and his two strange guests wended their way to make report to the king. The Indians proved tractable, and as they learned French, spoke of a great river upon which they customarily lived, having been visitors at the seacoast when captured by the French. Cartier hoped that this great river of which the Indians spoke might prove to be the channel he longed to find. He requested of the king permission to undertake a second voyage. This permission was graciously accorded. So great was the king's interest, that he visited St. Malo in person to inspect the preparations there being made. By the middle of May these preparations were complete; a fleet of three ships was outfitted; three days before sailing, the bishop blessed the crews and their commander at a solemn ceremony in the St. Malo cathedral. The nineteenth the little fleet put to sea. May of 1535 was unusually stormy; the ships were driven apart by gales. Finally, however, they all safely rendezvoused in one of the ports Cartier had found on his former voyage. Thence he set out to explore the bleak northern shores of the still nameless St. Lawrence Gulf. August 10 a bay on this north shore was named the St. Lawrence.[4] Coasting slowly along, the navigator found that the shores began to open, and at this point his Indian guides recognized the region and informed their captain that he was now in the mouth of the great river. Cartier still hoped the stream might prove to be a channel; great was his disappointment as

[4] The name "St. Lawrence" was very gradually extended to the gulf. The river was not so named for over a generation after Cartier. The Spanish historian López de Gomara was one of the first to apply in 1552-53 this name to the river. Even in Champlain's day it was commonly called the "Great River of Canada."

the estuary "went always narrowing clear to Canada." Canada, as thus named, was an Indian term for a locality on the great river in the vicinity of Quebec; this latter place, with its village, called by the Indian guides Stadacona, had been their early home. At their direction Cartier cast anchor off the island he first called "Isle de Bacchus," but later christened "Orleans." The great rock of Quebec towered above him; the Indian villagers received their lost chiefs like men returned from the dead.

The French were eager to explore farther along the river, but their Indian hosts either from cupidity or from fear attempted to detain them. It was the latter part of September before Cartier in his smallest vessel pushed up the St. Lawrence to its widespread, which he named Lac d'Angoulême. Here the explorers were obliged to leave their pinnace and take to the ship's boats; on the second of October they arrived at Hochelaga, the Huron village then on the site of Montreal. Above it towered the mountain which the French fitly named Mont Royal. The Indians led their visitors to the summit of this royal mountain, where was spread before their view a vast landscape wherein the two great branches of the river might be seen. The natives tried to describe to Cartier the geography of the land. They told him by signs that toward the southwest the river was obstructed by rapids, such as those of Lachine, whose boiling waters had stopped the passage of his own boats. Upon this river after passing the rapids one might voyage for many days. Pointing to the northwest they told of the other river, now known as the Ottawa, whereon one might sail for a month before "entering into two or three great lakes of water very wide; then, that one finds a fresh-water sea of which there is no

THE GREAT RIVERS 19

mention of having seen the end."[5] Thence came the red copper, such as Cartier had first seen at the mouth of the Saguenay; also silver, and yellow copper, or gold.[6] From these confused accounts of the Indians Cartier deduced a geographical error that had much influence on later cartography. He understood the natives to say that the Ottawa came from the same region as the Saguenay River;[7] he thereupon conceived a country named Saguenay, in form a great island, lying north of the St. Lawrence, bounded on the east by Saguenay River and on the west by the Ottawa. Somewhere in this region, he thought, lay the great fresh-water sea of unknown dimensions.

Cartier returned from Montreal, and wintered on St. Charles River near Quebec. Cold and disease attacked his sailors; after suffering greatly, the little band of pioneers in the spring prepared to return to France. May 3, 1536, Cartier raised a cross upon which he placed a scroll inscribed "Franciscus primus Dei gratia Francorum rex regnat," thus annexing the entire valley of the St. Lawrence to the crown of France. The wondering natives were then informed that they now

[5] Baxter, *Cartier*, 170-171, 189. Baxter thinks the reference was to Lake Ontario. It is clearly to the sources of the Ottawa, to Lake Nipissing, Georgian Bay, and Lakes Huron and Superior beyond.

[6] Stephen Leacock, *The Mariner of St. Malo*, Chronicles of Canada Series (Toronto, 1914), 78, thinks the Indians of that early day had some knowledge of the recently discovered gold and silver deposits of the upper Ottawa. Probably, however, Cartier misunderstood them. So far as known, the northern Indians knew no metal but the red copper of Lake Superior.

[7] Cartier had been given a large red copper knife at the mouth of the Saguenay River (Baxter, *Cartier*, 136, 206), which he was told came from its sources. This was doubtless Lake Superior copper; there was a portage route from the upper lakes to the Saguenay, and intertribal trade was active.

belonged to a great and mighty "master" across the sea. The Indian chief of Stadacona and some of his braves were embarked by the white men on board their ships in order to visit their new sovereign. In answer to the remonstrances of the villagers they were promised that their friends should return to them in a twelvemonth.

It was the sixth of July when Cartier's fleet cast anchor once more at St. Malo, bringing news of the discovery of a vast river and of the annexation of its territory to the kingdom of France. Unfortunately for Cartier, Francis I was again plunged into war with his rival Charles V. Admiral Chabot was absent leading an army in Italy; French frontiers were exposed to the danger of invasion. Two years after Cartier's return a truce was signed. Francis then took time to talk with his explorer and to interest himself once more in the lands beyond the sea. He spent much time poring over maps and charts, of which the Portuguese seemed to him the best; he conversed of the "river in the land of Cod, whither he has twice sent"; and was prepared to listen to Cartier's projects for further exploration. The Breton navigator proposed to the king that the region of Saguenay should be searched for gold and silver mines. He also suggested taking with him goldsmiths and other artisans to form a permanent colony.[8] For some reason these preparations were delayed until 1541. Then Francis determined to make a nobleman of the court, Jean François de la Rocque Sieur de Roberval, commander of the enterprise; while to Cartier was assigned the post of chief pilot.

[8] H. P. Biggar, "Charles V and the Discovery of Canada," in Royal Historical Society, *Transactions* (London, 1917), 149-150. The Spanish sent spies to watch Cartier's preparations of 1541, and hurried off two caravels to see what direction he would take.

FRENCH SHIP OF SIXTEENTH CENTURY
From map of Verrazano, 1529

Meanwhile all the Indians who had been kidnapped in Canada had died in France, except one small girl. Cartier took her back with him to her native land. Roberval's preparations not being completed, his pilot sailed without him May 23, 1541, and in due time cast anchor before Stadacona. He explained to the then chief the absence of his predecessor by claiming he had received so much honor in France that he preferred to remain there. The chief, not eager to be disturbed in his present honors, took the news calmly. Cartier chose as the site of his permanent colony the Cape Rouge River about twelve miles above Quebec. The explorer had brought with him small boats in which he planned to pass the rapids and to explore both branches of the great river above Mont Royal. In September, 1541, he essayed the discovery. He passed the first great rapid in safety; Indian hostility although veiled soon began to trouble him. He dared not continue farther into the strange country; from the second rapid he returned to his fort on the lower river. There he passed a winter full of distress, constantly fearful of Indian attacks, frequently in want of food and fuel.

The winter finally ended; yet Roberval, the governor of the colony, did not arrive. Cartier felt unable longer to endure the strain. He abandoned the fort, returned to his ships, and sailed down the river only to meet in a Newfoundland harbor Roberval outward bound with a cargo of colonists for the New World. For some unexplained reason Cartier would not return with his superior, but continued his voyage to France. Roberval, having recruited his colonists from the offscourings of jails and men of the street, established his colony on the site that Cartier had abandoned. Although better equipped and provisioned than his predecessor, Roberval had great trouble with his colonists and with the neighboring Indians. Francy Roy, as he named his new post, existed through the winter of 1542-43, and in the spring crops were sown and plans made for further exploration. June 5, 1543, Roberval, with an expedition of eight barks manned by seventy persons, set forth up the St. Lawrence River. Nine days later three of these ships returned with the news that one ship had been lost and several Frenchmen drowned. Five days later five more of the captains returned, leaving Roberval upon the upper river. What his experiences were and how far he penetrated we do not know, since at this point his journal stops abruptly.[9] All we do know is that Roberval in his turn became discouraged, and in the autumn of 1543 abandoned Francy Roy and returned to France.[10] Cartier may have gone that same summer with supplies for Roberval; but that is not certain. After this the discoverer of the St. Lawrence seems to have rested on his laurels and to have passed a peaceful and honored old age near his native port of St. Malo.

Thus ended the official expeditions sent by Francis I to North America. The great river of the north had been discovered and explored as far as its first rapids. The claim of France to the entire basin of the river had been asserted. The foundation for a French sphere of influence in the New World had been laid.

The discoveries of Cartier did not immediately appear upon contemporary maps. The map makers were chiefly in the employ of the kings of Spain and

[9] The extracts of Cartier's journal of his third voyage, and the voyage of Roberval, were first published by Richard Hakluyt, *The principall navigations, voiages, traffiques, and discoveries of the English Nation* (London, 1600). Hakluyt obtained these documents from the heirs of Cartier. They are republished in Baxter, *Cartier*, 219-242, and in Biggar, *Cartier*, 249-270.
[10] Baxter, *Cartier*, 50-51, 363-387.

THE GREAT RIVERS 23

Portugal, who were intensely jealous of any expeditions to the New World undertaken by rival monarchs. Cartier's own map, which is described in 1587 by his grandnephew as a sea chart still in use, has been lost.[11] The map made in 1541 by Nicolas Desliens of Dieppe shows a large indentation for the Gulf of St. Lawrence, whereon are a few of Cartier's names.[12] The well-known Sebastian Cabot map of 1544 makes the St. Lawrence River one of its most prominent features; the names are Portuguese, translated from Cartier's French. This map, however, shows no fork in the upper St. Lawrence.[13] A sketch map of Roberval's pilot, Jean Alphonse, in his *La Cosmographie* of 1545, shows the St. Lawrence only in its lower course; the Saguenay he makes a channel leading into a Sea of Saguenay at the north.[14] The map prepared in 1546 by Pierre Desceliers for the Dauphin has all the data furnished by both Cartier and Roberval. Roberval's portrait appears on the map, as well as colored pictures of animals and savages. This chart shows both branches of the upper river, the *sault* at Lachine, and places a country named Saguenay to the westward.[15] The Nicolas Vallard map of 1547, also made in Dieppe, has the name "G. lorens" on a small bay on the northern shore of the gulf. The upper portion of the river resembles that of the Des-

[11] Baxter, *Cartier*, 368-369.
[12] Reproduced in Hantsch and Schmidt, *Kartographische Denkmäler* (Leipzig, 1903). A copy is in the Wisconsin Historical Library, furnished by the New York Public Library.
[13] For the Cabot map, see *Canadian Archives Report*, 1897, 253; the American portion is in United States Bureau of Ethnology, *Fourteenth Annual Report*, 322.
[14] Alphonse's *Cosmographie* is in manuscript in Le Bibliothéque Nationale, at Paris. Baxter, *Cartier*, 253, reproduces the sketch map of the St. Lawrence.
[15] E. L. Stevenson has issued a facsimile of the Desceliers map. See also Biggar, *Jacques Cartier*, 224.

celiers map.[16] This became the common type for the maps of North America until the time when suggestions of the Great Lakes began to appear. The discovery of a great river, with the necessary expanse of territory which it drained, revived the idea that northern North America must be a part of Asia. The king's commission to Cartier for his third voyage in 1541 declared that he had "discovered the large countries of Canada and Hochelaga, making an end of Asia, on the western side." Jean Alphonse wrote that "these lands lie over against Tartary, and I doubt not but they stretch toward Asia, according to the roundness of the world. And, therefore, it were good to have a small ship of seventy tons to discover the coast of New France on the back side of Florida."[17]

The "back side of Florida" could not then be explored by the French, as Alphonse must well have known. He himself lost his life in 1557 in a naval battle with the Spaniards, whose explorers had by that time carefully examined the "back side of Florida" for their own purposes. As the French were the first on the great river of the north, so to the Spanish belongs the honor of first discovering the lower courses of the Mississippi. This discovery was, however, more by accident than by design, nor is it possible to say who was the first white man who found the great river. We have already noted that when the Gulf of Mexico appeared in outline upon the map of 1507, several rivers were shown entering its waters. Whether any of these represented the mouth of the Mississippi it is impossible to determine. The first official expedition to the gulf coast was that of Alonzo

[16] Reproduction in Winsor, *America*, iv, 87, and in Biggar, *Jacques Cartier*, 160, 259.

[17] Baxter, *Cartier*, 339. North America as a part of Asia appears on maps as late as 1562.

THE GREAT RIVERS

de Pineda in 1519. Whether he saw the mouth of the Mississippi is an open question. He placed upon the map, "Rio del Espíritu Santo," a name afterwards applied to the Father of Waters. Recent research, however, tends to the belief that Pineda's "Espíritu Santo" was the Mobile River.[18]

Eight years after Pineda's exploration Panfilo de Narvaez obtained a royal grant to the country lying between Florida and Mexico; there he hoped to find another Peru. In June, 1527, this grantee sailed from Spain with a large expedition to explore and, if need be, to conquer his kingdom. It was not until April 15, 1528, that Narvaez landed on the west coast of Florida, probably at Tampa Bay.[19] The next day he took possession of the country for the crown of Spain. Then Narvaez made his fatal mistake of sending away his ships, and of attempting a land march through the country. A rumor of a great city named Apalache, where gold and pearls were common, led the wanderers to a wretched thatched village of Creek Indians, somewhere in the northern arm of western Florida.[20]

The cruel treatment meted out by the conquistadors to the Indians, who were at first friendly, resulted in guerrilla warfare upon the expedition. Sickness also attacked Narvaez and many of his men. In this dilemma the explorers took the desperate step of building boats on which to escape. They had no shipwrights, tools, nor stores. Nevertheless necessity proved the

[18] E. G. Bourne, *Spain in America*, 137.

[19] There has been much discussion concerning the localities of Narvaez's expedition as related by Cabeza de Vaca. Lowery, *Spanish Settlements*, 177, 433-435, and Frederick W. Hodge, *Spanish Explorers in the Southern United States*, Original Narrative Series (New York, 1907), 19, both decide for Tampa Bay.

[20] Lowery and Hodge locate Apalache on the lakes of Leon and Jefferson counties, north of Tallahassee.

mother of their invention; nails, saws, and axes were formed from the stirrups, spurs, and crossbows of the cavaliers; palm husks and horsehair were twisted into ropes; resin was extracted from the neighboring pine trees; shirts were transformed into sails; and lastly, waterbags were improvised from the skins of horses which had been killed for food. Late in September five boats built in this fashion were ready to be launched; the two hundred and fifty survivors of the inland march set sail upon the waters of the gulf, "not a single one who went having a knowledge of navigation." Their aim was to reach Mexico, so they steered their course westward along the coast. Late in October, 1528, they cast anchor near a broad river "and took fresh water from the sea, the stream entering it in a freshet." So violent was the current that they were driven out into the gulf, and it was three days before they again found land. This, so far as can now be determined, is the first description of the mouth of the Mississippi. Its discovery was not soon known in Spain, however, since years passed before any of Narvaez's men returned to civilization. He himself was swept to sea and perished in the waters of the gulf. Four survivors of the expedition, after almost incredible adventures, found their way entirely across the continent,[21] and in 1536 returned to the City of Mexico. Cabeza de Vaca, one of these survivors who wrote the history of their wanderings, arrived in Spain in 1537 while preparations were being made for another great American expedition. Hernando de Soto, one of Pizarro's companions in Peru, had obtained a commission and was equipping with his

[21] For the various theories of the route of Alvar Nuñez Cabeza de Vaca and his companions, see Lowery, *Spanish Settlements*, 200-209, 457-458; also Harbert Davenport, "The Expedition of Panfilo de Narvaez," in *Southwestern Historical Quarterly*, October, 1923, and following numbers.

Peruvian riches an expedition to conquer North America. Cabeza de Vaca's stories aroused the interest to fever heat. Noblemen hastened to dispose of their property, public officials to sell their offices, in order to join the new expedition. So great was the concourse that many were obliged to remain behind, even when all these sacrifices had been made.[22]

The leader of this new adventure with six hundred followers landed, like his predecessor, in Tampa Bay. This was in May, 1539. For three years and over, this large body of men wandered through the present states of Florida, Georgia, Alabama, and Mississippi.[23] They were not explorers but marauders. They sought not to know the country but to exploit it and to enslave its inhabitants. By accident when in search of provisions they came upon the Mississippi River. May 8, 1541,[24] they reached a village whose exact site, because of the constant shifting of the river bed, cannot now be determined. The journalists of the expedition make scant mention of the discovery. "There," says Ranjel, De Soto's private secretary, "they saw the great river." "The stream was swift and very deep," writes the gentleman from Elvas; "the water, always flowing turbidly, brought along from above many trees and much timber driven downward by its force."[25]

[22] On the authorities for De Soto's expedition, see Lowery, *Spanish Settlements*, 458-460; E. G. Bourne, *Narratives of the Career of Hernando de Soto*, Trail Makers Series (New York, 1904), p. v-xx.
[23] The recent editors of the narratives of De Soto's journey place his farthest north at the head of the French Broad in North Carolina. Lowery, *Spanish Settlements*, 230.
[24] Bourne gives the date of discovery as May 8, in his *Spain in America*, 165; this date he has fixed upon from Ranjel's account. See Bourne, *Narratives of De Soto*, ii, 137. Lowery dates the discovery on March 2, in *Spanish Settlements*, 237-238.
[25] Bourne, *Narratives of De Soto*, i, 115; ii, 137.

The region from which so great a river came does not appear to have stimulated the Spanish imagination. It was gold, not timber, that they sought; a civilization ready made, not a region to develop. To them the Mississippi was but an obstacle on their route. A month was spent in constructing barges in which to cross the stream.[26] Once over, another twelvemonth was wasted in fruitless wanderings west of the great river. Finally the leader, in deep despondency at the difficulties that presented themselves, gave way to despair and died on the banks of the great river he had found. His fame has been enlarged by his romantic burial beneath its waters. His followers, now scarcely half of those who had landed in 1539, wandered for some time longer. At last they built for themselves boats,[27] and escaped down the stream to the gulf, and finally reached Mexico.

The Rio del Espíritu Santo, as the Mississippi was henceforth called by the Spaniards, appeared upon the Spanish maps along with the other gulf tributaries that De Soto had crossed in his wanderings.[28] Upon these maps the Espíritu Santo takes its rise in a chain of mountains which is made to stretch east and west across the continent from the highlands of the Carolinas to the Ozarks in Arkansas. No suspicion of the immense length of the Mississippi appears on any of the sixteenth-century maps. Instead, the St. Lawrence is frequently extended southward to rise on the northern border of

[26] Theodore H. Lewis, editor of the De Soto expedition in *Spanish Explorers*, Original Narratives Series, 204, places the crossing at Council Bend or Walnut Bend, Tunica County, Mississippi. The traditional site of De Soto's first view of the Mississippi is the lowest Chickasaw Bluff below Memphis.

[27] Lewis, *Spanish Explorers*, 249, locates the shipyard above the mouth of Arkansas River in Desha County, Arkansas. They embarked July 3, 1543.

[28] See contemporary map in *ibid.*, 132.

THE GREAT RIVERS

this same imaginary mountain uplift.[29] How great a river he had found De Soto never knew.

A third great river of North America was discovered by the Spaniards during this same period, in connection with the interior explorations of Francisco Vasques de Coronado.[30] When in 1540 this captain-general started for the pueblos of Arizona and New Mexico, a supporting expedition carrying provisions was sent out by the viceroy along the Pacific coast under the command of Hernando de Alarcón. Alarcón sailed May 9, 1540, and after coming to "the very bottom of the Bay" of California he "found a very mighty river, which ran with so great fury of a stream, that we could hardly sail against it." This river, the Colorado, the Spanish captain ascended for eighty-five leagues, much of the voyage being made by towing, with willing natives at the ropes. Alarcón called the stream Rio de Bueno Guia (River of the Good Guide) and ascended it until he came to "high mountains," when despairing of making connections with Coronado he returned to Mexico.[31] Coronado meanwhile sent a detachment under Garcia López de Cárdenas to endeavor to find Alarcón. "After they had gone twenty days they came to the banks of the river, which seemed to be more than three or four leagues in an air line across to the other bank of the stream which flowed between them." This was the first sight of the Grand Cañon of the

[29] See the maps of Sebastian Cabot, 1544; of Mercator, 1558; Zalterius, 1566; and Ortelius, 1570.

[30] Much has been published in recent years about Coronado. G. P. Winship, in Bureau of Ethnology, *Fourteenth Annual Report*; same author, *The Journey of Coronado*, Trail Makers Series (New York, 1904). F. W. Hodge also edits the narrative of this journey in *Spanish Explorers*.

[31] Alarcón's narrative is in Hakluyt, *Voyages*, ix, 279-318. Hodge thinks Alarcón sailed up as far as the bend in the Colorado in Mohave County, Arizona. See map in *Spanish Explorers*, 280.

Colorado; for three days the explorers rested upon its southern bank, making futile efforts to reach the bottom of the great gorge. They named it the Tison (Firebrand) River, because of the Indian custom of planting torches along its upper edge.[32]

It is curious that three of the great rivers of North America should have been found so near together in point of time, under such varying auspices—one by a Breton from France, one by a conquistador from Spain, a third by a sailor from Mexico. Thus in the first half-century of discovery, approach was made toward the interior of the continent where Wisconsin still lay unrevealed to the civilized world.

[32] *Spanish Explorers*, 308-310.

III. CONJECTURES CONCERNING THE GREAT LAKES

IN THE heart of the greatest city upon the Great Lakes there stands a symbolic representation of the beauty and beneficence of these inland waters, in the form of a lovely fountain, composed of five noble and gracious naiads who pour from one basin to the other the sweet waters of their guarding. High above them all towers Superior, the mighty shell of her lake tilted aloft to pour its gift into the shell of Huron, at whose right stands Michigan, aiding to fill the great basin Huron so proudly supports. Beneath and beyond, beautiful Erie stoops to catch the overflow from Huron's great shell; she in turn passes it on to Ontario, who, unmindful of her sisters above, stretches forth a yearning hand toward the mighty sea. Chicago's artist, Lorado Taft, has in enduring marble thus personified the most remarkable physical feature of the interior of North America.

No such phenomenon exists in the Old World. Neither in Europe nor in Asia are there vast bodies of fresh water forming the source of a great river. The conception, therefore, of the Great Lakes was yet to be born. The hints that were received from the Indians of the existence of these inland seas stimulated the imagination of sixteenth-century explorers and gave rise to fantastic conjectures concerning them. The enigma of the Great Lakes was not solved, however, until the seventeenth century.

The Great Lakes as we at present know them are the gift of the Ice Age. The glaciers did not, as was formerly supposed, scoop out their basins; these basins were the river valleys of pre-glacial epochs, which it remained for the great ice streams to fill. The gradual emergence of the Great Lakes from the fetters of the successive glaciers is a wonderful story; only in the age of what is known as the Wisconsin Drift—the final glacial advance—can the formation of the lakes be successively traced. As the ice receded, lobes of water were left to which geologists apply such names as Glacial Lake Chicago and Lake Duluth. These drained south and west through the Chicago-Illinois River valley into the Mississippi valley. In the Lake Algonquin stage, Superior, Huron, and Michigan were all one vast body of water draining east through the Mohawk valley and south into New York Bay. In what is known as the Nipissing stage the lakes had almost their present form, but drained through the Nipissing-Ottawa River into what was then the sea in the lower St. Lawrence valley, with a minor outlet along the line of the present drainage. Gradually the Nipissing-Ottawa outlet filled up; a watershed was raised between Lake Nipissing and the Ottawa River. The minor outlet became the principal and only one; the Great Lakes as we now know them emerged. Probably Niagara Falls did not appear until this final epoch of geological change. The glaciers in their retreat and disappearance left the Great Lakes; they, in their search for the sea, created the St. Lawrence River, the whole system affording a route into the heart of the continent.[1]

The French people, having in the first half of the sixteenth century discovered the St. Lawrence and learned of its two great branches, halted their efforts

[1] In this brief geological sketch the author, who boasts no science, has followed the account by F. B. Taylor, United States Geological Survey, *Monograph 53* (Washington, 1915), 316-469.

THE FOUNTAIN OF THE GREAT LAKES
Lorado Taft, Sculptor

CONJECTURES CONCERNING GREAT LAKES 33

at interior exploration for more than two generations. They turned their attention instead to colonizing on the more genial coasts of Florida. There in 1564 a considerable colony was established on the banks of the St. John's River. Francis Parkman has told in felicitous phrases the story of this Huguenot settlement, of its relations with the natives, and of its destruction by a band of fanatical Spaniards, who the succeeding year established the post of St. Augustine.[2] The Spaniards, expelling all intruders from their sphere of influence along the South Atlantic and Gulf coasts, maintained their supremacy in that region for two more centuries. Meanwhile France failed to grasp as its future domain the Atlantic coast plain, discovered by Verrazano and marked by the early map makers with the French flag. Nor were these shores early occupied by English colonizers. The daring English sea rovers of the sixteenth century touched here and there along the American coasts, but made no successful claim to permanent holdings. One of these seamen, the great Sir Francis Drake, on a map which he prepared after his voyage of circumnavigation in 1577-80, assigned to "Nova Albion" the interior of America and the entire Pacific coast.[3] It is curious to note that in the century following, Drake's "Nova Albion" and "Nova Francia" almost wholly exchanged places as spheres of influence, England clinging to the Atlantic coast plain first claimed by French explorers, while the latter explored the interior of America and carried the French flag from the Alleghenies to the Rockies, and along the entire length of the Great Lakes.

[2] Parkman, *Pioneers of France in the New World* (Boston, 1871).
[3] Zelia Nuttall, *New Light on Drake*, Hakluyt Society Publications, second series, xxxiv (London, 1914), p. lvi. The original map belongs to the Hispanic Society of New York.

The failure of France during the sixteenth century to grasp its opportunity in North America and to maintain its primacy along the Atlantic coast was due to the weakness of its rulers, and to the religious wars which in that period devastated the home land. Torn by dissensions between Huguenots and Leaguers, official France had neither energy nor ability to undertake voyages of discovery or plans for new settlements. Repulsed from Florida, the Huguenot leaders abandoned the project of overseas colonization, and for a generation the very name of America seemed forgotten. It was not, however, forgotten by the fisher folk and hardy mariners of Brittany and Normandy. Despite the civil wars that raged at home, they made their annual voyages to Newfoundland and the St. Lawrence Gulf, bringing thence the harvests of the seas and forests. How far their explorations went we have no certain means of knowing. The Gulf of St. Lawrence was completely mapped during the last half of the sixteenth century; there are also reasons to think that exploration inland along the St. Lawrence River did not cease with the departure of Cartier and Roberval. The fur trade as well as the fisheries flourished during this epoch; the tendency of rival traders was to follow their customers to their villages and hunting grounds. Both contemporary maps and contemporary descriptions seem to indicate some penetration during the latter years of the sixteenth century along the St. Lawrence toward the Great Lakes.

For instance, Francisco López de Gomara, in his *Historia General de las Indias*, published in 1552-53, speaks of "a great river, named San Lorenço, which some consider an arm of the sea. It has been navigated for two hundred leagues."[4] A few years later the Vene-

[4] So far as we have ascertained, Gomara is the first to apply the name St. Lawrence to the river.

CONJECTURES CONCERNING GREAT LAKES 35

tian editor Ramusio writes: "There is a great river called the San Lorenzo which some consider an arm of the sea, and which has been navigated for many leagues."[5] Vague reports of the existence of great inland seas in North America began to appear in conjectural form on the charts and maps of the period. One of the earliest of such maps, apparently drawn without any knowledge of Cartier's discoveries, is a mappemonde of the celebrated Venetian cartographer Jacopo Gastaldi, published in 1554. This map, now in the municipal library at Turin,[6] has upon it a large interior lake emptying into the Atlantic by a stream termed "R. de las yslas," which seems to be derived from the nomenclature of Gómez. The Gulf of St. Lawrence is well defined upon this map, but it has no river flowing into it.[7] Another map which seems to indicate Lake Ontario apart from its connection with the St. Lawrence is that of Le Moyne, who was with the French in Florida. The upper part of his map shows a large open lake, or sea, of which the northern shore does not appear.[8]

By the last third of the sixteenth century, the science of cartography had advanced considerably; two famous Flemings, Gerardus Mercator and Abraham Ortelius, made great progress toward accuracy. Mercator's marine chart of 1569 is the first, so far as we know, to

[5] Ramusio, *Voyages*, iii.
[6] A reproduction is in the Church Collection, Brown University Library, Providence.
[7] Harrisse and Winsor consider that Gastaldi's map of "La Nuova Francia" embodied in Ramusio, *Voyages*, iii, contains the first delineation of the Great Lakes. The recent discovery of Verrazano's manuscript proves that the so-called "lago" on that map is meant for New York Bay. Nor does the Forlani chart of 1565, nor the Zalterius of 1566, refer to the Great Lakes. The "lago" of these maps suggests Lake Champlain and the route thither via the Hudson River.
[8] Hakluyt, *Voyages*, ix, 112.

attempt the representation of the Great Lakes from the account in Cartier's narrative. Mercator follows this narrative very accurately. The great river running into the St. Lawrence Gulf has two large branches, the southern one of which extends south to an east and west mountain barrier. At the head of the northern branch are grouped three small lakes just west of which is a very large lake whose extent is concealed by a vignette. Beside this lake is written "Hic mare est dulcium aquarum, cujus terminum ignorari Canadenses ex relatu Saguenaiensium aiunt" ("This sea is of fresh water; the Canadians do not know its bounds, according to the report of the people of Saguenay").[9] Ortelius in his world map of 1570 follows Mercator only in part. He makes the sea west of the sources of the Ottawa an arm of the Arctic Ocean.[10] This change was apparently made to accommodate the theory of the Northwest Passage, which about this time was becoming so popular in England. Sir Humphrey Gilbert, the great promoter of search for this passage, cites Cartier and the fresh-water sea which he described; this, says Gilbert, "they presupposed to be the passage to Cataia [Cathay]."[11]

Gilbert's theory that the inland seas or lakes of North America might be the greatly desired passage through North America to China rested on the assumption that they were not merely the source of a single river system, but lay like great reservoirs at the summit of the continent, with streams discharging in more than

---

[9] The Library of Congress possesses a copy of this map; a reproduction appears in *Encyclopedia Britannica*, article "Geography."

[10] Ortelius, *Theatrum Orbis Terrarum* (Antwerp, Belgium, 1570), Map 1. A copy is in the Wisconsin Historical Library.

[11] Hakluyt, *Voyages*, ix, 171. Mercator adopted Ortelius' idea of opening the fresh-water sea into the northern passage in his map of 1587.

one direction. This geographical assumption is not so strange when it is remembered that there were no such great bodies of fresh water in the heart of any continent then known. It seemed theoretically probable to the sixteenth-century geographers that such reservoirs existed. Ortelius in 1570 represented Africa with a great interior lake, which not only was the source of the Nile but had another outlet into the Indian Ocean, and still a third flowing westward into the Atlantic. It was a fascinating possibility that the vast "Sea of Saguenay," of which Cartier had heard as the source of the St. Lawrence, might have an outlet to the western ocean. This theory conditioned the representations of geographers and the hopes of discoverers for at least a hundred years. We shall later see what effect it had upon Champlain's explorations. Not until the Mississippi was found running south across the continent was the theory of the Great Lakes as a fresh-water reservoir with an opening to the western ocean disproved and abandoned.

The possibility that the great interior lake of which so many rumors had been heard might be the long-sought passage to the western ocean was adopted by Richard Hakluyt, an Englishman intensely interested in geographical exploration. Hakluyt was a friend of Sir Humphrey Gilbert and of his half-brother Walter Raleigh. In 1583, at the solicitation of the latter, Hakluyt wrote a *Discourse Concerning Western Planting*, in which he advocated the theory that Cartier's fresh-water sea, whose limits were unknown, opened a way to the western ocean.[12] In the course of the investigations preparatory to writing his *Discourse*, Hakluyt visited France. There he talked with Breton pilots

[12] Hakluyt, *Discourse*, written in 1583, was first published n 1877 in Maine Historical Society, *Collections*, second series, ii.

and fisher folk who yearly visited the Canadian shores. Among them was a "Monsieur de Leau, an honest gent of Morleux in Britaine [Brittany] which told me this springe, in the presence of divers Englishemen at Paris, that a man of St. Malowe this last yere discovered the sea on the back side of Hochelaga."[13] This would seem to indicate that one of the St. Malo fur traders had penetrated to Lake Ontario. Possibly this explorer was one of Cartier's collateral descendants. Jacques Noel, grandson of Cartier's sister, wrote in 1587 to a friend in Paris that he had been at Hochelaga, where from the top of the mountain "I have seene the sayd River [St. Lawrence] beyond the sayd Saultes [Lachine Rapids], which sheweth unto us to be broader than it was when we passed it. The people of the Countrey advertised us, that there are ten dayes journey from the Saultes unto this Great Lake [Ontario]."[14]

Hakluyt, who has preserved for us these scraps of information concerning French enterprise, spent his life in collecting material on the English voyages of the latter half of the sixteenth century. Whenever a fleet arrived from attempting the Northwest Passage, or from harrying the Spanish main, Hakluyt hastened to the port and talked in person with the returned adventurers. He thus picked up tales of marooned sailors, and of wandering seamen, which, although not always reliable, are nevertheless full of suggestiveness. One of these narratives was that of David Ingram, who went

[13] Hakluyt, *Discourse*, 114-115.
[14] Hakluyt, *Voyages*, viii, 273-274; Baxter, *Cartier*, 367-369; Biggar, *Jacques Cartier*, 259-260, 313-314. The letters of Jacques Noel first appeared with the narrative of Cartier's third voyage in Hakluyt's second edition of his *Principall Navigations*, which was published in 1600. It seems probable that the editor secured these documents from Noel in person. Biggar thinks the lake referred to was Huron; for many reasons we think it was Ontario.

out in 1568 with Sir John Hawkins, when he tried to force the Spanish ports of Mexico to open to him for his trade in slaves. Although England was then nominally at peace with Spain, an engagement took place between the English fleet and the Spanish warships in the harbor of Vera Cruz. After the battle Hawkins' remaining ships were so crippled that he was forced to set on shore somewhere in northern Mexico a hundred of his seamen to accept whatever fate might overtake them. Of these marooned men only three survived the hardships of the wilderness or the miseries of Spanish prisons. One of these survivors was Ingram, who made his way overland to the northward, and was at last taken from New Brunswick to Europe on a French fishing smack. Ingram told Hakluyt many tales of his adventures among the savages of the interior of North America. Once, he said, "travelinge towarde the northe [he] founde the mayne Sea uppon the northe syde of Ameryca, and travayled in the sight thereof the space of two whole dayes."[15] Ingram told so many marvels concerning the wealth and treasure of the interior of North America, that Hakluyt became incredulous concerning the entire narrative, and omitted it from the second edition of his *Voyages*; none the less it is quite certain that, despite his untrustworthiness in details, Ingram did take the journey he described.

Hakluyt also picked up another narrative of interior America from one of the Spanish captives taken by Sir Francis Drake, when in 1586 he raided the West Indies and captured and sacked St. Augustine. This man, Pedro Morales, was taken at the latter place; he told Hakluyt that he had been in America six years, that

[15] George P. Winship, *Sailors' Narratives of New England* (Boston, 1905), 30. The editor uses the caption "Great Lakes" beside Ingram's statement which is cited above.

twenty days' journey west of Saint Helena (now Port Royal) were mountains whither some of his companions had been.[16] Morales and his comrades were eager to go to find these "rich mountaines, and the passage to a sea or a mighty Lake which they heare to be within four and twenty dayes travel from Saint Helena."[17]

These sailors' narratives need not be accepted in their entirety in order to believe that some hints of the existence of the Great Lakes are herein to be found. It is quite within the bounds of probability that Ingram may have skirted the coast of Lake Erie or of Lake Ontario, as he worked his way northeastward from Mexico to New Brunswick. Morales and his mates were no doubt correct in reporting the Indians' information of a "mighty Lake" twenty-four days' journey from Port Royal.

Hakluyt, to whom we owe these hints of early exploration along the Great Lakes, has also preserved a map which, published in 1587, shows a fresh-water sea (*mare dulce*) in the northern portion of the North American continent open to the north.[18] This map came to the notice of Jacques Noel, who in a letter dated at St. Malo, June 19, 1587, severely criticized it. "The

[16] H. E. Bolton and T. M. Marshall, *The Colonization of North America* (New York, 1920), 64.
[17] Hakluyt, *Voyages*, ix, 113-114.
[18] This map was first published by Hakluyt in his edition of *Decades* of Peter Martyr (*De Orbe Novo*). It is thus frequently spoken of as the Peter Martyr map, although it had no connection with that historian. For a reproduction of this map, see Hakluyt, *Voyages*, viii, 272. It had much influence on the map makers of the period. Both Ortelius in his later maps and Mercator's son Rumoldus in maps of 1587 and 1595 follow the Peter Martyr map with a large northern *mare dulce* (fresh-water sea). Giovanni Battista Mazza, an Italian geographer, introduces a *mare dulce* north of "Hochelas" on a map of 1684. Giuseppe Rosaccio, *Il Monde e sue parti* (Florence, 1595), indicates a lake as the source of the St. Lawrence.

Great Lake," he says, "is placed too much toward the North." Nor is the "River of Canada which is described in that Mappe" marked "as it is in my booke, which is agreeable to the book of Jaques Cartier."[19] In some way Hakluyt was informed of Noel's comments on his map, and immediately sought out the author. Noel so far convinced the Englishman of the validity of his criticisms, that Hakluyt omitted this map from the next edition of his *Voyages*, giving in its stead the letters of Noel and the hitherto unknown journal of Cartier's third voyage. He likewise designed from Noel's instructions another map[20] whereon the northern lake is omitted and the St. Lawrence rises in a large "Lake of Tadouac the boundes whereof are unknowne," directly west of Hochelaga. This we believe is the first map of Lake Ontario. Into its northern shore enters a river coming from another open and unknown lake, a first suggestion that there was more than one great lake in interior North America, and that these lakes were united by connecting streams.[21]

[19] Hakluyt, *Voyages*, viii, 273-274; Baxter, *Cartier*, 367-369.

[20] This map appeared in the 1600 edition of Hakluyt, *Principall Navigations*; it was the work of Edward Wright, engraved by Emerich Molineaux. It is supposed to be the map referred to by Shakespere in *Twelfth Night*, III,ii. We reproduce a portion showing Lake Tadouac from Hakluyt, *Voyages* (edition of 1903), i, 356, by permission of the publishers.

[21] Henry Harrisse, in *Terre Neuve* (Paris, 1900), 191-194, asserts that this Molineaux map reproduces Cartier's original map. But see John Brereton, *A Briefe and True Relation of the Discoverie of the North part of Virginia* (London, 1602), where Edward Hayes, the famous captain who was with Sir Humphrey Gilbert on his last voyage, in an appendix says: "the discoveries of Jaques Noel, who having passed beyond the three Saults, where Jaques Cartier left to discover . . . understood of the inhabitants that the same river did leade into a mightie lake, which at the entrance was fresh, but beyond was bitter or salt; the end whereof was unknown." This passage indicates that Hakluyt obtained his information of Lake Tadouac from Noel.

One other strange fiction concerning the lakes of interior North America appears on several of the maps of the late sixteenth century. That was a "Lake Conibaz," frequently represented with a large island in its waters upon which was placed an Indian village called Conibaz. This lake is usually placed far to the westward and sometimes discharges into a northern ocean by Conibaz River. The originator of this geographical anomaly was André Thevet, the celebrated French cosmographer. Thevet had met and talked with Cartier himself.[22] It thus seems probable that he obtained his suggestion for Lake Conibaz from Cartier's description of the Indian method of collecting wampum shells, which Cartier says they called "Cornibotz." Cartier said that in order to obtain these coveted shells the Indians slashed the thighs and other fleshy portions of the dead body of a captive and then sunk it into the depths of waters, when the shells would collect in the wounds.[23] Thevet, from this description and from Cartier's accounts of large interior lakes, evolved his "Lac de Conibaz," which he introduced upon his map of 1575.[24] Thevet's work was popular and several editions followed. His Lake Conibaz was copied by Cornelius de Judaeis on his map in *Speculum Orbis Terrae*, 1593; by Petrus Plancius in his *Orbis Terrarum*, 1594; by Cornelius Wytfliet in *Descriptiones Ptolemaicae augmentum*, 1597; by Mathias Quadus in *Novi Orbis pars borealis*, 1600; and probably by others. With the appearance, however, of the Molineaux map sponsored by Hakluyt, Lake Conibaz quickly disappeared from the interior of North America.

[22] André Thevet, *The Newfoundworld, or Antarctike* (London, 1568).
[23] Baxter, *Cartier*, 165-166.
[24] Thevet, "La Quanto Partie du Monde," in *La Cosmographie* (Paris, 1575), ii, 903.

HAKLUYT-WRIGHT-MOLINEAUX MAP OF GREAT LAKES, 1600

CONJECTURES CONCERNING GREAT LAKES 43

Hakluyt's new map had influence upon exploration as well as upon cartography.[25] Soon after it was published the London and Plymouth companies were formed for the permanent English occupation of North America. Hakluyt was himself interested in these corporations; his map was much used by those concerned in American colonization. It is supposed to have been the map which Henry Hudson had with him when in 1609, sailing under the auspices of the Dutch East India Company, he discovered Hudson River.[26] Before he left on this voyage of exploration Henry IV had been attempting to obtain Hudson's services for discovery under the French flag.[27] Had the French king been successful, New York and the Hudson River would have been French territory, and the subsequent history of New France and of America would have been vastly different.

While, however, Hudson was on the upper reaches of the river which bears his name, where he ascertained to his great disappointment that it was not the long-sought channel through North America to the western ocean, a young Frenchman was approaching the sources of the Hudson from the north, and leaving his name on the lake that unites New York and Canada. What earlier explorers had not succeeded in doing, Samuel de Champlain accomplished—the discovery of the sources of the St. Lawrence and the exploration of the Great Lakes of North America. With Champlain the period of conjecture ends, and that of careful, scientific exploration begins.

[25] A map drawn by Willem Janszoon Blaeu in 1605 for Henry IV shows in "Nova Francia" the St. Lawrence issuing from a large lake, which may be Hakluyt's Lake Tadouac. This unique map is in the Hispanic Society at New York.
[26] E. H. Hall, "Henry Hudson and the Discovery of the Hudson River," in American Scenic and Historic Preservation Society, *Fifteenth Annual Report*, 239-241.
[27] *Ibid.*, 256.

IV. DISCOVERY OF THE GREAT LAKES, 1598–1632

THE men of the Renaissance gave France a shadowy claim to portions of the North American continent. Frenchmen of the seventeenth century made good this claim and carried French sovereignty into the Mississippi valley. Between the two periods intervened the religious wars of France. These wars were in reality the growing pains of a great nation; from them France issued a full-grown modern state with a compact territory and a vigorous administration which for two centuries made her the leading power in Europe. The founder of France's greatness was Henry IV; during the time he was developing his kingdom he gave much attention to overseas exploration and also to the permanent occupation of New France. In the very year (1598) that the Edict of Nantes ended the sectarian strife throughout his kingdom, Henry granted a charter to the Marquis de la Roche to settle a colony in the New World. This undertaking was not the first of the kind that La Roche had undertaken. Fourteen years before, he had fitted out an expedition to colonize Newfoundland, where Sir Humphrey Gilbert the preceding year had come to grief. La Roche's fleet encountered near the coast of France a dreadful storm, and his largest vessel was wrecked off Brouage, where at that time dwelt a lad of seventeen who was to succeed where La Roche failed. During the interval between the first and second expeditions of the Marquis, Samuel de Champlain of Brouage had had many experiences on land and on sea. His native town had felt the shock of the civil wars. Condé, the great Huguenot leader, fortified Brouage, where in 1577 his party was besieged by the Leaguers under Mayenne and forced to an honorable surrender. Eight years later Condé besieged a royal garrison in the same town, destroyed its harbor, and gave it a blow from which it never recovered but gradually sank into an insignificant provincial village.

Champlain, Brouage's most famous son, early went to sea, learning navigation on small coasting vessels that plied between the ports of the Bay of Biscay. By 1589 he was serving in the Huguenot army and the next year followed the "white plume of Navarre" at the famous battle of Ivry. Later he was part of the naval arm of Navarre's forces; after the Peace of Vervins he assisted in carrying home the Spanish contingent which had been employed by the king's opponents in the vessel *St. Julien*, commanded by his uncle, who was pilot general of the transport fleet. At Cadiz the young French navigator was immediately interested in the sailors and officers who plied to the Spanish main. Great was his delight when the *St. Julien* was chartered to join the yearly Spanish flotilla to the West Indies, and Champlain himself was chosen to command. Although the Spaniards jealously guarded their American dominions from foreign visitors, the young French officer conducted himself so prudently that he was allowed all the privileges of a Spanish subject. Almost three years were passed by Champlain in Spanish America, going from island to island, visiting the mainland in both the northern and the southern continent. In order to make a report to the king, Champlain took full and accurate notes of all he saw, and upon his return prepared an account of his journeyings, which brought him to the notice of Henry IV.[1]

[1] The manuscript of Champlain's journal of his voyage to the West Indies was found in the nineteenth century at Dieppe. It

Henry IV was watching with attentive interest the possibilities of enlarging his kingdom by overseas colonies. La Roche's expedition of 1598, like his earlier one, having failed, the king in 1599 granted a trading monopoly in New France to Pierre Chauvin, a Norman merchant, on condition that he should plant there a permanent colony. Chauvin for some years had been crossing the ocean and gathering furs at Tadoussac. The year he obtained his grant he left a small group of sixteen men to winter at that bleak post in order to form the nucleus of a colony. Through incapacity and disease these men were reduced to great want, and the colony was the next spring abandoned. Meanwhile Chauvin had died. Aymar de Chastes, governor of Dieppe and one of Henry's old warriors, indicated a desire to aid in the development of North America. He proposed to the king that before settling another colony exploration should be made for a site in a milder climate. Chastes and Champlain had previously been comrades on the field of war; now with the prestige of his Spanish-American voyage upon him, Champlain was selected to undertake an expedition to the shores of New France. With him on this voyage was associated François Gravé Sieur de Pont (usually called Pontgravé), one of Chauvin's captains who was already familiar with the shores of the lower St. Lawrence.

The fleet left Dieppe the fifteenth of March, 1603. Champlain was now in the prime of life, enured to hardships, cool in danger, abounding in resource, and possessing a tenacity of purpose and a steadiness of will

---

is beautifully illuminated and adorned with water-color sketches of fruits, fish, animals, and Indians, one of which we reproduce, by permission of the John Carter Brown Library, which now owns this manuscript. It was first published in English translation in 1859 by the Hakluyt Society. It is included in Abbé C. H. Laverdière, *Œuvres de Champlain* (Quebec, 1870).

Prunes et tuche ou je touche comme les meures Est
de fort bon goust et des oÿ quil est tresboy pour guerir
les morseures de bestes venimeuses

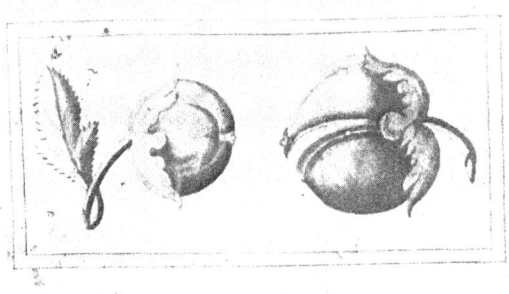

Il y a encor Duy autres fruict qui se nomme crollies des
grosseur Dune prune et est fort Fauluea et la goust comme
de poires muscadee

PORTION OF CHAMPLAIN'S MANUSCRIPT DESCRIBING HIS
WEST INDIAN VOYAGE

unusual among Frenchmen. Champlain was also gifted with religious enthusiasm and a vital imagination; he loved the wildness of the woods and was happier in the forests of America than at the court of the king. He had also the powers of a trained observer, and the simple, vigorous language of his descriptions makes the New World in all its pristine mysteries live again for the reader.[2] The voyage of 1603 was successful. Pontgravé dropped anchor at Tadoussac and was immediately absorbed in trade with the Indians, whom Champlain studied with much interest.[3] The latter had with him a copy of Cartier's journal, and recognized the sites the earlier explorer had visited as he himself advanced along the great river. On this voyage, however, he went no farther than his predecessor had gone—to the site of Montreal. Like him he ascended the "Royal Mountain" and listened to Indian accounts of the sources of the St. Lawrence. They told him that the left-hand branch was full of rapids, none so hard to pass, however, as the one at their feet, now called the Lachine. "Then," he writes, "they come into a Lake [Ontario] which may containe some eighty leagues in length, in which are many Ilands, and at the end of the same the water is brackish and the Winter gentle. At the end of the said Lake they passe a Sault [Niagara] which is somewhat high. . . . From thence they enter into another Lake

[2] Laverdière's work is the standard edition of Champlain's journals. The Prince Society (1878-82) published three volumes in an English translation. More recent English editions are those of W. L. Grant, Original Narrative Series, *Voyages of Samuel de Champlain* (New York, 1907); E. G. Bourne, Trail Makers Series, *The Voyages and Explorations of Samuel de Champlain* (Toronto, 1911).

[3] Champlain's narrative of this voyage was published as *Des Sauvages; ou Voyage de Samuel Champlain de Brouage, faict en la France Nouvelle, l'an mil six cens trois.* It contains reports of his conversations with the savages.

[Erie] which may be sixty leagues long, and that the water thereof is very brackish: at the end thereof they come into a Strait [Detroit River] which is two leagues broad, and it goeth farre into the Countrie. They told us that they themselves had passed no farther; and that they had not seene the end of a Lake [Huron] which is within fifteene or sixteene leagues of the farthest place where themselves had beene, nor that they which told them of it, had known any man that had seene the end thereof. . . . They say that the water is there excessive salt, to wit, as salt as sea water."[4] Twice more on this first voyage Champlain interrogated the natives about the lakes at the head of the St. Lawrence. They differed concerning their size and the nature of their water, some stoutly maintaining it was not salt, others declaring it grew saline as one advanced. Champlain calculated that from the farthermost point he himself had reached, four hundred more leagues would take him to the western ocean.[5] He also heard much of the copper mines somewhere upon these lakes. If one would set forth in the light Indian canoes he thought that "a man may see all that is to be seene, good and bad, within the space of a yeere or two."

Some years were to pass before Champlain could accomplish this voyage. We have, however, in his journal of 1603 a better description of the lower Great Lakes, of their size and connecting streams, than had yet appeared. This description is distorted by the explorer's prepossession that the Great Lakes must be a reservoir and that through them one could reach the western ocean. The report of salt springs near the western ends of Lakes Ontario and Erie, Champlain misinterpreted to mean the tides of the South Sea.

[4] Bourne, *Champlain*, ii, 200-202.
[5] *Ibid.*, 204-210.

Lescarbot had this same idea in mind when he wrote "of a great lake at the head of this river [of Canada], from which it issues, which is thirty days' journey in length, and at its head the water is salt, though fresh at the other end. I am almost led to believe that this is the same lake [as was described by Le Moyne], and that it flows into the South Sea."[6]

Champlain and Pontgravé returned to France after a summer of trading and exploring, reaching the port of Havre on the twentieth of September. There they were greeted with the unwelcome news that their patron Chastes had died. The king, however, graciously received Champlain, examined the maps he had drawn, and promised him a new patron for transoceanic enterprise. This latter patron, Pierre du Gaust Sieur de Monts, had already visited Tadoussac with Chauvin and had conceived a distaste for the climate of the St. Lawrence. In vain Champlain assured him that for "every ounce of cold at Quebec, there was a pound at Tadoussac." Monts would lend his powerful influence to the venture only on condition of colonizing in a warmer latitude. A settlement upon the St. Lawrence was thus postponed for five more years.

The king granted to Monts a region in North America extending south to the fortieth parallel; it therefore became Champlain's duty to explore the New England coasts, and to chart that region for France.[7] He, however, always persisted in his first preference, and after

[6] Marc Lescarbot, *The History of New France* (Champlain Society, Toronto, 1907-1914), i, 103. See account of Le Moyne, *ante*, page 35.
[7] Monts and Champlain in 1605 explored the New England shores as far as Cape Cod Bay. They entered Plymouth harbor, and skirted all around the bay. See Winship, *Sailors' Narratives*, 67-84. In 1604 Champlain named Mount Desert Island and explored the Penobscot.

the failure of an attempted colony in Nova Scotia, persuaded Monts "to settle on the great River Saint Lawrence." April 13, 1608, Champlain set sail for the St. Lawrence carrying furniture, clothing, tools, and workmen to build a factory, bearing himself a commission as lieutenant governor of the proposed colony. Pontgravé accompanied him to superintend the Indian trade. July 3 they disembarked at the foot of Quebec rock and began the "habitation" that was to be Champlain's home for so many years.

It was 1609 before he could undertake westward exploration; that year he discovered the Richelieu River, and the lake at its source that now perpetuates its discoverer's name. He describes it in all its virgin beauty, "a very large lake, filled with handsome islands, and with large tracts of fine land bordering on the lake." Near this he had that skirmish with the Iroquois Indians the consequences of which have been so greatly overestimated. The Five Nations were no doubt irritated with the French for their summary defeat by means of the alarming firearms; but to ascribe their hostility to an entire nation for a hundred years to the act of one man, even though he were the first Frenchman they had ever seen, is to place undue emphasis on a casual encounter. Henry Hudson's discovery the year of the finding of Lake Champlain, of the Hudson River and the subsequent Dutch colony settled upon its banks, in reality created the situation that ultimately brought about the Iroquois wars.

Champlain's voyage of 1609 had not led him toward the Great Lakes; it had, however, proved that there was no continuous channel between the St. Lawrence and New York Bay, and that in that particular the 1600 map of Molineaux was incorrect. The next year (1610) an unknown English pilot exploring and charting the

DISCOVERY OF THE GREAT LAKES 51

northern Atlantic region delineated the Hudson as leading directly to Lake Ontario, while he placed Lake Champlain quite distant therefrom. This map of 1610, which was not known until 1890, was prepared for James I by a surveyor whom he sent out to explore his American dominions. This action of James I alarmed the Spanish ambassador in England lest the people of that nation might even in time of peace be plotting to harry the Spanish colonies. He secretly obtained a copy of this map prepared for the English king, and forwarded it to his master, Philip III. The original of the map seems to have disappeared; the Spanish copy has lain unnoticed these many years in the archives of Simancas. From the rough sketch which was sent to Philip III we see that the maker of this English map was well informed concerning the latest explorations. He charted the Hudson River from Hudson's navigations; he drew Lakes George and Champlain apparently from Champlain's journal of 1609. He indicated all the eastern end of Lake Ontario and the Trent River portage from information, as he states, received from Indians. As Champlain's journal of 1603 is the first adequate description of the lower Great Lakes, the Simancas map of 1610 is the first drawing of Lake Ontario that in any wise approximates its true shape and proportions.[8]

Meanwhile Champlain was preparing for interior exploration by having French youths educated as Indian interpreters. In 1610 he sent Etienne Brulé, who was one of the immigrants of 1608, to winter among the

[8] Alexander Brown, *The Genesis of the United States* (Boston, 1890), 456; also Hall, in "Henry Hudson," 304. It would be a happy circumstance if the original of this sketch map in the Simancas archives could be found. We publish a portion of this sketch map by permission of Houghton and Mifflin, publishers of Brown's *Genesis*.

tribes that came each summer to traffic at Three Rivers. These Algonquian Indians lived in the angle between the two branches of the Great River, and Brulé must have wandered with them during the winter of 1610-11 along the upper reaches of the St. Lawrence, being so far as we certainly know the first white man to visit that region. He does not seem, however, to have gone as far as Lake Ontario. Through Brulé's skill as interpreter, Champlain in the trading concourse of 1611 learned more of the source of the great river. "They gave me," he says, "detailed information about their rivers, falls, lakes and lands. Four of them assured me that they had seen a sea at a great distance from their country"; these four Indians had probably been as far as Lake Superior. The policy of placing French youths in Indian villages was continued by Champlain in 1612. Nicolas Vignau went home with a tribe living on the Ottawa River. Brulé joined a band of Hurons who were going west to their villages in the present Simcoe County, Ontario. On this voyage he must have seen one or more of the Great Lakes.[9]

The assassination of the king, his patron, of which he heard in May, 1611, forced Champlain again to postpone his project of a western voyage. The remainder of 1611 and the entire year of 1612 were spent in France, where he published his journals and two maps showing all he knew of North America at that time. On one of the maps he delineated the entire valley of the

---

[9] Grant, *Champlain*, 185-187, 207-219, 302, 354. See also Sulte, "Valley of the Ottawa in 1613," in Ontario Historical Society, *Papers and Records*, xiii, 31-35; "Etienne Brulé," in Canada Royal Society, *Proceedings*, 1907, sec. i, p. 97-103. Sulte thinks Brulé went to Huronia in 1610-11; Champlain, however, says he was with Iroquet, an Algonquian chief, during that winter. Brulé's name is not mentioned in the account for 1612, but he said in 1618 that he had been eight years among the savages.

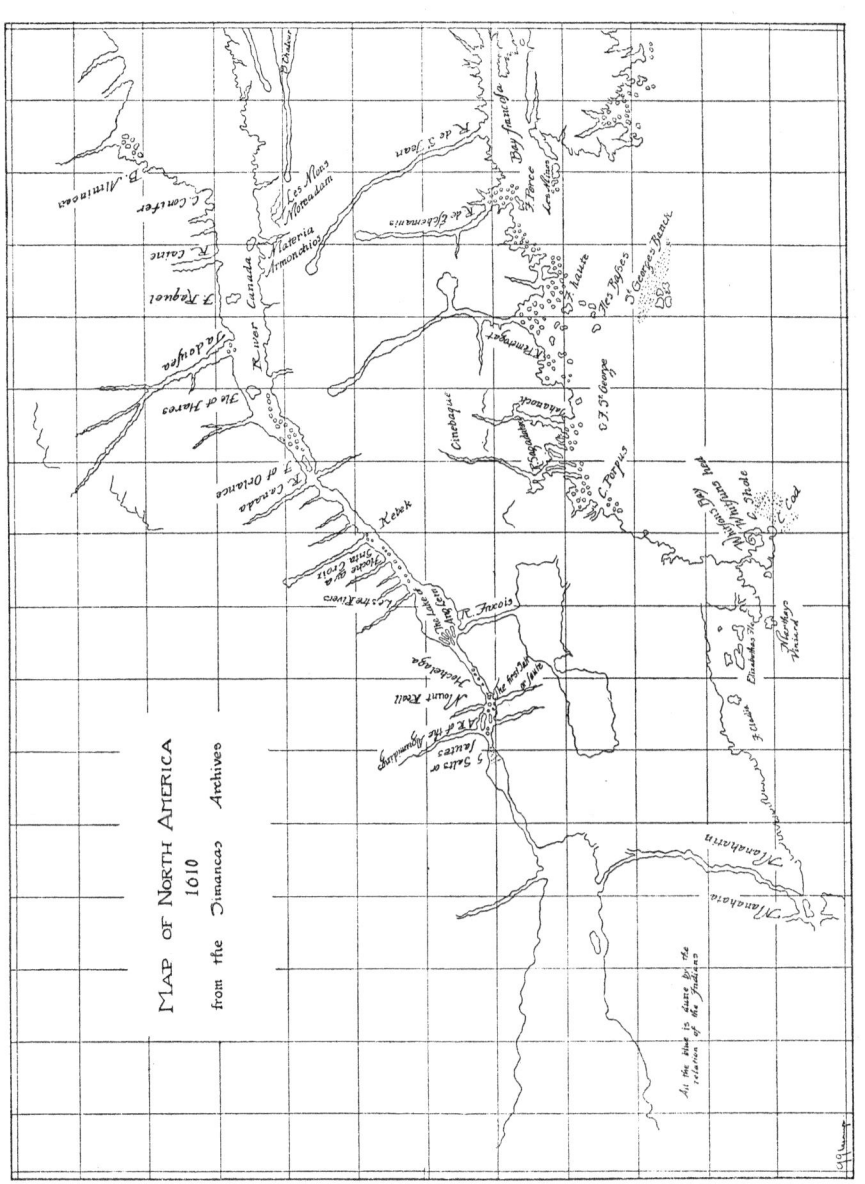

St. Lawrence up to and including Lake Ontario and an indefinite "grand lac" beyond emptying into it.[10] The Ottawa River was drawn parallel to the upper St. Lawrence, separated from it only by many islands. Lake Ontario's length was said to be fifteen days of voyaging in Indian canoes. This was by far the best map of the lower Great Lakes that had yet appeared.[11]

While Champlain was still in Paris he was surprised by a visit from young Vignau, whom he had sent the previous year to dwell with the tribesmen on the upper Ottawa. Vignau said he had been with the Indians to a northern ocean where he had seen the wreck of a white man's ship. This tallied so well with the account of Hudson's discovery of the great northern bay, that Champlain was jubilant. The route through North America would pass along the St. Lawrence, ice-bound for fewer months than Hudson's Strait. He hastened back to Quebec in the spring of 1613, and after the trading mart had been held near the Lachine Rapids, Champlain announced to his Indian allies that he would accompany them home. Vignau went with him, growing more and more silent concerning his exploits as they approached Allumette Island. There his former host convicted him of falsehood, proving that he had never left the Indian village nor seen a northern sea. Nor did the natives themselves admit that they had any knowledge of a route thither. Champlain in deep chagrin was obliged to retrace his steps, having accomplished nothing but the exploration of the Ottawa River.

[10] Reproduced in R. G. Thwaites, *Jesuit Relations and Allied Documents* (Cleveland, 1896-1901), ii, 56; Justin Winsor, *Cartier to Frontenac* (Boston, 1894), 104-105.

[11] Champlain also published a second map which shows nothing of the lakes, but does introduce a portion of Hudson Bay from a chart brought back by a companion of Hudson. See Winsor, *Cartier to Frontenac*, 106.

Two more years passed away without further westering. Meanwhile, Champlain returned to France and organized a company for the maintenance of his colony and addressed the States General on its behalf.[12] Then in 1615 he set forth once more for his "habitation," this time accompanied by four Recollect monks who went to begin missions for the savages. In undertaking this first mission to New France these devoted missionaries felt "a gladness of spirit which cannot be expressed." Father Joseph le Caron almost at once left with the Huron flotilla for their villages on Lake Huron, thus antedating Champlain's discovery of that lake by about three weeks. With the missionary went also twelve French *voyageurs* to assist the Hurons in their intertribal wars.[13]

At last the moment so eagerly desired had arrived for Champlain. July 9, 1615, with an equipment of two canoes, ten Indian paddlers, a white servant, and Brulé as interpreter, he left for the inland waters. The route up the Ottawa was already familiar as far as Allumette Island. Not far above that island his guides abandoned the Ottawa, ascended its branch the Mattawan, portaged into Lake Nipissing, and thence glided down French River to Georgian Bay. It was the last of July when Champlain finally emerged on the waters of that *mare dulce*, Sweetwater Sea, about which rumors had been afloat since the time of Cartier. Champlain recognized this lake as the one of which Cartier had heard, and gave it the name by which that explorer had called it (in French), "La Mer Douce." He also

[12] H. P. Biggar, *Early Trading Companies of New France* (Toronto, 1901), 94-98.

[13] Champlain also found a number of French traders among the Hurons when he arrived at their villages. He was thus by no means the first white man to see Lake Huron, but by virtue of making this lake known to the world his is the right of discovery.

DISCOVERY OF THE GREAT LAKES

realized after days of coasting southward along its shores, that it was not the same lake that lay above the rapids and falls of the main St. Lawrence. His destination was the Huron settlement, whence after a month's rest he went with a war party of that people through the Trent River portage and emerged at the eastern end of this second lake, to which he gave for the western Iroquois the name "Entouhonoron" (later softened into "Ontario"). Thus in the summer of 1615 Champlain discovered and named both of the Great Lakes concerning which conjecture had been afloat for eighty years.

He wished to complete the circuit of his discovery by returning down the St. Lawrence to Quebec. Unfortunately for this purpose he was slightly wounded in a battle with the enemies of the Hurons, and was forced by these savages to return with them to their villages on Georgian Bay. There he spent the winter of 1615-16, exploring in their vicinity.

The Huron Indians were among the earliest natives to make an alliance with the French in North America; this alliance had important connection with interior exploration. When Cartier in 1535 visited the St. Lawrence, the Indians he encountered at Stadacona, Hochelaga, and other villages were of the Huron branch of the great Iroquoian family. The Hurons and their kindred were then scattered from Quebec to Georgian Bay, with fishing villages as far east as Gaspé Bay. South of their habitat were other tribes who, although of related stock, were their enemies. These southern tribes later formed the confederacy of the Five Nations in central New York.[14] Between the time of Cartier

[14] See the Huron traditions of their early habitat, in W. E. Connelley, *Ontario Archaeological Report*, 1899, 92-109; appendix to report of Department of Education.

and the coming of Champlain, the Huron villages on the St. Lawrence were abandoned because of enemy raids, their inhabitants removing west and joining that portion of the tribe already located on the southern shore of Georgian Bay, protected on the southeast by Lake Simcoe. Thence they came each year to trade their furs for white men's goods. By the time Champlain visited them in the region now called Huronia, the Hurons consisted of a confederacy of from twenty to thirty thousand inhabitants living in eighteen towns, of which eight were strongly fortified by palisades.[15] They were a sedentary people, depending largely for food supply on agriculture, much advanced in civilization above the roving bands of Algonquian Indians who occupied the territory along the St. Lawrence and the Ottawa which the Hurons had abandoned. The word "Huron" was of French origin; the tribesmen called themselves the Wendat, from which the remnant of this tribe has received the name Wyandot.[16] In their seat in western Ontario the Hurons were surrounded by other kindred tribes. West of them in the Bruce Peninsula were the Tionnotates, called the Tobacco Hurons; south and east were the Neutrals, whose villages extended to Niagara River and beyond. The southern range of this latter tribe was the north shore of Lake Erie. South of that lake were the Erie, or Cat Nation, whose eastern neighbors were the Seneca, or western

---

[15] See sites of the Huron villages identified by Father Arthur Jones, in Ontario Archives, *Fifth Report*, 1908. Sulte, *Histoire des Canadiens-Français* (Montreal, 1886), ii, 21, thinks there were never more than twelve thousand Hurons; we give Champlain's estimate of their numbers.

[16] The Wyandot are in reality the descendants of the Tionnotates, the Petun or Tobacco Hurons; the Hurons of Lorette being the only descendants from the true Hurons of Champlain's time. See *post*, chapter vi.

Iroquois. With the Iroquois Confederacy the Hurons had been at enmity for many years. South and east of the Iroquois lay the Andastes, also of the Iroquoian family.

All around this closely compacted group of Huron-Iroquois natives roved Algonquian tribes who were in a much lower stage of civilization. Those of the St. Lawrence valley were in the hunter stage, knew little of agriculture, and were in general nomads. In the Ottawa valley these people had become more sedentary, an important village on Allumette Island and a group on Lake Nipissing approximating the higher barbarism of the Hurons. With these eastern Algonquian tribesmen the Hurons were at peace, as well as with those on the islands of Georgian Bay. Champlain met some of the latter in the Huron villages; he called them the *Cheveux Relevés* ("erect hairs") because of their fashion of wearing a crest of hair upon their heads. These tribesmen were the Ottawa of later history. Closely allied to them in the lower Michigan peninsula were the Chippewa and Potawatomi; the latter, "keepers of the sacred fire," were often confused with one of their bands, the Prairie people, or Mascouten. These latter, with their kindred the Kickapoo, Sauk, and Foxes, wandered in the Saginaw and Detroit region, and were at enmity with both the Hurons and the Neutrals.

Had Champlain during the winter of 1616 been able, as he wished, to visit the Neutrals, he would have discovered Lake Erie and the Niagara River. As events proved, he never knew of these connecting links between the lakes which he had visited. Nor was he more successful in exploring the north shore of Lake Huron, whence he might have discovered Lake Superior and Lake Michigan; he made an agreement with the Nipissing to take him thither, when an intertribal quarrel occurred which made it impossible to undertake a journey into the territory of tribes at war. Champlain was forced to content himself with instructions to his interpreters to continue western exploration. Then, after taking possession of the shores of Lake Huron for France, the great explorer returned to Quebec by the same route he had come out, never again to visit the West.[17]

How far his subordinates obeyed his instructions concerning further exploration it is not easy, in the absence of their reports, to determine. Some suggestive passages in contemporary documents afford reason to think that the early voyages from Huronia were widely extended. In 1618 Brulé, who had remained at Huronia the intervening three years, came down with the annual trading fleet. He related to Champlain the incidents of a journey to the Andastes, when he discovered the waters of the Susquehanna River, which he followed down to tidewater. He said nothing, however, about Lake Erie or the Niagara River. Brulé also reported that he had made a voyage to the northern shore of Lake Huron, along which he had coasted for ten days. Champlain chided him for not continuing farther in his voyage toward the West; the interpreter promised to do better in the future.[18] After this interview with his superior, Brulé went back again to his headquarters among the Hurons. There by his dissolute conduct he soon brought disgrace upon the name of Frenchmen. Nevertheless, he seems to have attempted to carry out Champlain's instructions for westward voyaging. This information we learn, not from Champlain, but from the

[17] For Champlain's description of this voyage, see Grant, *Champlain*, 276-332.
[18] *Ibid.*, 354-359; Sixte le Tac, *Histoire Chronologique de la Nouvelle France* (Paris, 1868), 107.

Recollect missionaries. The first of their order to visit the western villages returned to the St. Lawrence with Champlain, and it was six years before another ventured so far afield. Then in 1622 Father Guillaume Poulain visited the Nipissing, whose summer home was on the lake of their name but who wintered usually among their allies the Hurons. In 1623 Le Caron, the first missionary, went out once more to Huronia, accompanied by Father Nicolas Viel[19] and by a lay brother, Gabriel Sagard. The latter became the historian of the early Recollect mission.[20] These missionaries were inspired with zeal for exploration; Sagard planned to take a southern and Viel a northern journey westward from Huronia.[21] From the Frenchmen dwelling among the Hurons, Sagard obtained what information he could. In addition to Brulé, a youth named Grenoble told the missionaries that he had visited the place where the Indians were taking copper from a mine.[22] These interpreters also told Sagard that "above Mer Douce is another very great lake, discharging into it by rapids nearly two leagues broad named Saut de Gaston. This lake with the Mer Douce has an extent of thirty days' journey by canoe, according to the report of the savages, and according to that of the interpreter [Brulé?] it is four hundred leagues in extent."[23]

[19] Father Viel was drowned two years later by a vicious Huron, just as he was approaching civilization. This first martyr in New France gave name to the Sault au Récollet north of the island of Montreal.

[20] Gabriel Sagard-Théodat's first book was *Le Grand Voyage du Pays des Hurons* (Paris, 1632); his *Histoire du Canada* (Paris, 1636) is a second edition of the first, somewhat enlarged. They are among the rareties of French Americana. They were reprinted in 1865 and 1866.

[21] Sagard, *Histoire* (Paris, 1866), i, 265.

[22] *Ibid.*, ii, 328.

[23] *Ibid.*, iii, 589; *Le Grand Voyage* (Paris, 1865), 74.

These accounts, the first definite description of Lake Superior, indicate that Grenoble and Brulé had visited that region and had seen a copper mine, possibly on Isle Royale.[24] The name "Sault de Gaston," given in honor of the king's brother to the present Sault Ste. Marie, seems a clear indication that white men had visited this place.

Sagard and Viel never succeeded in going farther west than Huronia. Their associate, Father La Roche Daillon, went in 1626 with two interpreters, one of whom was Grenoble, to the country of the Neutrals. The missionary makes, however, in his report no mention of Lake Erie, but does describe the Lake Ontario-St. Lawrence route to Quebec as shorter than the customary one via the Ottawa River and Georgian Bay.[25]

Meanwhile, international complications occurred which put an end to the Recollect mission to the Huron tribesmen. Champlain after his voyage of 1615-16 devoted himself to consolidating and enlarging his colony. Quebec was rebuilt in stone, and in 1624 Champlain convened there the chiefs of the Iroquois, with whom he made a treaty of alliance which accorded the little colony a brief immunity from their attacks. The next year Cardinal Richelieu, who had become the power behind the throne in France, decided to reinforce the missions in Canada by a band of Jesuit fathers. Richelieu during the remainder of his life was much interested in developing New France. In 1625 he assumed for himself the entire charge of the marine

[24] A very interesting description of the remains of the prehistoric copper mines on Isle Royale is given by George R. Fox in *Wisconsin Archeologist*, x, 73-100.

[25] Chrétien Le Clercq, *First Establishment of the Faith in New France* (Englished and edited by John G. Shea, New York, 1881), i, 204-205.

department, with the office of grand master of navigation and commerce. The administration of the colonies was one branch of this department. Richelieu further provided for the growth of New France by revoking, in 1627, all previous concessions and privileges of trade, and concentrating the economic fortunes of the colony in the hands of the Company of New France, usually known as the Company of One Hundred Associates. This company was empowered and required to provide each year for the emigration of three hundred colonists, and for tools and equipment to enable them to till the soil. Champlain was reappointed governor of the colony. The fur trade also grew apace; in 1629 twenty Frenchmen came from Huronia, who had passed the winter among the tribesmen in that distant country.[26] Other young Frenchmen had gone to live among the Algonquian tribes, on the upper Ottawa and at Lake Nipissing. All looked favorable for the development of the colony, when suddenly English privateers appeared in the mouth of the St. Lawrence and demanded the surrender of all of New France. In the year 1628 Champlain, who at that time was not even aware of the breach between France and England, was able to hold the fort against the invaders. These invaders were English merchants formerly of Dieppe, who had secured letters of marque from the English king, expressly to secure possession of the colony on the St. Lawrence. Repulsed for the once, the Kirke brothers retired, only to return with reinforcements the next year.

Meanwhile the presence of the English freebooters had kept the supply ships from arriving at Quebec. Champlain had had great difficulties during the winter to supply his people with food. The arrival of the Huron flotilla in the spring was awaited with great anxiety.

[26] Laverdière, *Champlain*, vi, 231.

These newcomers brought no provisions; they did bring, however, Etienne Brulé, who at Tadoussac deserted to the English and piloted their ships up the St. Lawrence. Champlain and the aged Pontgravé were forced to surrender upon honorable terms. In great bitterness of heart the governor reproached Brulé for his treachery. Then, having made such plans as he could for the converted Indians and for the agricultural population, the great Frenchman, thinking his life work destroyed, embarked for France, while Brulé and some of the other youthful traders retired with the savages to Huronia. Before departing, Champlain handed to the English conqueror a map embracing the French claims and the extent of their discoveries.[27] This map was doubtless the same as that published with the new edition of his journals which he issued in France in 1632. Upon this map may be seen the great progress in western discovery which Champlain and his men, during a score of years, had accomplished. Both Lakes Huron and Ontario appear in their proper latitude with a river of some length connecting them, in which is marked "a very high fall where many fish come down and are stunned." West of "Mer Douce" [Huron] appears a "Grand Lac" discharging by the Sault de Gaston. The main features of the Great Lakes hereon begin to appear.[28]

By the time Champlain arrived in France Charles I and Louis XIII had arranged their differences; finally, by the treaty of St. Germain in 1632, Canada was restored to France. The next year Champlain was permitted to return to take charge of the colony to

[27] Laverdière, *Champlain*, vi, 295.
[28] We reproduce this map by permission of the publishers of Bourne's *Champlain*, the Laidlaw Brothers, successors to the A. S. Barnes Company.

CHAMPLAIN'S MAP OF NEW FRANCE, 1632

which he had devoted his life. With what emotions he must have recognized each familiar cape and headland as his vessel tacked up the broad bosom of the St. Lawrence toward Quebec! With him he brought a company of soldiers, the first royal troops in New France.

The return of Champlain was reported throughout the length and breadth of the Indian country. Soon canoes began to arrive filled with delighted savages. Many of the Indians had refused to traffic with the English, and had fallen back upon their primitive economy which had supported them before the white man's advent. Among the Hurons came some Frenchmen who for five long years had awaited the return of the fleurs-de-lis.[29] Brulé, however, was not among them. Having had a misunderstanding with a Huron, he had been struck down in anger and later killed. The Hurons were in great trepidation lest the great governor should take vengeance upon them for Brulé's murder. Champlain, however, assured them that the latter was not considered a Frenchman, since he had betrayed his people to the English, and that Brulé's death was a judgment upon him for his crimes. The superstitious Hurons, however, thought that a pestilence which fell upon them later was sent by the French to avenge the death of their interpreter.[30] So perished miserably the first explorer of the upper lakes.

Champlain lived but two years longer to advance his cherished colony. When he died on Christmas day of 1635, all New France mourned. America, as well as

[29] Some of these earliest Westerners whose names have been preserved were Du Verney, La Montagne, and Guillaume Chaudron. Chaudron died in Huronia between 1629 and 1632.
[30] Laverdière, *Champlain*, vi, 81, 265-267; *Jes. Rel.*, v, 239, 255; x, 79, 309-311; xii, 87; xiv, 17, 53; Sagard, *Histoire*, 430.

France, owes a debt of gratitude to Champlain. His memory belongs not only to the people of Canada, but to those of the United States who live along the Great Lakes. He was the man to whose enthusiasm, faith, and persistence the world owes the knowledge of these fresh-water seas at the source of the great river of Canada. With Champlain the earliest history of Wisconsin begins.

V. THE VOYAGE OF JEAN NICOLET, 1634–1635

DURING his last years Champlain made a final effort to solve the mystery of the Great Lakes, and to discover their possibilities as an ultimate route through the continent to the far East. For this purpose he chose a young Norman who had come to New France with him in the year 1618 and had served the usual apprenticeship among the Indians, learning their languages, customs, and the arts of woodcraft. Jean Nicolet was born at Cherbourg, then the third largest port of France, on that Norman peninsula that juts into the channel and faces the open ocean. Thus Nicolet was like Champlain himself a child of the sea; in his veins flowed the blood of the Vikings; his mother was Marguerite Delamer, who by her very surname showed herself to be a descendant of generations of sea-going ancestors. His father followed the more prosaic calling of mail carrying from Cherbourg to Paris and return. During the days of the civil wars in France this calling was no doubt one of adventure; but in 1598, the year of Jean's birth, the wars were ended and peace and prosperity under Henry IV spread over France.

We know nothing, except from inference, of Nicolet's boyhood. While he was growing up, Cherbourg increased yearly in importance; ships loaded with fish and furs frequently docked there after their long voyages to the Banks of Newfoundland. Mariners who had voyaged with Champlain and Monts returned thither to tell of the wonders of the New World, and of the great river of Canada whose source was hidden in the unknown depths of the continent. Nicolet no doubt accompanied his father upon some of his many journeys to Paris, and there after Henry IV's assassination in 1610 he may have seen his boy successor, Louis XIII, roll along in his gorgeous couch on his way to a bed of justice in Parlement. Like most youths Nicolet longed for adventure, and eagerly accepted Champlain's offer to accompany him to his trading post at Quebec, there to learn to be an interpreter for the company that maintained it. The founder of New France saw in the youth of Cherbourg those qualities of steadfastness and persistence that, combined with his love of adventure, adapted him to wilderness life. A congenial spirit existed between the older and the younger man—a like distaste for the sheltered life, a common love of the unknown, and above all a constant belief in the goodness and watchful care of God. Moreover, Nicolet had an aptitude for languages; "his nature and excellent memory inspired good hopes of him," says his biographer—hopes destined to be fulfilled in a high degree.

Upon reaching New France in 1618 Champlain sent his new recruit to live among the Algonkin Indians at Allumette Island—a tribe long in alliance with the French, whose former interpreter, Nicolas Vignau, had misled Champlain with his lying stories and caused his fruitless voyage of 1613. One may easily imagine Nicolet's sensations as he made his first journey up the Ottawa River in the canoes of the savages. He proved himself to be no idler and purveyor of worthless tales like Vignau, but won the good will of his savage hosts, and was soon adopted into their tribe.

Allumette Island was well placed for one who wished to learn the ways of forest wanderings and to obtain information about the tribes that dwelt in the interior. Its chief, the one-eyed Le Borgne, levied tribute on all canoes passing up or down stream, so that Indians who traded on the St. Lawrence stopped at this village and reported the happenings of their own distant habitats. The Indian youths also taught the young Frenchman the arts of forest life—how to hunt and trap for furs, how to handle a canoe in the boiling rapids of the Ottawa. Strange as it seems, however, they never taught him to swim, and years later, after voyaging for thousands of miles through incredible dangers, Nicolet lost his life through his lack of this accomplishment. While with the Island tribesmen, the only Frenchman within some hundred miles or more, he accompanied them in their wanderings in search of food and furs; "he tarried with them two years, alone of the French, and always joined the barbarians in their excursions and journeys, undergoing such fatigues as none but eyewitnesses can conceive; he often passed seven or eight days without food, and once, full seven weeks with no other nourishment than a little bark from the trees."[1] From this report of his experiences, it would seem that the young Norman not only had a strong physique and great powers of endurance, but was also gifted with a talent for vivid narration.

While Nicolet lived among the Islanders he went with four hundred of the tribe on a peace mission to the Iroquois villages. Thereafter he was interpreter at the famous conference of 1624, when peace was declared between these warring tribes and the French.[2] "Would to God," says his Jesuit biographer, "it had never been broken, for then we should not now be suffering the calamities which move us to groans, and which must

[1] Nicolet's fame rests upon his biography written in the year of his death by Father Vimont, Jesuit superior in New France. See *Jes. Rel.*, xxiii, 275-283; Louise P. Kellogg, Original Narrative Series, *Early Narratives of the Northwest* (New York, 1917), 11-16.

[2] Laverdière, *Champlain*, vi, 75-80; Le Clercq, *Establishment of the Faith*, i, 227.

be an extraordinary impediment in the way of converting these tribes."³ Nicolet's conduct was so correct and his skill as an interpreter so useful, that he was promoted soon after the peace negotiations to the position of official interpreter among the Nipissing, a larger tribe than that of the Islanders, whose friendship, because of their habitat on the route to Lake Huron, was of the utmost consequence to both missionaries and traders. Among the Nipissing, Nicolet had extraordinary success; unlike Brulé in the Huron country, he did not abandon himself to the vices of the savages; no breath of misconduct ever tarnished his reputation. While with the Nipissing "he passed for one of that nation, taking part in the very frequent councils of these tribes, having his own separate cabin and household, and fishing and trading for himself"; that is, he was recognized as a chief of the tribe and imposed his authority upon them, living none the less somewhat apart with more regard to the life of a civilized man than the tribesmen showed. Doubtless during these eight or nine years that he spent among the Nipissing he acquired a competence, for in 1637 when, his wanderings over, he espoused a daughter of the first Canadian colonist, he settled upon her as her dowry two thousand pounds.⁴

While Nicolet lived among the Nipissing, he gained much knowledge of the interior of the American continent and of the tribes that dwelt therein.⁵ The nearest neighbors of the Nipissing to the west were the tribes along the northern shores of Georgian Bay—the Missisauga, the Nikikoek or Otter people, the Amikouek or Beaver people, the Achirigouans, and at the Sault Ste. Marie the Paouitagouing, known to the French as

---

³ *Jes. Rel.*, xxiii, 277.
⁴ *Wisconsin Historical Collections*, xi, 20-22.
⁵ Sagard, *Le Grand Voyage*, 51.

Saulteurs, the ancestors of the present Chippewa.⁶
All these people were semi-nomadic, living chiefly by
hunting and fishing. The Ottawa, whom Champlain
had seen among the Hurons, dwelt on the Manitoulin
and other islands of Georgian Bay. They were progress-
ing into the agricultural stage of barbarism, but their
chief occupation was intertribal trade. The Ottawa
were friendly with a near-by group of wandering tribes,
the Sinago (Outaouosinigouek), Kiskakon (Kichka-
goueiak), and People of the Fork, who were later all
incorporated into the Ottawa confederacy.⁷ Closely
related to these latter tribes was a people now known as
the Potawatomi, called by themselves and their neighbors "Keepers of the Sacred Fires." In the nineteenth
century these three great tribes formed the triple
alliance of Chippewa, Ottawa, and Potawatomi.⁸ The
Hurons who sometimes traded with the Potawatomi
called them the Assistagueronons, or Fire People.
Gradually this name was applied by the Hurons and
white men to all the Algonquian groups lying west of
Lake Huron and dwelling in the lower peninsula of
Michigan as far south as Detroit River. The Jesuits
estimated this aggregation of tribal peoples at eighty
thousand souls.⁹

These Algonquian tribes, most of which afterwards
dwelt in Wisconsin, are now being classified by linguistic
affinities.¹⁰ From this study it would seem that the Sauk

⁶ *Jes. Rel.*, xxiii, 149-151.
⁷ *Ibid.*, 151.
⁸ *Handbook of North American Indians* (Washington, 1910), ii, 289, 471, 811.
⁹ *Jes. Rel.*, xviii, 233-235; xxvii, 25.
¹⁰ Truman Michelson, "Preliminary Report on the Linguistic Classification of Algonquian Tribes," in Bureau of Ethnology, *Twenty-eighth Annual Report*, 225-290. See also Alanson Skinner, *The Mascoutens or Prairie Potawatomi, Bulletin of the Public Museum of the City of Milwaukee*, iv, 9-15. Skinner proves that the Mascouten were an offshoot of the Potawatomi, but so long asso-

dwelling on Saginaw Bay, and the Foxes along the Detroit River, were of close kinship; and that the Mascouten and Kickapoo, who may have lived somewhat to the west of them, were likewise affiliated. All their languages are easily understood by members of the several tribes, while throughout their history they have always maintained a close alliance. Nearest to these latter tribes in language grouping stand the Shawnee, who in historic times dwelt in Kentucky and Tennessee; probably some of this tribe were living also in the southern portion of Illinois in times not long before they became known to white men.[11]

Southwest of these Algonquian of the eastern portion of Michigan dwelt the great tribes of the Miami and the Illinois, so closely related that their separation must have occurred at no very distant time before the coming of the whites.[12] The Illinois in the valley of their river, the Miami along the Wabash and eastern tributaries of Lake Michigan, had ceased to be nomads but still depended upon hunting for clothing and for a large share of their food.

The Huron tribe in closest contact with these western Algonquian was the Petun or Tobacco Hurons of Bruce peninsula; through their agency white men's goods had been introduced among the Westerners before the voyage of Nicolet. The Neutral Hurons, on the other hand, were at enmity with these people; while Nicolet was living among the Nipissing, they drove the Potawatomi northward to take refuge with the tribes not far from Sault Ste. Marie.[13]

---

ciated with the Kickapoo, Sauk, and Foxes that their social economy and language are more nearly related to the central than to the northern Algonquian.

[11] Clarence W. Alvord, *The Illinois Country, 1673-1818* (Springfield, 1920), 30-31.

[12] *Ibid.*, 33.

[13] Kellogg, *Early Narratives*, 23.

West of the Sault in the upper peninsula of Michigan and reaching down to the northwestern shore of Green Bay dwelt the kindred tribes of the Noquet and the Menominee. These were Algonquian in origin, their language, however, being allied to that of the Cree dwelling north and west of Lake Superior. It would seem probable, therefore, that they had migrated from the north before the Chippewa reached the Sault, and that they had lived so long in the habitat where white men first found them that they had forgotten any earlier home.[14] The Noquet, who gave their names to the bays opening north from the northern end of Green Bay, early disappeared as a tribe, probably coalescing with the Menominee. These latter must have taken their name after they came to live along Menominee River, where the wild rice grew abundantly and became their principal food. The Menominee appear to have been the oldest Algonquian dwellers in what is now Wisconsin. They were noted among the earliest travelers for their remarkable physical development and for their uniform friendliness toward the whites. It was the proud boast of the Menominee that they had never killed a white man, unless, it should be added, at the behest of other white men for whom they were allies in international wars. The Menominee still live on portions of the land that was theirs when Nicolet first visited them—a remarkable record of an unbroken residence in the same region.

With the exception of this small group of Algonquian peoples in the northeast, all of what is now Wisconsin was peopled by a tribe of an entirely different language

[14] The Menominee claimed to be autochthons in Wisconsin; the Chippewa had a tradition of migration from the St. Lawrence valley. *Holmes Anniversary Volume* (Washington, 1916), 199. See also Alanson Skinner, *Material Culture of the Menomini* (New York Museum of the American Indian, Heye Foundation, 1921), 24, 46, 371-372.

stock and customs—a people more barbaric, more fiercely proud and independent than the Algonquian, so intractable and so hostile that they have by some historians been designated as the "Iroquois of the West." These people were an offshoot of the great Siouan family, which during historic times occupied most of the basin of the Mississippi and of the Missouri. Some tribes of this family were encountered by De Soto on the lower Mississippi; others speaking a kindred language were found by the English in the foothills of the Appalachians; tribes encountered by Iberville on the coast of Louisiana were also of Siouan origin; while great branches of this family dwelt upon the headwaters of the Mississippi and along Green Bay when these regions first became known to the French. In their later history they became plains Indians, wholly dependent upon the buffalo and the horse. When first met by the whites, however, most of their tribes were sedentary and in part agricultural.

The original habitat of the Siouan peoples is one of the unsettled problems of American ethnology. A theory of a first home on the eastern slopes of the Appalachians with slow western migrations down the Ohio valley, a separation at its mouth with movements both up and down the Mississippi and out along the Missouri, has much to commend it.[15] In such a migration scheme the Wisconsin Siouan tribe, known to the Algonquian as the Winnebago, must have advanced up the Mississippi to the mouth of the Rock River, thence east and north along that river to its sources and beyond. Other recent investigations, however,

[15] The theory first proposed by Horatio Hale, of the original habitat of the Siouan nations on the eastern slopes of the Appalachians, was accepted by Brinton, Dorsey, Mooney, McGee, and Livingston Farrand. See Dorsey, "Siouan Sociology," Bureau of Ethnology, *Fifteenth Annual Report*.

locate the original Siouan habitat north of Lake Superior, whence by both its eastern and its western end advance was made into the Mississippi and Ohio valleys.[16] This theory seems to be corroborated in part by Winnebago traditions, which always describe the first home of their people upon Green Bay, instead of upon Rock River.[17] Moreover the Winnebago call themselves "people of the parent speech"; they are acknowledged as "elder brothers" by the Iowa, the Oto, and the Missouri, who would thus appear to have separated and wandered from the Winnebago, rather than the latter from among them.

Whatever the original line of migration, ethnologists are agreed that the Winnebago had dwelt a long time in Wisconsin before the coming of the whites. They have left many and unique monuments scattered over all the surface of southern Wisconsin in the form of mounds. These mounds are not merely for burial purposes; the greater number of them have no contents, but are built in the form of some animal, hence the term effigy mounds. This great series of sculptures or art works raised upon the soil of Wisconsin has created unusual interest from the time they were first observed. It is now believed that they were built by the Winnebago for ceremonial purposes, and that they represent the various elements of the clan or totemic system,

[16] Cyrus Thomas, "Some Suggestions in regard to Primary Indian Migrations in North America," in Fifteenth International Congress of Americanists, *Proceedings*, 189-205; *Handbook*, ii, 578. Edward S. Curtis, *The North American Indians* (1908), iii, 4; iv, 129-130, attempts to combine the two theories by assuming an eastern and southern origin, with a migration of certain Siouan branches north of Lake Superior before the occupation of Wisconsin and the upper waters of the Mississippi and the Missouri.

[17] *Wis. Hist. Colls.*, iii, 285; xiii 458, 466; *Journal of American Folk Lore*, xxvi, 300.

which was highly organized among the Winnebago.[18] The great number of these mounds, as well as the size of the trees growing upon some of them, indicates that this tribe had dwelt in Wisconsin two or three centuries before the voyage of Nicolet, and that their numbers then were much greater than those of the historic Winnebago.[19]

The prehistoric Winnebago of Wisconsin were in the early agricultural stage of development; animal food, however, especially the beaver, was particularly prized. They also used both fish and fresh-water mussels. From their Menominee neighbors they had learned to gather, store, and cook wild rice. They had chipped stone implements and a few bits of crude copper and lead; the latter metal, which they obtained themselves from the neighboring lead mines, was used almost wholly for ornamental purposes. Copper nuggets, beaten into a great variety of shapes for weapons, tools, and ornaments,[20] were secured by intertribal trade from Algonquian about Lake Superior. The Winnebago made pottery, but not with the potter's wheel; gourds, bark, and shells formed many of their vessels. They seem to have known no weaving, but plaited mats of rushes. Their garments were of skins; their lodges were built of poles, covered with skins or bark. Their only domestic animal was the dog.

[18] Paul Radin, "The Social Organization of the Winnebago Indians," in Canada Geological Survey, *Museum Bulletin No. 10* (Ottawa, 1915). The Winnebago village we reproduce is taken from Henry R. Schoolcraft, *Indian Tribes* (Philadelphia, 1851-57), ii, 80. It also appears in *Wis. Hist. Colls.*, xix, 300.

[19] About fifteen thousand mounds have already been listed by the Wisconsin Archeological Society within the boundaries of the present state. See the several surveys in the *Wisconsin Archeologist*.

[20] Charles E. Brown, "Native Copper Implements of Wisconsin," "Native Copper Ornaments of Wisconsin," in *Wisconsin Archeologist*, iii, 42-101.

A WINNEBAGO VILLAGE

Reduced from lithograph in Henry R. Schoolcraft's *Indian Tribes*

VOYAGE OF JEAN NICOLET 75

The Winnebago were very warlike and their relation to most of their neighbors was one of constant hostility. Cannibalism was practiced only on prisoners taken in war. Their prowess was great and the terror of their name widespread. "This," says an early report to the French, "was a very populous nation and these tribes believed themselves the most powerful in the universe; they declared war on all nations whom they could discover, although they had only stone knives and hatchets." The Ottawa, in their zeal for trade, sent messengers to tell the Winnebago of the French goods with which they could supply them. The Winnebago haughtily replied that they wished no dealings with the French. The Ottawa persisted, sending a second set of envoys, whom the Winnebago made prisoners, and afterwards killed and ate. The allies of the Ottawa rallied to avenge this misdeed and sent party after party to attack the faithless Winnebago. At last, harassed on every side, they agreed to accept peace and the articles of white manufacture the Ottawa had to offer.[21]

News of this different race of men dwelling in the far West reached French ears through both traders and missionaries.[22] Champlain had heard their name before he left Canada in 1629; upon his map of 1632 he placed the legend "le Nation des Puans [Winnebago]" beside a lake which discharges from the north into Lake Huron. In the former lake, Champlain placed an island on which is a mine of copper.[23] Nicolet among the Nipissing heard of these strange and distant people whose name was interpreted to mean "people of the

[21] *Wis. Hist. Colls.*, xvi, 4.
[22] Sagard, *Le Grand Voyage*, preface.
[23] See map, page 62.

sea."[24] The French, always eager to catch any hint of a route through the continent to the western sea, supposed that the Winnebago dwelt in the country whose streams flowed from the Great Lakes to that sea. Nicolet cherished the ambition of visiting this farthest western tribe of whom the French had yet heard. The Nipissing exaggerated their differences of custom and language to the degree that Nicolet thought they were of another race from the Indians.

Each summer when Nicolet went with this tribe to trade with the French, he reported to the governor what he had learned of the distant West. Meanwhile the English captured the colony, and during their occupation Nicolet remained among the tribesmen whom he governed. During this period also occurred the truce between the Ottawa and the Winnebago, and the way was thus prepared for westward exploration. When in 1633 Champlain returned to the St. Lawrence, he was greeted by his allied Indians with every mark of affection and respect. June 23 the Nipissing flotilla arrived bringing the interpreter, whose quiet steadfastness during the years of occupation was approved by the governor. Fifteen years of his life the young Norman had given to building up French reputation among the interior tribes. Now his reward was at hand. He was promoted to the position of clerk and interpreter in the Company of New France, with headquarters at the new post to be built at Three Rivers.[25] With what emotions he must have seen his charges

---

[24] The Algonquian word for this tribe, "Ouenibegous," was the same word that they applied to sea water. It really meant ill-smelling, or dirty; hence the French called the Winnebago "Puants."

[25] *Le Mercure Français*, xix, 825. Nicolet's name is not given but the promotion was accorded to the interpreter who had been a long time among the Nipissing.

depart, leaving him among men of his own race and language, after his long years of wilderness faring!

Unlike many of his successors, Nicolet's long sojourn in Indian cabins had not unfitted him for the society of civilized men. He married and settled at Three Rivers, founding a family that intermarried with the best of the colonials. He was much respected also by the churchmen, who wrote his obituary and highly praised his character. His death occurred in 1642 while he was on his way to Quebec, the boat in which he was traveling being swamped in the waves. "Save yourself sir, you can swim, I can not," he exclaimed to his companion. "I go to my God. I intrust to you my wife and daughter." It was a bitter cold night in October, and the water on the edges of the river had begun to freeze. His companion arrived half dead at the mission house; it was too late to rescue Nicolet. "His death," says the Jesuit historian, was "a loss to the whole country."[26]

After his death, the name and fame of Nicolet were forgotten for many years. Not until the middle of the nineteenth century, when the early history of the Northwest was being discussed, was the account of his discovery of Lake Michigan unearthed from the reports of the Jesuit missionaries.[27]

Nicolet undertook his now celebrated voyage at the behest of and under commission from Champlain. The veteran explorer realized that he could no longer venture to entrust himself to a birch-bark canoe, and to endure the hardships of wilderness voyaging. Nicolet, however, was now in the prime of life; his strong, vigorous body, his well trained mind, and his store of

[26] *Wis. Hist. Colls.*, xi, 17.
[27] On the history of the rediscovery of Nicolet as Wisconsin's first explorer, see *ibid.*, xi, 1-2, note.

woodcraft pointed to him as the logical person to be entrusted with this undertaking. Add to this his fine reputation among the tribesmen, his mastery of their languages and their customs, his eagerness to serve New France, and he became the ideal person of that day for the voyage Champlain contemplated. Champlain wished to test his theory that the route to the East lay through the Great Lakes. The English, when in possession of Canada, had so believed, and their king had granted a charter to one of his captains for land stretching from Canada to the California Sea, and declared that a discovery of a route thither "would proove an inestimable benefit for the Inhabitants of those parts, opening a neer way to China."[28] The retaking of Canada by the French, however, ended the British plans.

Champlain's instructions were for Nicolet to arrange a peace between all the western tribes, bringing them into the French alliance and opening the way for future trade and discovery. In pursuit of this design Nicolet carried with him "a grand robe of China damask, all strewn with flowers and birds of many colors," with the two-fold purpose of making an impression on the savage mind and of being prepared in case the distant Winnebago should prove to be Asiatics instead of Indians.[29]

Nicolet left the St. Lawrence with the trade flotilla of 1634,[30] with which was another white man, Father

[28] Sir William Alexander, "Our Encouragement to Colonies," Prince Society, *Publications*, viii, 185, 240-243.

[29] It seems hardly possible that Champlain with his knowledge of geography expected that his envoy would reach China on this expedition. He was apparently in doubt concerning these "people of the sea," and thought they might be a colony from the Orient.

[30] The date of Nicolet's voyage is nowhere stated. Sulte's arguments for the year 1634 are now generally accepted. *Wis. Hist. Colls.*, viii, 188-194.

Jean Brébeuf, on his way to the Huron mission.[31] They went together as far as Allumette Island, where Nicolet tarried to make arrangements for peace negotiations between the Islanders and the western tribesmen. From there he took the now familiar route to the Huron villages, a voyage occupying at least a month. Among the Hurons he made his final arrangements for his adventure, securing peace messages for the tribes he should encounter, and the services of seven Indians and a large canoe. About mid-August he left Huronia for the Ottawa villages on Manitoulin and other islands of Georgian Bay. So far the route must have been familiar to the explorer from his earlier voyages with the Nipissing, who frequented this region. From the Ottawa habitat the large canoe with its eight travelers, seven red men and one white, struck out into the unknown. Nicolet's Norman blood must have leapt within him, as like his Viking ancestors he breasted the waves through unknown seas, apparently as broad and untamed as the billows of old ocean. Along the dark, pine-clad shore of islands and mainland they crept into the open lake beyond, and then steered boldly north for the waters of the strait where the great Lake Superior pours its outlet into the lower lakes. Braving these waters to the foot of the rapids, Nicolet visited the Chippewa village at this place, saw the Indians' marvelous skill in spearing fish, and heard of the great inland [Superior] lake that lay beyond. But the "people of the sea," whom he was commissioned to find, dwelt, he learned, toward the sunset lands. So, abandoning the route to the northwest, he set the canoe toward the towering island of Michilimackinac, endowed by the superstitions of the savages with a certain mysterious sanctity. Thence on and on into the unknown, past the

[31] *Jes. Rel.*, viii, 99.

jutting point later to be named St. Ignace, hugging the forbidding northern shore of Lake Michigan, the explorer pressed his way. Now the vast expanse of the southwesternmost of the Great Lakes opened before him, a great sea of fresh water peopled by many tribes hitherto unknown. His guides informed him that the nation he sought lay at the end of a long, deep bay opening from the western side of the new-found lake. Along this bay dwelt more new tribes who were propitiated with gifts. "They fastened two sticks in the earth, and hung gifts thereon, so as to relieve these tribes from the notion of mistaking them for enemies to be massacred."

At the mouth of this bay lies a chain of islands where the traverse was customarily made to its southeastern shore. Here at the entrance of the bay the explorer paused and sent messengers to inform the people he sought of his approach. Then after allowing time for the announcement, he set forth along the pelucid green waters of this lovely inland waterway, amid pine-fringed islands and picturesque cliffs, toward the village of the mysterious people he had with such hazard sought.

Meanwhile, at the news of the approach of this strange visitor, all was excitement and animation in the native village. "They dispatched several young men to meet the Manitouiriniou—that is to say, 'the wonderful man.' They meet him; they escort him, and carry all his baggage. He wore a grand robe of China damask, all strewn with flowers and birds of many colors. No sooner did they meet him than the women and children fled, at the sight of a man who carried thunder in both hands—for thus they called the two pistols that he held."[32] Nicolet's dramatic landfall

[32] Kellogg, *Early Narratives*, 16. The narrative is doubtless in Nicolet's own words; it is a model of terse, vigorous description.

WISCONSIN LANDFALL OF JEAN NICOLET, 1634
From photograph of original canvas by Edwin Willard Deming

VOYAGE OF JEAN NICOLET 81

served its purpose in impressing the Winnebago with the marvelous character of their white visitor.[33] He no doubt had long been aware that the "men of the sea" were Indians like those he had known, except for differences of dialect and customs. His first task was to cement the desired alliance. All the interior chiefs were summoned; great feasts were held, at one of which were "served at least sixscore beavers"; and by means of the elaborate ceremonies the Indians love, a peace was made embracing the Winnebago, the French, and all their allied tribes. This diplomatic preliminary finished, Nicolet turned his attention to his other purpose, that of exploration and of finding a route to the western sea. Here all was confusion and difficulty. Through his interpreters he learned the names of great tribes that lay westward and southward, but nothing of a salt ocean whose shores he hoped to be able to visit. Finally he found tribesmen who told him that three days' journey away there was a great river issuing from the lake upon which he might sail to the great water.[34]

This report has generally been interpreted to mean

The scene has been represented by several artists, notably by Edwin W. Deming in a picture in the Wisconsin Historical Museum, which we herein reproduce. Another pictorial representation, by Albert Ballin, is in the State Capitol.

[33] The landfall of Nicolet has been in much doubt; rival places have erected monuments. There is one at Menasha and one at Red Banks. The Winnebago traditions point to the latter site: *Wis. Hist. Colls.*, iii, 204; xiii, 457.

[34] The Jesuit chronicler understood Nicolet to say as follows. "Sieur Nicolet, who has advanced farthest into these so distant countries, has assured me that, if he had sailed three days' journey farther upon a great river which issues from this lake [Michigan] he would have found the sea." *Jes. Rel.*, xviii, 237. It seems almost certain the Jesuit must have misunderstood Nicolet, who certainly would not have hesitated to take the three days' journey to test the theory. He must have meant he would have found *the way* to the sea, or he would have found "the big water," the Mississippi.

that if he had sailed three days beyond where he went on Fox River he would have reached the Mississippi; that would mean that he ascended the Fox as far as the portage. The report, however, explicitly states that the river issued from the lake. May he not have heard at Green Bay of the Chicago-Illinois exit from Lake Michigan[35] three days' journey from the Sturgeon Bay portage? This he would certainly interpret to accord with Champlain's belief that there were rivers issuing *from* the Great Lakes that led to the sea.

The season was now growing late; Nicolet's mission had been accomplished, his companions were eager to return to their country before the autumn storms. Leaving Green Bay, without further voyaging, they safely reached Huronia, where Nicolet passed the winter, returning to Quebec with the trading fleet of 1635.[36] Champlain was much pleased with his envoy's report; he regarded this voyage as the climax of his career; by its means he had carried the sovereignty of France into the interior so far that, as he wrote Cardinal Richelieu, New France extended more than fifteen hundred leagues in longitude.[37] Nicolet, his voyaging

[35] It is well known that in seasons of high water canoes passe from the Chicago to the Des Plaines without portaging.

[36] Most writers on Nicolet, notably C. W. Butterfield, *History of the Discovery of the Northwest by Jean Nicolet* (Cincinnati, 1881), believed that the explorer wintered in Wisconsin and visited all the tribes he enumerated in *Jes. Rel.*, xviii, 231-233. We do not think the text admits of this interpretation. "He returned to the Hurons, and some time later to Three Rivers," says Father Vimont on Nicolet's own authority. In the list enumerated as above are mentioned the "Naduesiu" and the "Assinipour." No one believes that Nicolet visited these tribes. His list is evidently given from Indian information to show that there were great peoples beyond the Winnebago. We think that Nicolet did not explore far beyond his landfall on Green Bay.

[37] *Collection de Manuscrits de la Nouvelle France* (Quebec, 1883), i, 112-113.

over, settled at Three Rivers, "where he continued his employment as agent and interpreter, to the great satisfaction of both the French and the savages, by whom he was equally and singularly loved."[38]

Champlain survived only a few months after Nicolet's return. His work was finished; he had laid firm foundations for the colony of New France, he had explored the sources of the St. Lawrence, he had revealed the mystery of the Great Lakes, but he probably died in the belief that there were but four of these inland seas, and that from them rivers ran to the west and entered the great South Sea. Nicolet's voyage was a tribute to Champlain's greatness. It reveals his faith in France as a colonizing power, his zeal for geographical knowledge, and his hope of federating and civilizing the Indian population of the New World. By his faith and vision he opened the continent to civilization.

Nevertheless, Nicolet's voyage, although it revealed the existence of Wisconsin to the world, was the end and not the beginning of an era in western history. With the death of Champlain the impulse for western exploration was exhausted, and the little colony on the St. Lawrence turned to purely local interests, while Indian wars in the interior forbade western voyaging. Nicolet had no successor for over twenty years, and Wisconsin and the upper Great Lakes remained as they had been before Nicolet's exploration—an unknown region, the home of barbarous savages and the haunt of the beasts of the forest. Nicolet's expedition was an episode whose importance has not been noted until recent times, and whose chief interest is due to the enterprise with which it was conducted, and to the fact that it rounded out the remarkable cycle of Champlain's exploits in discovery.

[38] Kellogg, *Early Narratives*, 16.

VI. TRIBAL WARS AND DISPERSION, 1635-1654

THE outstanding fact of the history of New France for thirty years after the death of Champlain was the enmity of the Iroquois. It was this enmity which prevented continued westward progress, which destroyed flourishing missions and drove the Jesuits from the West, which ravaged the homes of sedentary people and forced them to flee in every direction for a refuge. It was this enmity which, after the voyage of Nicolet, closed Wisconsin to French enterprise for twenty years, and made it an asylum for a vast aggregation of Algonquian tribesmen fleeing from the vengeance of their Iroquois foes.

Hostilities with the Iroquois were an inheritance by the French of the intertribal warfare which had raged in the century that elapsed between the discoveries of Cartier and Nicolet. During much of this period the Hurons and their Algonquian allies were in the ascendancy; the Iroquois tribesmen were comparatively few and rarely successful in raids.[1] Not until the organization of their confederacy of Five Nations did the Iroquois acquire a measure of confidence.[2] Even after that league was formed the Hurons were usually able to repel the Iroquois assaults, and frequently to carry the war into their enemies' territory.

---

[1] See legend of the origin of the enmity between these two groups, in E. H. Blair, *Indian Tribes of the Upper Mississippi Valley and the Region of the Great Lakes* (Cleveland, 1911), i, 42-47.

[2] The date of the formation of this confederacy is now placed at the latter part of the sixteenth century, probably in 1570. *Handbook*, i, 618; William M. Beauchamp, "A History of the New York Iroquois," in New York State Museum, *Bulletin No. 78* (Albany, 1905), 153.

When the French settled Canada, they were forced to choose alliance with one or the other of these two groups of warring natives. The Hurons appeared to them superior in intelligence and more amenable to teaching, while their Algonquian allies were the colonists' nearest neighbors. Upon the Huron confederacy, therefore, the French fixed their hopes as a field for both trade and missionary effort. Even in 1635 Champlain had so little dread of Iroquois enmity, that he wrote to Richelieu that one company of regular soldiers would enable him to subdue the Iroquois and make the French masters of the continent.[3]

Champlain's successor, Charles Hualt Sieur de Montmagny, had less success with this troublesome foe than the first governor. His governorship of twelve years (1636-48) was occupied with a succession of struggles with the wily Iroquois. They in the meantime obtained firearms from the Dutch traders who had built Fort Orange on the site of Albany. The contest for the control of the Iroquois trade took place in the very year of Nicolet's voyage. In the summer of 1634 six French traders visited the Iroquois cantons, offering goods of French manufacture for beaver skins. These tribesmen, however, would be satisfied with nothing but firearms in exchange for their goods; the sale of these weapons to the Indians was wisely forbidden by the French governor, so the Iroquois turned to the Dutch, from whom they could buy one arquebus for ten beaver skins. Six years later two thousand of their warriors were armed with these white men's weapons, and the tide of Iroquois conquest began to rise.[4]

Meanwhile the French were enlarging their rela-

[3] *Collection de Manuscrits de la Nouvelle France*, i, 112-113.
[4] J. F. Jameson, *Narratives of New Netherland* (New York, 1909), 47-76, 90, 131, 148, 168, 274.

tions with the Hurons by means of Jesuit missions, which were pushed with unflagging zeal in the decade succeeding Champlain's death. After the English in 1632 returned the colony to the French, the Recollect missionaries retired and the missions were entrusted solely to the care of the Jesuits. By them the Huron country was selected as the chief field for missionary effort, partly because of the fixed habitat of these tribesmen, partly because of their distance from the demoralizing influence of the fisher and sailor folk who visited the St. Lawrence. The missionaries also saw in Huronia a base for reaching the great population of the West. Thereupon the first missionary to visit Huronia after the return of the French went thither in 1634 in the same trade flotilla that Nicolet accompanied. He took the long, circuitous route of the Ottawa River and Georgian Bay, because even at this time the Iroquois were liable to attack any trading Indians or white men seeking the interior along the line of the lower lakes. The same year Father Brébeuf, the first Jesuit in these parts, was reinforced by two other missionaries, with whom went five young French laymen as assistants and woodsmen.[5] "By the beginning of October, 1639, we numbered here among these savages [the Hurons] twenty-seven Frenchmen, including our thirteen fathers." In 1640 the missions were enlarged to include the Neutrals, who were so called because both Huron and Iroquois enemies passed freely among their villages without harm to either group. From the territory of the Neutrals the northern shore of Lake Erie and the Niagara River were accessible. The visit of the Jesuits

---

[5] On the progress of the Huron missions, see *Jesuit Relations, passim*; also Father A. E. Jones, who gives a chronological record, 1615-50, in *Report of Ontario Bureau of Archives*, 1908, 269-402.

TRIBAL WARS AND DISPERSION

to this region first made known the presence of the last or fifth of the Great Lakes to be discovered, which they called "the lake of Erié, or of the Nation of the Cat [wildcat]." Soon after this visit is mentioned for the first time Onguiaahra, from which the modern word "Niagara" is derived.[6] This new information was represented on a map which appeared in Paris in 1643, entitled "Description de la Nouvelle France," published by Jean Boisseau. This map in its western features reproduces Champlain's map of 1632, with the addition of a small "Lac Derie" upon the stream connecting Lakes Huron and Ontario.[7]

The same year that the Jesuits entered the land of the Neutrals, Fathers Garnier and Pijart of the same order spent four or five months among the Petun Hurons, who, located on the Bruce peninsula, dwelt the farthest west of any of that confederacy. Among the Petun the Jesuits learned of a great aggregation of Algonquian tribes that lived across Lake Huron in what is now the lower peninsula of Michigan; they were called by the Hurons the Fire People or Assistogueronons.[8] With these tribes the Petun traded; but the Neutrals were their bitter enemies. These latter had secured from the Iroquois some of the firearms which had been purchased from the Dutch. Not long before the Jesuits visited the Petun, the Neutrals had attacked the western Algonquian, and created much confusion among the westerners. The Potawatomi fled northward to the Sault; other tribes were forced across to the eastern shore of Lake Michigan. There apparently the tribe called by the French Renards (Foxes) first received

[6] *Jes. Rel.*, xxi, 191.
[7] An original of Boisseau's map is in the New York Public Library. See facsimile in *Jes. Rel.*, xxiii, 234, and in Wis. Hist. Soc., *Proc.*, 1906, 156.
[8] See *ante*, chapter v.

their appellation of Outagami, "dwellers on the other shore."

In this new habitat the Outagami began hostilities with the Winnebago, who after Nicolet's voyage had been visited by some dreadful pestilence and had had their numbers much reduced. None the less they raised to attack the Outagami five hundred warriors, who were all lost in a tempest upon Lake Michigan. After this calamity, by an act of treachery the Winnebago got into difficulties with the Illinois. By all these means this once great tribe was almost wholly destroyed, only a few women and children being left of the large bands that welcomed Nicolet in 1634.[9] Thus Wisconsin's woods and watersides were almost depopulated, and the fierce Winnebago reduced to such impotence that they could offer no resistance to the invading Algonquian, who fled before their enemies in possession of the dreaded firearms.

The Jesuits were eager to carry their missions among the Algonquian of the West, and an opportunity occurred in September, 1641, that led to the first recorded visit to the Sault.[10] That year there was held on the shores of Lake Huron, sixty miles north of Huronia, a great feast for the dead, which occurs among the tribesmen at intervals about a decade apart. By the first of September two thousand savages had assembled and were engaged in games and combats which recall the mighty gatherings upon the distant Ægean described by Homer. The conditions of the primitive Indians, before their degeneration from white contact, are portrayed in the descriptions of this feast

---

[9] *Wis. Hist. Colls.*, xvi, 4-7; *Jes. Rel.*, liv, 15, 237.
[10] By "recorded visit" we mean one definitely described. Brulé and Grenoble's visits to the Sault, and even that of Nicolet, are known merely by inference.

by the Jesuits, several of whom were present at this great festival. At its close Fathers Charles Raymbault and Isaac Jogues accompanied to their home at the Sault a party of Chippewa Indians. The Jesuits on this visit gave to this beautiful flashing strait the name it has ever since borne—Sault de Ste. Marie, in honor of the Virgin Mary.

The visit of these missionaries had for its object the discovery of new tribes for gospel effort. The wandering habits of the northern Algonquian made it extremely difficult to maintain missions among them. At the Sault the Jesuits learned of a distant sedentary nation, "the Nadouessis [Sioux], situated to the northwest or west of the Sault, eighteen days' journey farther away. The first nine days are occupied in crossing another great lake that commences above the Sault; during the last nine days one has to ascend a river that traverses those lands. These people till the soil in the manner of our Hurons, and harvest Indian corn and tobacco."[11] This is the first description by white men of the Indian reports of the great Dakota people that dwelt beyond Lake Superior among the sources of the Mississippi.

The Jesuit visit to the Sault Ste. Marie had no immediate consequence for either trade or missions, since the next year aggressions against both Hurons and Algonquian by the Iroquois and the Neutrals grew more fierce. The latter attacked a palisaded village in lower Michigan, and after a siege of ten days carried it by assault, massacred all the warriors, and dragged eight hundred wretched women and children away as prisoners.[12] The Iroquois captured a frontier Huron village and put its inhabitants to fire and sword. They also took captive Father Jogues and several Frenchmen,

[11] *Jes. Rel.*, xxiii, 223-227; Kellogg, *Early Narratives*, 19-25.
[12] *Jes. Rel.*, xxvii, 25.

and inflicted upon them horrible tortures until they were rescued by the kind offices of the Dutch at Fort Orange. None the less these same Dutch traders continued to supply their Iroquois customers with firearms, which made possible their raids upon the French and their Indian allies.

The next year the Iroquois raided to the very gates of Montreal, which had been founded in 1642 as a religious-military colony to protect the settlements. The governor had no troops to send against them; he proposed as an expedient to arm the mission converts with firearms, but what were these few semi-civilized barbarians against the Iroquois hosts?[13] "They came," says the chronicler, "like foxes, attacked like lions, and fled like birds." "I would as soon," says another, "be besieged by hobgoblins as by the Iroquois. The one is scarcely more visible than the other."[14]

Cardinal Richelieu in 1645 sent a company of soldiers to New France, and a temporary peace was arranged with Iroquois deputies which seemed to promise great hope for both the colony and the missions. The Jesuits at this time planned to open a mission among the Winnebago,[15] and did actually begin instructions among the Algonquian tribes of the eastern and northern shores of Georgian Bay and also among the Ottawa on Manitoulin Island. With the two fathers that began this latter mission went Médart Chouart, later Sieur de Groseilliers, who in the years to come followed his first Indian neophytes into Wisconsin. This mission to the Algonquian was named St. Esprit, a name afterwards transferred to the Ottawa mission on the shores of Lake Superior.[16]

[13] *Jes. Rel.*, xxiv, 277-289; xxv, 27.
[14] *Ibid.*, xxvii, 71.
[15] *Lettres de la Reverend Mère de l'Incarnation* (Paris, 1876), i, 292.
[16] *Jes. Rel.*, xxviii, 229; xxx, 109-125.

From these Algonquian missions, which were maintained intermittently for five years, there issued the best description of the Great Lakes that had yet been penned. "The Great Lake of the Hurons," begins the *Relation*, "which we call la mer douce, four hundred leagues in circumference, one of which beats against our house of Sainte Marie,[17] extends from East to West and thus its width is from North to South although it is very irregular in form. . . . Other Algonquian Tribes [are] still further away, who dwell on the shores of another lake larger than la mer douce, into which it discharges by a very large and very rapid river; the latter before mingling its waters with those of our mer douce, rolls over a fall [sault] that gives its name to these peoples [Saulteurs], who come there during the fishing season. This superior Lake[18] extends toward the Northwest,—that is, between the West and North. A Peninsula, or a rather narrow strip of land, separates that superior Lake from a third Lake [Michigan], which we call the Lake of the Puants, which also flows into our mer douce by a mouth [Strait of Mackinac], on the other side of the Peninsula, about ten leagues farther West than the Sault. This third Lake extends between the South and the West, but more toward the West,— and is almost equal in size to our mer douce. On its shores dwell other nations whose language is unknown,—that is, it is neither Algonquian nor Huron. These peoples are called Puants."[19]

The geographical information furnished by the Jesuits began to be placed on the maps of the period.

[17] Sainte Marie was the main mission home among the Hurons, situated at the mouth of the Wye River, Ontario.
[18] This is, we think, the first use of the name "Superior" for this lake.
[19] *Jes. Rel.*, xxxiii, 149-151.

An undated map appeared with the term "lac Superieur" upon it;[20] while Sanson's map of North America in 1650 has the first outline of the Great Lakes, showing their true relation to one another.[21] Creuxius' map of 1660 gives the same lakes outlines as that of Sanson.[22] The progress of both missions and geographical discovery was rudely interrupted by renewed raids of the Iroquois. The peace of 1645 proved a mere truce, broken in the spring of 1646 by an attack on an outlying Huron village, and in the autumn of the same year by the murder of Father Isaac Jogues. The next year no caravan for trade or missions dared to ascend to Huronia, which was utterly cut off from the lower colony. July 4, 1648, occurred the destruction of a Huron settlement and the murder of Father Daniel in the very heart of Huronia. Now the Jesuits prepared for their doom. The fierce Iroquois wolves were abroad early in 1649. Two Huron towns were attacked before the snow was fairly off the ground. Fathers Brébeuf and Lalement were seized and tortured to death. The Hurons deserted their abode; some fled to the Petun, many to the Algonquian along Georgian Bay. Those who had become disciples of the missionaries crowded into the mother house of Ste. Marie; by May that was abandoned for an island in Penetanguishene Bay. By the autumn of 1649 the Iroquois were raiding the Petun

[20] This undated map in Depot de la Marine is copied in the Kohl Collection, Library of Congress. See Winsor, *America*, iv, 202. It cannot have been made earlier than 1649 or 1650.
[21] Nicolas Sanson d'Abbeville, *Amérique Septentrionale*, published at Paris in 1650. We reproduce the portion of the Great Lakes from a copy in the Wisconsin Historical Library.
[22] Creuxius, or Du Creux, was a Jesuit who wrote a history of New France, published in 1660. His map shows conditions in Huronia and the West before the destruction in 1649 and 1650 of the missions. François Du Creux, *Tabula Novæ Franciæ*, 1660. A facsimile of this map is in *Jes. Rel.*, xlvi, frontispiece.

TRIBAL WARS AND DISPERSION 93

territory, where two more missionaries fell as martyrs in defense of their neophytes. Even the winter, which usually furnished immunity in Indian wars, brought no respite to either Hurons or Jesuits. The enemy crossed on the ice to attack the island refuge, which was necessarily abandoned by the early summer of 1650. During a lull in the raids the remaining missionaries, with four hundred trembling, exhausted savage converts, retreated over the long route to the settlements on the St. Lawrence; there the remnants of the once great Huron nation were embodied in a mission village (Lorette) which still exists in the neighborhood of Quebec. The pagan Hurons were either slaughtered or adopted into the Iroquois tribes. Some of the Petun fled to the Ottawa on Manitoulin Island, and together they migrated west. The entire Huron territory and all the shores of Georgian Bay were utterly devastated and left without human habitations.

The Neutrals, with whom they had long been in alliance, next became the victims of the Iroquois war fury. In 1650 the first attack was made; the next spring a village with sixteen hundred Neutral warriors was captured by assault. The massacres that followed were appalling; all men and older women were killed. The young women and children were adopted into the attacking tribes. By these wholesale incorporations the numbers of the Iroquois were greatly increased.

The complete destruction of these two great tribes of the Hurons and Neutrals spread consternation throughout the entire West. All lesser tribal enmities were forgotten in the common danger from the terrible Iroquois. The Algonquian of lower Michigan abandoned the homes wherein they had dwelt for generations and fled to Wisconsin, where behind the barriers of Lake Michigan and Green Bay, and in the tangled swamps and dense woodlands, they hoped they might find safety. The decimation by pestilence, war, and drowning of the great Winnebago tribe had left the land beyond Lake Michigan almost uninhabited, save by the animals that therein abounded. To the refugees, however, these were less to be dreaded than the human enemy. "They accounted themselves more secure," wrote an old chronicler, "among the wild beasts than when exposed to the Hiroquois."

When and by what routes this great mass of Indian fugitives poured into Wisconsin we have no precise knowledge. Probably they came in many separate bands and without any order or system in their flight. All we know is that when the curtain of history again rises in Wisconsin, over twenty years after its discovery by Nicolet, all of central Wisconsin was the habitat of Algonquian tribes, such as the Sauk, Foxes, Mascouten, and Kickapoo, among whom dwelt a remnant of the Winnebago, who, powerless to check the invasion, had made friends with the newcomers and dwelt in amity with them. It has been conjectured that many of these central tribes fled into Wisconsin by the southern route around the lower end of Lake Michigan—all the more that in the early days of their sojourn in this region they were unacquainted with the use of canoes. On the other hand, we have definite information that some of the fugitives, such as the Potawatomi, crossed the Strait of Mackinac, and traditions in other tribes point to the same route. Whatever the means of ingress, the facts of the migration cannot be ignored, and they throw much light on our earliest history. If this interpretation of seventeenth century changes in the population of Wisconsin be accepted, there need be no longer discussion of the visit of Nicolet to the interior, or of the tribes, save the Winnebago, which he encountered in the vicinity of Green Bay. At the time of his voyage the Sauk, Foxes, Mascouten, and others were still in Michigan; the Potawatomi had not yet taken refuge at the Sault; the Menominee and their kindred the Noquet were, in all probability, the only Algonquian tribes in Wisconsin, which was peopled by Indians of Siouan origin who called themselves Otchagras, and were called by their later neighbors Winnebago.

The fugitives from the East were pouring in during all the decade which followed the destruction of the Huron missions in 1650, and doubtless much of the time they were wandering in heedless terror throughout many parts of Wisconsin; for when missionaries in the next decade first reached the shores of Chequamegon Bay, they were visited by many bands of these fugitives, who had as yet no settled homes or villages. We know comparatively little about their wanderings until after the peace of 1666, when they began to cluster about Green Bay and in the Fox River valley. One group of the fugitives we are able to follow; that is the Petun Hurons and the Ottawa, among whom the Jesuits had already had missions and in whom they never lost interest during the troubled years which followed their flight from Huronia. The remnants of these two tribes, now in close alliance, passed over Mackinac Strait and came to rest first on the islands at the mouth of Green Bay. There they had been preceded by the Potawatomi, after the latter's brief sojourn at the Sault. For these reasons these islands have been called both the Huron and the Potawatomi Islands. There the later comers dwelt about a year, and seem to have cultivated some of the land on the largest island, which is now known as Washington.[23]

[23] "Memoir of Nicolas Perrot," translated in Blair, i, 148-151; *Jes. Rel.*, lv, 103.

Meanwhile the Potawatomi had built for themselves a very strongly fortified village on the mainland. When the Jesuits heard of this large village, which the tribesmen called Méchingan, they planned to establish a mission therein, and gave it the name of St. Michel.[24] Circumstances, or rather the Iroquois hostility, made it impossible for them to visit this part of the West for several years, but the account they give in the *Relation* of this mission in embryo has led to misunderstandings concerning its history. The Jesuits report that in 1652 there were congregated at this village a thousand warriors of the Potawatomi and allied tribes. Their neighbors on the islands sent out in this year a scouting party in the direction of their old homes, who reported that they had discovered a war band of eight hundred Iroquois. Thereupon the Hurons and Ottawa abandoned their refuge on the island, united forces with the Potawatomi at their mainland retreat, and awaited the advance of the dreaded foe, in all eighteen hundred formidable warriors.[25]

The war party of the enemy did not in the year 1652 penetrate to the asylum of these tribes in Wisconsin. So in 1653 seven Indians in three canoes volunteered to reëstablish relations with the French, and to learn what the whites might know of the dreaded Iroquois. Not daring to attempt the Georgian Bay-Ottawa River route, the Indian party took a long northern course, through Lake Superior, north to Lake Nipigon, near which they found the Nipissing in retreat. Thence they sped from portage to portage through the great northland until they came to the headwaters of the St.

---

[24] The site of this great Potawatomi refuge has never been located; it must have been on the west shore of Green Bay, or a short distance from the bay.
[25] Blair, i, 151.

Maurice River, down which they glided to Three Rivers.[26] This was the first band of western Indians that had been seen in Canada for four years. They found the colony almost in despair; not a beaver skin had been brought for trade for over a year. In May, 1652, a Jesuit had been killed by the Iroquois in the far north toward the heads of the Saguenay. In August of the same year the local governor and fifteen Frenchmen had been captured at Three Rivers. Montreal had been in a state of continuous siege. Even while the western Indians tarried in the colony, Three Rivers was besieged for eight days and nights and another Jesuit was captured.[27] There were not more than a thousand people in all the settlements on the St. Lawrence. No help could come from France, where civil wars were desolating the homeland and Paris was in the hands of the Fronde.

Into the darkness of this darkest hour, when plans for abandoning the colony were being considered, there shot a ray of hope. An Iroquois embassy came bringing back a captive Jesuit and asking for peace. Astonishment reigned supreme; why should the haughty enemies humble themselves in the moment of their triumph? Not for many months was it known that the Iroquois humility was due to a defeat inflicted upon one of its largest war parties by the western tribesmen. An Iroquois disaster in far distant Wisconsin was the immediate means of saving the colony of New France.

After the departure in 1653 of the volunteers, the villagers of Méchingan prepared themselves for its defense. Well they might, for the largest war party yet sent out from the Iroquois cantons was now being equipped to follow the fugitives beyond Lake Michigan,

[26] *Jes. Rel.*, xxxviii, 181.
[27] *Jes. Rel.*, xxxviii, 191.

there to exterminate the entire band. But the way was long and hard; the fugitives had devastated the land as they retreated; when the great Iroquois party reached the Potawatomi stronghold, their whole number was weak with hunger. They were forced to beg food of their enemies. These latter agreed to supply the invading host, secretly adding poison to the gift. This act of treachery was discovered in time to save the invaders, who thereupon retreated in small bands which hunted the forests for subsistence. The Hurons wished to pursue, but the timid Ottawa restrained them; thus the merit for the defeat of the Iroquois passed to other tribes. One band of the invaders, which turned north, was attacked near the Sault by the Chippewa and their allies. With only stone knives and arrows they destroyed six score Iroquois carrying firearms, so that but one warrior escaped. The parties which retreated by a southern route fell among the Illinois, whom they never before had known. This populous tribe pursued the bands of the invaders as they retreated, and cut them down one by one. Only a few miserable fugitives ever returned from this first great Iroquois invasion of the region beyond Lake Michigan.[28]

Thus at this critical time for the colony of New France the western Indians had saved the day. The Iroquois, humbled by this great defeat, begged for a peace in which were included all the Indian allies of the French. The next year (1654) these allies came in triumph over the old Ottawa River route to trade. When the fleet was first seen from Montreal it was feared it was an enemy flotilla. Fear speedily turned to joy as the triumphant friends of the French swept down the rapids, their canoes gay with decorations

[28] Blair, i, 151-157.

TRIBAL WARS AND DISPERSION 99

and loaded to the brim with precious beaver skins. Plenty and prosperity once more visited the colony. Canada re-awoke to life and hope.

Despite the repulse of 1653 the Hurons could not shake off their dread of another Iroquois attack. The next year they with the Ottawa prepared for further flight to a still more distant refuge beyond the Mississippi. There they rested for a time among the Iowa; this branch of the Siouan family was then in process of becoming plains Indians, with an economy dependent upon the buffalo. The visitor Indians longed for woodland, and returned once more to the Mississippi, where they met the northern Sioux, who assigned them a home on an island in the upper Mississippi. There after stripping off the trees, so that it has since been called Pelée or Bald Island, they foolishly quarreled with their hosts the Sioux, and were forced to retreat into the thickest forests in Wisconsin. The Hurons built a village on the sources of Black River, while the Ottawa went to dwell beside Lac Court Oreilles.[29]

The Illinois, fearing, after the total destruction in 1655 and 1656 of the Erie people, that the Iroquois would take vengeance upon them, retreated across the Mississippi into what is now Iowa. Their kindred the Miami joined them there, but soon recrossed the great river into Wisconsin, where they found a home on the upper Fox.[30] As for the Sauk, Foxes, Kickapoo, and Mascouten, they wandered hither and thither in the Wisconsin forests, until in the next decade peace with the Iroquois permitted them to form settled villages on Green Bay, the Fox and Wolf rivers.

[29] Blair, i, 159-165. This lake was long known as the Ottawa Lake.
[30] Pierre Margry, *Decouvertes et Etablissements des Français dans l'Amérique Septentrionale* (Paris, 1876), i, 505.

By these events the Indian geography of Wisconsin became totally changed. Almost wholly Siouan at the time of Nicolet, this region became within the next twenty years the haunt of a vast number of Algonquian fugitives, whom the Winnebago, already reduced in power and numbers, were powerless to resist. The coasts of Lake Huron and the eastern shore of Lake Michigan were utterly deserted; the center of the Indian population in the West shifted to Wisconsin, which now became the goal for discovery, exploration, and exploitation.

VII. THE FIRST TRADERS, 1654-1670

THE Indian trade was the chief resource of the colony of New France. Agriculture developed slowly, but the fur trade grew by leaps and bounds. Indeed, the Indian trade was older than the colony, older even than the voyages of discovery. The daring fishermen who at the dawn of the sixteenth century crossed the Atlantic to fish off the coasts of the New World, at once began to barter with the natives and to add to the profits from fish those from pelts. By the time of Champlain's voyages the fur trade was well established on the St. Lawrence. Its center was then at Tadoussac. Each year the natives gathered there from all parts of the North and Northwest, and French ships brought them goods in exchange for their precious furs. Champlain removed the chief trading mart to the "habitation" at Quebec. Gradually the trade crept thence up the river. Enterprising traders would set out to meet the western tribesmen coming down the Ottawa and anticipate other purchasers. In 1634 Three Rivers was built as a fur trade center. After the founding of Montreal in 1642, the annual concourse for the western trade took place on the plains before its gates. There in the summer months great fleets of western tribesmen annually arrived, set up their skin or mat tents upon the open meadows, and prepared their packs of peltry for sale. All the merchants of the colony, even some from overseas, gathered for this annual fair. Booths sprang up as if by magic, merchandise that tempted primitive cupidity was displayed—knives and kettles, beads and bracelets, blankets and cloth, looking-glasses and combs—articles of French manufacture expressly for the Indian trade. The less scrupulous merchants offered brandy in exchange for furs, until the active efforts of the churchmen caused an attempt, which was never very successful, to prohibit the sale of liquor to the red men.

Not only regular merchants but the habitants and farmers attended the fur fair; these latter exchanged their farm products for skins. The Indians craved a taste of the colonists' bread; they enjoyed their cakes and confections; they purchased their vegetables and grain for the homeward voyage. Thus beaver and other peltry became widely distributed among all classes of Canadians. Ultimately, however, all skins were sold to the Company of New France; their agents were the only authorized exporters. They yearly fixed the price for which they would accept the various grades of skins. All New France prospered or suffered with the variations of the fur trade.

In 1645 a group of local merchants formed the Company of the Colony, which obtained valuable concessions from the Company of New France. For one-fourth of their gross receipts paid to the latter company, the former obtained what amounted to a monopoly of the furs brought by the western Indians. The purpose of the organization was to systematize the trade, but it also tended to eliminate small traders and the traffic of the habitants. Complaints of this new company at once went to France, all to no purpose while its dividends increased and the Company of New France shared in the general prosperity. This prosperity decreased as the Iroquois grew more warlike. The annual flotillas were frequently ambushed along the Ottawa River, stragglers were cut off, fear of these attacks diminished the numbers of the Indians who came to trade. Nevertheless, the company prospered until 1650, when the Huron settlements were absolutely destroyed. For four years no furs came from the West. The Company of the Colony was ruined; it became insolvent and finally dissolved. Even local fur gathering became impossible. Trappers and hunters were dogged at every step by the implacable Iroquois. The doom of the fur trade and of the colony itself seemed at hand. The governor, Jean de Lauson, was timid and avaricious; he did nothing to protect the colonists, his chief interest being to enrich himself and his family. To this end he consorted with the chief merchants and fostered fur trade interests.

The victory of the western Indians over the Iroquois in 1653 gave an opportunity for the renewal of the trade. The Ottawa, who had long aspired to act as middlemen for the western Algonquian, once more organized a summer fleet. Securing the accumulation of furs from all the refugee Indians of Wisconsin, they undertook in 1654 the long journey to the St. Lawrence, bringing, as we have seen, joy and hope to the disheartened colonists. When the Ottawa tribesmen reëmbarked for their distant homes in Wisconsin, the governor persuaded them to take back with them two young Frenchmen to make trading alliances with the surviving tribesmen of the West. These two traders were the first white men to visit Wisconsin waters after the voyage of Nicolet twenty years earlier.

They were absent on their journey to the interior for two years. In 1655 no flotilla came down. The following summer it was August before the Westerners arrived, bringing with them the two men who had gone out in 1654. They reported that there were great numbers of aborigines in the western country, and revealed the opportunities for the trade that lay in an alliance with these tribes.[1]

[1] *Jes. Rel.*, xlii, 219-233.

The identification of Lauson's two traders of 1654-56 has given rise to a controversial literature of considerable dimensions. About the year 1880 some curious manuscripts were found in the Bodleian Library at Oxford, which proved to be journals written in English of a quaint and unusual style by a French traveler in North America during the seventeenth century. He styled himself Pierre-Esprit Radisson, and described four voyages undertaken in New France partly by himself and partly in company with one whom he calls his brother, Médart Chouart Sieur de Groseilliers. He was in fact Radisson's brother-in-law, husband of his half-sister Marguerite. Radisson's journals are imperfectly dated; they were evidently written many years after the events they narrate. Nevertheless they have an air of verisimilitude and of first-hand description which makes them valuable historical sources.[2]

The discovery and publication of Radisson's journals awakened much interest among western historians. After Nicolet he was the first Frenchman whose account of voyages to the Northwest had been preserved. According to the various interpretations of his journals he may have been the first white man in Iowa, in Minnesota, and in the Dakotas, or in Manitoba, and possibly he was the first white man to visit the Mississippi River. The dates of his voyages have never been satisfactorily determined. His four voyages must have occurred sometime between 1652 and 1663. He arrived in Canada, as he says, in 1651; the next spring, while hunting, he was captured by a raiding party of Iroquois, carried to their villages, adopted into their tribe,

[2] The Bodleian manuscript has been edited and published under the auspices of the Prince Society. Gideon D. Scull, *Voyages of Peter Esprit Radisson* (Boston, 1885).

THE FIRST TRADERS   105

and finally rescued by the Dutch at Albany.[3] After this experience he returned to France. Having come back to Canada on May 15 of some year not mentioned, he began his "Second Voyage to the Upper Country of the Iroquois." The adventures which he had in his second voyage to the Iroquois could have occurred only after the peace of 1656. We know from the *Jesuit Relations* that a colony of French went July 26, 1657, from Montreal and passed a winter at Onondaga; that they escaped in March, 1658, by a curious stratagem of which Radisson gives many details. The two accounts are sufficiently parallel to force the conclusion that Radisson was a member of the Onondaga colony, and that his second journey to the Iroquois took place between the last of July, 1657, and March, 1658. With these two voyages dated (1652-53, 1657-58), we approach the problem of his two western voyages which he took, as he says, in company with his brother, Groseilliers.

His narrative states that they were absent on their first western voyage the space of three years. The similarities between Radisson's account of his experiences and those narrated by the *Jesuit Relations* of the two traders of 1654-56 have led many students to conclude that Radisson and Groseilliers were these two traders, and that in his narrative Radisson exaggerated the length of their voyage. Other historians place the first western voyage of Radisson and Groseilliers between

[3] Radisson says he arrived at Albany, October 29, 1663; from the context and headings this is clearly proved to be a mistake for 1653; Poncet, a Jesuit missionary who was at Fort Orange in September, 1653, mentions the bringing of a French captive to that place. *Jes. Rel.*, xl, 143. It is generally assumed that this captive was Radisson, all the more that he himself speaks of meeting a French priest at Fort Orange. This would date his first voyage as 1652-53.

the years 1658 and 1660; in either case three years could not have elapsed. We propose another hypothesis, which both makes allowance for a three years' voyage and identifies Lauson's traders of 1654-56. Let us examine in detail what Radisson says about his start on his first western journey. He states that on that voyage he left with an Ottawa trading fleet which was accompanied by twenty-eight other French traders and two Jesuit missionaries. The tribesmen, having recently acquired guns from the French, were very inexpert in their use and fired them at random; the Ottawa were also very careless about keeping together as a protection against the enemy. On the Ottawa River they were approached by an Iroquois from the shore, who gave them warning that his fellow tribesmen had prepared an ambush for them farther along the stream. The Ottawa thought the Iroquois was deceiving them; they paid no attention to his warnings and fell into the Iroquois ambuscade. After some sharp fighting the Ottawa finally escaped by means of a ruse, and stole quietly away in the night to continue their westward journey; they refused, however, to take the two Jesuits or the twenty-eight other traders with them; Radisson and his companion succeeded in going on with the fleet, while all the other Frenchmen were forced to return to the colony.[4]

We know, from the *Jesuit Relations*, that the first missionaries to attempt to go west after the destruction of the Huron missions started with the trading fleet of 1656. We also know that they had precisely similar adventures to those described by Radisson—that they were in a fleet which was warned by an Iroquois; that disregarding that warning they fell into an Iroquois

[4] *Radisson's Voyages*, 132-142; Kellogg, *Early Narratives*, 34-40.

ambush; that they and twenty-eight French traders who were with them were turned back by the Ottawa and returned to the colony.[5] These coincidences are so marked that we are forced to conclude that Radisson was in the Ottawa flotilla of 1656. He could not, however, have stayed in the West for three years at this time, since in late July, 1657, he was on his way to the Iroquois country, south of Lake Ontario.

This discrepancy may be reconciled by a study of the career of Radisson's fellow voyager, Groseilliers. He had been, as we have seen, in the Huron missions before their destruction, and had before 1650 visited the tribes that later fled to Wisconsin. After the destruction of the missions Groseilliers went to France, coming back to Canada, where on August 24, 1653, he was married at Three Rivers. Documentary evidence shows he was at that place until February, 1654; after that his name does not appear again until 1657. Groseilliers, with his previous knowledge of the Algonquian languages, was very probably a man whom Lauson would select to go west in 1654.[6] He may have taken Radisson with him at that time; more probably, since the latter was in France late in 1653 and since he describes as his *first* experience on the Ottawa River the events of 1656, Groseilliers went west in 1654 with a nameless companion, and upon his return to the colony with the fleet of 1656 he induced his young brother-in-law to go back to the western country for another year. Radisson, in relating his western adventures, speaks of both his own one year and Groseilliers' three years as if

[5] *Jes. Rel.*, xlii, 225-233.
[6] One more bit of evidence in favor of Groseilliers as one of Lauson's traders is that they baptized some dying Indian children. *Jes. Rel.*, xlii, 223. Groseilliers had been previously in Jesuit service as a *donné*. Radisson speaks as if Groseilliers were accustomed to baptize Indian children. Kellogg, *Early Narratives*, 55.

they had been together all the time. Groseilliers had lost his own journal during the voyage.[7] Radisson in his account endeavored to supply the deficiency. A study of the narrative of Radisson shows that he used the pronoun "we" in a very indiscriminating fashion. He often used it when narrating the adventures of the Indians with whom he conversed;[8] he also used it as meaning the French in general, as well as when speaking strictly of himself and Groseilliers. From all these considerations we think it probable that Groseilliers was one of Lauson's traders of 1654-56; that Groseilliers went west again in 1656 and was gone on these two early voyages from 1654 to July, 1657; that Radisson went up with him in 1656 and returned in time to start for the Iroquois country in 1657; that this was Radisson's first western journey.

If these facts are true, it makes it exceedingly difficult to arrange from Radisson's narrative any definite itinerary. Such an itinerary has been attempted by several scholars.[9] None of their conclusions seem to us to be satisfactory. It appears to us from his narrative

[7] Kellogg, *Early Narratives*, 61.

[8] The present writer believes that much of Radisson's narrative is a report of what he was told by the tribesmen, while still using "we" to designate the narrator. For example, all the paragraphs about the Christino, p. 50-53, are the narrative of a Saulteur chief.

[9] See Warren Upham, *Minnesota Historical Collections*, x, 449-594; refuted by J. V. Brower, *Minnesota*, in *Memoirs of Explorations of the Basin of the Mississippi* (St. Paul, 1903), vi. Henry C. Campbell, "Radisson," in *Parkman Club Papers, No. 2*, was the first to suggest that Radisson and Groseilliers were Lauson's traders of 1654-56. Benjamin Sulte does not accept this suggestion. He dates the first western voyage 1658-60, the second 1660-63. Can. Roy. Soc., *Proc.*, 1903, sec. i, 3-25; 1904, sec. ii, 223-230. I embodied my conclusions concerning Radisson in an article, "The First Traders in Wisconsin," published in the *Wisconsin Magazine of History*, v, 348-359.

that Radisson spent most of his year in a southern rather than in a northern climate. He seems to have visited Green Bay and to have gone from there south toward the Illinois country. When describing the people of the north he is relating what his Indian acquaintances had told him. Whether or not he saw the Mississippi when he visited "the great river which divides itself in 2" cannot be known.[10] We are not disposed to consider Radisson as the discoverer of the Mississippi River.

Radisson and Groseilliers undertook a second voyage to the West, this time clandestinely, without the permission of the authorities. In all probability this voyage occurred in 1658-60, since Radisson says that on their return they passed the place where Dollard and his companions had a few days before perished in the defense of Canada at the Long Sault. This was in 1660.[11] The route the traders took during this second western voyage is more easily determined than that of the earlier one. After arrival at the Sault Ste. Marie they entered Lake Superior, skirted its southern coast, portaged Keweenaw Point, and built a log building on Chequamegon Bay—so far as we know, the first white habitation in Wisconsin. Local historians think this was situated on the southwest coast near Shore's Landing.[12] In this log hut the traders left the bulk of their

[10] The great river of the West had been mentioned from Indian reports as early as 1654, both by the Jesuits and by Mère de l'Incarnation. See also a report apparently emanating from Radisson, in *Jes. Rel.*, xlv, 225-227.

[11] Benjamin Sulte admits that the return from the second western voyage seems, from the Dollard and Long Sault incident, to have occurred in 1660. He argues, however, without giving any reasons, that this passage has been transposed from the close of the first western to the close of the second western voyage, which he thinks took place in 1661-63. See reference *ante*, note 9.

[12] See article by Father Charron in Ashland *Daily Press*, April 13, 1925. A commemorative tablet has been erected near this site.

stores, going overland in the following winter to the village of their Ottawa customers on Lac Court Oreilles. They found these tribesmen in the midst of a famine, in which they suffered pangs all too graphically described by Radisson. A sleet storm providentially came to their rescue; the snow being crusted, the hunters could pursue the deer, who in their leaps broke through into the drifts and were easily captured. While at the Ottawa village a deputation arrived from the Sioux inviting the traders to visit their haunts. They had, however, made rendezvous for the Christino at the western end of Lake Superior near the site of the Wisconsin city of Superior. There they held a great council and thence they took the great Sioux trail overland to the villages of that tribe in eastern Minnesota, where they received a characteristic and enthusiastic welcome.[13]

Retracing their steps to Chequamegon Bay, they found that the Ottawa had arrived before them, and had built a village on the mainland. They thereupon built a second fort, supposedly on Houghton Point. It was at this time that Radisson broke or strained his leg, which was cured by rubbing with hot bear's oil. Another time, while he was camping by himself, his hut took fire and he escaped "all naked and lame," and was finally rescued when in extremities. At Chequamegon Bay the Christino visited them and brought great packs of furs. The traders quickly perceived that the

[13] J. V. Brower first suggested that the Isanti (or Knife) Sioux probably received their name because of the supply of knives furnished them by Radisson and Groseilliers. According to W. W. Folwell, *History of Minnesota* (St. Paul, 1921), i, 10, the traditional site of the village Radisson visited was at or near Knife Lake in Kanabec County.

north was the region in which the richest furs could be found.[14]

Early in 1660 the tribesmen and the traders met at the Sault for their descent to Montreal. One hundred canoes started, but news coming that the Iroquois were on the Ottawa River, forty turned back. The remaining sixty brought an immense cargo to Montreal, where they arrived safely, after Dollard and his brave men had saved the colony by sacrificing their lives to the Iroquois. Radisson and Groseilliers brought a great fortune from the West.[15] The governor, however, because they had gone without a license, confiscated their furs. Radisson and Groseilliers some time thereafter deserted to the English, told them of the rich furs of the northern country, and aided in organizing the Company of Gentlemen Adventurers to Hudson's Bay.

The remainder of Radisson's career does not belong to our story. He left the English service at one time and went back to the French, whom he led in a plundering expedition against the English forts on Hudson Bay. Later he went back to England, married there, was pensioned by the Hudson's Bay Company, and there died about 1710. Groseilliers likewise had many adventures in Hudson Bay, and probably accompanied his fellow adventurer to England. His family remained

[14] It is thought by some students of Radisson's journals, that he went overland in person at this time from Lake Superior to James Bay. I see no reason to believe in this extension of his trip.

[15] *Jes. Rel.*, xlv, 161-163. Radisson's journal for this last voyage is in *Wis. Hist. Colls.*, xi, 71-96. His estimate of the value of the furs they secured is $60,000, a vast amount for those times. Other estimates run as high as $400,000. See Reverend T. J. Campbell, S. J., *Pioneer Laymen of North America* (New York, 1916), ii, 61.

at Three Rivers, however, and many illustrious Canadians trace to this great traveler their ancestry.

The chief value of Radisson's journals lies not in the exact route or the exact dates of his travels, but in the remarkable picture he presents of the Northwest in its pristine conditions. That he visited the regions about Lakes Michigan and Superior at a very early time is not open to doubt. His narrative is thus unique, a picture of Wisconsin's natural features and aboriginal inhabitants before any white contact. The narrator had an eye for natural beauty. Around Lake Michigan "the country was so pleasant, so beautifull & fruitfull that it grieved me to see y^t ye world could not discover such inticing countrys to live in. This I say because the Europeans fight for a rock in the sea against one another." Radisson goes on to suggest that this lovely western land may in ages to come prove an asylum for millions of poverty-stricken Europeans who may here find a "laborinth of pleasure." In such passages he becomes the prophet of the future—an early land agent for the western valleys. In Lake Superior he found the coasts "most delightfull and wounderous"; a bank of rocks is "like a great Portall, by reason of the beating of the waves. The lower part of that oppening is as bigg as a tower"; this is the first mention of the pictured rocks and the arched portal of the south shore of Superior. The flora and fauna of the lands he visited interested him. In the winter "the snow stoocke to those trees that are there so ruffe, being deal trees, prusse cedars, and thorns, that caused y^t darknesse upon ye earth that it is believed that the sun was eclipsed them 2 months." He describes the wild rice and its harvesting, the many strange fishes and strange birds, like the pelican; the "staggs, buffs, elands and castors [deer, buffalo, moose, and beaver]." The buffalo he saw near Green Bay; but only by chance, he says, did they range as far north as Lake Superior.

From the wild beasts he turns to the wild men (for so he translates the customary French term for the Indians, *les sauvages*). He notes their domestic arts, weaving and making pottery; the calumets, the dress and ornamentation of primitive man are described exhaustively. Their organization, the councils held, the feasts, the games and dances, all receive attention. The respect paid to him and Groseilliers was marked. "We weare Cesars being nobody to contradict us." When entering the great Sioux village they were treated as were the royalties when Louis XIV's Spanish bride entered Paris. Nor would Radisson have exchanged the freedom of the wilderness for the restraints of court life. He epitomizes in his descriptions the vicissitudes of a fur trader's life—the long journeys in the unbroken wilderness, the tedious winters in snow-covered huts in the forest, the desperate chances for food or famine, the contact with untamed barbarians, their filthy habits and fickle dispositions—all endured not merely for love of gain, but for the love of the free life of the forest, for the pleasure of being "Cesars" in a primitive world. Radisson's journals are thus first-hand material for the ethnology of our Wisconsin Indians; as such they have been little used.

Radisson and Groseilliers may not have been the only traders among these tribes during their first years in Wisconsin; their names have been preserved for us by the accidental discovery of the former's journals. In 1656 thirty youths were ready to adventure with the western Indian trade flotilla. In 1657 and 1659 no canoes came down the Ottawa River, but numbers of trading Indians came in at Three Rivers and Tadoussac. White traders may have gone back with some of these.

Radisson appears to indicate that he met Frenchmen at the Sault.[16] Maps also show that knowledge of the Great Lakes region was increasing.[17] Creuxius' map of 1660 calls Lake Michigan, "Magnus Lacus Algonquinorum" (great lake of the Algonquian); it adds much information concerning Lake Superior, introduces Lake Nipigon and some rivers named for the northernmost tribes.[18]

In all the trading voyages from 1653 to 1660 the Ottawa were the leaders of the fleets and arrogated to themselves the monopoly of the trade with the French. Radisson and Groseilliers attempted to break that monopoly, but all to no purpose; the Ottawa frightened the other peoples with tales of Iroquois atrocities, and kept for themselves and their associate Hurons the right to introduce French goods in the West.[19] Upon the arrival of the Ottawa flotilla of 1660 at Montreal, bringing with it Radisson and Groseilliers from the West,[20] it was discovered that the way was clear for other Frenchmen to adventure with the returning tribesmen. The heroic defense of Dollard at the Long Sault[21] gave the colony a respite from Iroquois attacks which was quickly utilized by both traders and missionaries. Seven of the most reputable Canadians of the colony went up to Lake Superior in that year; accompanying them went the first missionary that ever penetrated to these regions. In 1656, as we have seen,

[16] *Jes. Rel.*, xliv, 201; xlv, 105; Kellogg, *Early Narratives*, 51.
[17] A lost map of 1658 indicated the new habitats of the western tribes. *Jes. Rel.*, xliv, 237-239.
[18] See *ante*, chapter vi, note 22; also report on the far West brought to Tadoussac by a Wisconsin Indian, in *Jes. Rel.*, xlv, 217-227.
[19] *Radisson's Voyages*, 164, 231-232; *Jes. Rel.*, xlv, 161-163.
[20] *Jes. Rel.*, xlv, 163.
[21] See Francis Parkman on Dollard's heroism, in *Old Régime in Canada* (Boston, 1875), chapter iii.

two missionaries essayed the dangerous voyage only to be driven back and one of them murdered. Now in 1660 the choice fell upon Father René Ménard, one of the survivors of the Huron missions after the great dispersion; he was accompanied by his *donné*, Jean Guérin, and was aided when possible by the French traders in the caravan. The leader among the traders was Antoine Trottier, who later settled at Batiscan, where he lived until 1706. With him was associated Jean François Pouteret Sieur de Bellecourt *dit* Columbier.[22] Other members of the party were Adrien Jolliet,[23] Claude David,[24] L'Espèrance, and Laflêche.[25] The name of the seventh man of this trading party has not been preserved.

The seven traders intended to be absent but a year; circumstances made it impossible for them to return until three years had passed. The Ottawa had, as we have seen, already removed their village from Lac Court Oreilles to Chequamegon Bay.[26] Thither the traders accompanied them, and passed the winter, which fortunately for their comfort was exceedingly

[22] *Jugements et Déliberations du Conseil Souverain de la Nouvelle France* (Quebec, 1883), i, 23-24; *Jes. Rel.*, xlvi, 143-145.

[23] Adrien Jolliet was born in France about 1641; his family removed to Canada before his younger brother Louis was born. Adrien was captured by the Iroquois in 1658, released the next year, and spent 1660 to 1663 in the trading excursion to Lake Superior. January, 1664, he married and April 23, 1666, made a contract for a second voyage to the Ottawa country. Thereafter he traded there until his death, sometime between 1669 and September 12, 1671. See Can. Roy. Soc., *Proc.*, 1920, sec. i, 75.

[24] Claude David was a physician, born 1621, married in 1649. He lived first at Three Rivers, later at Cap-de-la-Madeleine, where he was buried December 2, 1687.

[25] Probably these men were Pierre Levasseur *dit* L'Espèrance of Quebec, a Parisian mechanic; and some member of the Laflêche family related to Jean Richer, the Nipissing interpreter.

[26] See description of the experiences of the Ottawa and Hurons, in "Perrot's Memoir," Blair, i, 164-174.

mild. In the spring of 1661, having gathered a store of furs, they expected to accompany the Ottawa to the St. Lawrence, when suddenly this tribe announced its intention of abandoning the voyage that summer because of troubles with the Sioux. The Hurons, still in their village on the sources of Black River, were in famine conditions because they feared to hunt. By autumn of that year they had joined the Ottawa at Chequamegon.[27]

The French traders, forced to spend another winter on the bleak coasts of Lake Superior, prepared for the ordeal by laying in a store of provisions in order to escape the famine conditions of the preceding spring. All during the late summer and autumn of 1660 they fished in Chequamegon Bay. "It was a sight to arouse pity," writes the Jesuit chronicler, "to see poor Frenchmen in a Canoe, amid rain and snow, borne hither and thither by whirlwinds in these great Lakes, which often show waves as high as those of the Sea. The men frequently found their hands and feet frozen upon their return, while occasionally they were overtaken by so thick a fall of powdery snow, driven against them by a violent wind, that the one steering the Canoe could not see his companion in the bow. How then gain the port? Verily as often as they reached the land, their doing so seemed a little miracle. Whenever their fishing was successful, they laid by a little store which they smoked and used for provision when the fishing was over, or the season no longer admitted of fishing."[28]

Thus with fish and wild rice they made out to pass a second winter on the shore of Lake Superior. Surely, they comforted one another, the next summer they

[27] Ménard in the summer of 1661 was lost in trying to reach this Huron village. See next chapter.
[28] *Jes. Rel.*, xlviii, 121.

could go with the Ottawa to the settlements on the St. Lawrence. A vain hope, since in 1662 the Iroquois, who had been quiescent since their defeat on the Ottawa River in 1660, made up several war parties, one of which was designed to fall upon the annual trading expedition of the northern Indians. This Iroquois party, hunting for subsistence as it went, prowled along the shores of Lake Huron and reached the Sault before it encountered any enemy Indians. There "they were themselves surprised by a band of Saulteurs . . . who made their approach towards day break, with such boldness that after discharging some muskets and then shooting their arrows, they leaped, hatchet in hand, upon those whom their fire and missiles had spared."[29] The attacking party was composed not only of Saulteurs (Chippewa), but of Ottawa, Nipissing, and Beaver tribesmen. This was the second notable defeat inflicted on the Five Nations by the western tribes. It caused great rejoicing along all the Lake Superior shores, and gave its name to Iroquois Point a few miles beyond the Sault in Lake Superior.[30]

In the summer of 1663 a great concourse gathered for the trading voyage to Montreal; thirty-five canoes conveyed one hundred and fifty Indians and the seven white traders who had passed three years in these northern wilds. Neither Father Ménard nor Jean Guérin had survived to return to civilization. The venture had not been financially successful. Neither the Jesuits nor the traders obtained enough furs to pay the costs of the expedition.[31] The returning traders reported the existence of copper in Lake Superior, and brought back with them a large ingot prepared by the

[29] *Jes. Rel.*, xlviii, 75-79.
[30] "Perrot's Memoir," in Blair, i, 178-181.
[31] *Jes. Rel.*, xlvii, 307; *Conseil Souverain*, i, 23-24.

Indians. The difficulty of the route thither made it impractical to utilize this mineral wealth. Unless the passage of the lower lakes could be free from Iroquois attacks, the Lake Superior copper was inaccessible.[32]

During the absence of the seven traders in the far West, great changes had been taking place on the St. Lawrence, which gave the colony a permanence it had never before secured. Upon the death, in 1661, of Cardinal Mazarin, Louis XIV in person assumed the reins of government; he entrusted to the care of Jean Baptiste Colbert the colonial administration. Colbert was a man of vision; he also had had practical experience in developing the bases of prosperity—commerce and agriculture. During the first years of his administration the colonists in Canada chose one of their number as an agent to visit France, to represent the affairs and dangers of the colony, and to ask for a consignment of troops. Pierre Boucher, the chosen agent, drew up at Colbert's request a description of New France, of its resources both agricultural and mineral. This work created a new interest in the overseas dominion of the king, and made it appear not merely the trading post it had been supposed to be, but a rich possession well worth the cost of developing.[33]

Colbert took up the Canadian cause with vigor; he sent with Boucher on his return in 1663 a party of agricultural colonists, well equipped for their work. He also revoked the charter of the old Company of New France, many of whose provisions were detrimental to the development of the colony; he persuaded

[32] Pierre Boucher, *Histoire du Canada* (Paris, 1664). This is the earliest history of Canada; reprinted in Can. Roy. Soc., *Proc.*, 1896, sec. i, 99-168. The report on copper is p. 167-168.

[33] Benjamin Sulte, "Pierre Boucher et Son Livre," introduction to book as reprinted. See preceding note.

the king to send a royal agent to report on the needs of Canada, and best of all for immediate defense, he sent a detachment of regular troops. Sieur Gaudais-Dupont, the royal commissioner,[34] and the Chevalier de Mézy, the new governor, with one hundred troopers and many new colonists arrived about a month after the return, in 1663, of the Lake Superior traders.

An international event of the next year promised relief for New France from the menace of the Iroquois. New Netherland, whose traders had kept these hostiles so well supplied with arms and ammunition, was in 1664 ceded to Charles II of England, the ally and the pensioner of Louis XIV. Hope sprang up that the raids of these Indians might be controlled. The same year Colbert created *La Compagnie des Indes Occidentales*, which embraced all of France's possessions in America. He also sent a great nobleman, the Marquis de Tracy, as lieutenant general for all North America. June 30, 1665, Tracy debarked at Quebec amid salvos of artillery and the great rejoicing of the habitants. About the same time came some companies of the regiment of Carignan-Salières, which the king had designated for the garrison of his American possession.[35] By the close of 1665 there were thirteen hundred French officers and soldiers among a colonial population that numbered scarcely more than three thousand souls.

As the first four companies of these veteran troopers advanced up the St. Lawrence, they met on August 3

[34] See his instructions May 1, 1663, in *Edits et Ordonnances Royaux* (Quebec, 1854-56), iii, 23-27; Englished in *New York Colonial Documents*, ix, 9-13.

[35] This famous regiment had originally been enlisted in Savoy by the Prince de Carignan; it came to Canada fresh from wars with the Turks. Several of its officers became seigniors in Canada, among others the ancestor of Charles de Langlade of Wisconsin. See Sulte, "Le régiment de Carignan," in Can. Roy. Soc., *Proc.*, 1902, sec. i, 25-95.

near Three Rivers the annual fleet of trading Indians from the far West. In all their experiences on European battle fields they had never seen a sight like that of the hundred canoes that darkened the surface of the river, propelled by flashing paddles in the hands of the wild Indians of the upper lakes. These red men were flushed with triumph, having beaten off two attacking parties of Iroquois; they approached their trading mart, shouting their songs of victory and firing their fusees in a delirium of joy and excitement. Their canoes were piled high with packs of furs, which they had obtained by their intertribal trade. With them were several French traders, of whom one was probably the youth Nicolas Perrot, who was later to be identified for many years with the western trade. These traders had collected their peltry in Lake Superior, around which they estimated that the tribesmen were numerous enough to muster one hundred thousand warriors.[36]

The Ottawa on their return took back to the West six French traders whose names we do not know, and the second Jesuit missionary to the Northwest, Father Claude Allouez. The latter was commissioned to announce to the western Indians that the French king had taken pity on them and had sent his warriors to subdue their enemies. The news created great excitement in the far West; deputations from tribes that had never before seen a Frenchman flocked to Chequamegon Bay. In the description of this gathering we hear of some of the Wisconsin Indians for the first time by their modern names.[37]

Nor were the tribesmen disappointed in their hopes. As a result of two invading expeditions into their own

---

[36] *Jes. Rel.*, xlix, 241-249; "Perrot's Memoir," in Blair, i, 175-176.

[37] *Jes. Rel.*, l, 249, 289, 309; li, 27, 43, 47, 53, 61.

THE FIRST TRADERS

country, the Iroquois, humbled and frightened, came to Quebec in the summer of 1667 to beg for peace. After hostages had been exchanged and peace assured, the Marquis de Tracy embarked for France. Canada was now governed by Daniel de Rémy Sieur de Courcelles and Jean Talon, known as the "great intendant." Talon's administration was an epoch in the history of the colony. Colbert continued his favor, sent over more colonists, the first horses in New France, and many cattle. If the authorities encouraged agriculture rather than the fur trade, the peace with the Iroquois operated to increase the numbers of Indians that came to the St. Lawrence, and the amount of furs they were able to take. It also permitted the tribesmen to form permanent villages along the shores of Green Bay and Lake Michigan. Those who had heretofore been wandering in the interior of Wisconsin chose some favored places upon Wisconsin's lakes or rivers, and built the villages that have become historic. As a result of this peace, also, the center of trading operations in the West shifted from Lake Superior to Green Bay. The last company of traders who visited Lake Superior during this epoch went there with the trading flotilla of 1667. Among these were Adrien Jolliet and eight associates who were outfitted by a French merchant firm of La Rochelle, comprising one Armand and Jean Peré; the latter or junior partner made the contract in Montreal August 10, 1667. He himself became one of the explorers of the far Northwest and, as we shall see, first visited the West in 1668. Some accident befell this party of traders who came to Lake Superior in 1667; two of the party were drowned, the fate of the others is not known. The three survivors, Corneille Tecle, Mathurin Normandin, and Robert Cachetière, applied in 1670 to the courts for an equitable division of the profits of the association.[38]

The same year that these traders undertook their voyage to Lake Superior there also went west a youth who has been called "the greatest Frenchman of the West" during these earliest years of exploitation and exploration.[39] Nicolas Perrot was in many respects the successor of Jean Nicolet; he operated in the region of Nicolet's discoveries; he was regarded, like Nicolet, as a "wonderful man" by the tribesmen, over whom he had unbounded influence; like Nicolet also, he was the first Frenchman ever seen by many of the tribes around Green Bay—those Algonquian tribes who had come to take the places of the dwindling and dispossessed Winnebago. Perrot formed a series of alliances with the tribes of central Wisconsin and the upper Mississippi, which laid the foundation for the French sovereignty in the Northwest. He deprived the Ottawa of their monopoly of the western trade; he also discovered the lead mines upon the Mississippi and built upon that stream several posts, at one of which he took possession, for the king of France, of all the country of the Sioux.

Concerning Perrot's early life we have but little information. Charlevoix says he was a man of good family and of some education, whom necessity obliged to enter the service of the Jesuits. While among the missionaries he learned several Indian languages.[40] When he left the service of the Jesuits he entered that of the Sulpitians of Montreal, where he passed at least

[38] *Conseil Souverain*, i, 634; *Jes. Rel.*, liv, 151; *Canadian Archives Report*, 1905, i, p. lii-liii.
[39] Sulte, "La Baye Verte et le Lac Superieur en 1665," in Can. Roy. Soc., Proc., 1912, sec. i, 3-33.
[40] Pierre François Xavier de Charlevoix, *History of New France* (Englished and edited by John G. Shea, New York, 1868), iii, 165.

two years.[41] While in that city in 1667, he made an agreement with two Montreal merchants for a voyage to the Ottawa country in company with Toussaint Baudry. Whether this was Perrot's first visit to the Northwest we do not know. It appears probable that he had been west before. According to his contract, he and Baudry were to have one half of the furs they might obtain, the outfitters having the other half.[42]

Perrot and Baudry went out with the returning Ottawa fleet in 1667, and seem to have spent the first year of their trading voyage around the shores of Lake Superior. At Chequamegon, then the center of the Ottawa trade, they met a delegation of Potawatomi from Green Bay, who begged the traders to visit their village in person so that they, like the Ottawa, might have the advantage of direct contact with the French. The traders decided to accept this invitation; however, when Perrot and Baudry arrived at the Potawatomi village in the early summer of 1668, they found that a large number of those tribesmen had gone for the first time to visit Montreal. The Frenchmen were received by those who remained at home, with great cordiality. They were treated like gods; tobacco smoke from the sacred calumet was blown upon them and their goods, they were carried on the shoulders of stalwart savages,

[41] It has usually been assumed, following the notes of Father Jules Tailhan, editor of Perrot's memoir, that Perrot made his historic voyage to Wisconsin in 1665. This we think is disproved by two facts: first, his name appears in the Canadian censuses of 1666 and 1667 as at the Sulpitian convent at Montreal; secondly, he did not come to Green Bay until the year the first Potawatomi visited the St. Lawrence, which was in 1668.

[42] Original document in possession of Chicago Historical Society. The Montreal merchants were Jean Desroches and Isaac Nafrechoux. Baudry signed by a mark. We reproduce the last page of this document showing Perrot's signature, by permission of Caroline McIlvaine, librarian of Chicago Historical Society.

and the women and children from a respectful distance proclaimed them spirits.[43]

The tribesmen who had come, upon the news of the peace with the Iroquois, to build their villages upon the shores of Green Bay lived in what was for them a terrestrial paradise. The virgin soil was exceedingly fertile and produced large crops of maize, of beans, and of squashes. The bay and the rivers abounded with game, which fattened on the wild rice. So plentiful were the ducks, that the Indians caught them in nets and snares as they alighted to feed. Pigeons were caught in the same way in the woods; one man hidden in a hut of branches would sometimes snare six hundred in a morning. The waters also swarmed with fish; the Menominee were adept in spearing the sturgeon as they ran up the river to spawn. Weirs were constructed in the several rivers emptying into the bay; these weirs were furnished with bells which rang when a fish entered the nets stretched across the hurdles of the weir.[44] In the winter the tribesmen left their summer villages and went in small family groups to hunt bear and beaver in the forests.[45]

Perrot found living about Green Bay (then and during all the French régime called La Baye des Puants) a few Winnebago and Menominee, and several groups of Sauk and Potawatomi. The latter he characterized as affable and intelligent, hospitable, and

[43] Bacqueville de la Potherie, *Histoire de l'Amérique septentrionale* (Paris, 1753), ii, 87. Translated in Blair, i, 309-310; *Wis. Hist. Colls.*, xvi, 34. La Potherie knew Perrot in Canada; most of his history is based on Perrot's own journals.
[44] Bells were among the articles of European manufacture much prized by the Indians. In pre-Columbian times metal bells were found in Central America, but not among the more northern tribes. Rattles had probably been used by the Algonquian Indians before they obtained French bells.
[45] La Potherie, in Blair, i, 304-305; *Wis. Hist. Colls.*, xvi, 35-36.

PERROT'S CONTRACT FOR WESTERN TRADE, 1667

desirous of appearing well in their neighbors' eyes. The
Sauk were more brutal and unruly, good hunters, but
very unskillful with a canoe. He was first received in a
mixed village of Potawatomi and Sauk, with a few
Winnebago.[46]

While the two traders were visiting at the village
of the Potawatomi a quarrel arose between them and
the Menominee, one of whom was slain while visiting
a Winnebago family in the village. This quarrel seemed
likely to lead to an intertribal war, it being a point of
Indian honor for the tribe to avenge the death of one of
its members, unless some recompense should be made
by the guilty persons. Perrot offered to act as mediator,
and to satisfy the demands of the Menominee for the
death of their kinsman. He went overland to the
Menominee village,[47] where he was received with universal
joy. The youth of the village turned out to meet
him in warlike array, and their yells and contortions
would have frightened any but the stoutest heart.
Perrot responded by firing his gun, which caused them
to think him a visitant from the sun. He was carried
by the warriors into the village in triumph, the women

[46] The site of this village we think, after careful comparison of
the traders' and missionaries' records, must have been on Oconto
River. See Wis. Hist. Soc., *Proc.*, 1905, 151; *Wisconsin Archeologist*,
xi, 140-143; xviii, 97-98. There were other Potawatomi villages
about Green Bay formed no doubt about this same time; one is
known to have existed on Washington Island, one on the Lake
Michigan shore at or near the present Kewaunee. Perrot probably
visited all these villages. Sites of villages probably established
by the Potawatomi may yet be seen on the lake shore of Door
County, notably one near Jacksonport.

[47] The Menominee village lay on the southeast bank of
Menominee River, some distance above the mouth, probably near
the rapids. *Wisconsin Archeologist*, xvii, 37-38. Large fishing
camps existed on the sites of Marinette, Wisconsin, and Menominee,
Michigan. It was probably at the permanent village that
Perrot made his alliance with this tribe.

and children breaking off branches of the trees to clear his path. Later the Indians danced the calumet for him; and after he had made the blood atonement by presents to the father of the Menominee who had been killed by the Potawatomi, he made an alliance between the Menominee and the French, which included all their Indian allies. This alliance the Menominee kept so faithfully that they were always known as the friends of the white men.

When Perrot returned to the Potawatomi village he found the tribe much agitated concerning the fate of the young men who had gone on the momentous voyage to Montreal. The flotilla of 1668 was the largest and most varied of any that had yet gone down the Ottawa River to trade; in all there were six hundred Indians of several different tribes.[48] It was the first infringement of the Ottawa monopoly. The Potawatomi thoroughly enjoyed themselves and the novel sights of civilization. They ran in and out of the habitants' cottages, marveling at their domestic arrangements, their food, and their dress. When the governor regaled them with white bread, prunes, and raisins, their delight was unbounded.

Anxiously as their return was awaited at home, their approaching canoes were first taken for those of an enemy, since they appeared firing their newly acquired guns. When the panic had subsided, the returning delegation was received with great honors. At the news that two Frenchmen were in their tribal village, the joy of the voyagers expressed itself in a triumphal march headed by the chief, who later harangued the village on the wonders he had seen on the St. Lawrence.[49]

[48] *Jes. Rel.*, li, 263-265.
[49] La Potherie, in Blair, i, 309-316; *Wis. Hist. Colls.*, xvi, 35-38.

THE FIRST TRADERS 127

The Potawatomi now undertook the rôle of middlemen for the Green Bay tribes, which the Ottawa had formerly claimed for the entire Northwest. They sent messages to the Outagami, Miami, Illinois, Kickapoo, and Mascouten, that it would no longer be needful for them to make the long journey to Chequamegon Bay. They, the Potawatomi, were prepared to supply them at Green Bay with French goods. Only the Outagami at first showed a disposition to avail themselves of this opportunity. They established a new village within thirty leagues of Green Bay.[50] Meanwhile Perrot and Baudry were somewhat alarmed lest their chances of securing beaver and of making alliances with the primitive tribes should be filched from them by the Potawatomi. They thereupon took advantage of a delegation from the Outagami who came to visit the Sauk, and went home with the former to their new village. If they went by canoe they ascended the Oconto River until it approaches Lake Shawano, then portaged to that lake and followed the Wolf to the Fox village. If by land, an ancient trail followed much the same route. The Frenchmen found the Outagami in a most primitive stage of barbarism, "destitute of everything. These people had only five or six [French] hatchets, which had no edge, and they used these by turns for cutting their wood; they had hardly one [French] knife or one [steel] bodkin to a cabin, and cut their meat with stones." This report of the first traders in the Fox

[50] The site of this Outagami (Fox, Renard) village, the name of which was Ouestatimong, has been much discussed. It was somewhere on Wolf River, in Waupaca or Outagamie County. See Wis. Hist. Soc., *Proc.*, 1905, 153; *Wisconsin Archeologist*, xv, 5, 18-19. The present writer inclines to believe that the site explored in 1915 by George R. Fox near Leeman, on Wolf River, agrees best with the descriptions of the earliest visitors to this village. It was abandoned about 1680 for a site on Fox River.

village shows to what extent French goods had already passed from tribe to tribe, until this remote people was furnished with a few blunt hatchets and with several knives and bodkins. "Want," our trader continues, "had rendered them so hideous that they aroused compassion. Although their bodies were large, they seemed deformed in shape; they had very disagreeable faces, brutish voices, and evil aspects."[51] Other early travelers did not find these tribesmen so physically uncouth; they all, however, speak of their mental traits—that they were arrogant, avaricious, thieving, and quarrelsome. They were, as we shall see, the Wisconsin tribe which longest maintained its primitive independence, and was the last to succumb to French influences and to yield submission to white men. Their courage was greater than that of the other surrounding tribes, as well as their determination to live as their forefathers did, uncontaminated by white contact. To this end they not only fought the French for two generations, but they reared as many children as possible, and trained them for the same fierce resistance to civilization. By far the most fierce, the Outagami were certainly the most interesting of the Wisconsin aborigines. Their own impressions of the first white men they met were distinctly unfavorable, although in time Perrot gained so much influence over their councils that, had he been retained as French agent in the West, the Fox wars would undoubtedly never have occurred.[52]

[51] La Potherie, in Blair, i, 318; *Wis. Hist. Colls.*, xvi, 39.

[52] On the early history of this tribe, see Kellogg, "The Fox Indians during the French Régime," in Wis. Hist. Soc., *Proc.*, 1907, 142-188. Perrot found six hundred cabins in the Outagami village. Allouez enumerated only two hundred. Possibly Perrot included some neighboring tribes, who had come to dwell with the Outagami. See *Jes. Rel.*, liv, 219; lv, 219. The Fox Indians always considered Perrot as their benefactor and father, since he first brought them iron. See *post*, chapter xii.

THE FIRST TRADERS 129

After his visit to the Outagami, Perrot passed the ensuing winter in the vicinity of Green Bay, probably engaged in trapping the beaver so plentiful in that region. The next year he undertook a second journey to interior Wisconsin, this time to the upper Fox River, where the Mascouten and Miami had recently built a village on a lovely upland looking afar across the valley of the winding stream.[53] These tribesmen since the great dispersion had been living across the Mississippi River. News of peace with the Iroquois and of opportunity to obtain French goods had induced them to venture into Wisconsin, and to plant a village where there was every advantage for aboriginal economy. Besides the fertility of the soil for their crops, the land produced spontaneously many edible roots. The abundant trees furnished sugar sap, acorns, wild plums, and apples, while grapevines heavy with wild grapes festooned the branches. The game that frequented the river's banks and widespreads was even more plentiful than on the lower river. A lovely, never-failing spring at the foot of the bluff on which their village stood furnished abundance of wholesome water; while the stagnant places along the banks of the Fox were thick with reeds for the squaws' skillful fingers to fashion into mats.[54] Clay was at hand for pottery, osiers for basketry; best of all, the buffalo roamed the land, and his flesh furnished meat, his hides blankets, his tongue the choicest morsels, even his hoofs were used for ornaments.

The Potawatomi disparaged these inland peoples, hoping to keep the trade and the traders in their own

[53] The site of this village has been identified near Berlin in Green Lake County. Wis. Hist. Soc., *Proc.*, 1906, 167-182.
[54] Reed mats were used for many purposes—to cover the cabins, for carpets, bedclothes, and tablecloths, for coverings of bundles, for seats and other furniture in the cabins.

hands, all to no purpose. Perrot and Baudry could by no means be turned from the journey.[55] They were received with great enthusiasm by their new customers; were met with the ceremonial calumet; "a large painted ox-skin, the hair of which was as soft as silk" was spread for the traders to rest upon. Attempts were made to carry the wondrous guests, who protested that since they could shape iron, their legs were strong enough to walk. At the summit of the plateau the great Miami chief came to meet them, at the head of more than three thousand men;[56] his entourage sang the calumet song, presenting the ceremonial pipe to the sun and then to the two strangers. Feasts, dances, and speeches followed. Perrot made alliance with these peoples for the French crown. Financially the visit was very successful; the traders acquired many fine beaver robes in exchange for their kettles and knives. Trade with these primitive tribes was likened by Perrot to the riches of Peru. "The savages could not understand why these men came so far to search for their worn-out beaver robes; meanwhile they admired all the wares brought to them by the French, which they regarded as extremely precious."[57]

[55] There is no account of the means by which the journey was accomplished. Probably the traders went on foot along the Fox River, carrying their packs. The Potawatomi had canoes, but as they opposed the journey, the Frenchmen probably had to walk; upon his arrival a Mascouten rubbed Perrot's back, legs, and feet as if to relieve his fatigue.

[56] Perrot's numbers seem exaggerated; this was, however, the largest Indian village ever known in Wisconsin. The Jesuits estimated it after some accessions at 20,000 souls. *Jes. Rel.*, lix, 221. The position of the principal chief among the Miami was unusually exalted. He was reverenced almost like a divinity.

[57] La Potherie, in Blair, i, 307. The used beaver robes, greased and made supple by being worn next to the skin, were the most valuable and brought the best prices.

THE FIRST TRADERS

While Perrot and Baudry were visiting interior Wisconsin during the early summer of 1669, several other Frenchmen arrived at Green Bay as emissaries of the intendant Talon. Talon, the most energetic of the early rulers of New France, determined to seek an easier route to Lake Superior than the customary one via the Ottawa River. He was eager to exploit the copper mines of that region, having seen a large ingot which Father Allouez brought down in 1667. The intendant thereupon commissioned Jean Peré, who had learned from one of his Indian customers that there was an easier route to the Ottawa country along the Great Lakes, to explore the new route. Conveyed by his Indian guides, Peré ascended the St. Lawrence, skirted the northern shore of Lake Ontario, portaged along the Oshawa-Lake Simcoe route to the bottom of Georgian Bay, and thence proceeded northward through that bay and Lake Huron to Sault Ste. Marie.[58] Peré's voyage seems to have been begun in 1668 and to have lasted three years. He made a thorough exploration of Lake Superior and its northward connections, and located a copper mine.[59] Meanwhile Talon in 1669 sent supplies and reinforcements to Peré by the usual Ottawa River route. In command of this expedition went Louis, younger brother of Adrien Jolliet, a Canadian by birth, who had taken minor orders in the Seminary at Quebec, but who now entered upon the adventurous life of explorer.

When Jolliet arrived at the Sault in the summer of 1669, he found that the Jesuits had established a mission house there the autumn before, in the charge

---

[58] Galinée's map is the only evidence we have of Peré's route. Its editor adopts the route here outlined for this voyage. See *Canada and Its Provinces* (Toronto, 1914), i, 83.

[59] *Jes. Rel.*, lv, 237.

of a young priest of Laon, Father Jacques Marquette. Marquette and Jolliet may have met before; at this time doubtless they renewed the friendship which was to serve so well in a future voyage of discovery. Jolliet learned at the Sault that the Algonquian tribes had again become embroiled with the Iroquois, that a small party of the latter coming from a raid on southern Indians had been ambushed and captured by a band of Chippewa. It was necessary that these captives should be rescued and returned to their kinsmen according to treaty terms, or the settlements as well as the fur traders would feel the vengeance of the Iroquois. Father Allouez at Chequamegon had succeeded in ransoming some of these captive Iroquois, and had already gone to carry them to Montreal to deliver them into the hands of the governor. Jolliet likewise, knowing there could be no peace until this quarrel was settled, abandoned any attempt to join Peré in Lake Superior, bought the one remaining Iroquois from the villagers at the Sault, and started to return with the rescued captive to the colony. The Iroquois captive suggested to Jolliet that they should voyage by way of the lower lakes, along which he could be their guide. The explorer and one French companion accepted this offer, and made the first recorded voyage of white men through the straits of Detroit into Lake Erie and along the shores of that lake.

Jolliet's Iroquois guide felt much uneasiness when he reached the waters of Lake Erie, lest he should once more fall into the hands of prowling enemies which infested that region. He thereupon insisted upon landing and taking a trail along the north shore of the lake, which led them to the western end of Lake Ontario. There they arrived September 23 at an outlying Iroquois village named Tinawatawa.[60] The next day there arrived at this same distant village another party of white men who were making a voyage of exploration along the Great Lakes. This party was headed by François Dollier de Casson, superior of the Sulpitian convent at Montreal. With the consent of the governor and the intendant of New France, he was taking a voyage of exploration preliminary to the founding of a western mission for his order.[61] Attached to his party, yet independent of its purpose, was a young Norman adventurer, Robert Cavelier de la Salle, who two years before had come from France, and was eager to explore the interior of the continent. Thus unexpectedly in the heart of the forest met the two men who were to become the discoverers and explorers of the Mississippi River. Jolliet described to the Frenchmen the new route along which he had come from the Ottawa country; he told them where he had left his canoe, and advised the missionaries to visit the far West and to begin a mission to the Potawatomi on Baye des Puants. Thither he had already sent six young traders who had accompanied him to the Sault. Jolliet then continued his route and brought his ransomed captive safe to Montreal.

Meanwhile at Tinawatawa the exploring party broke apart. La Salle parted from the missionaries, who, taking Jolliet's advice, set out for the shore of Lake Erie. Finding it too late in the autumn to pursue their journey, they went into winter quarters late in October and awaited the spring in order to continue

[60] Kellogg, *Early Narratives*, 191-192. Tinawatawa was in Beverly swamp near the present Westover, Ontario.
[61] Sulpitian missions had already been commenced on the north shore of Lake Ontario for the Iroquois. Casson wished to convert some far western tribes.

their voyage.[62] The winter of 1669-70 was a hard one throughout all of North America; the snows were deep and the frosts bound the streams in fetters. It was with difficulty that the little band of explorers on the north shore of Lake Erie kept from freezing, and it was late in the spring before they were able to launch their canoes upon the shores of the great lake. They depended for their guide upon René de Bréhant de Galinée, the second missionary of the party, who was a trained cartographer and who had studied all the available maps of the region. Galinée was familiar with Sanson's map of the lakes.[63] He was surprised therefore, upon reaching the end of Lake Erie, to find no salt water, but only continuous fresh-water seas. Passing through the Detroit River, Lake St. Clair, and the St. Clair channel, the explorers entered Lake Huron, which Galinée thought the largest lake in all America.[64] It was the twenty-fifth of May, 1670, when this small party of daring voyagers finally reached the mission house at the Sault.

The voyaging missionaries were treated with courtesy by the Jesuit fathers at the Sault, but the latter had no idea of encouraging the Sulpitians to undertake missions in the Northwest. The Jesuits informed them that a mission to the Potawatomi had already been begun by Father Allouez. Casson thereupon determined to return to Montreal over the Ottawa River route.

[62] Winter quarters were near Fort Dover, Ontario. Kellogg, *Early Narratives*, 194-196. The outlines of the buildings set up during the winter of 1669-70 are still visible, and July 5, 1922, a monument was unveiled near this site, under the auspices of the Ontario Historical Society.

[63] See *ante*, page 92.

[64] He called it "the Fresh Water Sea of the Hurons, or in Algonkin, Michigan." He included the present Lakes Huron and Michigan in one great body of water. See his map, Ontario Historical Society, *Papers and Records*, iv, p. xxxi-xxxvi.

Since one of his canoes voyaged as far as the entrance to Green Bay, his party had visited all the Great Lakes and made the first complete circuit thereof.[65] Galinée's map, although only a sketch of the route he and his companions had followed, is an advance upon any previous map of the Great Lakes. Lake Superior is not given, the southern shore of Lake Erie, nor the eastern coast of Lake Michigan, which is made a part of Lake Huron. Green Bay is called "Baye des Poteotamites." The Chenaux and Mackinac islands appear along the north shore of Lake Huron.

Meanwhile what of Perrot and Baudry, whom we left on their return to the Potawatomi village on Green Bay? Jolliet's six traders who had arrived in their absence stirred up animosity among the savages, and quarreled with the chief over payment for his furs. Perrot exerted his influence to compose the difficulty, while some of the Potawatomi voyaging to the Sault complained of the white traders and invited the "black robe" to visit their village and arbitrate their grievances. Father Allouez accepted their invitation with alacrity, and in December, 1669, made his first visit to the tribes about Green Bay.[66] After the missionary had departed the next May, Perrot and Baudry made arrangements to return to Montreal with the furs they had gathered. Five traders in all accompanied the flotilla, which was by far the largest that had ever left the upper country, comprising nine hundred natives, among whom were members of several tribes that had never before been to Montreal. Chief among these

[65] Galinée's narrative makes no mention of Green Bay; on his map, however, he shows the islands at its entrance, and states that he did not go beyond these islands.

[66] La Potherie, in Blair, i, 319-321; *Jes. Rel.*, liv, 197-201; Kellogg, *Early Narratives*, 142. Allouez's visit is described in the succeeding chapter.

newcomers was a delegation of the Outagami, who went to complain to the governor that the Iroquois had attacked a large winter camp of their people near Chicago, and had massacred the men and carried captive the women and children. So great was the concourse of savages, that there was a plethora of furs, and prices were much lowered in consequence. Perrot soon had a chance to add to his reputation by acting as interpreter.[67] So far as appears, Baudry never undertook another western trading voyage. He made his home at Pointe aux Trembles, married, and there died in 1694.

The governor in 1670 composed the difficulties between the Iroquois and the western Indians. The former sent back their Outagami captives, and traders continued to flock into the Northwest. Even when the Sulpitians were at Sault Ste. Marie in 1670 there were twenty to twenty-five Frenchmen in the vicinity of the mission. Few of these traders have left any account of their adventures; most of them were illiterate Canadians who signed their contracts with their mark. It is only from such typical narratives as those of Radisson and Perrot, aided by incidental references in the missionaries' reports, that the life of the earliest traders among the Wisconsin Indians can be reconstructed.

Most of these nameless traders left little mark on the history of Wisconsin. They came and went without record, bringing in French goods, taking away precious furs, leaving in the minds of the aborigines strange impressions of white men's ways. Some of the traders were cruel and thoughtless, and created prejudice against all white men; the awe in which Nicolet and Perrot had been held quickly vanished, and the traders

---

[67] "Perrot's Memoir," in Blair, i, 210-220; La Potherie, in *ibid.*, 336-342.

who ingratiated themselves with their dark-skinned customers were the most successful. The Frenchmen quickly learned the art of adaptability which characterized them during all their intercourse with the Indians.

The fur trade had a profound influence on the history of New France, conditioning it throughout its entire existence; but great as the importance of the trade was to the white men, it did not revolutionize all their habits and mode of living as it did those of the red men. It is only in the accounts of these first traders, such as Radisson and Perrot, that we can learn from historical documents anything of the primitive economy of the Indians of Wisconsin. By the time the missionaries reached these tribesmen their former mode of life had already been profoundly altered by the fur trade. They quickly forgot the arts of barbarous life and became dependent upon French goods, and upon the traders who brought them. Iron and brass implements replaced stone knives and hatchets, and the art of fashioning the latter was soon lost. Blankets and cloth of French manufacture replaced the clothing of skins for which the white man was so eager. Metal kettles and cooking utensils superseded the earthenware pots and the gourds that had been previously used by the Indian women; and steel needles, awls, and bodkins replaced those of bone and shell. The energy of the tribesmen was turned more and more to the chase. Whereas in former days the Indian hunted only to supply the immediate wants of himself and family for food and clothing, he was now forced to obtain many more animal pelts in order to purchase from the white trader the manufactures which had now become necessities to him and his. Hunting became his one employment, and as the game became more scarce and retreated before the onslaught of the red hunter deeper into the woods, he was forced to range farther and farther from his village into the depths of the forest. It thus came to pass that most of the winter was spent in the woods, while the summer was idled away around the hut of the white trader. Thus the whole life of the Indian was changed; he acquired new wants, new habits, and new vices. He became in large measure dependent upon the visiting traders, and must, in event of their not seeking him, take the long journey to the St. Lawrence to supply his wants. He became in truth a subject of the French king, since he was dependent upon that ruler's subjects for his living. He lost his proud independence as a son of the forest, and became an ally of the French rulers and a customer of the French trader. It was only when international rivalries arose in the fur trade that the Indian was able to free himself from absolute dependence upon the French traders, who had altered the whole economy of his life.

VIII. THE MISSIONS, 1660-1675

NO PHASE of Wisconsin history has received more attention, and none has been less impartially considered, than the work of the French missionaries among the native population. Notwithstanding all that has been written on these missions, this study is undertaken with a sense of blazing at first-hand a way through an uncharted historical wilderness, so large is the body of tradition that has grown up around this subject, and so numerous are the unfounded assumptions that have been made. The attempt has been to lay aside all prepossessions and to make a resurvey from the sources alone; thus to determine what the missionaries themselves have said about their work. It is believed that only by this method historical perspective may be obtained. The conclusions hereafter presented will serve, we hope, as a stimulus to further careful study of the sources.

The one great source for the history of the early missions is the *Jesuit Relations*, annual reports compiled by the superior at Quebec from the accounts furnished him by the missionaries in the several fields. This report, or relation, was first sent to the provincial of the order in France, who prepared it for publication, when it was issued in an annual volume for the patrons of the society. The relations were intended to stimulate the benevolence and interest of their readers. They soon became immensely popular, had a large sale, and passed from hand to hand among the devotionally-minded people of all Europe. Notwithstanding this popularity, perhaps because of it, complete sets of the *Jesuit Relations* are very rare. Several attempts were made in the nineteenth century to republish these documents; this was finally accomplished in the last years of the century under the editorial care of Reuben G. Thwaites, who in his Cleveland edition of *Jesuit Relations and Allied Documents* has given a definitive form to this important source for early French history in America.

Unfortunately for the purposes of our study, the publication of the *Relations* ceased with the year 1673, at the time the central Wisconsin missions were being opened.[1] Thereafter we have to depend upon the few hitherto unpublished summaries which are issued in the Thwaites collection, and upon chance references in the reports of travelers and the secular documents of the time. These are scanty and insufficient, so that the later history of the Wisconsin missions can only be inferred.

In order properly to interpret the history of the missions one must understand the missionaries' use of the fundamental terms for their work. The term "mission" was used in the seventeenth century in a sense different from what we understand by it today—"an organization usually including a church, established for the conversion and spiritual improvement of a certain district."[2] The early Jesuits used the term in no

---

[1] The publishing of the *Jesuit Relations* was stopped because of the struggle of the French church with the Papacy. As an incident thereto, the Pope in 1673 required that all reports of mission work should have the authorization of the Congregation of the Propaganda. The French laws forbade the publication of any volumes with this stamp. The Jesuits, who were Ultramontane in their policy, thereupon suppressed their *Relations*. In Canada these reports were prepared for a few years after their publication ceased. The Thwaites edition gives from the manuscripts these later relations, which are fragmentary and unsatisfactory so far as the Wisconsin missions are concerned.

[2] *Webster's New International Dictionary of the English Language* (Springfield, Mass., 1916), 1382.

such limited or definite sense. To them a mission was the "substance of things hoped for," a desire or prophecy of what could be seen only by the eye of faith. If only one dying infant of a tribe were baptized, the first fruits of that mission were thought to be garnered for heaven. If any members of a tribe expressed a wish to hear the gospel message, thereafter the mission for that tribe was spoken of as commenced. For instance, the mission for the Illinois was included in the annual list of western missions while that tribe was dwelling in central Iowa and the nearest missionaries were on Chequamegon Bay, where they had talked with a few of the Illinois tribesmen come thither for purposes of trade. The Potawatomi village near Green Bay was in 1658 hopefully christened the mission of St. Michel by Father Dreuillettes, then upon the Saguenay River, where he heard from some wandering Indians of this new village in the far West.[3] Allouez in 1667 described missions for the Sauk, the Foxes, the Potawatomi, and other northwestern tribes, while he was dwelling upon Chequamegon Bay among the Ottawa, who were there visited by a few stragglers from among these tribes. Later he speaks of his mission of St. Marc in central Wisconsin after a three days' sojourn in the Outagami village.[4] Thus any contact with a native tribe was considered the beginning of a mission, whether there had been any acceptance of the missionary's message, or any substantial plan for continued contact.

In the next place, it is necessary to consider the way the reports, or the *Relations*, were prepared. They were written not solely for the eye of the superior of the Canadian missions, but always with the thought in mind of stimulating the interest and the benevo-

[3] *Jes. Rel.*, xliv, 245.
[4] *Ibid.*, li, 27-45; liv, 225-227.

lence of the readers. The appeal was to the religious emotions. Sufferings and hardships were thrown into relief, the death of a martyr was the greatest possible glory. Since the readers craved to hear of great results, of savages converted and baptized, of whole tribes forsaking their idols and superstitions and turning to the true God, the temptation to enlarge upon every success was very great. To the credit of the western missionaries it should be said that they nobly resisted the temptation to exaggerate their work, and the *Relations* on the whole present a reliable account of what really happened in the western wilderness. The faithful priests report their failures as well as their successes, and it is entirely from their own reports that we infer the slight influence that the missions had on the Wisconsin tribes. None the less in reading the *Relations* one must make allowance for the audience to whom they were addressed—a credulous, devout constituency, eager for emotional reactions. Even in reading the reports of modern missionaries, an allowance must be made for the human equation of the writers and readers, in a society so much more enlightened than that of three centuries ago.

This brings us to the consideration of the larger subject of the soil out of which these missions grew, and the motives that impelled such devotion and exertions for the benefit of distant savages. France in the seventeenth century was the greatest Catholic country in the world. After the Protestant schism and the religious wars of the sixteenth century, France and Spain were the chief bulwarks of the older church. As the latter country declined from its high estate, France rose to become not only the greatest political but the greatest religious power in Europe. There ensued a notable revival of enthusiasm for the Church and for religious activity of every sort. The Huguenots, discredited after the revocation of the Edict of Nantes, had become an unimportant element of the population. The prime ministers of France for two successive generations were cardinals or princes of the Church. The religious revival expressed itself in a sense of personal responsibility for the upbuilding of the Church; a desire for sacrifice and salvation was a dominant force in social life. Seventeenth-century France was a society of great and startling contrasts and of opposing forces. On the one hand, luxury and ostentation grew as they had never done before, display and refinement became the chief objects of life among the upper classes; but on the other hand, as the court and its followers became increasingly frivolous and extravagant, a considerable portion of the population revolted from these aims and sought refuge in a life of devotion and self-sacrifice that in its turn assumed an extreme character. Society was penetrated by the so-called *devots*. Even the king and the courtiers had frequent recourse to penance, and were ready to interest themselves in enterprises for the relief of the destitute and for the spread of religion among the pagans of all lands. The latter portion of the sixteenth and the early part of the seventeenth century saw the rise of an immense foreign missionary activity, in which the Jesuits played a leading part. During that period Spanish Jesuits began the evangelization of South America,[5] of Asia, and of Africa. French zeal turned its thoughts to the races of North America, upon whose northeastern border their king had acquired a foothold.

This missionary movement was supported by almost

[5] The Franciscan order had the privilege of conducting the missions of Mexico, including Texas and New Mexico. In the eighteenth century these were extended to California.

every class in France; the king himself bestowed lands and an annual stipend upon the Jesuit missionaries, to whom in 1632 he confirmed the right of converting North America. Pious donors added lands and annuities; the aristocracy especially aided the missionary projects and made large donations to the funds of the several societies.[6] But it was among the upper middle class that the most constant and efficient help was found. These bourgeois families, grown rich during the civil and religious wars, were a sturdy, sober-minded, and religiously-inclined people. They gave liberally not only of their substance, but from their ranks was recruited the personnel of the religious orders, and in giving their sons and daughters to the Church they gave their best gifts. So great was the enthusiasm for the religious vocation that monasteries and convents were filled to overflowing, the missionary and preaching orders grew by leaps and bounds. Finally the government was forced to interpose lest the population of France should be depleted by too widespread celibacy. Scarcely a family of note but counted among its members some servants of the Church; thus the interest in the growth of religion at home and abroad became a matter of vital family concern.

In a society so constituted the martyr became the hero. He who left all for the service of God, who voluntarily resigned all that civilization could offer for the sake of preaching to the heathen, who suffered untold discomforts, fearful tortures, and a dreadful death, rendered the highest service not only to God but to his king and country. Such motives appealed to the noblest souls among the French youth. The missionary orders were filled with high-minded, eager young men,

---

[6] Thomas Hughes, *History of the Society of Jesus in North America* (London, 1917), ii, 249, 350.

THE MISSIONS

seeking as a mark of divine approbation the crown of martyrdom. The Jesuits thus had ample material for missionary recruits, and their activities were followed with an interest hardly paralleled in the history of missions. The kinsfolk and friends of the Jesuits in North America were legion, and the publication of each *Relation* was an event not only in the religious but in the social world.

It was under such a stimulus that the missions of New France began, auspiciously at first, among the Huron tribesmen. The great interest thereupon awakened, and the hopes for permanent success, were overthrown when by the close of the first half of the seventeenth century these promising missions were utterly destroyed by the Iroquois warriors. True several of the missionaries became bright stars in the galaxy of the martyrs; but new fields must be found for the continuation of the missions of New France. Attempts were made to penetrate to the conquerors' habitat and to subdue these fierce tribesmen by the gospel message. These tentatives were, however, dangerous to the colony as well as to the missionaries themselves. In the course of a long series of efforts Iroquois missions were established and certain converts attracted thence to the mission colonies on the St. Lawrence; but no Iroquois tribe was ever Christianized by the Jesuits. Opportunity was also sought among the numerous peoples of the far West; especially was it desirable to seek the "lost sheep" of the Huron mission, the remnant that had escaped the fury of their enemies and had taken refuge in the forests of Wisconsin. The earliest western missions were thus a direct outgrowth of the Huron disaster and an attempt to conserve the remnants of that destroyed mission.

It was six years after the final abandonment of

Huronia before an opportunity came of sending missionaries to the far West. Then in 1656 the Ottawa who came to Montreal to trade agreed to carry two "black robes" with them to their western refuge. This first effort met with disaster at the hands of the Iroquois. Of the two missionaries who started with the Indians, one was killed on the Ottawa River by a prowling band of Iroquois; the other fleeing for his life came back to Montreal.[7]

Four years later the way again opened for the commencement of the western missions. Two fathers were again chosen from among the veterans of the Huron mission; but at Montreal one was refused passage by the savages, and only Father Ménard with his *donné* Jean Guérin secured a place in the canoes of the outgoing fleet. René Ménard was in 1660 a man fifty-six years of age, of a delicate constitution, already worn by years of service in the western wilderness. Born in 1604, he had entered the Society of Jesus in 1624, had been designated in 1640 for the Canadian mission, and had dwelt in Huronia until its abandonment. For two years also he had lived and suffered among the Iroquois (1656-58); thus he had no illusions concerning the dangers and hardships involved in the present undertaking. He realized that the appointment was for him a death sentence, and wrote to a friend: "In three or four months you may include me in the Memento for the dead, in view of the kind of life led by these peoples, of my age, and of my delicate constitution. In spite of that, I have felt such powerful promptings and have seen in this affair so little of the purely natural, that I could not doubt that if I failed to respond to this opportunity I should experience an endless

[7] *Jes. Rel.*, xlii, 221, 225-245; Blair, i, 157-158. See also *ante*, chapter vii.

remorse."[8] On his way up the St. Lawrence to Montreal he met the bishop of Canada, who said to him: "My Father, every reason seems to retain you here; but God, more powerful than aught else, requires you yonder."[9] These words were to him an accolade of Christian knighthood. They allayed his every misgiving.

The Indians who had promised to care for Father Ménard quickly broke their word. On the difficult journey up the swift Ottawa they forced him to paddle constantly, to disembark in the roughest places, and to carry heavy burdens around the numerous portages. Savages have but slight compassion; the predicament of a comrade usually evokes their mirth. They laughed when the "black robe" sank beneath his burden, when he cut his bare feet and one of them became swollen and painful. Food was scarce, and the father was allotted the worst portions and the smallest share. The seven French traders who accompanied the flotilla,[10] as well as his own *donné*, were separated from the missionary. Finally in Lake Superior a serious accident befell him. The canoe in which he and three Indians were traveling was broken by a falling tree. None of the other canoes would stop for the unfortunates stranded on a gravelly beach. At last, after six days of privation, they were rescued and carried on to the foot of Keweenaw Bay, where they arrived the fifteenth of October. This being the saint's day of Ste. Thérèse, the bay was given her name.

The remainder of the party had already gone on to Chequamegon, where the Ottawa from Lac Court

[8] *Jes. Rel.*, xlvi, 79-81; Latin MS. in Wisconsin Historical Library.
[9] *Jes. Rel.*, xlviii, 259.
[10] See *ante*, chapter vii.

Oreilles had begun to form a village.¹¹ One band only remained for the winter at Keweenaw, under the chief Le Brochet. He was a surly brute, "proud and extremely vicious, possessing four or five wives." When Ménard, following the promptings of his conscience, rebuked the chief for his polygamy, he "treated the poor Father very badly, and finally forced him to leave him and make himself a hut out of fir-branches. Heavens, what an abode during the rigours of Winter!" Fortunately it was an exceedingly mild winter; the bay did not freeze until February, nor did the wine for the mass congeal in the father's poor hut.¹²

March came and with it aid for the missionary. The traders who had come from Canada with him now sought him out and took him back with them to the great village on Chequamegon Bay. "I must," he writes, "push on to the last post, the Bay of St. Esprit, 100 leagues from here."¹³ The lake was still bordered

¹¹ The site of this village was almost certainly on Fish Creek at the bottom of Chequamegon Bay. *Wis. Hist. Colls.*, xiii, 430, 439.

¹² *Jes. Rel.*, xlvi, 127-143. Le Brochet later became a firm friend of the French. Blair, i, 175.

¹³ Previous studies of Ménard's journey, such as that of Henry C. Campbell, *Parkman Club Papers, No. 11* (Milwaukee, 1897); R. G. Thwaites, *Wisconsin* (New York, 1908), 45-46; and the writer's own "Story of Wisconsin," in *Wisconsin Magazine of History*, ii, 420, make Ménard start on his final journey from Ste. Thérèse Bay. A rereading, however, of Ménard's own letter, *Jes. Rel.*, xlvi, 141-143, has changed my point of view. This letter was evidently begun March 1, 1661, at Ste. Thérèse Bay and completed later at St. Esprit on Chequamegon Bay. In it the missionary particularly describes the voyage begun Easter Saturday (April 20, 1661) to Portage River, through Portage Lake and the bogs to the lake beyond, whence he and his companions coasted for five days to St. Esprit Bay. See also *Jes. Rel.*, lii, 205, where it is stated in 1669 that Ménard instructed the Ottawa "in the place where they are now," namely, Chequamegon Bay. The present writer embodied this new light on Ménard's career in an article entitled "The First Missionary in Wisconsin," published in *Wis. Mag. of Hist.*, iv, 417-475.

with ice when they arrived; but the Indian women were already planting their cornfields and the young hunters preparing for the summer chase. Here the missionary was received with deference; he baptized a few savages, as well as ministered to the French.[14] On Ascension Day, May 23, a Huron messenger arrived with the sad tidings that his tribe, then dwelling on Black River, were dying with hunger; since their enemies were so pervasive they dared not venture forth to hunt. They proposed to abandon their village and take refuge with their former comrades the Ottawa at Chequamegon Bay. In their extremity Ménard saw his opportunity. These dying Indians must be baptized and hastened to Paradise. By three of the traders going inland with the Huron envoy, Ménard sent a present to Chief Sastaretsy,[15] requesting permission to visit his village. The traders were absent some time;[16] upon their return they endeavored to dissuade the missionary from undertaking the journey, all to no purpose. "God calls me thither and I must go, although it should cost me my life." Before his departure Ménard finished the letter to his superior which he had begun in March at Keweenaw Bay.[17]

Pierre Levasseur *dit* l'Espèrance, who had just returned from the Huron village, volunteered to accompany the missionary.[18] They were guided by some young Hurons who were returning to their village. Leaving Chequamegon on the thirteenth of July,[19] they

[14] *Jes. Rel.*, xlviii, 123.
[15] The hereditary title of the Petun Hurons. See *Wis. Hist. Colls.*, xvii, 279.
[16] For their probable route, see *Wis. Mag. of Hist.*, iv, 422.
[17] *Jes. Rel.*, xlvi, 145; it is here dated June 2, but see *ibid.*, xlviii, 277, where the proper date, July 2, is given.
[18] Ménard's companion is said to have been "the armorer," who was L'Espèrance of the traders' party.
[19] The text says June, but see *ante*, note 17.

took the land trail to Lac Court Oreilles, then called because of the previous village of that tribe upon its banks, Ottawa Lake.[20] The Huron guides, impatient at the slow progress of the old man along the wilderness road, soon abandoned the Frenchmen, promising to send guides to meet them at the lake. There the two travelers waited for a fortnight, their slender store of provisions fast dwindling away. L'Espèrance finally found an Indian canoe on the lake shore and proposed to continue the journey. Stepping into the frail craft, they trusted themselves to the rushing waters of the lake's outlet. Soon they swung into the main Chippewa, where the river grew swifter and swifter. Ménard's companion had some skill in paddling, and guided the tiny vessel in safety until he reached the mouth of the stream, whose source lay near the Huron village. This river he recognized from his previous voyage, and up it he turned the prow of his canoe.[21] Which of the eastern tributaries of the Chippewa it may have been we can only conjecture. Probability points to the Jump River, but it may have been the Yellow River of Taylor County. Both streams are full of rapids, in one of which the canoe was caught and whirled down stream. Ménard, to lighten his companion's labors, considerately stepped ashore, while the armorer bent all his strength to breast the rough rapid. Safely up in quiet water, he waited for the father to emerge from the dense forest. Becoming alarmed at the delay, the

[20] For the probable route of this trail, see *Wis. Mag. of Hist.*, iv, 423.

[21] Ménard was mounting a stream when he was lost. Blair, i, 173; Charlevoix, *History of New France*, iii, 49. See also accompanying map, reproduced from that known as "Parkman No. 4" in the library of Harvard University. Note that the site of the missionary's death is placed south of Chequamegon Bay, whence he had set out. The author of this map is not known.

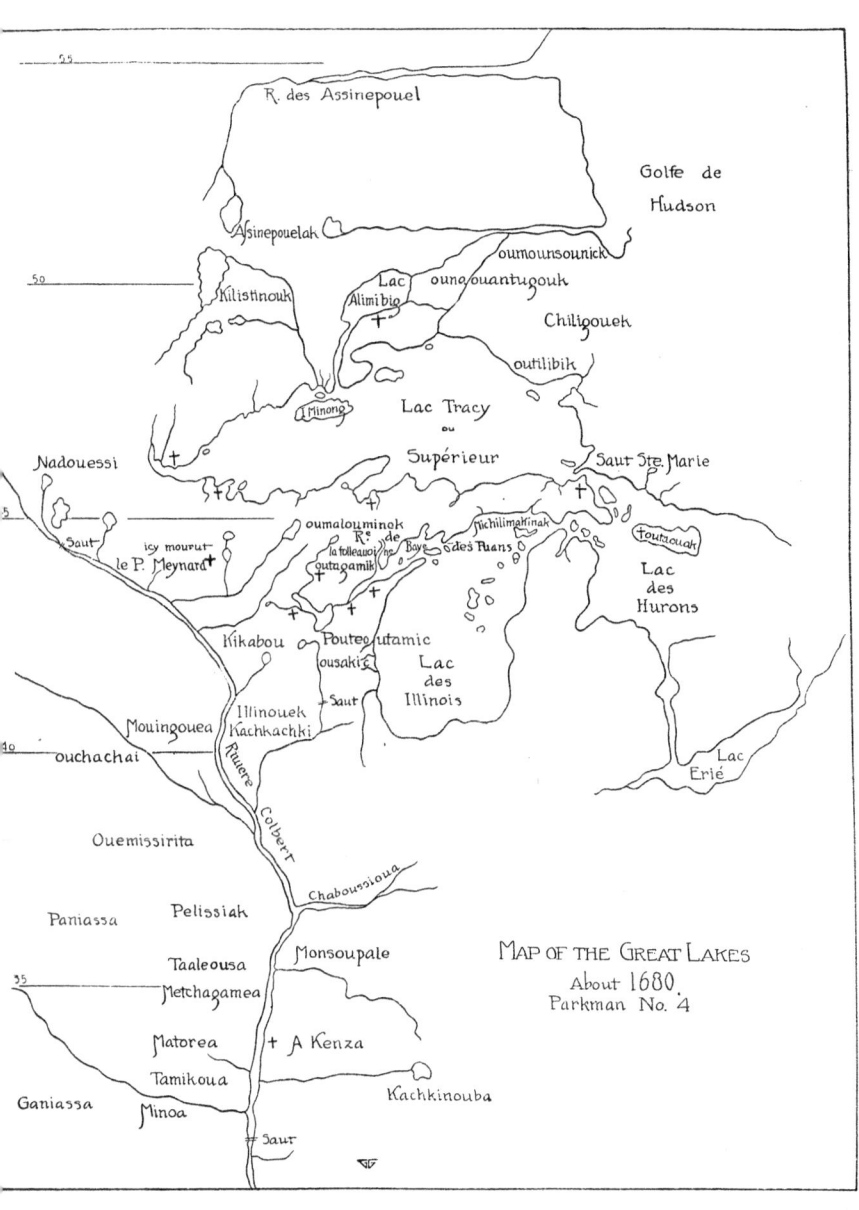

THE MISSIONS

Frenchman fired his fusee and shouted to guide the footsteps of his companion. All in vain; only the echoes answered his summons. L'Espèrance now became seriously alarmed and ran back through the woods in search of the old man; then he himself became frightened at the menace of the forest, where every step involved him in a tangle of trees and undergrowth. Help must be sought to find the lost missionary; the Huron village was close at hand. Thither he hurried, only in his turn to become lost, so that it was the second day before he finally reached the Hurons. With them he could communicate only by signs; he managed to convey to them the fact of the loss of the "black robe," when one Indian agreed to go to the father's rescue. After a brief absence he rushed back with a false alarm of approaching enemies. "At this cry the pity felt for the Father vanished, as well as the inclination to go to search for him." In vain the Frenchman besought and bribed the savages to undertake the rescue; the Hurons were obdurate in their refusal to search for the missing missionary. Days passed and no news came from the silent forest. L'Espèrance went back to Chequamegon and reported the loss, whence a son of Le Brochet carried the news to Quebec. A report was later current that some of Ménard's effects were seen in a cabin of western Indians. This was never substantiated. His colleagues in Canada believed that he had been lost, not murdered; that he laid down his life in the dense pineries where the sun scarcely penetrates, and where an old man with little strength would easily become confused and lose his way.[22] Let us hope that his end was peaceful, and

---

[22] An unpublished Latin manuscript, of which a copy is in the Wisconsin Historical Library, entitled "Life and Death of Father René Ménard," speaks especially of the density of the forest where he was lost.

that he died consoled by a vision of the crown of martyrdom for which he had so earnestly prayed.

Thus perished in the heart of our northern forests the first missionary to Wisconsin. His faithful servant, Jean Guérin, also met death in the West, having been accidentally shot by one of the French traders. As we have seen, these traders were financially unsuccessful in their adventures. The Jesuits also lost heavily on their furs, and the expedition was to them an economic as well as a personal loss.[23]

The next essay at missionary work among the Ottawa was more successfully planned. Warned by experience, the superior chose for this new effort a younger man, in the prime of life, who had come to Canada in 1658. Claude Jean Allouez spent the next quarter-century among the tribes of the western country, and was known as the apostle of the Ottawa missions. Allouez was a member of a family in central France who had already given an older son to the religious vocation. Claude's earliest inclinations led him to follow in his brother's footsteps, and after a successful career as a teacher, he sought and obtained appointment to the missions in New France, desirous of emulating the illustrious members of his order. After his arrival in Canada he was stationed at Three Rivers, where he knew Ménard, the traders Radisson and Groseilliers, and some of the seven traders of 1660-63.[24]

Allouez left Three Rivers for the West on August 8, 1665, in a flotilla of canoes filled with four hundred tribesmen and six French traders. His first experiences on the outward journey were almost as painful as those

[23] *Jes. Rel.*, xlvii, 307.

[24] A manuscript in the Chicago Historical Society is a receipt by Madame Groseilliers for a sum of money lent her by Father Allouez.

of Ménard; he was once abandoned on an island in the Ottawa River. Having been rescued by the traders, he threatened the Indians with the displeasure of the governor, from whom he was carrying messages to the western savages. Cowed by his commanding tone, the savages thereafter treated him with less contumely, and even accorded him certain privileges and honors. The Sault was reached by the beginning of September, and then a full month was passed in coasting Lake Superior to Chequamegon Bay. There the reëstablished mission was maintained for over five years.

Changes had occurred since Ménard's sojourn on the bay. The Hurons had come thither and built a village,[25] where they raised corn and tobacco, prospered in their fishing, and were once again rehabilitated after the famine days on Black River. The Ottawa village on Fish Creek had grown by the accession of large numbers of wanderers, so that by the time of Allouez's arrival there were seven different tribes with eight hundred warriors clustered around the beautiful shores of Chequamegon. These were mostly primitive savages who had never seen a European.[26] Allouez had built for his mission a bark chapel and a hut in which he himself dwelt.[27] He ministered impartially both to the pagan tribesmen and to the Ottawa and Hurons who had before heard the gospel. Among the latter he found slight traces of any remembrance of or interest in the Christian doctrines.[28]

With apostolic zeal Allouez bent to his task, but despite his effort the results were meager. Finding the tribesmen prejudiced against the baptism of dying

[25] For the probable site of the Huron village, see *Wis. Hist. Colls.*, xiii, 433, 440.
[26] *Jes. Rel.*, l, 273.
[27] See *Wis. Hist. Colls.*, xiii, 431, 439-440.
[28] *Jes. Rel.*, l, 307-311.

infants, he determined to baptize all whom he could find in a state of innocence, and waylaid and administered the rite to more than two hundred children. The elders and the youth alike treated the missionary with insolence and scorn, broke down the walls of his chapel, stole his possessions, and repelled his teachings. In all these trials his patience and fortitude did not fail. In the spring of 1667 he determined to visit the Nipissing, then in retreat north of Lake Nipigon. In a small canoe, with two Indian guides he skirted the entire coast of Lake Superior, making observations which were later utilized for the remarkable Jesuit map of Lake Superior.[29] Allouez was always an intrepid explorer as well as a lover of natural beauty. His descriptions of his journeys add a vivid chapter to the literature of early travel in Wisconsin. His letters also give us much knowledge of the Indian movements of his time. The Algonquian fugitives from Michigan were in a state of unrest and without settled habitats. They were dependent upon the Ottawa tribesmen for trade goods, and numbers of them came each year to the shores of Chequamegon Bay, where Allouez met and described the Potawatomi, Illinois, Sauk, Foxes, Sioux, Chippewa, and Cree tribesmen. The Illinois related to him that they had taken refuge west of a great river called the "Messipi," the first mention by this name of the central stream of North America.[30] Among all these tribes Allouez baptized an occasional person, and so began the "mission" for each group.

After two years of such experiences Allouez became convinced that if real progress was to be made he must

---

[29] This map is published in *Jes. Rel.*, lv, 94; also in Wis. Hist. Soc., *Proc.*, 1906, 188. Probably Allouez had Marquette's aid in the making of this map.

[30] *Jes. Rel.*, li, 47, 53.

THE MISSIONS   155

have more assistance. He needed an economic basis for the mission; husbandmen to sow and harvest, carpenters to build a more adequate shelter, and above all, a companion missionary to share his joys and sorrows. To this end in the summer of 1667 he went with the Ottawa tribesmen on their annual visit to the St. Lawrence. At Quebec he remained but two days, nevertheless he obtained some of the aid he desired. Father Louis Nicolas was sent out with him; the laborers he had engaged, however, failed to secure places in the returning canoes.

Allouez's report of the vast extent of Lake Superior and of its copper mines led to the exploration of Peré and Louis Jolliet, which we have already recounted. The missionary himself sought the immaterial rather than the material riches of this region. Yet despite his devotion he made but little headway. Father Nicolas was no fitting colleague for the resourceful Allouez. The cold weather and the scarcity of every civilized comfort appalled his soul. Early the next spring he returned to Quebec with a party of tribesmen who, attempting to break the Ottawa monopoly, went to trade with the Frenchmen, taking the missionary as interpreter.[31]

Allouez in the meantime continued his assaults upon the citadel of heathendom in the Northwest. His policy of baptizing children who were well, reacted so favorably that the Indians believed the rite assured their children a long life; but the Jesuit superior disapproved of this wholesale conversion of children who might soon exhibit all the marks of pagans, and cautioned the missionary against continuing such methods.[32]

[31] *Jes. Rel.*, li, 151; Mère de l'Incarnation, *Lettres*, ii, 374. Nicolas was at the Iroquois mission 1670 to 1675, after which he returned to France and abandoned the order.
[32] *Jes. Rel.*, li, 259-265; lii, 213.

Disappointed by his failure to induce the Ottawa to become Christians, Allouez determined to remove his mission to Sault Ste. Marie, where the Chippewa showed more docility and where all the French traders held rendezvous. He thereupon called a council of the Ottawa at Chequamegon and announced to them his decision by loosening his shoes and shaking off their dust among them. The savages were dismayed; they superstitiously feared that the abandonment of the "black robe" might presage their rejection by all white men. They pressed him to stay, and one village of the tribe promised *en masse* to obey the missionary. That winter the chief and one hundred of the Kiskakon Ottawa were baptized. This was the foundation of the permanent Ottawa mission, which after its removal to Mackinac was maintained throughout the French régime and was ministered to by several able missionaries.

Meanwhile the Sault mission was begun by Nicolas' successor, Father Jacques Marquette. When in 1668 he was chosen for the northwest mission, Marquette was the youngest Jesuit in the colony, having been born at Laon, June 1, 1637. He had already spent eighteen months in New France and had proved at Three Rivers his ability to acquire the Indian languages.[33] In bidding adieu to his friends at this place, Marquette abandoned forever all touch with civilization, and began a career that was to end in undying fame.

His outward voyage up the Ottawa River was crowded with the usual incidents. Among the tribesmen in the fleet were Potawatomi from the shores of Green

[33] Not much is known of Marquette's early life. His father was a magistrate of Laon; among his mother's family were noted churchmen. He himself had wished from boyhood to become a foreign missionary.

Bay, who were making their initial venture to Montreal. May they not on this occasion have told the young traveler something of the great river which five years later he explored? Arrived at the Sault, Marquette found that a tiny log chapel and a hut for his residence had already been prepared for him by French *voyageurs*. The savages at this place were gentle, and he might have baptized the entire village had not prudence dictated that they should first receive some form of Christian instruction.[34] The winter passed quickly; and the spring was cheered by the arrival from Chequamegon of Father Allouez on his way to report to his superior at Quebec. Allouez's voyage was for diplomatic as well as for religious reasons. All the French allies were included in the peace that had been made with the Iroquois. None the less the dwellers at the Sault had captured a party of the latter, and were proposing to burn their captives when Allouez arrived at their village. Horrified at the prospect of another intertribal war, he rescued the prisoners and started with them for Montreal to accommodate the difficulty.[35]

Meanwhile Marquette passed the summer of 1669 at the Sault, where he received a visit from his future companion Louis Jolliet, and also from a Shawnee Indian who "gave them marvelous notions of the South Sea, from which his village was distant only five days' journey—near a great river which, coming from the

[34] *Jes. Rel.*, lii, 213. The site of the Jesuit chapel at the Sault is thought by local historians to have been near the foot of Bingham Avenue. Stanley Newton, *The Story of Sault Ste. Marie* (Sault Ste. Marie, Mich., 1923), 58-59.

[35] It was with another prisoner of this same band that Jolliet made his journey in the same year. See previous chapter; also *Jes. Rel.*, lii, 199; Blair, i, 334-336.

Illinois, discharges its waters into that sea."[36] Thus coming events cast their shadows before.

Marquette, however, was destined to serve a long apprenticeship in wilderness faring before his voyage of discovery accorded him a lasting fame. The autumn of 1669 found him on his way to Chequamegon Bay to continue Allouez's mission of St. Esprit. After his arrival on the thirteenth of September he had no white companion during the entire winter that followed. The mission did not prosper greatly during this winter of 1669-70. The Kiskakon Ottawa, whom Allouez thought were evangelized, showed tendencies to relapse, despite all Marquette's admonitions. During the winter he had opportunities to learn the Illinois language from some visitors of that tribe; he also made overtures to the Sioux by sending them gospel messages and pictures.[37] After a short visit to the Sault in the summer of 1670 Marquette returned for one more solitary winter at St. Esprit, which proved to be the last of the mission at that site.

Meanwhile the western missions were developing in another portion of Wisconsin. When Allouez returned from the St. Lawrence in the autumn of 1669, he was accompanied by Father Claude Dablon, a veteran Jesuit who had been appointed the superior of the northwest missions. Dablon had already served among the Iroquois and had taken a hazardous journey toward Hudson Bay; he was a man of herculean bodily frame, and of vigorous intelligence. He was especially

---

[36] Blair, i, 336. The "South Sea" of the Shawnee Indian was either the South Atlantic or the Gulf of Mexico; Marquette understood him to mean the "South Sea" or the Pacific Ocean, still cherishing the hope that the great river might become the route *through* North America.

[37] *Jes. Rel.*, liv, 169-195. See also R. G. Thwaites, *Father Marquette* (New York, 1902).

interested in discovery and expected to utilize his sojourn in the West to that end. Dablon's appointment was probably occasioned by the activity of the Sulpitians, who were at this time preparing an expedition for the discovery of the Great Lakes and the commencement of a mission on Green Bay. The Jesuits, unwilling to share their western field, determined to forestall them there; so Allouez left the Sault, November 3, 1669, escorted by two canoe-loads of Potawatomi then returning from their second visit to New France.

Since the time of Nicolet the Indian geography of the country bordering on Green Bay had greatly changed. Now that peace with the Iroquois had been made, Algonquian tribes were making themselves homes in this favored region, were planting corn, erecting huts, and already trafficking with French traders. When Allouez and his guides passed up Green Bay, they were hailed first by the Menominee Indians from their river and asked for food. Thence they continued along the bay to the Potawatomi and Sauk village where the traders dwelt; there they arrived on the evening of December 2. Here were eight Frenchmen for whom on the next day Allouez celebrated mass, and named the mission for the day, St. François Xavier.[38] The traders were soon away with the wintering bands of Indians, while Allouez prepared his winter quarters and his food supply. For the latter he depended chiefly on frozen fish; occasionally a friendly Indian brought him some meat; once as a great delicacy the missionary was offered the fat of a newly-slain bear. Accustomed as he was to wintering in the wilderness,

[38] See description and diagram of Allouez's route, in Wis. Hist. Soc., *Proc.*, 1905, 143-156. Mr. Neville writes that in 1921 he identified what he thinks is the exact site of the Oconto River village. These traders were Perrot, Baudry, and the six that Jolliet sent thither. See preceding chapter.

Allouez found his sojourn on Green Bay less rigorous than his former winters on Chequamegon Bay. In February, Green Bay closed over and the ice was firm enough to bear a man; then the missionary crossed to a village on the south shore, and found there a few Potawatomi whom he attempted to convert. On his return he was almost lost in a blizzard, and saved by what he considered divine providence.

Spring, however, came at last and with it the Indian hunters returning to their villages. Allouez prepared to visit the tribes in the interior. First he went by canoe to the Outagami village on Wolf River,[39] via the foot of the bay, Fox River, and Lake Winnebago. He called the river "des Puans" for its former Winnebago habitants. He remarked therein quantities of game feeding on wild rice; but he saw no Indians, fear of the Sioux keeping the whole region uninhabited. The twentieth of April was Sunday and on the shore of Lake Winnebago the first mass in interior Wisconsin was celebrated.[40] Five days later the Fox village was reached, where the inhabitants were in deep distress owing to an Iroquois attack upon a winter camp of their tribe near Chicago, when a hundred women and children had been slain or captured. The savages saw in Allouez's coming an opportunity for a French alliance against their enemy. Allouez mistook their emotion for evidence of penitence, and prophesied success for this mission, which he named St. Marc.[41] After a three days' visit he again set forth, this time for the village of the Mascouten and Miami on the upper Fox, whence some messengers had come to condole with the bereaved Outagami.

[39] For this site, see references in chapter vii, note 50.
[40] Sunday, April 24, 1921, a tablet in commemoration of this event was unveiled in the park at Oshkosh by the Winnebago County Historical Society.
[41] *Jes. Rel.*, liv, 219-227; Blair, i, 349; *Wis. Hist. Colls.*, xvi, 65.

Spring was now abroad in the land, and to Allouez the river on which he embarked was very beautiful. After three days on its winding course, he left his canoe and walked over an ascending slope to the site where the Miami, with the Mascouten, had recently built a village. The missionary, like the traders who had preceded him, was here received with distinguished honors and treated as a manitou. The gentleness of these tribesmen delighted the "black robe," who in their docility placed his hopes for their conversion; the mission he there began was later known as St. Jacques.

Allouez tarried but two days among these villagers; then made a twelve-mile detour to visit a Kickapoo-Illinois group, who told him of the "great river named Messi-Sipi," from beyond which they had lately come. By the end of April he was once more at his starting point on Green Bay, whence on the sixth of May he went overland to the Menominee and began the mission of St. Michel Archange.[42]

Then having laid the foundations of what appeared to him as four most promising missions, he embarked, May 20, 1670, with one Frenchman and one savage in a canoe, which reached headquarters at the Sault after the disappointed retirement of the Sulpitians, Dollier de Casson and Galinée.[43] These travelers had found two Jesuit missionaries at the Sault in a "pretty fort" surrounded by a cedar palisade twelve feet high and a clearing planted to wheat. The chapel was thronged by French traders, and to the visitors the missionaries

---

[42] *Jes. Rel.*, liv, 227-235. The mission to the Menominee was begun May 8, the day of the apparition of the archangel Michael. The Catholic mission to the Menominee still bears its earliest name of St. Michael.

[43] See *ante*, page 134.

appeared to minister to the white rather than to the red men.[44]

Reinforcements for the western missions arrived in the autumn of 1670, in the persons of Father Gabriel Dreuillettes, a veteran of twenty-seven years' service, and Father Louis André, the youngest and latest comer from France. Dreuillettes spent the next nine years at the mission at the Sault, retiring to die two years later at Quebec. The good old priest was very kindly and sympathetic; he tried to alleviate physical suffering and even sprinkled the Indians' planting grounds with holy water to secure for them good crops. André, who was enthusiastic and garrulous, was assigned first to the scattered villagers of the Lake Huron islands. There he found that a great evil had come with the white men to the Northwest—a visitation of smallpox, the first attack of that dreaded scourge which destroyed so many entire tribes.

Dablon, the superior of the Ottawa missions, now determined to go with Allouez to his missions around Green Bay. His descriptions of Wisconsin in its autumn garb have become classic; to him it was a paradise and the rapids of the Fox were likened to the difficulties in the road of those who sought that blessed land.[45] In that stream the fathers found and destroyed a spirit stone, which was to them a hated idol. At the Mascouten-Miami village they met several Illinois and heard of the great river "rising in the North and flowing toward the south." Upon Dablon's return to the Sault, Allouez transferred his headquarters and the mission

[44] Kellogg, "Galinée's Narrative," in *Early Narratives*, 205-207.

[45] Dablon's description is in *Jes. Rel.*, lv, 95-225; see also *Wis. Hist. Colls.*, xvi, 80-82.

THE MISSIONS

of St. François Xavier to the neighborhood of Red Banks on the southeast side of Green Bay.[46]

Dablon rested for several months upon his homeward route at the island called by the tribesmen Michilimackinac,[47] whither in the summer of 1671 the entire Indian population from Chequamegon Bay transported itself. The Hurons and Ottawa, always fickle and restless, had picked a quarrel with their formidable neighbors the Sioux. In their fear they fled, and Marquette, their gentle mentor who "had more to suffer than achieve," accompanied them. The mission of St. Ignace, begun on the island by Dablon, was soon transferred by Marquette to the present point of that name on the north shore of Mackinac Straits.[48]

Dablon was informed by the earliest canoe from the St. Lawrence that year of 1671, that he had been chosen superior for all the missions of New France. He thus departed from the Northwest, but ever afterwards maintained a deep interest in that region. In his place came Henri Nouvel, who released André for work with Allouez in Wisconsin. There the two missionaries built, the fall and winter of 1671-72, the first permanent mission house on Fox River, which has given its name to De Pere. Dablon's keen eye had noted the preceding year the availability of this place for missionary headquarters, within reach, as he says, of ten different tribes and fifteen thousand savages, and had chosen it for a mission site.[49] We have no description of the buildings, which were doubtless like those of the Sault, of logs with a protecting palisade. This rude abode sheltered

[46] Jesuit map of Lake Superior 1670-71. See also Neville, in Wis. Hist. Soc., *Proc.*, 1905, 154.
[47] *Jes. Rel.*, lv, 101, 157-167, 173-175.
[48] See Thwaites, "Story of Mackinac," in *How George Rogers Clark Won the Northwest* (Chicago, 1903), 210-211.
[49] *Jes. Rel.*, lvi, 91, 121-123.

for many years the cultivated French gentlemen and scholars whose devoted piety brought them to these solitudes. Allouez and André now divided the Wisconsin mission field, the latter confining himself to the villages on the bay side, the former devoting his time and efforts to the villages in the interior.

André preached and sang in Chouskouabika and Ossauamigonong, visited the Menominee, and noted the sturgeon-fishing in their river.[50] Allouez's field was the larger and the more difficult; the Outagami were sullen, and the dwellers in the Mascouten-Miami village were constantly changing.[51] In the summer of 1672 Father Nouvel came to inspect the new mission house at De Pere;[52] and the next year Father Philippe Pierson, a Belgian Jesuit, took Marquette's place at St. Ignace when the latter departed on his trip of discovery. There Father Pierson remained as missionary to the Hurons for the ten succeeding years.[53] Thus by 1673 there were six missionaries in the Northwest, serving a territory that extended from Sault Ste. Marie to the villages on the upper Wolf and the upper Fox rivers in central Wisconsin.

Perhaps it may be well at this point, where the full reports of the western missions terminate,[54] to attempt a brief summary of what had so far been accomplished.

[50] Chouskouabika was on the Pensaukee, according to the Misses Grignon (Patrick papers in Wisconsin Historical Library); Ossauamigonong was Suamico. André's letters are fascinating reading. *Jes. Rel.*, lvi, 129-139; lvii, 265-301; *Wis. Hist. Colls.*, xvi, 83-84, 86-87.

[51] *Jes. Rel.*, lvi, 139-147; lviii, 21-43, 59-65; *Wis. Hist. Colls.*, xvi, 84, 87-88.

[52] *Jes. Rel.*, lvii, 251; lviii, 21.

[53] *Ibid.*, lix, 71; lx, 209-211. Pierson is the only Jesuit whom Father Hennepin mentions. He did the colony the service of preventing the Hurons from removing *en masse* to the country of the Iroquois.

[54] See *ante*, note 1.

The mission at St. Ignace gave promise of permanence; the Hurons and one clan of the Ottawa had been partially Christianized, and the mission begun on the Straits of Mackinac was maintained throughout the French régime. The mission at the Sault, maintained chiefly for the French, suffered a great accident in 1674. In a tribal quarrel the mission house was burned, the missionary barely escaping with his life.[55] Thereafter headquarters were transferred to St. Ignace, and although the Sault mission was rebuilt and maintained for some years longer, it never became influential with the neighboring tribesmen. In Wisconsin, the Lake Superior mission was completely abandoned, and all attention turned to the tribes around Green Bay. Of these the Menominee, Miami, and Mascouten were somewhat influenced by the "black robe"; the Potawatomi, Sauk, Foxes, and Winnebago were almost wholly untouched by the gospel message. St. François Xavier mission was the permanent headquarters; temporary chapels were built and crosses erected at other villages during the time of the missionary's visits.

André at Pensaukee, after a three months' visit, baptized ten adults and nine children; at St. François Xavier he wrote: "I do not despair of baptizing some this year or next."[56] After several months among the Menominee, he might, he said, have baptized most of the tribe, but thought they should be tested longer, and so conferred this rite on twenty-two children and two dying adults. Among the Potawatomi he baptized forty, mostly children.[57] Allouez's experiences were similar to those of André. He found the Outagami "self-willed beyond any thing that can be imagined," and they privately in-

[55] *Jes. Rel.*, lviii, 255-263; lix, 71-73.
[56] *Ibid.*, lvii, 299-301; *Wis. Hist. Colls.*, xvi, 86-87.
[57] *Jes. Rel.*, lviii, 273-289.

formed some Iroquois visitors that they were about to drive the "black robes" from their country. Some Sauk coming from the bay reported that "only children pray to God."[58] At the mission of St. Jacques, on the other hand, the chapel was so thronged that the bark mats gave way before the pressure for admission. The Miami were divided, one portion of the tribe listening respectfully to the missionary, another part scorning his message. In this mission there were one hundred and fourteen baptisms, mostly children or youths. At St. François Xavier, Allouez baptized thirty-four, all children except one sick man.[59] So far not one notable convert had given adherence to the missionaries. Late in 1673 the dying Miami chief asked for baptism, but to Allouez's bitter disappointment passed away before the missionary could reach his side.[60] The results, therefore, of the missions in Wisconsin were inadequate and disappointing; most of the warriors were unfriendly, and showed no inclination to accept the white man's religion.

There was one tribe, however, whose promise as a field for gospel efforts had been notable since the beginning. This was the Illinois, and the mission, begun as a dependency of St. François Xavier by Allouez and Marquette, became the most permanent and effective of any of the western missions.[61] Marquette has usually been accredited with the beginnings of this work; there seems to be evidence, however, that Allouez had already made a journey to the Illinois villages before Marquette's first visit.[62] After his voyage of discovery

[58] *Jes. Rel.*, lviii, 43-59.
[59] *Ibid.*, 21-43, 59-65; *Wis. Hist. Colls.*, xvi, 87-88.
[60] *Jes. Rel.*, lviii, 269-271.
[61] See Alvord, *Illinois*, 223-224, on the course of the Illinois mission.
[62] Allouez met a number of Illinois at the Mascouten village and endeavored to have the tribe remove to the neighborhood of

in 1673 Marquette spent a year at St. François Xavier, resting and preparing his maps and reports.[63] By October, 1674, he began his memorable last journey along the Lake Michigan shore in order to reopen the mission among the Illinois tribes. Two of the men who had been with him on his previous voyage, Pierre Porteret and Jacques Largilliers, volunteered to accompany him. Taking the Sturgeon Bay portage, they slowly coasted the western shore of the lake, noting the natural features and landing frequently to hunt and to rest. Apparently they camped under the bluffs of Milwaukee, explored the entrance to Root River, and stopped near the Pike. At the last camp they met a hunting party of Mascouten. They passed the present state line about December 1, ice and snow impeding their progress; and by the time Chicago was reached the missionary was seriously ill.[64] His companions built for him a small hut, and there they passed a dreary winter, visited once by some French-Canadians sojourning among the Illinois. By the last of March the missionary was able to proceed to the great Kaskaskia village.[65] He was there received with distinguished honors; a great council was held, and on Holy Thursday

---

De Pere. Failing in that, he went overland to the Kaskaskia village on Illinois River, reaching there before Marquette's return from his voyage of discovery. *Jes. Rel.*, lviii, 265.

[63] See *post*, chapter x.

[64] This voyage is the earliest along the east littoral of Wisconsin a description of which has been preserved. *Jes. Rel.*, lix, 165-211; Kellogg, *Early Narratives*, 262-280. For a recent article on Marquette at Chicago, see *Illinois Catholic Historical Review*, iv, 115-134. Jacques Largilliers settled at Kaskaskia and died there in 1714. MS. in the Wisconsin Historical Library.

[65] This was opposite the present "Starved Rock." See map in Kellogg, *Early Narratives*, 228. The two hundred and fiftieth anniversary of the events of Marquette's landing at Chicago and his opening mission to the Illinois were celebrated at Chicago in December, 1924, and April, 1925. See *Illinois Catholic Historical Review*, vii, 195-226.

and Easter Sunday Marquette preached and performed mass. The auspicious beginning of this mission gave Marquette joy, but he realized that its continuation was not for him. He urged his faithful companions to bear him back to St. Ignace. The Illinois in large numbers escorted them to the lake shore; then the frail canoe with the dying missionary set forth along the southern and eastern coasts. Not granted the privilege of reaching his mission home at the head of the lake, he died May 15, 1675, at the mouth of the river which still bears his name. Thus at the age of thirty-eight Marquette obtained the coveted crown of martyrdom and placed his name beside that of Ménard among the martyrs of the cross in the Northwest.[66]

It fell to the lot of Father Allouez to continue the Illinois mission, his place in the Wisconsin missions being taken by Father Antoine Silvy.[67] For fourteen years more after Marquette's passing, Allouez traversed the western country, following his neophytes to their wintering camps and removing the missions as the savages changed their village sites. The Miami and Mascouten finally concentrated on the St. Joseph River in southern Michigan; there Allouez founded the mission of that name, and there early in 1689 he died.[68]

[66] Two years after the missionary's death some of his Ottawa Kiskakon converts took up his body and carried it to St. Ignace, and buried it beneath the mission chapel. In 1877 there was found at St. Ignace what seemed to be the remains of Father Marquette. *Michigan Pioneer and Historical Collections*, ii, 134-145; Chicago Historical Society, *Reports*, special meeting, April, 1900, 264-272. Part of the relics of Marquette are at Marquette University, Milwaukee.

[67] Allouez did not at once leave Wisconsin for Kaskaskia; he made to the latter place three missionary visits before finally, in 1678, he departed, leaving his Wisconsin missions in Silvy's care. *Jes. Rel.*, lx, 149-167.

[68] *Jes. Rel.*, liv, 322; Margry, i, 59-64. The site of this mission was within the boundaries of the present city of Niles, Michigan. A Jesuit cross stood thereon until recent years.

THE MISSIONS   169

This mission of St. Joseph became one of the permanent mission sites in the West; during the eighteenth century it was maintained principally for the Potawatomi, and thus continued the work begun at St. François Xavier. From the unpublished *Relations* we obtain a few reports of the mission workers through the decade of the seventies; after that there are no reports, and only an occasional random mention of the missionaries.

In 1676 Dablon estimated that in all the Ottawa missions—that is, the missions of the far West—there had been baptized three hundred and sixty-seven persons, only sixty of whom were adults. "The remainder are children, most of whom have gone to Heaven since baptism."[69] While this increased the church triumphant, it gave but little promise for the church militant in Wisconsin. Three years later the baptisms had doubled and ten missionaries were among the missions of the Ottawa country.[70] A fine chapel was finished at De Pere, with which the Indians were so impressed that they offered tobacco to its resident deity.[71] This period seems to mark the high tide of the missions in Wisconsin; from this date both the number of workers and the conversions declined rapidly. In 1683 there were but seven missionaries in the entire Northwest, four of whom were almost disabled from age and disease.[72] By 1711 this number was reduced to two, but was soon increased to a customary four or five.

Among the faithful missionaries who followed Allouez and Dablon in Wisconsin should be remembered Louis André, apostle to the Menominee. For fourteen years this blithe, intrepid little Frenchman voyaged

[69] *Jes. Rel.*, lx, 197; for the letters of the missionaries, see *ibid.*, 197-213.
[70] Unpublished MS. in Wisconsin Historical Society, giving statistics for 1678-79.
[71] *Jes. Rel.*, lxi, 71, 153.
[72] *Ibid.*, lxii, 215.

from village to village around Green Bay, never losing his courage or hope, instructing, warning, disputing with his savage flock. His mode of living brought on what he called "gout," and though almost disabled he continued to hobble from one tiny hut to the next, teaching his neophytes to sing, arousing their interest by sacred pictures, faithful, firm, and loyal to his convictions of duty and of God. Finally in 1684 André was recalled to serve as professor in the college at Quebec. He had no successor among the bay tribes, who after his departure were unshepherded.[73]

The central mission at De Pere was presided over from 1676 to 1679 by Father Charles Albanel, one of the Jesuit explorers who had aided in enlarging the possessions of Louis XIV in the New World. It was said of Albanel that he "would rather travel than make converts." On a journey to Hudson Bay, Albanel was captured by the English and kept imprisoned for two years. After his exchange he came to Wisconsin, where it was reported he meditated new explorations. The infirmities of growing age and the commands of his superior kept him at the residence at De Pere until he was transferred to Sault Ste. Marie, where he died in 1696.[74] It was during his incumbency that the new chapel was built for the St. François Xavier mission.

Of Father Antoine Silvy, who came to aid and succeed Allouez in the interior missions, we have but little knowledge; his residence in Wisconsin was not more than two years, when he was transferred to Tadoussac, after which he had a term of service on Hudson Bay. One letter of this missionary gives his

---

[73] André's letters are worth reading. Aside from those cited *ante*, note 50, see *Jes. Rel.*, lviii, 273-289; lx, 201-205. See also lxi, 73.

[74] We have no letter from Albanel written from De Pere; but a good report of his first year there is in *Jes. Rel.*, lxi, 151-153.

first impressions of his field at St. Jacques.⁷⁵ Father André Bonneault, who took Silvy's place in Wisconsin, was only three years in Canada. We have no account of his impressions of Wisconsin.

Father Nouvel, superior for over twenty years of the De Pere mission field, was for much of that time the only missionary in Wisconsin. He had already traveled extensively in the missions northeast of the St. Lawrence, and while at St. Ignace took a long journey through the present state of Michigan. It is believed that he died in 1702 at the De Pere chapel. He was the missionary to whom Perrot presented the ostensorium, the great treasure of this early mission house.⁷⁶

When Father Nouvel began to fail in health, a young priest was sent to his aid, who proved to be the last incumbent of St. François Xavier. This was Jean Baptiste Chardon, who spent twenty-seven years in the West, returning to die at Quebec in 1743. Father Chardon had an excellent talent for languages and labored devotedly to maintain his mission. Nevertheless he had small success with the Wisconsin Indians. For a time he was with the Potawatomi at St. Joseph; but after the French fort was built at Green Bay his house was placed near the commandant's, where he acted as chaplain for the garrison, and frequently as interpreter in Indian councils. It would appear that he abandoned De Pere before going to St. Joseph, and that he left Wisconsin when the French fort was destroyed in 1728.⁷⁷

⁷⁵ *Jes. Rel.*, lx, 207-209.
⁷⁶ This relic, the oldest authentic testimonial of French occupation, is now in the Wisconsin Historical Society Museum. See its description in *Wis. Hist. Colls.*, ix, 199-206; also *post*, chapter xi.
⁷⁷ On Chardon, see *Jes. Rel.*, lxvi, 281-285; *Wis. Hist. Colls.*, xvi and xvii, *passim*.

A mission to the Sioux was twice attempted: once in 1683, when Father Pierson, under Duluth's escort, visited that tribe; later in 1727, when after elaborate preparations Fathers Michel Guignas and Nicolas de Gonnor went to Lake Pepin with a trading company and commenced the mission of St. Michel Archange. The missionaries were obliged to flee in 1728, although Guignas later went back for five years at the Sioux post.[78] We have no account of their success in converting the Sioux tribesmen, but must believe that it was small. Father Joseph Marest was with Perrot at the Sioux post in 1689, probably as chaplain of the expedition.[79]

Charlevoix, a Jesuit priest on a government mission in 1721, found the state of the western missions very unsatisfactory. At Mackinac he said the missionaries had very little to do, as the Ottawa Indians were not much disposed to receive their instructions. At Green Bay the missionary had very slight success with the Sauk, and was hoping to do more for the Winnebago village; even at St. Joseph there were few Christians, and the missionary was subjected to great hardships.[80]

What were the causes of the decline in interest and enthusiasm, and the ultimate failure of the work begun with so much earnestness and supported with such zeal? In the first place, the interest in and enthusiasm for missionary effort suffered a sharp decline in France. This may have been due in part to the lack of the stimulus of the yearly volumes of *Jesuit Relations*; but

[78] *Wis. Hist. Colls.*, xvii, 7-15, 22-28, 36-55, 244, 271; Folwell, *Minnesota*, i, 45-47.
[79] *Wis. Hist. Colls.*, xi, 35-36.
[80] Charlevoix, *Journal Historique* (Paris, 1744), 279, 292, 312. The English edition of 1761 has recently been reissued by the Caxton Club of Chicago, under the editorship of the author of this volume.

THE MISSIONS

the difficulty went deeper than that. The French crown was engaged in a struggle with the Papacy over the question of the regale, or the independence of the national church. The Jansenists, who were the strong opponents of Jesuitism, were very powerful in the latter half of the seventeenth century. Gallicanism was growing at the expense of Ultramontism. Fewer and fewer of the better class of French youths entered the Jesuit order; desire for sufferings and martyrdom in distant lands declined. The civil authorities of New France frequently deplored the lack of new missionaries.[81] In 1683 only one arrived in Canada. The missions were poorly manned, and with the decline in numbers came a decline in the character and influence of the missionaries who did come. The missions became stereotyped; the tribes that had accepted Christianity brought their children to be baptized, occasionally attended mass and confession, but made no difference in their customary mode of life. Except by the token of a crucifix or a silver cross, a Christian savage was scarcely distinguishable from a pagan. For the Jesuit scheme did not involve civilizing the Indians. They did not as a rule encourage the use of the French language. As for the introduction of French customs and habits, they set their faces against these as a flint. The savages were to be maintained in their simplicity and ignorance, only to be taught to worship the true God.

This policy was opposed to the governmental plan for the native population. The French authorities advocated assimilation and civilization. They wanted the young Indians educated and taught to take their places in the body politic. The Jesuit opposition to this viewpoint, frequently covert, often declared, was one of the strongest reasons for the distrust of their order among

[81] *Wis. Hist. Colls.*, xvi, 392, 396.

the ablest of the Canadian governors and colonists. The Jesuits desired to preserve the West, especially, from exploitation, to cultivate their missions for the natives only, where the missionaries might rule supreme and keep their flocks from the demoralizing influence of the lawless and licentious French traders, as well as from the domination of the French commandants. In other words, they wished to make a Paraguay of the great central valley of North America, an Indian kingdom wherein the missionaries would rule supreme.

There is no doubt that the missionaries had just cause of complaint of the debauchery introduced by the white traders among the simple savages. It was the same tale as that of missions everywhere; the white men's vices and the white men's liquor did more harm to the aborigines than all the teachings of the missionaries could do good. To their credit be it said, that the Jesuits everywhere and unalterably opposed the liquor traffic, the licentiousness of the *coureurs de bois*, and the unjust exploitation of the Indians by the traders. No doubt these conditions were great hindrances to the success of the western missions. But the failure had a deeper cause, in the character of the northwestern Indians and in their resistance to change and influence.

The Indian was very proud and independent, and was deeply satisfied with his own condition, customs, and beliefs. He showed no desire for imitation of a higher civilization, nor envy for the white man's mode of life. His invariable reply was that the Great Spirit had made the white man and the red man different; that what was good for the former was not good for the latter; let each go his separate way and preserve his own traditions. The missionaries, unable to influence the chiefs and warriors, turned to the women and children. Their reports are full of the piety of the young women and girls. This only increased the distance between the "black robe" and the men of the tribe. Their ideals were incompatible; every boy wished to become a great warrior; hatred of enemies was the highest tribal virtue; meekness and obedience were scorned. Even small children were not corrected, in order that they might grow up self-dependent and lead a free existence.

To the Indian the missionary was always a mystery; with the white trader who brought him goods and mingled with him on terms of equality he made friends. The trader's motives he understood and as a rule respected. The "black robe," on the other hand, was a being aloof. Try as he might he could obtain no comradeship with the Indian. The latter's complacency with his own manners and mode of life, especially with his religious conceptions, erected a barrier between him and this mysterious personage who made strange signs over dying babies, devoted hours to saying mass and to reading books the Indian could not understand. He felt certain that there must be some sinister motive in the conduct of this unasked-for guest. The missionary's meekness and patience only increased the Indian's contempt. Dislike and distrust either resulted in indifference and neglect or quickened into persecution. Seldom did the missionary gain any influence in the Indian councils; when he did it was as a white man, a messenger of Onontio, not as a "black robe," a servant of the white man's manitou. Thus the very virtues of each group rendered them contemptible to the other. The ideals of the North American Indian and the French Jesuit were incompatible; the former could not yield without denial of his highest motives. Thus the Jesuit never became in the Great Lakes region the father and leader of a band of faithful neophytes, as did the missionaries of South America and Mexico. The tribes most docile to missionary training, such as the Illinois, lost their manliness and sank in the aboriginal scale until they became the prey of more virile enemies and are now extinct. Some tribes, however, such as the Hurons and the mission Iroquois, retained their warlike qualities while nominally following Christian ceremonies. "Praying Indians," as they were called, they never became docile to missionary dictation.

What the missions might have become if continued as they were begun, by high-souled men of commanding genius, we cannot say; the red men might have been elevated to the Christian standard by substituting milder qualities for their outstanding barbaric virtues. As it was, the fierce independence and proud complacency of the Wisconsin tribesmen proved a barrier which the Jesuits could not overpass. The missions came and went, and the religion of the tribesmen was comparatively unchanged.

Not only the characteristics but the migrations of the Indians contributed to this result. La Salle in 1680 and Cadillac in 1701 changed the Indian geography of the Northwest. The Miami and Mascouten left Wisconsin forever; the Potawatomi moved south and east around Lake Michigan. At Mackinac but a remnant of the tribesmen that visited the chapels of St. Ignace remained at that place. The Fox wars broke up the missions for the Sioux and closed the mission house at De Pere, finally leading to abandonment by the missionaries of what is now Wisconsin. None of the Wisconsin tribes became Christian.[82] For a century after the

---

[82] Some memories of Christianity were preserved among the Menominee. This tribe, however, always kept a close relation to the white settlement at Green Bay, and intermarried with the French at that place.

FRENCH SHIP OF
SEVENTEENTH CENTURY
From map of Franquelin, 1688

withdrawal of the last Jesuit missionary from Green Bay, no messenger of the Christian faith ever visited that region.

Yet, with all this seeming failure, the Jesuit missions must not be called valueless. Granted that their influence on the Indians was not permanent; nevertheless, the presence of the Jesuits in the western country tended toward civilization. As chaplains for the garrisons and the French expeditionary forces they filled a needed want; their presence acted as a restraint upon the lawless conduct of the French traders and *voyageurs*. At the time of treaty or council with the Indians they were frequently utilized as interpreters, and often as ambassadors from the governor to the tribesmen. The governors of the eighteenth century considered it good policy to maintain missionaries at these distant posts. They sometimes detected and reported incipient Indian conspiracies against French sovereignty. In a few cases their influence was sufficient to counteract these movements and to restrain the tribes within the French alliance. As white population grew around the frontier posts, the Jesuits gave to these settlers pastoral care, marrying, baptizing, and burying these people, even educating their children and acting as their guardians.

For present-day historians the reports of these trained and educated observers are invaluable. Their writings form the basis of our knowledge of Indian ethnology and linguistics; their descriptions are our best sources for primitive Wisconsin; even their scientific observations of eclipses, parhelia, tides, flora, and fauna are valuable. In map making many of these men were highly trained; their descriptions first disclosed our region to the world of geographers and savants, their enthusiastic accounts made France aware of the value of her possession on the upper lakes. Without the Jesuits our knowledge of early Wisconsin history would be fragmentary.

We are also indebted to them for examples of pure lives nobly devoted to an unselfish purpose. Whatever we of today think of their methods or their results, there is but one verdict for their motives. None would withhold the meed of praise for these men who, for the sake of conscience and a religious ideal, abandoned the comforts of civilization and plunged into a pathless wilderness, endured such hardships and sufferings as can hardly be imagined, and were prepared to lay down their lives rather than to be "disobedient to the heavenly vision." As long as courage, persistence, and zeal in a holy cause shall be considered noteworthy, so long will the story of the early missions of Wisconsin hold an honored place in its first history.

IX. ANNEXATION, 1671

IN THE years 1670 to 1672 Louis XIV, in order to enlarge his kingdom on its eastern frontier, was preparing for a war with the Dutch Republic. All the forces of his realm were employed to provide for the success of this expedition. French diplomats made treaties subsidizing England, Sweden, and some of the German states (five such treaties were actually concluded in the year 1671); French economists secured the funds to reconstitute the army and to pay the subsidies demanded by the treaties; French officers reorganized the royal armies and rebuilt the royal navy. Then upon the declaration of war in April, 1672, a medal was struck in honor of the monarch, upon which he was allegorically represented as the sun shedding his beams upon a grateful world. All Europe was moved by these acts of the Grand Monarque. The balance of power, so carefully built up, was being destroyed to satisfy the ambition of a ruler who wished to be the greatest upon earth. A few years later obsequious courtiers formally bestowed upon him the surname of "The Great"—this because he had annexed to his kingdom a few hundred square miles of European territory wrested by force from weaker nations.

Meanwhile in New France a territory of unknown extent, the key to the richest valley in the world, a district abounding in minerals and fur-bearing animals for immediate exploitation, with potentialities greater than those of all France, was in 1671 taken possession of for Louis XIV. No medals were struck in honor of this event, nor was mention made thereof save in the annals of Jesuits and traders, and in a few colonial state papers that were read only by the colonial officials.

With the annexation of the region of the Great Lakes, New France became the largest and richest colonial possession in the world. The value was, however, potential, dependent upon the peopling of this region by those who could develop its productive powers and utilize its possibilities. The subjects of Louis XIV, dazzled by the splendors of his court and his enterprises in Europe, showed little inclination to emigrate. Even the valley of the St. Lawrence, now in occupancy for over sixty years, held but five thousand colonists all told—less than a single Indian aggregation in central Wisconsin. Meanwhile the English colonies along the Atlantic coast were peopling rapidly, and at the very time the agents of the French king were proclaiming the annexation of the interior of North America to his crown, British explorers from Virginia were pushing westward toward the same interior valley.[1] Then began a race that continued for over eighty years, and terminated in favor of the more populous colonial group. For a time, however, the French sovereign profited by the fact that he was the first to make formal proclamation of annexation of the interior region.

Louis XIV has received the merited name of the "well-served." In Old France as in New, his agents were active in increasing the royal prestige and developing the resources of the realm. Men of genius in administration like Colbert, in finance like Louvois, in diplomacy like Lionne, gave their services ungrudgingly to the enlargement of French power. In Canada the king was also well served. A series of able governors throughout the seventeenth century toiled for the upbuilding of prosperity and the increase of French territory. Side by side with the governor labored the intendant—an

[1] Alvord and Bidgood, *The First Explorations of the Trans-Allegheny Region by the Virginians, 1650-1674* (Cleveland, 1912).

officer especially designed to promote the royal ascendancy and to check undue pretensions on the part of the governor. The intendancy was not established in New France until after the Company of New France had ceded its governing rights to the crown; then the first intendant, Jean Talon, was appointed—the ablest of all these officials in Canada. For the first three years of Talon's administration (1665-68) his efforts were devoted to the concerns of the local colony on the St. Lawrence. When, however, he returned in 1670 from France to Canada for a second term, he came with far-reaching plans for discovery and annexation.

Talon recognized that the Iroquois were the chief obstacle to the growth of New France. He repeatedly asked for more troops to subdue their insolence, and to punish them for the attacks they were making, in contravention of the peace, upon the French-allied Indians in the West.[2] Among these was a Wisconsin tribe which had not yet made a treaty of allegiance with the French governor, but which had been visited by French traders and missionaries. The Outagami took the opportunity of the trading expedition of 1670 to journey to the St. Lawrence and to ask for Onontio's protection. They accompanied the flotilla of their allies the Potawatomi, who were taking to the authorities some of the raiding Iroquois whom they had captured. Nicolas Perrot was also in this company, and at the governor's council acted as interpreter for the western tribesmen. After the usual negotiations and speeches, the Outagami were accepted as "children" of the French king and promised for the future his protection.[3] Talon and the governor-general, Courcelles, saw in this occasion an opportunity to humble the Iroquois. They forced these latter to

[2] See *ante*, chapter vii.
[3] "Perrot's Memoir," in Blair, i, 210-220; *Jes. Rel.*, liii, 39-57

return the Outagami prisoners;[4] and in the summer of 1671 Courcelles made a swift voyage up the St. Lawrence to the entrance of Lake Ontario. The Iroquois were greatly alarmed; they had thought the rapids of the St. Lawrence insurmountable. They now saw French troops at the door of their cantons, and hastened to make their peace with the invaders. Courcelles assured them that his visit had no hostile intent, but the warning served upon these trouble-makers was efficacious, and kept them in partial subjection for a decade. The governor's expedition also broke up, for the time being, a clandestine trade which the Iroquois were encouraging between the Dutch traders of Albany and the western Indians.[5]

Talon now decided to take steps more adequately to secure the upper country from foreign traders and untrustworthy tribesmen. He first suggested to the king that it would be an easy matter, during the negotiation of the treaties of peace, for France to obtain possession of the port of Manhattan and the fort at Orange, and thus to have the Iroquois and the Dutch traders under his control. The favorable moment had, however, passed when Talon's memoir reached France. Peace had been concluded between the two crowns, and the Hudson River posts had been assigned to the English. Talon then proposed to build two posts on Lake Ontario, to be linked by a "sort of a galley," which project he thought would "make the first openings towards Florida across the interior"; and to annex the region of the upper Great Lakes.[6] Colbert, the French premier, had hitherto opposed these distant expeditions, and

[4] *Jes. Rel.*, liv, 263-269; lvi, 143.
[5] E. B. O'Callaghan, editor, *Documents Relative to the Colonial History of the State of New York* (Albany, 1853-87), ix, 75-85.
[6] *Ibid.*, ix, 65-66. This is, so far as we know, the first proposal for shipping-vessels on the Great Lakes.

had urged the rulers of New France to bend their energies to upbuilding the agricultural interests of the colony. When, however, reports reached his ears of the great mineral wealth of Lake Superior, he was ready to sanction an expedition thither, both for exploration and for annexation of that rich region to the crown of France. Such a measure had been urged upon him for some time by the far-seeing Talon, who wished not only to overawe the western natives by a sight of French splendor, but also to serve notice on other European nations who were colonizing North America that France intended to claim the interior valleys as her own.

When Nicolas Perrot returned from the West in 1670 with his reports of alliances made for France with the many tribes then clustered around Green Bay, Talon determined that Perrot was the best person to arrange with the western Indians for an annexation ceremony. To make such a pageant more imposing, however, Talon chose as its chief figure a young nobleman, François Daumont Sieur de St. Lusson, whose name is associated with only this one episode in western history; then so far as the Great Lakes region is concerned he drops from sight.[7] St. Lusson was commissioned to spend two years on his western voyage, to visit all the missions in that region and report on their conditions, and in general to promote the king's interest in the far Northwest.[8] Perrot was sent in advance to notify the tribes that the royal delegate was on his way. St. Lusson's official flotilla left Montreal early in October, 1670; this was later in the year than any western expedition had yet started. In consequence, when Lake

[7] Benjamin Sulte, "Les Français dans l'Ouest en 1671," in Can. Roy. Soc., *Proc.*, 1918, i, 19, has found a few additional facts about St. Lusson. He died before 1675, when his widow remarried; the years between 1672 and his death were spent in Acadia.

[8] Mère de l'Incarnation, *Lettres*, ii, 530.

Huron was reached the weather was too cold to permit the voyagers to proceed farther. They were forced to take up winter quarters among the Amikwa Indians on the north shore of Georgian Bay.⁹

The entertainment furnished to these unexpected guests during the winter of 1670-71 was unique in the annals of the Northwest. If we may credit the accounts, the time was largely spent in hunting the moose, the *orignal* of the Canadian colonists. Twenty-four hundred of these great beasts were captured and slaughtered on Manitoulin Island without the aid of firearms. Perrot declares they were taken with native snares, probably in a great park or pen such as the plains Indians often used to round up vast numbers of deer and bison. Occupied in this way, the winter passed quickly. Ice was not yet out of Georgian Bay when Perrot left camp, pushed his canoe on a sledge to open water, and set forth to summon the Wisconsin tribes to the ensuing ceremony at the Sault. As he went toward Green Bay he met Father Allouez coming thence from his second winter of missionary effort in that region. He told Perrot that the awe and enthusiasm with which the white men had at first been welcomed had worn away. The tribesmen were dissatisfied with the French alliance; some of them resented the treatment they had received the previous summer at Montreal; even the traders had recently been subjected to insult, and the missionaries had been scorned in the villages of the bay whither he had just come.¹⁰ Perrot, nevertheless, continued his voyage, trusting to his own

⁹ St. Lusson's official report is in Margry, i, 96-99; an English translation is in *N. Y. Colon. Docs.*, ix, 803-804, and *Wis. Hist. Colls.*, xi, 26-29. Perrot's account is in Blair, i, 220-225, 342-348. The Jesuits' account is in *Jes. Rel.*, lv, 105-115, and Kellogg, *Early Narratives*, 213-220.
¹⁰ Blair, i, 221-222, 343; *Jes. Rel.*, lv, 185-191, 219-221.

influence to induce the Wisconsin Indians to a better frame of mind. In this he was wholly successful; the news of the coming of "Metaminens" (Little Corn), as the tribesmen called him, was joyfully received. The chiefs and warriors, away from their villages on fishing expeditions, hurried home to meet their favorite white man and listen to his message. Especially the Potawatomi gave him good greeting and promised at once to send an embassy to the Sault to partake in the French ceremony.

It was now the month of May, and Perrot undertook once more the now familiar journey up Fox River to notify the Mascouten and Miami of his mission. The Potawatomi offered to escort him and to protect him from the ravaging Sioux. At the great Miami village the messenger of the king was received with all the honors the tribesmen knew how to offer. A mimic battle was staged on the plain below the village, when Perrot by raising the calumet brought an end to the flight of arrows passing over his head, and prepared for a ceremonial entrance into the village itself. The great chief received him in person, assigned him a guard of fifty warriors, and ordered a game of lacrosse to be played in his honor. Accompanied by the Miami chief Tetinchoua, Perrot returned to the Potawatomi village on Green Bay and prepared for the voyage to the Sault. Representative delegations from the Sauk, the Winnebago, the Potawatomi, and the Menominee tribes accompanied him. At the last moment illness prevented the Miami chief from going, when his tribe and those of the Kickapoo, Mascouten, and Outagami withdrew their delegations, asking the Potawatomi to act in their stead.

The Wisconsin Indians and Perrot arrived at the

Sault by the end of May.[11] There they found that St. Lusson had reached the mission house before them, and that the Indian delegations from the north had begun to arrive. Talon reported that seventeen nations gave formal allegiance to the French king.[12] The pageant took place June 14 on the southwestern bank of the Sault rapids a mile and a half from their head. The native village and the mission palisade were in full sight. Two large trees had been prepared for erection on a little height: one with a crosspiece to represent the missions, the other bearing on a broad escutcheon the royal arms of France.

It was mid-June in this northern region when summer poised in early beauty over the land. Around the group of natives upon the hill stretched the dark pine forest; in the foreground the mighty river sang its wilderness song. Forth from the gate of the mission house issued the procession of Frenchmen; first came

[11] Blair, i, 346; but see *ibid.*, 222, which is evidently incorrect as to date.

[12] The Jesuits reported that fourteen tribes were present. The report gives fifteen. See list in *Wis. Hist. Colls.*, xi, 27, identified as follows: Achipoés, the Chippewa; Malamecks, the Catfish (Marameg) band of the Chippewa; the Noquets, from the bay of that name; Banabeouiks, misprint for Ouinibeouiks (Winnebago); Makomiteks, possibly the Sauk, otherwise this tribe is not mentioned; Poulxteattemis, the Potawatomi; Oumalominis, the Menominee; Sassassaoua Cottons, misprint for Nessouakoutoun, the Ottawa of the Fork, then living on Green Bay (*Jes Rel.*, lviii, 289); Christinos, the Cree; Assinipoals, the Assiniboin; Aumonssonites, the Monsoni; Outaouois Bouscouttons (should be one name), the Ottawa of Manitoulin Island; Niscaks, probably the Nipissing; Masquikoukioeks, probably the Amikwa. The tribes from Green Bay agreed to get the assent of their neighbors, the Illinois, Mascouten, Outagami, and others. The Chequamegon Bay Hurons and Ottawa endorsed the occupation later in the summer (Blair, i, 225), making seventeen tribes who gave formal assent to the French sovereignty. See Talon's report in *N. Y. Colon. Docs.*, ix, 72.

the Jesuit priests, with their long black robes, holding crucifixes aloft and singing a Latin hymn. Then followed the traders in motley array of hunting shirts, bright sashes, gay *capots*, and embroidered moccasins, Perrot the interpreter among them. Lastly came the delegate of the king, in the gorgeous uniform of a French officer, bright sword unsheathed, with the royal ensign of the fleurs-de-lis borne aloft upon his glittering helmet. On swept the procession to the chosen hill. Around, the native envoys stood in all their savage finery—bodies greased and painted, heads crowned with feathers and horns, strings of bears' and moose's teeth about their necks, fur robes carelessly flung about their limbs. With them they bore the sacred calumets never absent on any occasion of ceremony.

With dignity and decorum, although with deep wonderment within their breasts, the natives watched the little group of aliens mount the height, bless the cross, and raise it aloft amid the chanting of the *Vexilla*. Then St. Lusson signed to the assembled chieftains to draw near. Perrot explained to them the nature of the ceremony, and that they had now become the subjects of the great father beyond the seas. In his regard for them he had sent them tokens of his care. At this, porters brought forward and opened bales of presents—blankets, French cloth, coats, hats, *capots*, knives, mirrors, and a hundred objects to arouse the barbarians' delight. Not to be outdone in generosity, the chiefs in their turn pressed forward and threw at St. Lusson's feet heaps of rich furs. The delegate then caused the tree bearing the royal arms to be erected amid the singing of the *Exaudiat* and the chanting of Latin prayers. Then as a climax St. Lusson performed the emblematic ceremony of possession. Stooping to the ground, he broke off a bit of turf which he raised aloft, and in a loud voice proclaimed, "In the name of the Most High, Most Mighty and Most Redoubtable Monarch Louis, the Fourteenth of the Name, Most Christian King of France and Navarre, we take possession of the said place Sainte Marie du Sault, as also of Lake Huron and Superior, the island of Caientoton [Manitoulin], and of all the other countries, rivers, lakes, and their tributaries contiguous and adjacent thereto, those discovered and to be discovered, bounded on one side by the Northern and Western seas, and on the other side by the South Sea, this land in all its length and breadth." Three times he repeated these words amid a chorus of "Vives le Roi," and a musketry volley from all the Frenchmen present. Perrot and Allouez then explained the ceremony to the watching chiefs, who came forward and signed the official record with their totemic marks. Four missionaries were present and added their signatures to the same record: Father Dablon, superior of the western missions; Allouez, veteran of the same missions; André and Dreuillettes, newcomers at the Sault. Marquette, however, who had spent the winter on Chequamegon Bay, did not arrive in time for the pageant. Fourteen traders from the St. Lawrence colony were also present and signed the *prise de possession*.[13] The first signature was that of Perrot, who called himself a *seigneur* [Sieur de Perrot]; next came the name of Jolliet;[14] Largilliers and Porteret, who were soon to accompany the discoverers of the Mississippi, also affixed their signatures. Among

[13] Sulte, "Les Français dans l'Ouest en 1671," in Can. Roy. Soc., *Proc.*, 1918, i, 19-21.
[14] Sulte thinks the one who signed "Jolliet" was Adrien, not Louis; but a document of September 12, 1671, shows that Adrien was then deceased, after service with La Salle. So the trader at the Sault in 1671 was in all probability Louis. Can. Roy. Soc., *Proc.*, 1920, sec. i, 75.

the other traders were several who became well known in the West during the next two decades, such as Jacques Maugras and Pierre Moreau *dit* La Toupine. The ceremony was now completed except for the great bonfire that was lighted in the evening and illumined the dark forest with its gleams, as the sparks of civilization lighted fitfully the darkness of native barbarism. The day closed with a final chant of a great Latin hymn.

The fashion set on this fourteenth of June, 1671, was followed by most of the later explorers of interior America. Duluth in 1679 took possession of the Sioux country; La Salle in 1682 performed a similar annexation ceremony at the mouth of the great central river; finally in 1689 Perrot, who had had so large a share in the pageant at the Sault, staged a like taking possession on the upper Mississippi, the only one actually enacted on the soil of what is now Wisconsin.[15] None the less the pageant at the Sault, with its phrases of lands "discovered and to be discovered," was not only the prototype for later action, but was in itself the most comprehensive as well as the widest known of such French ceremonies, and its record the most influential in maintaining French claims to the western country.

The other parts of St. Lusson's commission were not so well carried out as the pageant. So far as we know, he visited none of the missions but that at the Sault; he did make a short voyage into Lake Superior to discover copper, but all to no purpose.[16] His was the decorative part of the expedition, and not the practical one. Talon, however, avowed himself well pleased with the results, all the more that the gifts of beaver and other furs presented to the delegate more than paid the expenses of the enterprise. Talon saw with a pro-

[15] *Wis. Hist. Colls.*, xi, 33-36; Kellogg, *Early Narratives*, 330.
[16] Blair, i, 348; Margry, i, 95, 255; *Jes. Rel.*, lv, 237.

phetic eye what the taking possession portended. "This portion of the French monarchy," he wrote, "will become something grand." The seaboard colonies of the English would be hemmed in, and if they attempted to expand westward could be treated by the French as usurpers.[17] It now remained to carry on the exploration so favorably begun, to discover the great river of which so much had been heard, and to open the regions of the vast interior to French enterprise and civilization. Talon at once began to make preparations for these efforts, and his arrangements for further discovery proved to be his last gift to the western expansion of New France.[18]

[17] *N. Y. Colon. Docs.*, ix, 72-73.

[18] The natives were distrustful of the paper they had signed; no sooner were the Frenchmen out of sight than they withdrew the nails of the escutcheon, extracted the paper from behind it, and burned the *prise de possession*, fearing it was some kind of spell which would bring death upon them. Blair, i, 347. On the American side of the Sault Ste. Marie stands a granite obelisk erected to commemorate this ceremony of France's taking possession of the Northwest.

X. EXPLORATION OF THE MISSISSIPPI VALLEY, 1671–1682

TALON'S projects for exploration were not restricted to the great interior valley. He hoped to obtain control of Hudson Bay, to discover a land route to the western ocean and also a southern passage leading to the West Indies. Ambitious as he was, he realized that such a program could not be accomplished in one lifetime by a single individual. "Such discoveries," he wrote, "must be the work either of time or of the King."[1] He recommended to the latter the project of a Dieppe sailor who proposed to circumnavigate America and to penetrate to China in the same voyage.[2] Talon also fitted out an expedition to seek Hudson Bay by land.[3] The project which he had most at heart, however, was the discovery of the Mississippi River, a name already familiar in Canada by the reports of missionaries and fur traders. Talon selected as the leader of this expedition Louis Jolliet, already a veteran in western exploration and the discoverer of the deep-water route from Mackinac to Lake Ontario. Dablon, as superior of the Canadian missions, assigned to Marquette the office of chaplain. It was also arranged that the outfitting was to be done at the mission of St. Ignace; but before the start was made Talon and Courcelles had both been recalled to France.[4] Louis XIV at this time sent to rule his overseas colony the ablest governor New France had had since the days of Champlain. It fell to the lot of this new governor, Louis de Buade

[1] *N. Y. Colon. Docs.*, ix, 67, 71-73.
[2] *Ibid.*, 67.
[3] Margry, i, 93-94; *Jes. Rel.*, lvi, 149-217.
[4] Talon had requested his own recall.

Count de Frontenac, to carry on the policy of expansion Talon had advocated and to annex the Mississippi valley to the crown of France.

Like his predecessors Frontenac saw in the Iroquois the chief obstacle to his success. Like his predecessors he also invaded their territory, but unlike them he did not after his expedition leave these tribesmen to their own devices, but placed in their midst a pledge of future action by building on the north shore of Lake Ontario the fort to which he gave his own name.[5]

While Frontenac was occupied in overawing the Iroquois and regulating the fur trade, which was again in danger of slipping from the French grasp,[6] Talon's projected expedition set out to discover the Mississippi. Jolliet probably knew the western country as well as any living Frenchman; it would seem that he had already been as far as the Mascouten village on the upper Fox, then the farthest west of French exploration in Wisconsin.[7] The choice of Marquette to accompany this expedition of discovery seems to have given umbrage to some of his colleagues in the western missions. Allouez had long desired to be the apostle to the Illinois; Marquette was young and comparatively untried, why might his opportunity not wait until a later time?[8] Nevertheless his youthful ardor was one element that determined his choice—that and his skill in map-making and his knowledge of Indian languages.

[5] Margry, i, 195-238; *N. Y. Colon. Docs.*, ix, 95-114.
[6] *N. Y. Colon. Docs.*, ix, 65, 89.
[7] Ernest Gagnon, *Louis Jolliet* (Quebec, 1902), 27; Margry, i, 255.
[8] It is nowhere explicitly stated that the other missionaries of the West were envious of Marquette's preferment; but it is strange that they contrived to avoid meeting him, sometimes by only a day or two, as he passed through Wisconsin; and as we have seen in the previous chapter, Allouez, during his absence, inaugurated the Illinois mission.

For his own part Marquette was overjoyed at the opportunity. At his mission on Chequamegon Bay he had met some visiting Illinois, had heard of the great river which they had crossed in their journey, and had made some progress in learning the Illinois language. Now at St. Ignace he welcomed Jolliet with enthusiasm on his arrival, December 8, 1672, with their commission. The winter was spent in preparations, among which was the drawing of a map from the knowledge acquired from the Indians. "We were not long in preparing all our equipment," Marquette wrote in his journal; "Indian corn, with some smoked meat, constituted all our provisions; with these we embarked—Monsieur Jollyet and myself, with five men—in two bark canoes, fully resolved to do and suffer everything for so glorious an undertaking."[9] We know the names of only two of the *voyageurs* who accompanied the expedition; these were Pierre Porteret and Jacques Largilliers, who were present in 1671 at the pageant at the Sault, and later accompan ed Marquette on his final journey, and cared for him at his death.

It was the seventeenth of May when the little flotilla left St. Ignace, freighted with so many hopes, discarding so many fears—since the Indians sought to dissuade the explorers from their enterprise by stories of dangers that would be encountered, monsters which lurked along the stream, rapids that would swallow their frail barks, and heat that would roast them alive. Jolliet knew enough of interior North America to discount the natives' exaggerated reports, and the discoverers set forth with light hearts. As far as the Mascouten village

---

[9] Kellogg, *Early Narratives*, 229; also Kellogg, "Marquette's Authentic Map Possibly Identified," in Wis. Hist. Soc., *Proc.*, 1906, 183-193. Concerning this latter article, see *post*, note 29.

all was familiar; this was reached without hazard on the seventh of June.

While these young Frenchmen were thus adventuring for king and country in the wilds of North America, their king in person was leading a vast army toward the border of the Netherlands. Contrast the two expeditions—the tiny canoes of the *voyageurs* slipping swiftly along the Wisconsin waterways; the great state coach of Louis XIV and all the royal family lumbering on to the siege of Maestricht, accompanied by the paraphernalia of a royal progress and the equipment of a mighty army. Yet the world has well nigh forgotten that in June, 1673, Louis XIV captured the Dutch fortress; it will never forget that in that month Jolliet and Marquette first saw the Mississippi River.

Marquette was delighted with their reception by the villagers on the upper Fox. The Miami he found "the most civil, the most liberal, and the most shapely. . . . The Maskoutens and Kikabous are ruder and seem peasants in comparison with the others." Guides were furnished by the Miami to lead the explorers through the wild-rice mazes of the upper Fox.[10] When the portage was reached the guides carried the canoes across, and left the travelers to go on alone.[11] The expedition had now "left the waters flowing to Quebeq, four or five hundred leagues from here, to float on those that would henceforth take us through strange lands." Now was disproved the theory that rivers ran from the Great

[10] Kellogg, *Early Narratives*, 233-235. On Marquette's mistake concerning the distance, see Father Arthur E. Jones, in Wis. Hist. Soc., *Proc.*, 1906, 175-182.

[11] The site of their crossing has been marked by the Wau Bun (Portage) Chapter of the Daughters of the American Revolution. The tablet, unveiled in 1905, reads: "This tablet marks the place near which Jacques Marquette and Louis Joliet entered the Wisconsin River June 14, 1673."

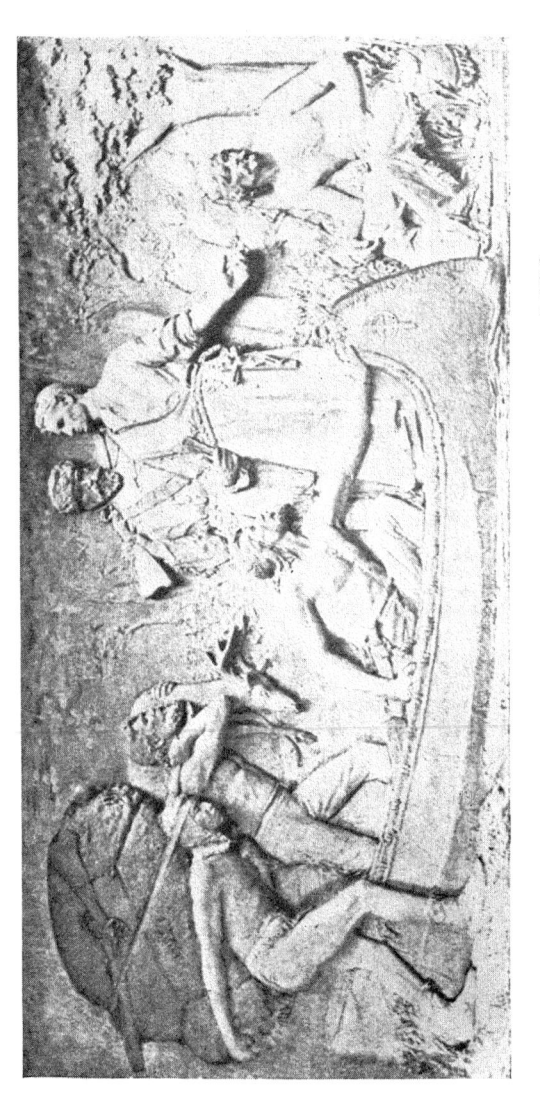

JOLLIET AND MARQUETTE AT PORTAGE, 1673
Bronze relief by Herman A. MacNeil

Lakes toward the western sea, while at the same time the most convenient portage route from the basin of the Great Lakes to the waters of the Mississippi was found.

The westward-flowing stream on which they embarked Marquette was told by his guides was named the Meskousing or the Miskous.[12] His description gives the characteristic features of our central river. "It is very wide; it has a sandy bottom, which forms various shoals that render the navigation difficult. It is full of islands covered with vines. . . . After navigating about thirty leagues, we saw a spot presenting all the appearances of an iron mine."[13]

It was the seventeenth of June when the mouth of the Wisconsin was reached and their canoes entered the long-sought river. "Here we are, then," writes Marquette, "on this so renowned River. . . The Missisipi."[14] A pleasant month had been spent on the Fox-Wisconsin portage route; another month on the

[12] This form of the river's name was changed to "Miskonsing" in a report appearing under Jolliet's name in Margry, i, 259. The "n" was evidently a typographical error for "u." Hennepin completed the transformation in his *New Discovery*, printing "Misconsing" and "Mesconsin" on pages 622, 643, 666; and "Ouisconsin" or "Misconsin" on page 221. Thereafter the stream remained the "Ouisconsin" during the French régime.

[13] Kellogg, *Early Narratives*, 235-236.

[14] Marquette wished to name the river "Conception," in honor of the Virgin Mary. Jolliet first called it "Buade River," for Frontenac's family name; later at Frontenac's suggestion he changed the name to "Colbert River," for the great French minister. Fortunately, however, the Indian name under which it was first mentioned persisted. In June, 1923, the quarter-millennial celebration of the discovery of the Mississippi was observed at Prairie du Chien and in the river cities of Iowa. A commemorative tablet was erected by the Knights of Columbus on the south bank of the Wisconsin near its mouth. See *Wis. Mag. of Hist.*, vii, 113-114; also *Illinois Catholic Historical Review*, July-October, 1923.

great river brought them to the southern limit of their voyage. After leaving the Mascouten village, they saw no vestiges of inhabitants until June 25; then at the water's western edge they descried human tracks, and landing with the peace calumet in hand they found a village of the Peoria tribesmen,[15] where they were graciously entertained with feasts and dances. The explorers setting out the last of June, their canoes soon came abreast of the cliffs near Alton, on which were painted the Piasa monsters.[16] Soon they were involved in the swift currents where the Missouri enters, the only rapids they mention on their route. The Missouri River Marquette called the Pekitanoui, and hoped "by its means to discover the Vermillion or California Sea."

Twenty leagues below the Missouri came in an eastern stream, on which the explorers understood the Shawnee lived. This they no doubt learned from the Monsoupelia tribe, whose village they found on the east bank some distance below the Ohio. Marquette left with the latter tribe a Latin letter for whom it might concern, which ultimately found its way to Virginia.[17] Somewhat farther south on the western bank were met the Michigamea, some of whom understood the Illinois language. From them they heard of the Quapaw at the mouth of the Arkansas River, at whose village

[15] This village had been supposed to have stood on the Des Moines River; it is now thought by many Iowa historians to have been on the Iowa River. *Iowa Journal of History and Politics*, 1903, 3-16.

[16] These pictographs were visible as late as 1848. See Illinois State Historical Society, *Transactions*, 1908, 114-122.

[17] *American Historical Review*, xxv, 676-680. The editor, Professor Alvord, thinks the Monsoupelia were a band of Chickasaw. Since Marquette noted resemblances to the Iroquois, it seems more probable that this village was one of Cherokee or Tuscarora origin.

they reached the southern limit of their voyage. They were now convinced both by Indian reports and by the course of the stream that they had traversed, that the Mississippi discharged its waters into the Gulf of Mexico. Between the Arkansas and the Mississippi's mouth they might meet Spaniards, with whom the French were then at war. They decided to turn northward, which they did on July 17, one month from the day they first saw the great river, and two months from that of their departure from St. Ignace.

Concerning the long, toilsome voyage upstream Marquette's journal says but little. Taking the advice the Indians had given, Jolliet returned by way of the Illinois River, finding on its upper waters some of the Peoria, who had come back from the trans-Mississippi to dwell in their own land. The explorers also visited on the upper Illinois a large Kaskaskia village, where guides were found for the Chicago portage to the waters of Lake Michigan. By the end of September they once more saw white faces at the mission house at De Pere. There Marquette remained to recuperate from the fatigue of his long voyage, while Jolliet appears to have spent some time exploring the southern and eastern shores of Lake Michigan,[18] before arriving in 1674 at the mission at Sault Ste. Marie *en route* to Canada. If, as seems probable, he returned thither by the deep-water route he had discovered in 1669, he may have stopped at Fort Frontenac and have related his discovery to its commandant, La Salle.

So far all had gone well with Jolliet, but when in very sight of Montreal his canoe overturned in the

---

[18] This statement is an inference from Jolliet's maps, which not only show features of Lake Michigan's southern and eastern coasts, but contain titles which speak of explorations in 1673 and 1674.

fierce rapids of the Sault St. Louis, his *voyageurs* and a young Indian slave were drowned, all the souvenirs of his voyage were lost, including a chest with his journals and his maps. He himself was finally saved after four hours' battling with the waves.[19]

The governor at Quebec received Jolliet after his rescue with much condescension. While deploring the loss of his journal, the explorer assured Frontenac that another copy of it had been left at Sault Ste. Marie.[20] A strange fatality seems to have attended the records of Jolliet. Hardly had he departed from the Sault, when the mission house and all its contents were burned.[21] Thus the second version of his journal perished by fire, as had the first by water. From memory Jolliet prepared several maps. The first, dedicated to Frontenac, on which the great river was called from his family name "Buade" and the valley "La Frontenacie," contains a cartouche with a letter from the explorer to the governor.[22] Another map was thereafter prepared to send to France, whereon at Frontenac's suggestion the great river and the valley it drains were named for Colbert, the French minister.[23] On the margin of this map is a letter urging the colonization of the newly discovered country.[24]

[19] *Jes. Rel.*, lviii, 93; Margry, i, 258; Harrisse, *Notes*, 322; *Canadian Archives Report*, 1905, i, p. xxxiv. This last document states that the shipwreck occurred before July 7, 1674.

[20] Margry, i, 258.

[21] *Jes. Rel.*, lviii, 255-263.

[22] A manuscript copy is in the John Carter Brown Library, which may be Jolliet's original chart. See reproduction in *Jes. Rel.*, lix, 86.

[23] The original of this map drawn for Colbert is in the Depot des Cartes in Paris. A photographic facsimile is in the Clements Library at the University of Michigan. The letter is printed in Margry, i, 257-262; *Jes. Rel.*, lviii, 107; *N. Y. Colon. Docs.*, ix, 121.

[24] In the John Carter Brown Library are two manuscript maps known as the "larger" and "smaller" Jolliet maps, repro-

The Jesuits did not fail to make much of this discovery by one of their order and a Canadian educated in their schools. Jolliet himself prepared a report for their superior, Father Dablon, who sent it at once to France. In this account the discoverer laid stress on the importance of the newly found region for colonization, and the possibilities of easy transportation by means of a canal at the Chicago portage.[25] October 10 Jolliet wrote a similar letter to Bishop Laval, then visiting in France.[26]

Marquette did not hear of Jolliet's loss of his papers and maps until sometime in September, 1674. He at once prepared his own journal and sent it to the Jesuit superior before leaving for what proved to be his last journey to Illinois.[27] This journal has been preserved as Marquette wrote it, and since it is the only extant record of the expedition the belief has gone abroad that Marquette, not Jolliet, was the leader. The priest himself never made such a claim, and in Canada Jolliet was always known as the dis-

---

duced in Winsor, *America*, iv, 212-214. I think, after examination and from various evidence, that these were drawn some time after 1674; as was likewise Jolliet's map of the Great Lakes, in *ibid.*, 215. The so-called "Carte Generalle" ascribed to Jolliet (*ibid.*, 218) is now known to have been drawn in 1681 by Franquelin.

[25] There are two manuscript copies of Jolliet's letter to Dablon, one in the Jesuit Archives in Paris, one in a Latin version in Rome. This latter is printed in Douniol, *Relations Inédits* (Paris, 1861), i, 193-204. Camille de Rochemonteix, *Les Jesuits et la Nouvelle France au XVII Siecle* (Paris, 1895), iii, 10-11, says it is less correctly transcribed than the French copy in Margry, i, 262-270. The latter is printed in *Jes. Rel.*, lviii, 93, where it is dated August 1, 1674, which is probably the true date of its writing; the other version is dated October 25, probably the date of its forwarding by Dablon.

[26] This letter is now in the library of St. Sulpice in Jolliet's handwriting; it is printed in Harrisse, *Notes*, 322-323.

[27] *Jes. Rel.*, lix, 165; Kellogg, *Early Narratives*, 262. See description of Marquette's manuscript, in *Jes. Rel.*, lix, 294-299.

coverer of the Mississippi.[28] Marquette's journals, abridged and edited, first appeared at Paris in 1681, in the *Recueil de Voyages*, of Melchisédech Thévenot; with this was issued a map supposed to be Marquette's. Prototypes of this map have since been found in manuscript in several forms,[29] and from the title are called the Manitoumie maps.[30] These maps seem to have been drawn by the Jesuits to exalt their order's share in Jolliet's discovery. Marquette's own holograph map was found in Montreal in the last century, and first published in 1853.[31]

[28] Marquette's early and tragic death enhanced his fame. See *ante*, chapter viii.

[29] See Wis. Hist. Soc., *Proc.*, 1906, 181-193. The present writer therein published an article identifying as Marquette's a map in the Parkman collection at Harvard University Library, of which an original copy was located in Paris. I wish to revise my former conclusions, since I now think that Marquette never drew but one map, which is in Montreal; that he began that map at St. Ignace before setting forth, and that later he added the courses of the Mississippi. The map known as "Parkman No. 5," of which there are several variations, was, I believe, prepared under the auspices of the Jesuits, in order to advance their claim to the newly discovered country. On these maps is represented an idol or manitou, such as the Jesuits overthrew in 1670 and again in 1672 in the Fox River, and the entire region is thereon called "La Manitoumie." Kellogg, *Early Narratives*, 228. These maps are the prototype of the one appearing as Marquette's in Thévenot's *Recueil*. Peter A. Porter, of Buffalo, believes the Manitoumie maps were adapted from an original left in the West by Jolliet. I cannot concur in this opinion, but consider it probable that they were prepared by one of the western Jesuits from data given by Marquette. The course of the Mississippi on all these maps is, however, less accurate than that laid down on Marquette's holograph map.

[30] See the reproductions of two of these Manitoumie maps in Wis. Hist. Soc., *Proc.*, 1906, 184; and Kellogg, *Early Narratives*, 228. There is a copy of one of these maps in the John Carter Brown Library at Providence. After examination I think the latter is a modern copy made from the original in the Bibliothèque Nationale, Paris, of which the one in *Early Narratives* is a photograph.

[31] John G. Shea, *Discovery and Exploration of the Mississippi Valley* (New York, 1853); *Jes. Rel.*, lix, 108. See also *Iowa Journal of History and Politics*, 1903, 9-13.

Jolliet's great discovery did not bring to him either profit or opportunity. Frontenac was, in fact, embarrassed by the success of the expedition. The ministers of the king were not friendly to such distant explorations, unless they resulted in the discovery of rich mines or some immediate source of profit.[32] Jolliet endeavored to propitiate the all-powerful Colbert by the insertion of his name on the map of the river he had discovered, and by giving the entire valley the title of La Colbertie. All, however, to no purpose; for when the discoverer petitioned for a small concession in the new regions he had added to the French crown, he was refused and obliged to content himself with the grant of the barren island of Anticosti, in the mouth of the St. Lawrence; and so far as appears he never went back to the great West which he had done so much to reveal to the world.[33]

The reason for this treatment of Jolliet was his previous connection with the Jesuits, and the missionaries' attempt to claim the discovery as their own. Frontenac was determined that he himself, and not the religious order, should profit by the expansion of the colony he governed. He immediately set on foot plans for the exploitation of the great West. From his fort on Lake Ontario he sent in 1676 his engineer Randin into Lake Superior to carry presents to the tribesmen of that region, and to control its profitable trade. We have no account of Randin's journey, except what is embodied in his excellent map of the West.[34]

[32] Margry, i, 256-257.
[33] *Ibid.*, 324, 329-336.
[34] *Ibid.*, ii, 252; *N. Y. Colon. Docs.*, ix, 142. Randin's manuscript map is in the John Carter Brown Library and has not been published. It shows knowledge of Jolliet's discoveries, but none of La Salle's. The map was thus drawn no later than 1678. See, however, Harrisse, *Notes*, 209-210, who dates it much later.

THE FRENCH RÉGIME

Frontenac soon found other agents for his purpose, two of whom have become famous in the annals of the West. They were Daniel Greysolon Sieur Duluth,[35] and Robert Cavelier Sieur de la Salle.

Frontenac considered his governorship of New France as a species of exile and also as an opportunity to recoup his ruined fortunes. The royal instructions forbade his participation in the fur trade; Frontenac was confident, however, that delinquencies in this line would be overlooked at court. The fur trade of the colony, moreover, had fallen into a ruinous condition. The great flotillas of western Indians that formerly came to the St. Lawrence each year were dwindling away. The horde of traders that sought the western country carrying goods to the tribesmen made unnecessary their long, hazardous voyage to Montreal. The governor was determined to suppress illegal trading. He induced the king to declare the death penalty for traders who went from the colony without the governor's permission.[36] Then arose the institution of the *coureurs de bois*, for not until the trade had been declared illegal could the unlicensed traders be classed as outlaws. Some of them carried their furs to the English at Albany, where they obtained not only protection

---

The name has been spelled "Raudin"; the research department of the Canadian Archives has sent me proofs that this officer was Hugues Randin, who came to Canada with the Carignan regiment. He held a fief on the St. Lawrence in 1672-73; drew plans for Fort Frontenac in 1673; visited Lake Superior in 1676; and died before 1681.

[35] The French form of the name was "Dulhut." See the accompanying document, with the signature of the explorer. I have decided to use the Anglicized form "Duluth."

[36] Talon had issued ordinances against woods running. *N. Y. Colon. Docs.*, ix, 65; *Bulletin des Recherches Historiques* (Levis, Canada), xxv, 170; *Edits et Ordonnances Royaux*, i, 73.

Pou La somme de vingt robes
que Jay eu du sieur hebert tant en
Peleterie qu'ils mont envoyés par
ozogoua que pour celles quil a deffendu
avec Les Srs LaMouville Lariviere
de Tours et mon Domestique Bosseron
aussy bien que pour les marchandises
que iay prises pour la paix, dans
la Communauté, et lesquelles dittes
vingt robes ie donne ordre aud. Sr
hebert de les prandre au retour dispo—
Traitte faitte cette annee soit du
Costé du nord ou du Costé du Sud
sur ma part des peleterie que sont
au Sault S.te marie fait a michelimakinak
ce 8e mars 1681   Dulhut

si mieux n'ayme led. Sr. hebert
prandre lesd. vingt robes sur les
peleterie quil fera cest esté prochain
fait aud. Lieu et le d. Jour que Dessus
                            Dulhut

but better prices than the French would give.[37] Others remained in the western country beyond the reach of laws and officers. It was claimed that the Jesuit missionaries protected these Frenchmen and shared the profit of the illicit trade.[38] But as this claim was made by their enemies, it must not be accepted without further substantiation.

The regulation of the fur trade consisted in the issuance of licenses called congés, twenty-five of which were granted under bonds to reliable persons each year. These were in the nature of pensions, the needy of the colony being assigned these congés with leave to sell them to merchants who wished to utilize them. Each congé permitted its holder to send one canoe-load of goods, worth about three thousand francs, to the western country. For such a canoe eight *voyageurs* were needed. The initial outlay was thus considerable, as the congé sold for from eight to twelve hundred francs, and the *voyageurs* must have some advances before they could be secured. The trader, therefore, was usually obliged to obtain aid from some of the outfitters and merchants of the colony. This was furnished on the basis of a half-share of the proceeds of the venture. Profits were, in the early days, enormous—the furs frequently selling for twelve hundred per cent of the advances made for the expedition. In 1674 Nicolas Perrot, who until this time seems not to have been in the West after he accompanied St. Lusson, secured a congé and returned to Green Bay.[39]

The principal menace to the western fur trade was the enterprise of the Albany traders, which was largely

[37] *N. Y. Colon. Docs.*, ix, 90; Margry, i, 241; Helen Broshar, "The First Push Westward of the Albany Traders," in *Mississippi Valley Historical Review*, vii, 228-230.
[38] *N. Y. Colon. Docs.*, ix, 120; Margry, i, 303, 322-324.
[39] Blair, i, 228-229.

forestalled by the erection of Fort Frontenac; but Frontenac's plans were threatened within his own colony by the opposition of the intendant, Jacques Duchesneau, who came in 1675 to take the hitherto unfilled place of Talon. The new official allied himself with the party in the colony which opposed the governor, and upon his recommendation an edict was secured from France, dated April 15, 1676, revoking all congés for the western fur trade and imposing heavy penalties for any infraction.[40] Frontenac's plans, however, did not rest upon an open market in the West; he intended to obtain from the court in France monopoly concessions for his favorites, and with that in view La Salle was sent in 1674 to Paris with such recommendations and introductions as obtained for him a grant of Fort Frontenac as a seigniory with exclusive permission to trade. Three years later La Salle again went to court with more extended plans for exploiting the western country; but before describing these plans, let us examine conditions in the West, and observe what affected further exploration and discovery.

Since the time of Jolliet great changes had taken place in the tribal geography and in the places frequented by the traders. The Iroquois were tampering with the western tribesmen and offering their services as middlemen for the Albany traders. In order to aid in these plans they had induced a band of Miami to come nearer to their habitat, and these latter had gone around Lake Michigan and built a village at its southeastern end, on the St. Joseph River.[41] Meanwhile many other bands of tribesmen had been persuaded by the *coureurs de bois* to settle in the fertile Fox River valley, and an aggregation of twenty thousand was

[40] *Edits et Ordonnances Royaux*, i, 86.
[41] Blair, i, 349-350; *N. Y. Colon. Docs.*, ix, 129.

reported in 1677 as dwelling on the upper Fox—a larger number than the present inhabitants of this particular site.⁴² With the Indian method of food purveying this number was greater than could be supported, and famine conditions soon arose. The different bands of the Miami and Mascouten began to scatter and build new villages. The Ouiatanon settled near Chicago;⁴³ the Crane clan of the Miami built a village on the Fox River of Illinois. A part of the Mascouten settled on Milwaukee River, while some of the tribe still remained at their former village where Marquette had seen them. About this time also the Foxes left their home on the upper Wolf River and built a village near Butte des Morts, when the river which had formerly been called the Puans or Winnebago River now began to be called the Fox.⁴⁴ Even the Menominee, who had been constant friends of the white men and had welcomed them at their villages on Green Bay, got into a quarrel with some of the Jesuits' servants, and one or more of these latter were killed. The Menominee no longer dared to go to Montreal to trade, and when a pestilence fell upon them they thought it was invoked by the missionaries as a measure of revenge. All the Wisconsin Indians ceased going to the St. Lawrence and fell back on their primitive economy and such goods as they could obtain from the *coureurs de bois* or through intertribal trade with the Iroquois.⁴⁵

Between the discovery of Jolliet and Marquette and the expeditions of La Salle and Duluth, a period of five years intervenes, in which we have no record of exploration; yet the maps of the period show an increas-

⁴² *Jes. Rel.*, lix, 225; lxi, 149.
⁴³ *Ibid.*, lxi, 73, 149; R. G. Thwaites, editor, *Hennepin's New Discovery* (Chicago, 1903), i, 307.
⁴⁴ *Ibid.*, 166; Wis. Hist. Soc., *Proc.*, 1907, 151-152.
⁴⁵ *Wis. Hist. Colls.*, xvi, 101-102; Margry, ii, 78, 116.

ing knowledge of the Great Lakes and the paths to the Mississippi. The question arises whether there were not some unrecorded reconnaissances within that epoch, and whether we may not be justified in inferring that some such unnoticed voyages took place. For instance, La Salle was at Fort Frontenac for over two years between his first and second visits to France, and there is some reason to think he may have made a trip around the lakes before he received his concession for settling the Illinois valley. One contemporary historian asserts that he made such a voyage in 1676; and certainly his report in 1678 of the lakes region to the French king reads like the description of an eyewitness.[46] In his plans for the voyage of 1679 he seemed familiar with the general features of the upper lakes, especially with Lake Michigan. Some biographers of La Salle have argued that he obtained his knowledge of the West after he left the Sulpitians on the eastern end of Lake Erie in 1669, when he is thought to have visited the Ohio, and believed by some to have gone as far as the prairies of Illinois. This portion of La Salle's career is quite obscure, and the more recent writers on this subject reject the Ohio voyage entirely.[47] He may, as we have seen, have obtained his information of the Illinois from Jolliet; but a Great Lakes voyage in 1676 from Fort Frontenac is not improbable, all the more that at that date the route was sufficiently well known not to occasion much comment, and that any person would wish to see the region into which he was to venture and for which he proposed to make such great sacrifices. Whether, however, La Salle had visited the Great Lakes in person or not, before his second visit to

[46] La Potherie, *Histoire*, ii, 134-135; see also Blair, i, 351.
[47] Alvord, *Illinois*, 78; Charles A. Hanna, *The Wilderness Trail* (New York, 1911), i, 143.

France, he was able with the aid of the powerful influence of Frontenac to impress the French court with the importance and value of the great central valley, and to secure from the king a patent permitting him to explore, settle, and exploit this region. Armed with the royal grant, La Salle arrived at Quebec late in the summer of 1678; but before his arrival another of the band of noted western explorers had set forth on his first voyage to the upper country, without royal consent, and with only the tacit permission of Frontenac.

The voyages of Duluth have received far less attention than those of La Salle, in the first place because they were undertaken in a somewhat clandestine fashion, and Duluth was technically open to the charge of being a *coureur de bois*; and secondly, because Duluth was without self-assertion and left few records or descriptions of his exploits. His plans were perhaps as far-reaching as those of the better known explorer, and he obtained a greater measure of success by the power of his personality, by his ability to deal with men, both white and red, and by his single-hearted devotion to the best interests of New France and to the establishment of French sovereignty in interior America. His failures were due to an excess of generosity, as when he abandoned his project of penetrating to the western ocean, in order to rescue one of La Salle's expeditions from the unfortunate position it had fallen into because of imprudence and mismanagement. Duluth was far more generous than La Salle, who bitterly accused Duluth of unfair practices, of interfering with his monopoly, and of enticing away his men; while the truth was that La Salle himself was violating the provisions of his patent—which forbade trading in beaver in the northern regions—and was so unpopular with his employees that they deserted to Duluth, who was always beloved and respected by all Frenchmen in the West.

Concerning Duluth's early life not much is known. He was born in 1636 at St. Germain-en-Laye, but was brought up at Lyons, whence he was often called Le Lyonnais. He belonged to a noble family, and was bred to the profession of arms. At an early age he was enrolled in the King's Guard, wholly composed of noble youths. What was the motive that led him to abandon, at the age of thirty-six, the life of the French court and to emigrate to the overseas colony of New France, we can only conjecture. He had an uncle then living at Montreal, Jacques Patron by name, who was one of the best known and wealthiest merchants of Canada. Probably Daniel Duluth came thither in the expectation of improving his fortune. After two years in Canada he was recalled to service, and took part in the expedition of 1674 into Flanders, where at the battle of Seneffe he served as the squire of a great nobleman, the Marquis de Lassay. This duty accomplished, Duluth late in the same year 1674 returned to the colony, bringing with him at this time a much younger brother, Claude Greysolon Sieur de la Tourette. At Montreal the brothers bought a home and lived there quietly for the next four years. No doubt they heard much in those years of the western regions. Jolliet had but just returned from his epoch-making voyage; the Jesuits were sending new missionaries to the upper country; traders came and went with stories of adventure and profit to be found there; delegations of the western tribesmen each year visited Montreal with their tales of distant regions and great rivers leading to the sea. Duluth's ambition was fired to discover a route to the western ocean. He probably talked with Randin, and planned to continue his work of pacifying and making alliances with the tribes of Lake Superior as a preliminary to his discovery, for he was convinced that the continent could best be crossed from that direction.[48]

Ever since the flight in 1671 of the Hurons and Ottawa from Chequamegon Bay, an Indian war had been raging which had closed Lake Superior to the French traders. Duluth's first task was to bring about a secure peace. For that purpose he wintered in 1678-79 with the Chippewa near Sault Ste. Marie, and having secured the good will of their most prominent chief, set out in the spring of 1679 with his escort to seek the Sioux. No more dangerous mission could be conceived, but the steadfast French soldier wrote to the governor that "he feared not death, only cowardice or dishonor."[49] His party was composed of young men of like reckless courage, some of them like himself scions of the nobility.[50] Taking their lives in their hands, they went forward to a rendezvous arranged with the Sioux at the western end of Lake Superior.[51]

[48] The first expedition to reach the Pacific Ocean overland, that of Sir Alexander Mackenzie in 1792-93, followed the route Duluth planned to take via the Ottawa River, Lake Superior, the portage from the western end of this lake to the great northern plains. Mackenzie thus finished the exploration which Duluth began.

[49] Margry, vi, 26-34, prints Duluth's letter written to Frontenac, dated April 5, 1679, in which he describes his adventures of the preceding winter.

[50] We know the names of the following: the brothers Pepin (for whom Lake Pepin was named), Sieur le Maistre, Paul la Vigne, Sieur Bellegarde, and Sieur de la Rue. Technically they were *coureurs de bois*, since the expedition was not authorized by the government and they had no traders' congés.

[51] According to La Salle, the *voyageur* who arranged the Sioux rendezvous was one of his own employees named Faffart. He had probably been one of Randin's party in 1676. The site of this meeting at Fond du Lac of Lake Superior cannot be definitely determined. It may well have been within the radius of the great city that now bears Duluth's name.

This fierce tribe received the French messengers graciously, and after making peace between the two most powerful tribes of the Northwest, the Chippewa and the Sioux, the explorer was escorted in triumph to the home of the latter tribe on the headwaters of the Mississippi. There in the Isanti village on Lake Mille Lac he erected, on July 2, 1679, the royal arms and took possession of the Sioux country for Louis XIV.

Duluth was certainly deceived about the width of the continent at this point. He had conceived the idea that the Sioux village was not far distant from California, and that there was danger that other Europeans might forestall France among these tribesmen. He named the lake on which it stood "Buade," for the governor, and called the village itself "Izatys."[52] He questioned its inhabitants carefully about their neighbors, and went himself to two other Sioux villages, where he likewise erected the royal standard. Both of these villages lay to the east of the Isanti. When he departed from his Indian hosts, with whom he made a firm alliance for the French, he appears to have left three of his men with the savages, and to have given them directions to explore as far west as possible. These *engagés* visited a tribe of the Sioux who had been on the warpath twenty days' journey westward to a great lake the waters of which were salt. Duluth, to whom his men brought some of the salt, naturally concluded that the war band had been as far as the western ocean, knowing nothing of such a phenomenon as Great Salt Lake.

[52] Margry, vi, 34; Kellogg, *Early Narratives*, 330; see also map in *ibid.*, 342. Hennepin's map of 1683, part of which we reproduce, shows the king's arms on a tree trunk near this village. This token of Duluth's visit Hennepin probably saw himself. The village name "Izatys" (another form of "Isanti," or "Issati") was misread as "Kathio" by early Minnesota historians. But see Folwell, *Minnesota*, i, 22-24.

HENNEPIN'S MAP, 1683, SHOWING ROYAL ARMS FASTENED TO A TREE

What tribe of the Sioux was visited by Duluth's men? From the map of Franquelin drawn from information furnished by Duluth, it would seem that it was the Teton, since the only tribe whose name is given on the western edge of the map is called the "Tintons." Hennepin also speaks several times of the "Tinthona," and places them on his map the farthest west of all the kindred tribes; so from all these indications it seems highly probable that Duluth's men went from the Isanti village on Mille Lac westward to some of the Teton bands, who had been on the warpath as far as Great Salt Lake. Just where this tribe may have dwelt when first visited by these Frenchmen, we do not know; there is some evidence to place their village on Big Stone Lake, in which case Duluth's men must have crossed what is now Minnesota, and may have been the first white men to enter Dakota.[53]

Before, however, Duluth could plan for westward faring, he had to keep his rendezvous with the tribes of the north, to whom he had sent an envoy before visiting the Sioux. On September 15 a great council was again held at the head of Lake Superior, wherein the Sioux and the Assiniboin, who had been at war for thirty years, were reconciled. Both tribes promised to send delegations to visit Frontenac the coming summer. An epidemic of smallpox in the colony, however, frightened them away.[54]

[53] Kellogg, *Early Narratives*, 333. See the name "Tintons" on the Franquelin map of 1688 (frontispiece). For the habitat of the Teton, see *South Dakota Historical Collections*, ii, 22. Note also on the map the names of the Sioux tribes east of Lake Buade. The Sougatiskiton were no doubt the Sisseton; the Houetbatons, the Wahpeton.
[54] *N. Y. Colon. Docs.*, ix, 129. It may have been that Duluth built a fort that winter on Minnesota soil. See Folwell, *Minnesota*, i, 22-23.

Duluth now determined to explore a water route to the Sioux country, and thence to push westward toward the salt water he had heard of from his men. He thereupon ascended the Brule River of Wisconsin, cutting down *en route* a hundred or more beaver dams; then portaged to the St. Croix, and by July had run down that stream to its mouth. Arrived at the Mississippi, he learned to his displeasure that the Sioux, with whom he had the year before made a treaty of alliance, were holding captive three white men. Such conduct on their part made his westward explorations impossible. Duluth, more than any other of the early explorers, realized the danger of allowing any Indians to take liberties with the lives or freedom of white men. The fate of one might become the fate of all. To Duluth's energetic measures of retaliation it was due more than to any other agency that the French of the Northwest were safe in Indian territory.

Abandoning his own plans he set forth in a light canoe, and near the mouth of the Wisconsin River[55] overtook a hunting party of the Sioux with whom were two of the white captives. One of these he recognized as a Recollect monk, who proved to be Father Louis Hennepin, a chaplain of La Salle's party.[56] Hennepin's companions—Michel Accault, the leader of the expedition, and Antoine du Gay Auguel, called Le Picard—were likewise in durance among the Sioux.[57] They had

[55] Eighty leagues below the St. Croix. The Wisconsin is 170 miles below that stream. A French league is 2.76 miles, but the explorers' distances are not very accurate.

[56] Duluth and Hennepin had probably met at Montreal before either left for the West, since the friar had come to Canada in 1675. By a curious coincidence both had been in 1674 on the battle field of Seneffe.

[57] Hennepin, who was very vain, hated to admit he had been a captive. But see *New Discovery*, 293-305; La Salle's statement

been sent by La Salle, of whose western expedition Duluth now probably heard for the first time, to explore the upper Mississippi and to build a fort at the mouth of the Wisconsin.[58] Now for four months they had been at the mercy of the savages' caprices, had been dragged to Lake Mille Lac, carried on hunting expeditions, and effectually prevented from fulfilling their instructions. Duluth at once returned to the great Sioux village where he had arranged the French alliance, called a council, and reproached the chiefs for their breach of faith. With a haughty gesture he rejected their peace calumets, spurned their excuses, and demanded the release of the French captives,[59] whom he at once carried away to civilization and safety.[60]

The return journey was made by the Wisconsin and Fox rivers, the first recorded voyage over that route from west to east.[61] During this long summer voyage Hennepin no doubt related to Duluth his adventures and those of his chief since the latter's return in 1678 from France, with concessions for settling the Illinois country.[62] He told of the building of the ship on Cayuga

---

that Hennepin was once about to be burned, Margry, ii, 251-260; and Duluth's direct statement that they were slaves—that is, prisoners—Kellogg, *Early Narratives*, 331-332.

[58] La Salle stated that such a fort was actually built. Margry, ii, 254; *Wis. Hist. Colls.*, xvi, 110. We have no reason to believe that such was the fact.

[59] Kellogg, *Early Narratives*, 332-333.

[60] La Salle never made acknowledgment to Duluth for this rescue; instead, he complained that the latter had encroached upon his fur trade privileges. *Wis. Hist. Colls.*, xvi, 107-110. See Duluth's defense, in Kellogg, *Early Narratives*, 333.

[61] See Hennepin's description in *New Discovery*, 305-310.

[62] For La Salle's great project for the West, see Margry, i, 329-336. Jolliet asked for only twenty colonists per year and licenses to trade. La Salle's plans were imperial in scope; his concession, signed May 12, 1678, granted him only the trade in buffalo robes, and expressly forbade participation in the beaver

Creek above Niagara Falls, and of La Salle's sending Duluth's cousin, Henry de Tonty, in advance to Detroit to gather furs.[63] Fifteen more of his men had been hurried to Green Bay for the same purpose. Hennepin himself had come out with his chief in the *Griffon*, the first sailing vessel on the Great Lakes. This stately vessel had aroused much wonder and alarm among the native population. In safety, however, it reached the opening of Green Bay and anchored off the Potawatomi Islands. There it was heavily laden with valuable furs which were to be sent back by La Salle to pay the expenses so far incurred in this enterprise. The *Griffon* never was heard from again. Her fate to this day has remained a mystery. She has usually been supposed to have foundered in the autumn gales; La Salle, however, claimed to believe that her pilot and crew scuttled her, secured her cargo, and joined Duluth. Another rumor reached the colony that the ship had been boarded by hostile Indians, her crew massacred, and the bark burned.[64] Such a fate overtook the *Tonquin* on the Pacific coast in 1811. If it occurred to the *Griffon*, the perpetrators were never detected, which may in part account for the critical conditions in the West during the next few years.

After the departure of his vessel eastward, La Salle

---

trade of the Ottawa country. La Salle did not regard this latter restriction in the least. He loaded the *Griffon* with furs from Green Bay and sent Accault for furs among the Sioux.

[63] There are several accounts of La Salle's expedition of 1678-80. The official account is in Margry, i, 437-544; that of Zenobius Membré is in Le Clercq, *Establishment of the Faith*, ii, 114-157; Hennepin's own is in *New Discovery*, 110-181. The best brief account is that of Tonty in Kellogg, *Early Narratives*, 286-297. We spell Henry de Tonty's name as he did himself.

[64] La Salle's suspicions are recounted in Margry, iii, 324-327; the rumor of the Indian massacre, in Blair, i, 353; Charlevoix, *History of New France*, iii, 204.

EXPLORATION OF MISSISSIPPI VALLEY 215

and his party voyaged in Indian canoes southward along the Lake Michigan shore. At or near Kewaunee, on October 1, 1679, they landed at a big village of Potawatomi. These were the only tribesmen they encountered until they came upon a large hunting party of Outagami at the southern end of the lake, who made hostile demonstrations, and were only overawed by a show of force. The autumn was very stormy, and the little canoes with their fourteen white voyagers were tossed like cockleshells on the great swells of the lake. There was great difficulty in landing through the surf. Father Gabriel de la Ribourde, the oldest of the chaplains, suffered greatly on this stormy voyage. La Salle's plan was to reach the mouth of St. Joseph River, where he expected Tonty to join him after a hurried trip to the Sault to arrest some deserters. While awaiting his lieutenant, La Salle and his party built a log fort at the mouth of the river, and there they rested and recruited their strength. Tonty coming down the east shore of the lake was shipwrecked on that coast, fortunately near enough to obtain succor from La Salle. In December the reunited party mounted the St. Joseph River, finding near its source a village of Miami and Mascouten, who showed them the portage route to the Kankakee, one of the headstreams of the Illinois.[65] By the third of January, 1680, the expedition reached Peoria Lake, where it halted and built a post which La Salle named Fort Crêvecoeur.[66]

All along the route the Indians had been hostile, stirred to opposition, La Salle thought, by the Jesuit

---

[65] This was one of the important routes from the Great Lakes to the Mississippi valley. It passed through St. Joseph County, Indiana, above South Bend.

[66] Probably named for a fortress captured by Turenne in 1672, where Tonty may have seen service.

missionaries. Certainly these men could not have seen the approach of this expedition with complacency; it must have seemed to them the ruin of all their plans for converting and controlling the savages. Nevertheless La Salle no doubt exaggerated the hostility of the Jesuits. The western tribesmen for other reasons were in a turbulent humor, and La Salle had not acquired sufficient skill and diplomacy to conciliate them as Duluth was then doing in the North. La Salle's later successes with the Indians came from their admiration of his boldness or their fear of his power. Nor did he have greater success with his subordinates; his men were constantly seething with revolt and deserting at the slightest pretext. Only in his lieutenants did he evoke faith, especially in the young Italian, Henry de Tonty. From Fort Crêvecoeur, La Salle, after dispatching his little party to the upper Mississippi, felt himself obliged to return to Fort Frontenac, leaving Tonty in command.

All this and much more Friar Hennepin related to his rescuer on their voyage through Wisconsin. Stopping but a brief time at St. François Xavier mission, the travelers pushed on to St. Ignace, where they spent the winter and where Duluth learned that he had been proscribed by the Canadian intendant, and declared the leader of a lawless body of *coureurs de bois*.[67] Duluth's proud spirit could not brook such an unjust accusation; he immediately prepared to conduct his own defense in Canada. Leaving St. Ignace by the end of March,[68] he presented himself to Frontenac at the

[67] *N. Y. Colon. Docs.*, ix, 131-133, 141-142, 145, 153-154, 159-160; Margry, ii, 251, 253. Duluth always repudiated the charge of being a trader. See Kellogg, *Early Narratives*, 333; Margry, vi, 36.

[68] Note the document with signature dated Michilimackinac, March, 1681, a facsimile of which is herein published by permission of the Chicago Historical Society.

earliest possible moment. His achievements had not been inconsiderable; he had reopened Lake Superior to French enterprise, annexed the Sioux country, built several forts, made alliances with great tribes, and opened a route toward the west. The utility of his exploration far surpassed what La Salle had as yet accomplished. Duluth, however, has never had a biographer; and as he himself made brief and few reports, his fame has not been equal to his merits. Frontenac received him with great kindness, invited him to his own table while keeping him a nominal prisoner to satisfy the intendant.

Meanwhile what of his relative, the young Italian explorer whom La Salle had left to guard his forlorn hope in Illinois? Well would it have been for Tonty if he, like Hennepin, could have obtained the powerful protection of Duluth. Hardly was La Salle away, when the garrison mutinied, destroyed Fort Crêvecoeur, and hastened off to join the Iroquois. Tonty, with two chaplains and three remaining men, was obliged to seek refuge in the great Kaskaskia village on the upper Illinois. There a more dreadful misfortune overtook these refugees when a war party of Iroquois burst into the valley and carried death and ruin in every direction.[69] Tonty was wounded in a brave endeavor at a parley with the furious warriors, nominally at peace with the French and their allies. There was nothing for the six Frenchmen to do but to retreat, and no asylum nearer than the mission house at De Pere. Many are the tales of frontiersmen wandering through deep woods and enduring severe hardships; none surpass in interest the record Tonty has left us of his anabasis in the Wisconsin woods. The first day out old

[69] For the causes which led to this irruption of the Iroquois, see Alvord, *Illinois*, 85-86. See also Hanna, *Wilderness Trail*, i, 158.

Father Gabriel, as he stepped aside to pray, was murdered by a prowling band of Kickapoo. There was no opportunity even for ascertaining his fate, which would be that of the remainder of the party did they not press on. One small canoe bore them by way of the Chicago portage to the shores of Lake Michigan; finally on November 1 their frail craft was wrecked somewhere north of the site of Milwaukee. Again left in the woods Tonty, still suffering from his wound, pressed forward, he and his comrades living only upon the scanty fare of the forest—wild garlic, grubbed up from under the snow. Finally they reached the Potawatomi village, to find the entire band had gone hunting and left only such provisions as could be gleaned from their harvested cornfields. Having assembled a little heap of food, sufficient, Tonty thought, to last them to Mackinac, and having found a canoe, they were preparing to embark when, during a brief absence, one of their men who had been lost for some days stumbled upon the food supply and devoured it nearly all. "We had much pleasure in seeing him," writes the urbane Tonty, "and much regret to see our provisions partly consumed." There was but one hope left to the starving and weakened men, that of finding some band of hunting savages, which was finally accomplished at the Sturgeon Bay portage. There with some French traders Tonty passed the remainder of the winter. But for the accident in the Potawatomi village he might have reached St. Ignace in time to have spent some weeks with Duluth. As it fell out, it was June, 1681, before he arrived at Mackinac, and Duluth had been away for three months. Father Membré, the Recollect survivor of Tonty's party, went to the Jesuit mission at St. François Xavier and was there cared for until spring.[70]

[70] Kellogg, *Early Narratives*, 294-296. See also Kellogg, "A Wisconsin Anabasis," in *Wis. Mag. of Hist.*, vii, 322-339.

At St. Ignace, Tonty was found by La Salle, who had come west in the earliest spring, had visited the ruin left by the Iroquois in the Illinois valley, and had mourned Tonty as dead. Their joy at reunion was tempered by the failure of their hopes. Relief, however, soon came for the harassed explorers. The king had granted an amnesty to the *coureurs de bois*, announcing forgiveness for those who would come in and give themselves up. This he was forced to do or see Canada depopulated of her finest youth. In 1680 six hundred were outlaws in the western woods.[71] Frontenac sent to Mackinac a messenger in the person of Sieur de Villeraye to announce the king's clemency. The governor's representative proceeded to Green Bay, and at a great council extorted reparation from the Menominee for the murder of the Jesuits' servants.[72] The lives of Frenchmen were once more safeguarded. The woods were emptied of their outlaw white men.

La Salle with renewed courage bent to his purpose; to combat the Iroquois he now proceeded to form a strong federation of western tribesmen. He drew together a great group of Algonquian Indians—Illinois, Miami, Mascouten, Kickapoo from the vicinity; Abenaki and Mahican from the far east; Shawnee from the south.[73] Central Wisconsin was denuded of inhabitants;

[71] *Edits et Ordonnances Royaux*, i, 248-249; *N. Y. Colon. Docs.*, ix, 140; *Bulletin des Recherches Historiques*, xxv, 172-173. Duluth took advantage of this ordinance to absolve himself from the technicality of being treated as a *coureur de bois*.

[72] *Wis. Hist. Colls.*, xvi, 101-104; Blair, i, 231.

[73] See map in *Jes. Rel.*, lxiii, frontispiece. Note Parkman's description of La Salle's Indian community: "La Salle looked down from his rock on a concourse of wild human life. Lodges of bark and rushes, or cabins of logs were clustered in the open plain or along the edges of the bordering forests. Squaws labored, warriors lounged in the sun, children whooped and gamboled on the grass. Beyond the river, a mile and a half to the left, the banks were studded once more with the lodges of the Illinois." *La Salle*, 295.

the Algonquian aggregations moved into Illinois. Thence La Salle and Tonty were enabled to visit the mouth of the Mississippi, to plant there the royal arms, and to annex the basin of that stream, which now became permanently Louisiana.[74]

A new era opened for the West; it had now been explored, its largest river discovered, its chief portage paths traversed, its territory annexed. The fur trade was again licensed and outlaw trading suppressed. Its Indian tribesmen were collected under direct French influence. All promised well for progress when a new disaster befell all New France. Count de Frontenac was recalled and his place filled by an elderly, unwise, untried governor, Antoine Lefebre Sieur de la Barre.

[74] Note the progress in importance of the early names for this region: "La Manitoumie," "La Frontenacie," "La Colbertie," "La Louisiane"—for an Indian spirit stone, for the governor of New France, for the prime minister of France, and lastly for the king.

XI. IROQUOIS WAR AND THE WEST, 1682-1689

THE Iroquois raids of the fifth and sixth decades of the seventeenth century profoundly affected Wisconsin's destiny by driving into its territory large numbers of Algonquian Indians, who were soon followed by French traders and missionaries. The Iroquois wars which covered the last two decades of the same century in like manner changed the Indian geography of Wisconsin. During their course many of the intruding tribesmen, who were beginning to exhaust the available food supply, migrated from this region. Meanwhile, because of the Iroquois peril, those of Wisconsin's Indians who remained became increasingly dependent upon French traders for their weapons and ammunition; French garrisons were sent to build forts at strategic positions; lead mines were discovered and opened for additional war supplies. Wisconsin became an important portion of the French empire in America.

These results were not obtained without difficulty. Time and again it seemed that the Iroquois would prevail, would drive the French from the Northwest; three times flotillas of English traders accompanied by their Iroquois customers penetrated to the upper Great Lakes; more than once the western tribesmen formed embassies to arrange an Iroquois alliance—an alliance that meant death to every Frenchman in the western country. These dangers were averted by a group of remarkable leaders, able, alert, influential, and courageous. Among them were Duluth, Tonty, Perrot, and La Durantaye.

The second group of Iroquois wars may, from their European significance, be divided into those when the

French and English were nominally at peace (1682-89); and those after the English Revolution, when France and Great Britain were parts of European coalitions at enmity one with another (1689-98). This chapter is concerned with the earlier period. The Iroquois wars sprang out of the exigencies of the fur trade. No sooner had the traders taught the Five Nations the desire for white men's goods, than the supply of furs with which to purchase them diminished. The country of the Iroquois was quickly denuded of fur-bearing animals; in order to satisfy their wants they had to range farther and farther afield. Soon they encountered opposition from tribes already occupying these hunting grounds. Iroquois policy thereupon insisted that these tribes be conquered and their lands appropriated. The opposing tribesmen themselves were either massacred or incorporated into the Iroquois confederacy.

In pursuit of this policy the Five Nations had ruined one after another the Hurons, the Neutrals, the Andastes, and the Eries. They had depopulated the territory northwest, west, and south from their habitat. Still their demands were not satisfied. They then ranged farther west and attacked the Algonquian tribes of the upper Great Lakes. Here they met an obstacle which hitherto they had found unimportant, namely, the French alliance. Until this time the French had defended the St. Lawrence valley, but not the outlying regions. Now La Salle, Tonty, Perrot, Duluth, and La Durantaye taught their allies to stand their ground, to build defensive forts, to pursue and capture numbers of the invaders, to fling defiance at the encroaching bands. Fort St. Louis on the Illinois, Fort Ignace at Mackinac, were rendered impregnable to an Indian enemy. From Canada itself successive invasions entered the home territory of the Iroquois; in these expeditions large numbers of the western Indians bore a prominent part.

After the Iroquois invasion in 1680 of the Illinois valley during a period of nominal peace, Governor Frontenac demanded that the Five Nations should make reparation. A great council was held at Montreal, wherein were delegates from all the northwestern tribes. The Westerners asked and received from Frontenac permission to defend themselves if attacked, but not to carry war parties into the Iroquois cantons, since he did not then despair of bringing the Five Nations to a sense of responsibility for the peace they had formerly signed.[1] At this stage of the negotiations Frontenac was recalled to France, leaving to La Barre, utterly unfamiliar with Indian diplomacy, the work of keeping the peace. La Barre called to his counsel the leading men of the colony, and they unanimously decided that the Iroquois could be brought to terms only by a show of force. The governor thereupon represented to the king that more troops and arms must be furnished to Canada or "the country is lost."[2]

In pursuance of his scheme for subduing the Iroquois, La Barre encouraged the western Indians to act offensively as well as defensively. The western country was immediately thrown into a turmoil. Officers and traders everywhere prepared for war. La Salle, who had returned from the mouth of the Mississippi, expecting to go at once to France, turned back from Mackinac at the threat of war, in order to assist Tonty to put the Illinois in a state of defense. They built at this time Fort St. Louis on the impregnable rock on the Illinois River near Utica, sent their men to erect an outlying post at Chicago, and bound together a great Algon-

[1] *N. Y. Colon. Docs.*, ix, 163-164, 168, 193.
[2] *Ibid.*, 196-197; *Jes. Rel.*, lxii, 157-165.

quian confederacy against the Iroquois power.³ These measures defeated the Iroquois raids of 1682⁴ and animated the spirit of the western Indians. Then in August, 1683, La Salle took what proved to be his final farewell of the land for which he had hoped and suffered so much, and set forth for France. Thereafter this man of imperial ideas disappears from northwestern history, to meet five years later a tragic death on the plains of Texas. His plans were too extensive to be accomplished by the means at his command. To operate over so vast a region as he prepared to occupy, required as a base a colony of denser population than that of New France, as well as better means of transportation. His successor in the Illinois was Henry de Tonty, who confined himself to maintaining his post, defending it against the Iroquois, encouraging settlement, and building up a small unit of civilization in the Illinois valley. With less breadth of vision and less ambition for great enterprises, Tonty nevertheless succeeded where La Salle had failed.

Tonty's cousin Duluth was more like La Salle in the eagle view of his task. He proposed to add an empire to New France by exploring and annexing the headwaters of the Mississippi, by finding routes thither from the uppermost of the Great Lakes, and by exploring thence a route to the Pacific. Not so successful a courtier as La Salle, however, on his visit to Paris he obtained neither concessions nor assistance in his project of discovering a land route to the western ocean. Nothing daunted, he made plans on his own behalf, obtained a

[3] For Fort St. Louis, see *Report of Illinois Park Commissioners*, 1912, 31-35; see also preceding chapter for the Algonquian Confederacy. On the Chicago post, see Margry, ii, 186; and a letter from La Salle dated September 1, 1683, in Chicago Historical Society, printed in *Canadian Archives Report*, 1905, i, p. lx-lxi.

[4] Margry, i, 611; *Jes. Rel.*, lxii, 71-95.

license for trade in the West, and by the summer of 1683 he arrived at Mackinac ready for a plunge into the unknown.[5] He found the West seething with revolt. The first task must be to reclaim the western tribes for the French alliance; already French traders had been killed on Fox River and in Lake Superior; such men as Zacherie Jolliet and Pierre le Sueur, who were operating in the West, must be safeguarded from Indian treachery.[6] The route through Lake Superior was especially dangerous. Duluth determined to make his way thither by the Fox-Wisconsin and the Mississippi, and to enlist the cooperation of the Sioux before entering Lake Superior. He arrived at the mission house at De Pere in September with a party of thirty men, for whom Father Philippe Pierson went as chaplain. Perrot had made the Fox River route safe; so Duluth, passing that way, ascended the Mississippi until he reached the Sioux, who gave him an eager welcome. His old friends among this tribe now renewed their allegiance, broken in 1680, and assured Duluth of their loyalty to the French alliance. Thence he set forth for Lake Superior, probably building at this time a small supply post at the St. Croix portage, the earliest fort in interior Wisconsin.[7]

Duluth planned to control the fur trade of Lake Superior by uniting all its neighboring tribes in the French alliance before pushing westward for exploration. In pursuance of this plan he sent his brother, Claude Greysolon Sieur de la Tourette, northward to negotiate with the Assiniboin and Cree, who were accustomed to trade with the English on Hudson Bay.

[5] Margry, ii, 309-310, 332; vi, 35-36.
[6] *Conseil Souverain*, ii, 594; *Canadian Archives Report*, 1905, i, p. xxxv.
[7] *Wis. Hist. Colls.*, xvi, 111; Franquelin's map of 1688, frontispiece.

La Tourette was successful in gaining the good will of these tribes, and built on Lake Nipigon at the mouth of Ombabika River a post called Fort La Tourette.[8] Meanwhile, Duluth was counciling with the Assiniboin at the Kaministiquia portage, where to facilitate his westward exploration he built another supply post, probably on the site of his earlier post of 1679.[9]

Before, however, he could leave Lake Superior a case of Indian treachery must be punished. He had learned while at the Sault that two Frenchmen had been killed at Keweenaw Bay and their bodies concealed. When the evil deed was discovered, no one dared to arrest the murderers because of their powerful relatives in the great Chippewa confederacy. Duluth, with his customary promptness and courage, at once undertook the task. Aided by Jean Peré, whom he found trading in Lake Superior, he seized the guilty assassins, took them under guard to St. Ignace, and after a fair trial forced their own tribesmen to execute the murderers. Such high-handed justice cowed the tribesmen; no more could they hope to expiate the death of white men by the gift of a few beaver skins. Thenceforth for many years Frenchmen were safe on the waters of Lake Superior, and a wholesome respect for white men's justice was instilled into the savages' minds.[10]

Duluth now once more attempted his cherished plan of pushing westward toward the western sea. He had arrived at the Kaministiquia portage, and was making there his preparations when a messenger from Mackinac summoned him to join an expedition against the

[8] Margry, vi, 50. The fort is shown on the following maps: Jaillot, 1685; Franquelin, 1688, frontispiece.

[9] Thwaites, editor, *Lahontan's New Voyages* (Chicago, 1905), i, 316. See also *ante*, chapter x, note 54.

[10] *Wis. Hist. Colls.*, xvi, 114-125.

Iroquois. La Barre after two years' waiting was prepared to move against the common enemy.

Meanwhile the other French officers in the West were suppressing disaffection and consolidating French interests. La Barre had sent as commandant-in-chief for the upper country an experienced soldier, Olivier Morel Sieur de la Durantaye, a former officer in the regiment of Carignan.[11] La Durantaye first put Mackinac into a state of defense, enlarging and strengthening two small palisaded forts at this place; then, accompanied by Nicolas Perrot, he set out to adjust the distracted affairs at La Baye. No one knew as well as Perrot how to deal with the turbulent tribesmen; by a master stroke of boldness he offered to sacrifice himself to their resentment. "Put me in your kettles, ' he demanded, "and satiate yourself with the flesh you have wanted."

"What son," replied the Indian orator, "will eat his own father, from whom he has received life? Thou has given us birth, since thou has brought us the first iron."[12]

La Durantaye and Perrot were soon able to reestablish the allegiance of the tribes around Green Bay. While engaged in these negotiations they were startled by the arrival of fifteen white men, who had been found by a group of Outagami hunters in a starving and nearly naked condition on the southern coast of Lake Michigan and brought to their village. These men belonged to a large trading expedition headed by René le Gardeur Sieur de Beauvais, who, it

[11] Margry, ii, 332-333.
[12] *Wis. Hist. Colls.*, xvi, 102-103. There seems to have been no post at Green Bay, except the buildings around the mission house at De Pere. Probably Perrot had a warehouse or magazine at this place. Deborah Martin, "Border Forts of the Great Lakes," in *Wisconsin Club Woman*, February, 1923, 3.

was an open secret, was La Barre's agent for western exploitation. He and his men had been set upon and pillaged by the Iroquois near the St. Joseph portage; their lives, however, had been spared, since the Iroquois had not yet openly broken their treaty with the French.[13] La Durantaye feared that this Iroquois war party, now well equipped with arms, would do still more mischief in the West. His fears were soon justified when a messenger arrived from the Illinois, bringing word that the Iroquois were besieging Fort St. Louis. La Durantaye at once set out in person for the relief of that post.[14] He arrived too late to assist at the siege, for after six days' intensive fighting the enemy departed without having done much damage, except to capture some wandering Illinois, who later escaped.[15] After conferring with the officers at Fort St. Louis, La Durantaye retired by way of the Chicago portage, where he rebuilt and enlarged La Salle's small post, and left in it a garrison which was maintained for several years.[16]

The attack upon Beauvais's party and the seizure of his goods angered the French governor to the point of exasperation. He made vigorous efforts to undertake the punitive expedition into the Iroquois country which he had been preparing ever since his arrival in Canada. As a first precaution he wrote to the English governor of New York to desist from selling arms and ammuni-

[13] *Wis. Hist. Colls.*, xvi, 110-113; Margry, ii, 338-345.
[14] Tonty had been relieved as commandant at Fort St. Louis by the Chevalier de Baugy. It was Tonty, however, who successfully defended the fort on the occasion of the Iroquois attack.
[15] Kellogg, *Early Narratives*, 305-306; Margry, i, 613-614; *Canadian Archives Report*, 1885, p. xliv.
[16] The question of a French post at Chicago has been much discussed. For evidence, see Tonty's statements in Kellogg, *Early Narratives*, 305, 307; Franquelin's map of 1688, frontispiece; and references *ante*, note 3.

tion to the savages, then sent to La Durantaye at Mackinac to prepare a flank attack on the Iroquois territory. The western Indians were loath to undertake a new Iroquois war; they knew only too well the danger of stirring that nest of angry wasps, who swarmed everywhere upon the warpath, and made the lives of all their enemies unsafe. It took all the arts of Perrot and the powerful influence of Duluth to persuade the Ottawa and their allies to join the expedition. Finally, however, they set out in a flotilla of canoes, four hundred vigorous warriors. On Lake Erie they were joined by the Green Bay contingent of one hundred Winnebago, Sauk, Fox, and Menominee tribesmen. This was the first war party of Indians to traverse the Great Lakes at the behest of the white man.

The expedition of 1684 was a failure from the beginning. La Barre in notifying the English governor had foredoomed his enterprise. Dongan not only warned the Five Nations, but sold them liberal war supplies. La Barre never got beyond the eastern end of Lake Ontario; there, with most of his soldiers sick, he was forced to sign a peace with the enemy, a disgraceful peace, by which he abandoned the French allies in the West to Iroquois fury, in exchange for a brief immunity for the St. Lawrence colony. The Westerners first heard of this fiasco at Niagara. In despair they broke into small groups and made the best of their way homeward.[17] When the news of

[17] Contemporary accounts of La Barre's expedition of 1684 are: Abbé de Belmont, *Histoire du Canada*, in Literary and Historical Society of Quebec *Transactions*, i, 18, 37; Thwaites, *Lahontan*, i, 66-87; Cadwallader Colden, *History of the Five Nations of Canada* (London, 1755), i, 73; McIlwain, *Wraxall's Abridgment of the New York Indian Records* (Cambridge, Mass., 1915), 13-14; Blair, i, 232-242. See also Parkman, *Count Frontenac and New France under Louis XIV* (Boston, 1877), 89-115.

La Barre's failure reached France, he was at once recalled, and a far abler governor, Marquis Denonville, was sent to Canada in his stead.

French prestige in the West now touched its lowest point. The astute western chiefs knew that they had been betrayed. They only awaited the opportunity to go over to the Iroquois and to transfer their trade to the English. That opportunity soon arose. A French deserter, Marion *dit* La Fontaine, who came in to Albany offered to lead the way to the Ottawa country. Captain Johannes Roseboom accepted his offer and fitted out an expedition in eleven canoes, which in the autumn of 1685 reached Mackinac in safety. The usual trading season at this post had closed. The French officers had scattered to other posts. Duluth had gone to Lake Superior, Tonty had started on his search for La Salle at the Mississippi's mouth, La Durantaye was at Chicago adjusting a quarrel between the Illinois and Miami, Perrot was at Green Bay composing another intertribal quarrel.[18] La Fontaine was well known at Mackinac, where the English merchant made a splendid trade, and easily obtained the Indians' promise to visit him at Albany in company with the Seneca. This first English flotilla on the upper lakes returned triumphantly to Albany, believing that the French monopoly of the Great Lakes was broken.

The French officers in the Northwest were much alarmed. They reported the invasion to their governor, Denonville, who protested to the English governor of New York against permitting his traders upon the upper lakes. "'Tis a hard thing," wrote Dongan curtly, "that all Countryes a Frenchman walks over in America must belong to Canada." The French must see to their own monopoly. Duluth was once

[18] Kellogg, *Early Narratives*, 306-307; Blair, i, 356-363.

more summoned from his western exploration to build a fort, which he called St. Joseph, on the St. Clair River. The Toronto portage, however, was left unguarded, and through this entrance French renegades and Indians led a second expedition in 1686. Seven Dutch traders reached Mackinac, and again succeeded in taking away a full cargo of beaver.[19]

While Mackinac was the scene of these English exploits, French traders were making great progress in the heart of Wisconsin, and several fur trade posts were therein established. After La Barre's disgraceful fiasco Perrot went down to the colony, obtained a large invoice of trade goods, and a commission of some sort for commanding at Green Bay.[20] Perrot had now the opportunity he had long sought, of attempting "some discovery of importance." He first followed on Duluth's track, and the autumn of 1685 found him on the upper Mississippi. Overtaken by cold weather before he could mount to the Sioux country, he built a wintering post "at the foot of a mountain, behind which was a great prairie abounding in wild beasts." Although it was chosen for utility, the French trader must have recog-

[19] *N. Y. Colon. Docs.*, iii, 436, 476, 514, 527; ix, 277, 287, 336; Blair, i, 250; ii, 21-25; Alvord and Bidgood, *First Explorations in the Trans-Allegheny Region*, 437; *A Brief History of the Ancestors and Descendants of John Roseboom* (Cherry Valley, N. Y., 1895), 21-23; Helen Broshar, "The First Push Westward of the Albany Traders," in *Mississippi Valley Historical Review*, vii, 232-235. For Duluth's post, see *Wis. Hist. Colls.*, xvi, 125-127.

[20] Blair, i, 242; ii, 252; *Wis. Hist. Colls.*, x, 60, 299. The nature of Perrot's commission has been much discussed. As he was not an army officer, he could not have had the rank of Tonty or La Durantaye. La Barre, however, saw the importance of securing his interest because of his powerful influence with the Indians of what is now Wisconsin. No doubt Perrot was also acting for La Barre in the fur trade. He named his upper Mississippi post St. Antoine for his patron, who in all probability gave him the ostensorium in order to secure the Jesuits' interest.

nized the beauty of the site, beside the mountain that steeps itself in the water—Mount Trempealeau, facing the cliffs behind which each night the sun drops in golden glory.[21]

The winter passed slowly, its only incident being an alliance with the Iowa tribesmen. Then when the ice ran out of the Mississippi, the white men abandoned their temporary post, built for themselves canoes, and ascended to Lake Pepin, where they erected Fort St. Antoine.[22] There Perrot began a brisk trade with the Sioux, which netted him large profits.[23] Denonville, upon his arrival at Quebec, ordered the Mississippi trader to return to the colony, but Perrot evaded the orders upon one pretext or another until the spring of 1687. In the meanwhile he built Fort St. Nicolas at the mouth of the Wisconsin,[24] and held councils at the De Pere mission house with all the Wisconsin tribesmen. On this visit to De Pere Perrot presented to the mission the chased silver ostensorium, which still exists, the most splendid as well as the earliest relic of the French régime in our state. It must have been imported from France, and no doubt was ordered by Perrot while he was in the colony in 1684-85. It may

[21] See Wis. Hist. Soc., *Proc.*, 1915, 111-123, on the discovery of this post. See also *Wis. Mag. of Hist.*, vii, 340-344. The remains at Trempealeau are the only ones of a French post so far found on Wisconsin soil. In honor of Perrot the new state park, embracing Trempealeau Mountain, has been named Perrot Park.

[22] Fort St. Antoine was in Pepin County, north of the mouth of Chippewa River. See accompanying map drawn for Draper in 1887, and discussion in *Wis. Hist. Colls.*, x, 369-371. No remains of this post have yet been found.

[23] Blair, ii, 25.

[24] Considerable controversy developed over the site of Fort St. Nicolas. *Wis. Hist. Colls.*, x, *passim*. It seems to have been located at or near Prairie du Chien. Gardner Stickney, "Nicolas Perrot," in *Parkman Club Papers, No. 1.*, p. 12, note; Franquelin's map of 1688, frontispiece.

THE PERROT OSTENSORIUM

have been forwarded to him by his patron La Barre. Upon its oval base is engraved "Ce soleil a este donne par M.ʳ Nicolas Perrot a la Mission de St. Francois Xavier en la Baye des Puants 1686."[25] It was used to take the place of a crude copper or lead ostensorium that had been made at the mission house itself.[26]

Perrot has related at considerable length his experiences among the Wisconsin Indians during this period of his command. The tribes about Green Bay were hereditary enemies of the Sioux, and were incensed at the French for carrying thither goods and firearms. At one time when Perrot had been absent for some weeks, he returned to find Fort St. Antoine besieged by a motley army of Foxes, Kickapoo, and Mascouten, who were purposing to break into the fort and plunder the storehouses for arms to be used against the Sioux. Perrot found his little garrison of fifteen men weary with keeping at bay their importunate allies. He thereupon sent word to the invaders that he wished to see their principal chiefs only. Six having been admitted to his presence, he ordered them seized and threatened to execute them if they would not command their forces to retire. Then as these fierce chiefs weakened in their purpose, he made them a few presents and told them that the gate to the Sioux country was barred to them, when this large concourse slowly dispersed.[27]

[25] *Wis. Hist. Colls.*, viii, 199-202. This beautiful silver altar-piece was found at Green Bay in 1802 and preserved by the Grignon family until the opening of the first Catholic church in 1823, when it was used in the service. The priest Father Badin carried it to Detroit about 1828, where it was recognized and recovered for the use of the Green Bay diocese in 1838. The bishop of Green Bay has deposited it in the State Historical Museum.

[26] Margry, ii, 179.

[27] Blair, ii, 16-20.

By such methods as this Perrot succeeded in holding the fort and conducting trade with rival tribes to his and his patron's great advantage. He was still on the Mississippi when news reached him that an Iroquois war party had massacred a Miami village near Chicago. Great was the consternation in the West, and the Jesuits were accused of being party to the massacre since Father Allouez had urged the Miami to settle in that vicinity.[28] On account of this fresh injury, and to avenge ancient wrongs, the Westerners were eager to join the punitive expedition which the new governor set on foot in 1687 against the Seneca, the westernmost and most numerous of the Iroquois confederates.

While the French governor was planning to punish the Seneca, the English traders were preparing a new expedition to the upper lakes. Johannes Roseboom led the first division of twenty canoes with fifty *voyageurs*, wintered in the Seneca country, and when the lakes were opened in 1687 started for Mackinac. A second division under the charge of Major Patrick McGregory left Albany in the early spring, all unaware of the French preparations for a war expedition.

Denonville had at command eight hundred regulars, with Canadians and mission Indians enough to double that number. He counted on an equally large contingent from the West. The chief difficulty was the danger of miscarriage in operating over so vast a territory. "The distances are terrible," he reported to France. The plan of campaign "looks very well on paper, but the business remains yet to be done." The western division was officered by the same leaders as those of La Barre's expedition. Perrot collected the Wisconsin Indians, and leaving a small garrison at Fort St.

[28] Blair, ii, 16.

Antoine hastened to De Pere, where he stored his peltry, and started for Mackinac at the head of one hundred Potawatomi, Menominee, and Winnebago. The Miami, panting for revenge, had gone in advance. The Foxes, Kickapoo, and Mascouten went overland and rendezvoused at Duluth's post on St. Clair River. Thither Tonty also brought two hundred Illinois and Shawnee. The Mackinac contingent, coming down Lake Huron to the same post, arrested the English traders under Roseboom; in Lake Erie the entire force of Westerners captured Major McGregory. At Niagara the expedition halted to await orders from Denonville, who was already at Fort Frontenac.

The western division of this expedition comprised the largest army of these tribesmen ever brought together, and probably the fiercest and most unstable combination that could be imagined. Only the experience and ability of such officers as Tonty, Duluth, Perrot, and La Durantaye could control tribes so insubordinate and quarrelsome. Fortunately their stay at Niagara was not prolonged. Orders came from Denonville to join him at once on the south shore of Lake Ontario. The two wings of the army met on July 4 at Irondequoit Bay and prepared for the invasion of the Seneca canton. These Indians were waiting for the French governor and his forces in a cunningly laid ambuscade; nevertheless, the French and allies after a sharp skirmish dispersed the hostiles, leaving many dead upon the field. The French also lost several men, while Father Enjalran, the Mackinac missionary, was seriously wounded. The Seneca now burned their nearest village and fled. Denonville then destroyed and devastated all their country, and on his retreat built a post at Niagara, where a garrison was maintained for over a year.[29]

Denonville's expedition, although better conducted than La Barre's three years earlier, was only a partial success; the Seneca were indeed severely punished, but the other Iroquois groups were aroused to sharp sympathy with the woes of their confederates and sent out more war parties than ever. When the western contingent went home Tonty and Duluth took command, Perrot and La Durantaye going to the colony. Duluth had obtained permission for further western exploration; his post on St. Clair River was therefore placed in the charge of a new officer, the now famous Baron de Lahontan. When the Westerners arrived at Mackinac, bad news awaited the traders; the mission house at De Pere, in which was stored a fortune in furs, had been set on fire by malcontents and entirely consumed.[30] Perrot was ruined; when the news reached Canada the governor allowed him, in return for his services, to take out a license for the next year free of cost; Denonville also recommended La Durantaye, Tonty, and Duluth for promotion and reward.[31]

While Perrot during the winter of 1687-88 was in the colony, he met the king's hydrographer, Jean Baptiste Franquelin, to whom he gave much information about the countries west of the Great Lakes. From Tonty and

[29] For the best modern account of Denonville's expedition, see Parkman, *Frontenac*, 139-157. Printed sources are *N. Y. Colon. Docs.*, iii, 436-437, 527; ix, 300, 316, 336-344, 358-369; Blair, i, 250; ii, 21-25; Belmont, *Histoire*, 39-46; Kellogg, *Early Narratives*, 306-312; Thwaites, *Lahontan*, 118-133; *Journal redigé par le Chevalier de Baugy* (Paris, 1883), 53-127. See also Judge Girouard, "L'Expedition du Marquis de Denonville," in Can. Roy. Soc., *Proc.*, 1899, sec. i, 87-101.

[30] Blair, ii, 25. The ostensorium may have been buried to save it from this conflagration.

[31] *N. Y. Colon. Docs.*, ix, 343, 350-351, 354, 370.

Duluth, Franquelin also secured information which he embodied in his great map of 1688, the most complete map of New France issued in the seventeenth century.[32]

The summer of 1688 found Perrot and Duluth once more at La Baye, again employed in adjusting disputes between rival tribesmen. The Foxes had declared that no goods should be carried to the Sioux. Duluth opposed to their threats three hundred well-loaded guns, and they capitulated to superior force. Duluth then, by the Fox-Wisconsin route, visited the Sioux country, thence went on to the Assiniboin, leaving Perrot to follow, after adjusting all tribal feuds at Green Bay.

Duluth and his brother La Tourette were employed during the succeeding year in asserting French sovereignty over the far Northwest, in interfering with the monopoly of the English Hudson's Bay Company, and in tapping for the French the greatest fur-bearing country on the continent. La Tourette at his post on Nipigon Lake had the embarrassment of success; he called in so great a host of customers that he had not goods enough to supply them, and in the spring of 1689 he set out for Montreal in order to obtain an enlarged amount; he brought down word also of the great mineral wealth of the north country.[33] Duluth himself proceeded to his former post at Kaministiquia, prepared once more for the overland discovery he had planned for ten years. But this was not to be. Early in the summer of 1689 he received a summons to return to the colony, from whence he never again revisited the West. The exposure and hardships of an explorer's life had told upon his frame, and he had contracted a painful disease which made further voyaging impossible. By July 22 he was at Montreal, signing a fur trade con-

[32] See frontispiece.
[33] *N. Y. Colon. Docs.*, ix, 343-344.

tract for partnership; the next year he was promoted to a captaincy, when he was reported "highly honorable, a brave and experienced officer, active in business matters, of high repute, and devoted to the service."[34] This was high praise, but not undeserved. Duluth made one more expedition into the wilderness, when in 1696 he was sent to command for Count Frontenac at the fort that bore his name. There Duluth must have met many of his old comrades of western fame as they journeyed down from the upper country and reported the successes and failures of the fur trade, the progress of French discovery in Lake Superior, and the hopes still held of finding a land route to the western sea. But the brave old explorer knew that such triumphs were no more for him; his was the easy chair, the comforting fire, and the pleasure of remembering past adventures. After the death of Frontenac, Duluth lived quietly in his own house in Montreal, whence in 1710 his brave spirit was released from his tortured frame. He had added to New France an empire in the Northwest, had explored the routes from Lake Superior to the Mississippi, had ventured farther west than any of his confrères, and had made French alliances with the greatest and most populous of the northwestern tribesmen. Well does the noble city at the head of our greatest lake bear the name of this nobleman of Old and New France—Daniel Greysolon Sieur Duluth.[35]

Duluth's successor in command of his post of St. Joseph on St. Clair River was a man of another mould and temper. Clever, cynical, inconstant, veering hither

[34] *Canadian Archives Report*, 1899, Suppl., 26.
[35] Kellogg, *Early Narratives*, 327-328; William McLellan, "A Gentleman of the Royal Guard," in *Harper's Magazine*, September, 1893; "Death of Dulhut," in Can. Roy. Soc., *Proc.*, 1903, sec. ii, 39-47.

and thither with each wind of rumor, Louis Armand Baron de Lahontan has had a much wider fame than the Sieur Duluth. Lahontan came to New France in 1683 with reinforcements for La Barre's army, and participated in the expedition of 1684 and in that of Denonville in 1687. After the latter he came west for the first time, and found himself heavily bored by the inaction of a winter's sojourn at his wilderness post. When spring came he abandoned the post at the first excuse, fired the fort, and retreated with his garrison to Mackinac. Here he found orders to return to the colony, but alleging that the year was too far advanced —it was then September—for a safe passage down the lakes, he planned an expedition into the farther West, in which he claimed to have made important discoveries.[36] Just where he went and what he saw has never been definitely ascertained, but it seems certain that his description of eastern Wisconsin is quite accurate, and that in his narrative we have a pen picture of conditions in our region in 1688.

After describing Green Bay with its mouth choked with isles, Lahontan says he came on September 29, 1688, to a "little deep sort of a River" where were several native villages and a Jesuit house. "This is a place of great Trade for Skins and Indian Corn, which these Savages sell to *Coureurs de Bois* as they come and go, it being the nearest and most convenient Passage to the River of Missisipi." The Indians of this place regaled their interested visitor with native dances, "their ridiculous Musick," and a famous feast of white fish, partridges, the breast and tongue of a deer, the feet of a bear, and the tail of a beaver—these being considered the choicest morsels of each kind of game. He especially enjoyed the taste of maple sugar which

[36] Thwaites, *Lahontan*, i, p. xx-xxv, 152-166.

was offered him, and after the feast he was entertained with more songs and dances.[37] This traveler makes no mention of permanent residents or a French post at Green Bay. It seems certain that all activity there centered at the Jesuits' house.

The next day Lahontan started west, his narrative giving a detailed and interesting picture of the Fox-Wisconsin route and of the Indian villages seen thereon. The Fox River he characterized as "Muddy, full of Shelves, and inclosed with a steep Coast, Marshes, and frightful Rocks." The "Ouisconsinc" he said runs from the northeast to the southwest, "and its sides are adorn'd with Meadows, lofty Trees and Firs." After reaching the Mississippi, Lahontan indulged in pages of description of a voyage to an imaginary river which he calls "Long," with unknown tribes thereon. Whether this journey was intended as a satire like Gulliver's voyage to Liliput, or was a deliberate fabrication, has never been determined.[38]

Meanwhile, what of Perrot, whom we left that same summer of 1688 at Green Bay, adjusting tribal feuds? Sometime that autumn he reached his post on Lake Pepin and found the little garrison he had left there safe and well. The Sioux had been restless and had childishly appropriated some of the French goods, which they refused to return. Perrot determined to teach them a lesson they would not soon forget. Pouring some brandy into a cup of water, he set it on fire, telling them that he would in like manner set fire to their lakes and marshes if they did not return the

[37] Thwaites, *Lahontan*, i, 167-170; Deborah Martin, "Border Forts of the Great Lakes," in *Wisconsin Club Woman*, February, 1923, 4-6.

[38] Thwaites, *Lahontan*, i, p. xxxviii-xli. Lahontan's book had a tremendous vogue in Europe and passed through many editions and translations. See bibliography in volume cited, p. li-xciii.

stolen goods. The trick was successful, and soon long lines of Indians were seen hurrying back to Fort St. Antoine with bundles and packages containing the articles they had coveted and willfully appropriated.[39]

In the spring Perrot staged another ceremony which greatly impressed his Indian customers. Before Perrot left Canada orders had been received from Seigneley, the French premier, to take possession again of the western country for France, because of the conduct of the English governor of New York in asserting his right to trade therein.[40] Denonville commissioned Perrot to arrange this matter, since he had participated in a similar ceremony eighteen years earlier at the Sault Ste Marie.[41] Perrot waited for spring weather so that he might conduct his pageant in the open air. At Fort St. Antoine, on the eighth of May, when the tiny leaves of the forests were showing the first hints of green, the ceremony took place. We have no such detailed report of it as we have of the pageant of St. Lusson, but no doubt the methods were similar, and the occasion was made impressive to the watching Indians by all the solemnity and splendor that could be produced by a handful of Frenchmen at this wilderness post. One Jesuit priest, Father Marest, was present; Boisguillot came up to participate from the fort at the mouth of the Wisconsin. Several traders and young Canadian gentlemen were in attendance. The banks and bluffs of the Mississippi echoed and reëchoed to the salvos of musketry, the shouts of "vive le roi," and the chants of the Latin hymns, when Louis XIV was proclaimed king "of the Baye des Puants [Green Bay], the lake and rivers of the Outagami and the Mascouten

[39] Blair, ii, 30-35.
[40] *N. Y. Colon. Docs.*, ix, 372.
[41] See *ante*, chapter ix.

[Lake Winnebago and the lower and upper Fox], Ouiskonche River, that of the Missicipi, the country of the Nadouesioux [Sioux], the rivers St. Croix and St. Peter [Minnesota River], and other places more remote."[42]

In the eighteen years that had elapsed between the taking possession at the Sault and that at Fort St. Antoine, French discovery and occupation had made great progress. In 1671 the Sault was practically the farthest western foothold of New France. By 1689 the eastern half of the Mississippi valley had been traversed, the portages thither from the Great Lakes threaded, the region well mapped. By 1671 a few traders and missionaries had visited Wisconsin; in 1689 the entire region was occupied with strategically placed posts and missions, its tribesmen subdued and drawn into the French alliance. In 1671 interior Wisconsin was an unknown land; in 1689 it was an integral portion of the French empire in North America—a rich source of wealth, a known region of great importance to New France.

[42] Margry, v, 33-34; English translation in *Wis. Hist. Colls.*, xi, 35-36, not quite correct.

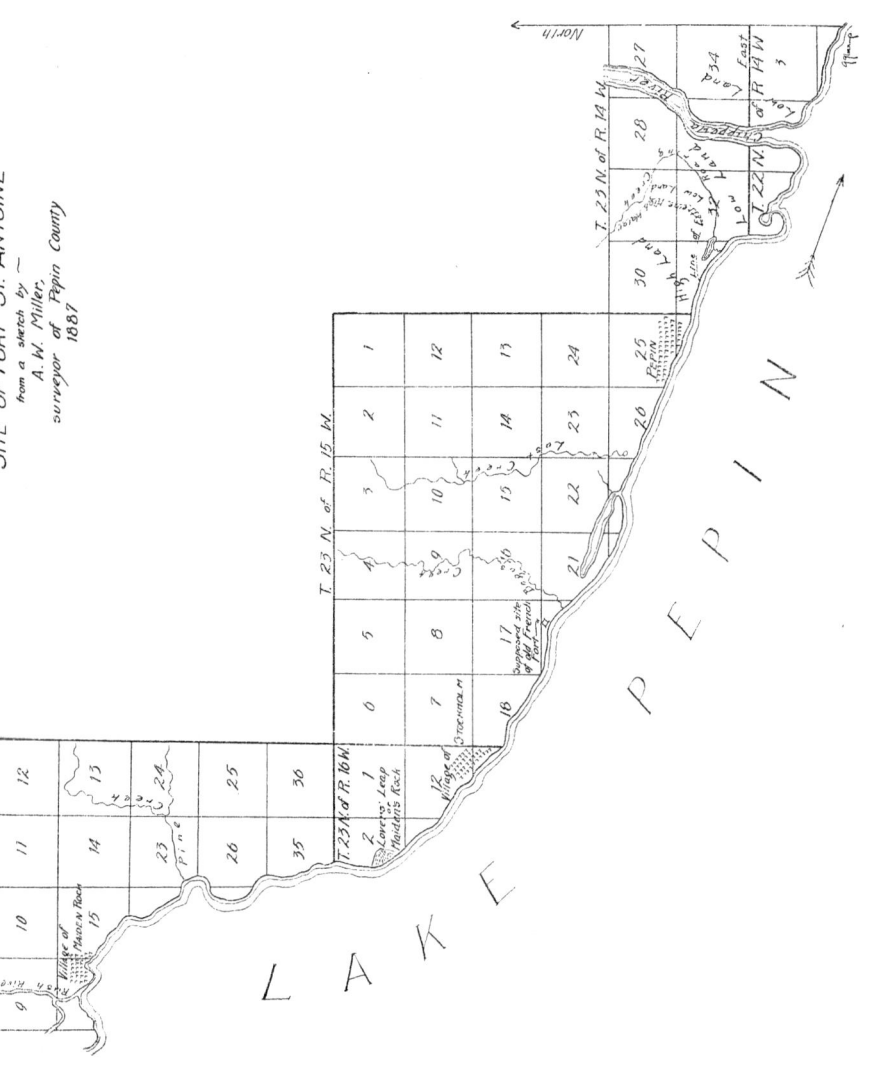

XII. THE WEST EVACUATED, 1689-1701

THE enterprise of the British traders and their evident intention to share in the trade of the upper Great Lakes and the Mississippi valley led not only to renewed diligence on the part of the French officers in the West, but also to the reassertion of French sovereignty in this region. The chief factor in the situation was the cheapness with which the English furnished goods to the Indians, the bargains the latter could obtain either at Albany or through the Iroquois middlemen. A gun could be bought of the English for two beaver skins; at Montreal five were charged for the same weapon. A blanket at Albany sold for a single beaver; at Montreal two beavers were charged for such a covering. It was not, therefore, surprising that such bargains tempted the western tribesmen, or that the Canadians feared to lose the entire profitable business. In time of peace between the crowns of France and England it was difficult to preserve the French monopoly in the West. In time of war there was the danger that the French allies would go over *en masse* to the Iroquois-English trade combination.

It was, therefore, with consternation that the western officers learned that a revolution had occurred in England, which had brought the French king's arch enemy, William of Orange, to that throne. Cautious rather than imaginative, the Grand Monarque had not dreamed that his subsidized ally, James II, could so easily be deposed and driven into exile. France and England were again plunged into war, known in colonial history as King William's War, which greatly affected the destinies of Wisconsin, and seemed for a time to foreshadow complete disaster for the French in North America. Louis XIV took the precaution to send to command in Canada his ablest officer, the one man capable of defending New France and preserving French dominion in this new crisis—the Count de Frontenac.

It was a forlorn hope that the old count, now in his seventieth year, undertook. Even before the news of the English revolution had reached Canada the Iroquois were threatening its very existence. Laying their plans with deep duplicity, they deceived Denonville by promises of peace, and induced him to send for the western allies to join in a treaty. Perrot was summoned from the upper Mississippi, Duluth from the far shores of Lake Superior, to bring the Algonquian chiefs to a great council. Before they had arrived, however, the Iroquois's cup of iniquity was full. The first days of August, 1689, an army of their warriors fifteen hundred strong fell upon the settlements on the exposed portions of Montreal Island, killing, pillaging, and burning at every step. No quarter was shown to French men, women, or children. Two hundred perished at the first stroke. Their fate was happy compared with that of the prisoners, some of whom were tortured before the eyes of their compatriots, others reserved for a more frightful death in the Iroquois cantons.

New France was wild with terror at the massacre of Lachine. Denonville courageously advanced to Montreal, animated the troops, counseled and consoled the habitants, and received as they came in the delegations of western Indians. He could not hide from their keen eyes the truth that the white men feared the Iroquois and were unable to protect either themselves or their allies. The Westerners returned to Mackinac in a sullen mood, firmly determined to ally themselves

THE WEST EVACUATED 245

with the enemy, to massacre the French in the western country, and to take their trade to the English.¹ "These Indians propose," wrote the Mackinac missionary, "to bring [here] at once both the Iroquois and the Fleming [Dutch merchants]—the Iroquois as master in war; the Fleming as master in trade and in commerce."²

The officers at Mackinac counseled together and asked for volunteers to run the terrible risk of reaching the St. Lawrence, and carrying word to the governor of the crisis in the upper country. Not only the hazards of a winter's journey must be braved, but the dangers of an ambush by prowling bands of Iroquois who infested all the routes from the Northwest to Canada. Zacherie Jolliet, younger brother of the explorer, and one companion undertook the desperate venture, and succeeded in reaching Quebec by the last of December, 1689, with the message of disaffection in the West. The Count de Frontenac had but just returned from France, and found all Canada in confusion and alarm; nevertheless he realized the disaster implied in Jolliet's message and responded immediately to the need. The fighting spirit of the old warrior flared up in his response to the disaffected tribesmen. He sent Jolliet back with the message that their ancient father had now returned and was fully able to protect them, that he was preparing to teach the Iroquois a lesson, and that they would soon hear of their punishment.³ Nor did he leave the matter to words alone. He chose one of his ablest officers, Louis de la Porte Sieur de Louvigny, and sent him to Mackinac with a relief party of nearly one hundred and

¹ *Jes. Rel.*, lxiv, 23-39; *Wis. Hist. Colls.*, xvi, 134-135.
² *Jes. Rel.*, lxiv, 29.
³ *N. Y. Colon. Docs.*, ix, 448-451.

fifty Canadian soldiers. Perrot was dispatched with the same contingent, but Duluth was retained for advice and assistance in the colony itself.[4]

Louvigny's detachment had the good fortune to defeat an Iroquois war party on Ottawa River and to capture one chieftain alive. As the relief party neared Mackinac, the captive was placed in the bow of a canoe and forced to sing as he approached, in the fashion of a victorious return from an Indian raid. All Mackinac rushed to the beach to see the canoes come in, and received the Frenchmen with demonstrations of joy and volleys of musketry.[5] The plotters among the tribesmen were deeply impressed with the recovery of the Canadian morale, and with the dangers of coquetting with an Iroquois alliance; all the more that Governor Frontenac had sent them a message that the Iroquois cantons were merely muskrat cabins in a marsh, which he now proposed to drain and burn.[6] They abandoned their rebellion, when the French at Mackinac breathed freely once more and the ordinary processes of trade were resumed.

Perrot, or "Little Indian Corn," to give him his Indian nickname, was sent to Green Bay to quell the disaffection in that quarter. The Foxes, who had always had a secret leaning toward the Iroquois alliance, were planning to please the enemy by putting to death the French traders, who, all unwitting of the national disaster, were about to bring down their year's furs from the upper Mississippi. In turbulent humor several of this tribe had visited the mission house, and had held a naked sword over the head of the

---

[4] *N. Y. Colon. Docs.*, ix, 463, 465; *Wis. Hist. Colls.*, xvi, 135. For a sketch of Louvigny, see *Wis. Hist. Colls.*, v, 108-110.

[5] Blair, ii, 44-53; *Wis. Hist. Colls.*, xvi, 135-144.

[6] Blair, ii, 50.

Jesuit blacksmith, threatening him with instant death if he did not repair and sharpen their tomahawks. Then with these weapons they had returned to their village and laid an ambuscade for the expected French traders from the Northwest. A friendly Winnebago chief, powerless to aid the French except by strategy, reported to the Foxes that Perrot was advancing against the renegades of Green Bay with an army of twelve hundred French and Indians; thereupon these tribesmen abandoned their ambuscade and retired precipitately to their village.

The Winnebago chief then hastened to the entrance of Green Bay to meet Perrot, who was coming, not with an army, but with his own unaided wits to counteract the savages' treachery. The Frenchman gave the friendly chief a gold-braided jacket to recompense him for his useful deceit; then taking advantage of the situation, Perrot ordered him to tell the Foxes that he had sent back all but a few of his men, that he had plenty of ammunition, that he knew of their plots, and that he would not answer for the consequences if he met *en route* any such deceitful tribesmen as they had proved to be.

The ruse succeeded admirably; the great Fox chief did not dare wait for Perrot's coming, but hastened off on a western raid, leaving word with the remnant in his village that he loved Perrot and that every honor was to be shown him.[7] After a like success in cajoling the Miami, Sauk, Potawatomi, and Mascouten, Perrot advanced up the Fox River, and at the village of the Fox Indians was received with every token of endearment and repentance. Two youths "entirely naked, armed as warriors" advanced and laid two packages of beaver at his feet, exclaiming that if these were insuffi-

[7] Blair, ii, 54-56; *Wis. Hist. Colls.*, xvi, 143-144.

cient to atone for their nation's fault, they would suffer death as a sacrifice to appease the Frenchman's wrath.[8]

Having secured the submission of all the Bay tribes, Perrot set out for his Mississippi posts, and at the portage encountered a canoeful of French traders *en route* from the Sioux country. Frontenac had given orders that all white men trading in these distant places must come in to Mackinac both for their own protection and in order to aid in war expeditions that might be necessary. Fort St. Antoine was, in all probability, abandoned at this time because of these orders. Certain it is that we hear of it no more, and that Perrot was stationed in more southern posts for the next succeeding years.

We first hear of him in a fort on the Mississippi somewhere opposite Dubuque, at a place "very advantageously situated for security from attacks by neighboring tribes."[9] The next year he was ordered to come still nearer the center of western interests, and built a post among the Miami on the Fox River of Illinois.[10]

Meanwhile, Count Frontenac was pushing a vigorous offensive against the English colonies and justifying his choice as governor in these critical times. His officers carried fire and sword into New York, and spread terror to the gates of Albany, while the governor himself repulsed a powerful New England fleet from the

[8] *Wis. Hist. Colls.*, xvi, 147-149.
[9] *Ibid.*, x, 330-333; xvi, 151; Blair, ii, 59, 66.
[10] Blair, ii, 103; *Wis. Hist. Colls.*, xvi, 161; *N. Y. Colon. Docs.*, ix, 570; Margry, v, 72. This post, formerly believed to have been on the Kalamazoo River, Michigan, is now thought to have been situated at the "Maramech" of Franquelin's map of 1684, and the "Maramec" of the Franquelin map of 1688, near Fox River of the Illinois. See J. F. Steward, *Lost Maramech and Earliest Chicago* (Chicago, 1902), 22-29, 70-75. The word "maramech," although Algonquian for a fresh-water fish, was no doubt the clan title of one branch of the Miami.

walls of Quebec. The news of these actions was speeded to Mackinac by a special messenger, Sieur de Courtemanche.[11] It was a desperate hazard this young officer ran, for the Iroquois war bands infested every portion of the country between Montreal and Mackinac. Courtemanche, however, was a native Canadian, a descendant of daring explorers, and by his adroitness and address he with his ten followers won their way through to their destination, and brought good cheer to the harassed officers of the Northwest. All negotiations between the western tribesmen and the Iroquois were broken off, and war parties were continually raised for raids into the enemies' territories. So successful were these western attacks, that the Seneca abandoned their habitat and withdrew to the canton of the Cayuga.[12]

Never in all the stress of danger on the St. Lawrence did Frontenac forget the needs of the West; he knew well that should the dam of French control in that region break, the colony itself would be swept out of existence by an engulfing flood of renegade Indians. Regulars, who could be ill spared from the defense of Canada, were sent to garrison the little western posts where the veteran officers kept their guard—Louvigny at St. Ignace, where he rebuilt and strengthened the Mackinac post;[13] Tonty and La Forest in the Illinois, where a new post was built about this time on Lake

[11] Augustin le Gardeur de Repentigny de Courtemanche was a grandson of Jean Nicolet; born in 1663, he served with distinction during Frontenac's rule, and was sent by his successor as an envoy in 1706 to Boston. There his manner and personality evoked very favorable comment. He appeared several times in the West in the decade following this journey of 1691, for which see *N. Y. Colon. Docs.*, ix, 496, 516; Margry, v, 53.

[12] *N. Y. Colon. Docs.*, ix, 516.

[13] Margry, v, 54.

Peoria.[14] The Miami tribesmen, who had dangerous connections with the western Iroquois, and leanings toward English trade, were kept under surveillance by the Sieur de Mantet at Chicago and Courtemanche on St. Joseph River.[15] In 1693 a large raiding party of Iroquois was defeated in an attack on this latter post, by which victory Courtemanche saved the farther West from invasion.[16]

Once enlisted in the French cause, the western tribesmen acted their part valiantly. Raiding parties went out from the northern tribes and frequently brought in prisoners and scalps. When Tonty was taunted with the supineness of the Illinois, he had an affidavit made that these Indians had brought in nearly five hundred Iroquois scalps since the war began.[17]

All these raiding parties, however, seriously interfered with the fur trade; even when furs were collected at the interior posts the danger of shipping them to the colony was too great to be encountered. For three years after Frontenac's return not a trade canoe came down from the West. All Canada was in straits; complaints of the governor's policy were heard on every side. In 1693 Frontenac sent a message to the western officers to bring down the furs at any hazard. Perrot and Tonty rendezvoused at Mackinac and raised so large a fleet that they could defy the menace of the Iroquois. As this great flotilla of canoes swept down the Ottawa and out into the St. Lawrence, the inhabitants were at first greatly startled and alarmed. The cry

[14] Alvord, *Illinois*, 100.
[15] Margry, iv, 9; v, 54, 61, 71; *Mich. Pion. and Hist. Colls.*, xxxiii, 47.
[16] Margry, v, 71-72.
[17] *Ibid.*, iv, 5, note; *N. Y. Colon. Docs.*, ix, 532, 535-537; Blair, ii, 85-88.

went up that the Iroquois were upon them. When, however, they ascertained that the invaders were friendly tribesmen, and that they had brought the greatest harvest of furs that had ever come from the western country, the mercurial spirits of the population rose with a bound. The governor became the most popular person in Canada. Proud noble that he was, he did not disdain to come in person to Montreal, and mingle freely with the crowds at the great fur fair on the plains without the walls of that city. He was received with loud huzzas, pronounced the savior of the country, the friend of its debtors, and the harbinger of prosperity. All Canada speculated in furs, and beaver skins became the currency of the day.[18]

The Westerners returned home, elated with their reception and confirmed in their alliance with the French nation. With the return fleet Frontenac sent Pierre le Sueur as successor to Duluth to command in Lake Superior. Le Sueur was born in 1657 in Artois, France, and came to Canada while still a youth under the auspices of the Jesuits, who sent him to their mission at Sault Ste. Marie as *donné*, or assistant. The lure of the fur trade was too great for the youth to resist, and in 1680 he was denounced as a *coureur de bois* in Lake Superior. Two years later he was actively trading among the Sioux on the upper Mississippi, where he became very popular with these tribesmen and is thought to have given his name to Minnesota River, originally called the St. Pierre.[19] By 1689 Le Sueur was with Perrot at Fort St. Antoine, when the latter took possession of the Sioux country; quite prob-

---

[18] Blair, ii, 105-107; *N. Y. Colon. Docs.*, ix, 562-563, 568-570; Charlevoix, *History of New France*, iv, 237-242.

[19] *Conseil Souverain*, ii, 594; *Canadian Archives Report*, 1905, i, p. xxxv.

ably he continued trading in the country of these tribesmen until the great fur fleet went down to Canada in 1693; he returned with a commission to reopen the routes from Lake Superior to the Mississippi, and to bring, if possible, the Sioux within the circle of the French alliance. In pursuance of this policy Le Sueur built a post in 1693 on Chequamegon Bay, on the south shore of Madeline Island,[20] which was, so far as known, the first white man's dwelling in this region since the time of Marquette. The next year Le Sueur built another post at the southwestern end of Duluth's old route via the Brule and St. Croix rivers, probably on Pelée, now Prairie, Island.[21] For two years Le Sueur traversed the western end of Lake Superior and the upper waters of the Mississippi in the interest of New France, and so successful was he that in 1695 a great Sioux chief—the first to visit the St. Lawrence—came down to make alliance with Frontenac. With him Le Sueur also brought an hereditary enemy in the person of a Chippewa chief, who ratified peace between their two nations in the presence of Onontio. Thus were these two great barbarous tribes incorporated among the allies of France, an unstable pact among "a race unsteady as aspens and fierce as wild-cats, full of mutual jealousies, without rules, and without laws, for each was a law unto himself."[22]

[20] Le Sueur's post is thought to have stood on the southwestern shore of Madeline Island, about a half-mile east of Michel Cadotte's post of a century later. The corner posts and chimney of Le Sueur's fort were uncovered some years ago. A tablet was erected in 1925 to mark this site.

[21] Folwell, *Minnesota*, i, 39. This region at the mouth of the St. Croix became in the eighteenth century the battle ground between the Sioux and the Chippewa. In the seventeenth century, however, the Sioux were in full possession.

[22] Parkman, *Frontenac*, 145.

Nous soussignés François de Bourguillon & pierre le sieur sommes convenues de demeure Jacob De ce qui suit a scavoir que moyenant la somme de trente cens livres En argent que moy audit S[r]. De Bourguillot nous demeurerons quittes De Pour les complices Le sieur payeray des premiers effetz qui me viendron. Et oultaoüov[?] que nous aurons En ensemble. De son Repais jusques a ce jour tant de ce qui a Concerne la Communauté de Societé que nous avons Eües Ensemble que pour alimens De Nourir autres affaires + fait Double a montreal le 8e aoust 1695 Ensresence De ...ouvicus Byre reveau Lieutenant general En la justice Du Dmont Real

Truchreau

BOURGUILLOT Lesueur

SIGNATURE OF LE SUEUR, 1695
From a document in the Chicago Historical Society

"The savage's mind," wrote Perrot, "is difficult to understand; he speaks in one way and thinks in another. If his friend's interest accord with his own, he is ready to render him a service; if not, he always takes the path by which he can most easily attain his own ends."[23] This disposition of the tribesmen Perrot constantly had to combat. Although he was skilled in Indian diplomacy, the Mascouten twice pillaged his bales of goods, and finally seized and were about to burn him alive, when by a ruse he escaped to friendly Winnebago and Outagami villages. The latter tribesmen were desirous of attacking the Mascouten for this insult to their friend, but "he obliged them to suspend their anger for the sake of the French nation," saying it would be more pleasing to him if they wreaked their vengeance upon the Iroquois.[24] By these and other inducements he urged continual war parties to set out toward the east. These attacks so told upon the morale of the Iroquois, that in 1694 they sent an embassy to Frontenac to beg for peace. The wary governor realized that this embassy was a mere ruse to secure a temporary immunity; nevertheless the rumor ran through the western country, stimulated no doubt by La Barre's earlier treachery, that Onontio was about to make peace with the common enemy and to abandon his Indian allies. Thereupon Frontenac sent for a western embassy to come to Montreal. Upon their arrival he assured them that he was incapable of such treachery; that the Iroquois envoys had just left him, crestfallen at the ill success of their plans. The western chiefs were now persuaded that all their hope lay in clinging to the cause of France.[25]

[23] *Wis. Hist. Colls.*, xvi, 152.
[24] Blair, ii, 83-89.
[25] *N. Y. Colon. Docs.*, ix, 577-584.

With the returning chieftains the governor sent in this year of 1694 a new commandant for the West in the person of Antoine de la Mothe Sieur de Cadillac. With his advent a new force came to the support of the western commandants and new vigor was infused into the prosecution of the war. Cadillac was no stranger to Indian warfare, having been for years in charge of the eastern provinces of New France in Acadia and Maine.[26] Between him and the Count de Frontenac there was a community of spirit, and the latter trusted the "adroitness, firmness and tact" which Cadillac showed in his management of tribesmen. Cadillac on his part was not pleased with his new appointment. "Mackinac," he wrote, "is the most terrible place imaginable. . . . Neither bread nor meat is eaten there, and no other food to be had there but a little fish and Indian corn."[27] His opinion of Mackinac and the West underwent considerable modification in the three years of his residence there. He became an enthusiastic promoter of western expansion, and ultimately, as we shall see, founded one of its most important settlements.[28]

Even during this period of intercolonial and intertribal warfare the English traders did not cease their efforts to tap the great fur reservoir of interior America. Undismayed by the fate of Johannes Roseboom and Major Patrick McGregory, who not only had their goods confiscated, but were themselves thrown into prison and were released only after protest from the English government, Albany traders found their way

[26] *Maine Historical Collections*, vi, 273-274.
[27] *Mich. Pion. and Hist. Colls.*, xxxiii, 72-96; *N. Y. Colon. Docs.*, ix, 587.
[28] Cadillac's memoir on Mackinac is in Margry, v, 75-132; that portion translated in *Wis. Hist. Colls.*, xvi, 350-363, is misdated. It should not be 1718, for it refers to the period of Cadillac's command, 1694-97.

during this period of warfare among tribes who were classed among the allies of the French. La Salle had, as we have seen, confederated around Fort St. Louis not only the neighboring Indians, but portions of the Shawnee confederacy from the south, and the Mahican from the east. From them he had drawn his personal attendants, who accompanied him on his journeys to Fort Frontenac and to the mouth of the Mississippi. Tonty, more farseeing than his leader, had questioned whether these tribesmen might not be employed in leading strange traders into these western wilds, and the event proved his fears were justified. After La Salle's death and the break-up of his colony, some of the Shawnee drifted eastward and offered to show the way into the Ohio valley. Arent Viele, the interpreter for the Five Nations, was sent with them and for two years traversed the waters that discharge into the Ohio. Upon his return laden with rich furs, a delegation of western Indians came with him, and settling near Minisink made a connecting link between the western tribes and the English. Tonty was alarmed at Arent's tampering with the Miami, and with the knowledge which the Dutch traders acquired of the routes to the Mississippi.[29]

Not only red vagrants but white deserters turned traitor to French interests and led the British into the western valleys. Martin Chartier, who had also been with La Salle on the Illinois, deserted from his service and joined the Shawnee. After several years of wandering he and his band approached the Maryland government, and asked for a settlement in one of the back counties of that province.[30]

[29] *N. Y. Colon. Docs.*, iv, 51, 96-97; *Wraxall's Abridgment*, 19, 22, 24; Margry, iv, 4; Helen Broshar, "The First Push Westward of the Albany Traders," in *Mississippi Valley Historical Review*, vii, 236-240.

[30] Hanna, *Wilderness Trail*, i, 126-134.

Still more serious was the disaffection of a trusted employee of Tonty, who had come west in the train of Baugy in 1683. Jean Couture was a carpenter from Rouen, and being of a roving disposition quickly adapted himself to the life of an American *voyageur*. Tonty took Couture with him on his fruitless voyage of 1685 to the Mississippi's mouth in search of La Salle. At Couture's request Tonty granted him a concession in his seigniory on the Arkansas, and it was Couture who came overland in 1688 and informed his master of the fate that had overtaken La Salle on the Texan plains. Dissatisfied with the meager returns of the Arkansas post, or eager for new adventures, Couture set out sometime in the early nineties and found his way to the tribes dwelling east of the Mississippi. In all probability he mounted that river to the Ohio, thence ascended the Tennessee to its headwaters in Cherokee territory, whence there was already a well-worn traders' path to the Spanish trading posts in Florida.[31]

Couture, however, had no notion of throwing himself into the hands of the Spaniards; he had heard enough of their methods at his post on the Arkansas. Instead he made his way to the colony centering at Charleston, and there created a genuine sensation by his account of gold mines he had discovered, and of the pearl fisheries of the Mississippi River. Companies were formed to explore for mines; but the English, like the French, found greater riches in beaver skins than in precious metals, and soon established strong trade relations with both the Cherokee and the Chickasaw, an alliance which had a disastrous effect on the French in the great valley during all their years of control.[32] The

[31] Franquelin's map of 1688, frontispiece.
[32] Margry, iv, 4; Verner W. Crane, "The Tennessee River as the Road to Carolina: The Beginnings of Exploration and Trade," in *Mississippi Valley Historical Review*, iii, 3-18.

immediate danger, however, was that the English would find a road from these southern tribes to the region of the Great Lakes, a route which one Englishman claimed to have found.[33]

As a barrier to this penetration and as a bulwark in maintaining the western Indians in the French alliance, stood the few small posts about the Great Lakes commanded by the experienced and able officers we have already noted. The French government now, however, proposed that these posts should be evacuated, the officers and garrisons recalled, and the upper country abandoned to the missionaries and aborigines—a measure that nearly wrecked the French empire in the West. May 21, 1696, the king issued a royal ordinance revoking all licenses for the fur trade, prohibiting all colonials from carrying goods to the western country, violation of which edict would be punished by condemnation to slavery in the galleys.[34]

The immediate cause of this sweeping reversal of policy was economic. Duluth, Perrot, and Le Sueur had been too successful in opening the great resources of Lake Superior and the upper Mississippi for the French trade. The flood of beaver was so great that the farmers of Canada reported that the skins on hand were sufficient for ten years to come. According to the regulations for the fur trade all the beaver must be sold at a fixed price to the king's officials, called farmers. These officials then marketed the furs in France and Europe and from their sales paid a portion into the royal treasury. The market distinguished be-

[33] Dr. Daniel Coxe. See Alvord and Bidgood, *First Explorations of the Trans-Allegheny Region*, 232, note.

[34] *Collection de Manuscrits de la Nouvelle France* (Quebec, 1884), ii, 219-221. The king's letter is dated May 26, the edict May 21. *Canadian Archives Report*, 1899, Suppl., 317; see also *N. Y. Colon. Docs.*, ix, 636-639.

tween six sorts of beaver. Winter beaver greased was the best; this consisted of the beaver captured when its pelt was the thickest, and worn by the savages until the long hairs fell out and the skin was soft and supple. The second variety was the half-greased winter beaver; next in value came the greased summer beaver; soft, called *veule*, beaver; dry winter beaver; and, lastly, dry summer beaver. The last-named variety was often badly dressed, and contained holes where the animal had been shot or speared. An especial kind called muscovite was prepared for the Russian trade, consisting of fine winter skins ungreased, with long hairs left on. With the exception of this variety, most of the beaver was used for making hats.[35] Large numbers of beaver hats were made in Normandy; the royal revocation in 1685 of the Edict of Nantes banished hundreds of Huguenots, who were the chief hat manufacturers of the kingdom; thus the market for beaver declined just when the greatest amount began to come from the western country. The fur trade farmers complained to the king; the remedy he adopted was to check the supply at its source, and by scarcity to raise the price.

Other and more potent influences than the distress of the merchants of furs brought out this edict. For fifty years two parties had struggled for ascendancy in New France, with two different policies concerning the western country. That of the governor, backed by the merchants, the army officers, the explorers, and concessionaires, who wished to develop the great West by means of French enterprise, was opposed at every step by the party of Jesuit missionaries, usually headed by the intendant, supported by the bishop and the agricultural portion of New France. The latter party wished to keep the young colonists in the St. Lawrence

[35] Margry, v, 138-153; La Potherie, *Histoire*, i, 267-269.

valley tilling its fields and developing its industries. They saw in the reckless life of the woods the ruin of Canadian youth and of the Indian tribesmen. These two groups may be styled the imperialist and antiimperialist parties of New France.

The anti-imperialists had now secured the ear of the king, through the influence of his Jesuit confessor Père la Chaise, and of his wife Madame de Maintenon, whose piety interested her in Canadian missions. The missionaries represented the great evils connected with the fur trade, among them the constant sale of liquor to the tribesmen notwithstanding stringent regulations against it. But, retorted the imperialists, the Indians, if not furnished with French brandy, will take their furs to exchange for English rum.[36] "How will you be able," demanded Cadillac of the Mackinac missionaries, "to endure the daily exposure of these Neophytes for whom you feel so much affection, to the excessive use of English rum, and to the imbibing of Heresy."[37] The missionaries retorted that not until the great horde of traders and *coureurs de bois* had invaded the West did the Indians learn to crave liquor.[38] They also complained of the profligacy of the young Frenchmen, whom the freedom of the wilderness and the license of savage life led to scandalous excesses. Either the brandy-traders or the missionaries must go, wrote the zealous superior of the western missions.[39] Such representations finally determined Louis XIV to withdraw all traders from the Great Lakes region, and to resort to the earlier method of urging the Indians each year to come down to Canada to trade.

[36] Margry, i, 405-420.
[37] N. Y. Colon. Docs., ix, 648.
[38] Mère de l'Incarnation, *Lettres*, ii, 445, 533; Margry, i, 410.
[39] Jes. Rel., lxv, 191, 201, 215-217.

The promulgation of this edict caused the greatest consternation in Canada. Frontenac, who was on the eve of departing for an expedition into the Iroquois country, saw in this edict the reversal of all his plans for the development of New France, and augured the swift loss of the western country. Given, however, a certain discretion as to the time and manner of enforcement, he temporized with the ordinance, and was two years in carrying it into full effect. The decree did not call for the immediate withdrawal of the garrisons, but a council held at Quebec agreed that no commandant or other officers could exist in the Ottawa country without the privilege of trading. Thus by the close of 1698 the western posts were abandoned, all the traders and *coureurs de bois* called in. Only the "black robes" were left to dwell in the Indian villages and to guide the Indian diplomats upon their difficult path. Cadillac had been relieved at Mackinac in 1697 and had gone to France, Alphonse de Tonty commanding there as his successor. The younger Tonty, Perrot, Le Sueur, Courtemanche, and Mantet evacuated their posts in 1698 and returned to the colony, leaving the land wherein they had labored so long and successfully in building up French authority, to desolation and ruin.[40]

One exception was made to this sweeping edict of abandonment in favor of the veteran officer Henry de Tonty, who with his partner La Forest was allowed to retain his post in the Illinois, but without a garrison, with the permission for beaver trading withdrawn, and with a limitation of their supplies to two

[40] Perrot never returned to the West. He later petitioned that his three sons might visit the Ottawa country to collect his debts. Chicago Historical Society, Schmidt Collection, No. 231. Le Sueur tried in vain to get permission to return. *N. Y. Colon. Docs.*, ix, 696. See facsimile of document with his signature and that of Boisguillot, facing page 252.

canoes a year.⁴¹ These conditions made the French post in Illinois unprofitable. La Forest returned to service with his regiment, while Tonty after a fruitless journey to the Assiniboin Indians in the far North was fain to content himself with the era of small things in the Illinois valley. In 1698 he went down to Montreal to convey in person the two canoe-loads of merchandise permitted by his concession. The bishop of Canada took advantage of this opportunity to dispatch a new mission to the far West. The Jesuits were in control of the Great Lakes region and had sent missionaries whenever practical to the upper Mississippi; but the great tribes of the lower Mississippi had not yet been reached by gospel messengers, and it was this region which a group of young Parisian devotees, called the *Societé des Missions Etrangères*, planned to occupy. The expedition was equipped at considerable expense and headed by a nobleman, François Jolliet de Montigny. Three other missionaries accompanied him, and founded as many missions on the lower Mississippi as their ardor and their adaptability permitted. We are chiefly interested in the narrative of their outward journey furnished by Father Jean François Buisson de St. Cosme, who gives the first detailed description of the western shore of Lake Michigan since the days of La Salle.⁴²

The party left Mackinac on September 15, 1698, and reached the mouth of Green Bay six days later. They would have liked to reach the Mississippi by the Fox-Wisconsin route; but the Fox Indians, having no Perrot to control them, opposed all passage of French

⁴¹ *N. Y. Colon. Docs.*, ix, 700; Alvord, *Illinois*, 109. Henry de Tonty ceded to his brother Alphonse half of his concession in the Illinois, September 10, 1698. See *Louisiana Historical Quarterly*, vi, 576-579, for a facsimile of the document of cession. Henry was never married, so Alphonse and his children were his nearest kin.

⁴² Kellogg, *Early Narratives*, 337-361.

canoes which might carry goods to their enemies, the Sioux. September 28 the flotilla of canoes crossed the mouth of Green Bay from island to island and paddled down the lake coast of Door County to a Potawatomi village, which probably stood on the site of the modern Kewaunee. This village was about to be abandoned for a new site on Green Bay. After purchasing provisions at this place, the flotilla passed on to another small Potawatomi village where a Jesuit missionary had recently wintered and planted a large cross. This would seem to have been at the mouth of Manitowoc River, and the mission and the cross may have given it its present name. There the canoes were windbound for two days, and it was the ninth of October when the little flotilla entered Milwaukee River, which our annalist called the "Milouakik."[43] There the expedition found a mixed village of Foxes, Mascouten, and Potawatomi. The Frenchmen stayed two days, feasting on the wild ducks which were swarming in the marshes. Their next stop was at Kipikaoui, the mouth of Root River. They had been told that by ascending this stream they might portage to the "Pesioui" River (the Pistakee or Fox River of Illinois) and avoid the tedious and stormy lake passage and the Chicago portage. Investigation, however, proved that the upper reaches of Root River were dry; so concluding that the Pistakee would also be low, they had no alternative but to follow the lake shore to Chicago. *En route* their canoes were nearly swamped, and St. Cosme gives a vivid description of the high rolling waves that rush in from Lake Michigan with the autumn winds.

[43] The first mention of this river appears in the narrative of Membré (1679), where it is spelled "Melleoiki." Le Clercq, *Establishment of the Faith*, ii, 133.

THE WEST EVACUATED 263

We will not follow these travelers farther; but while they were voyaging along this tempestuous inland sea, the tempestuous career of the great governor of New France was drawing to a close. During the preceding summer he had received word of the signing of the treaty of Ryswick, whereby the two crowns of France and England came to an agreement, and Louis XIV recognized the legitimacy of William and Mary as sovereigns of Great Britain. Frontenac was ordered not only to announce the peace throughout the New World, but, a still more difficult task, to persuade the Indian allies of the two European nations to lay down their arms, to forego their passion for revenge, and to remain at peace with those against whom they had been so long urged to wage relentless war. The English, moreover, claimed a suzerainty over the Iroquois tribesmen which neither Frontenac nor their own chiefs would admit. "Consider [that] you are the Subjects of the Great King of England under whose Gov^t you have been time out of mind," declared the then governor of New York, Earl Bellomont, to the assembly of their chieftains.[44] "We are the masters on our own lands," was the proud Iroquois reply to this demand.[45] Irritated by the English claim, the great Iroquois chieftains went to see Count Frontenac, who gravely told them that he was their "father," while the English governor was only "brother." "A father is nearer of kin than a brother. Shall not a father chastise his children when he sees fit?"

Indeed sore was the chastisement that Onontio had inflicted upon his rebellious Iroquois "children." The Five Nations had lost more than half of their warriors. They were no longer able to carry the war into the West,

[44] *Wraxall's Abridgment*, 32; Parkman, *Frontenac*, 425.
[45] Charlevoix, *History of New France*, v, 83.

but were obliged to defend themselves against the reiterated attacks of the western tribesmen, and were in desperate need of peace. Before it could be consummated the old count died (November 28, 1698), leaving as a legacy to his successor, Louis Hector Count de Callières, the negotiations for the peace.

The preliminaries of this peace were long and tedious, occupying in all three years. Numerous councils were held, wherein were delivered many of the figurative and passionate orations beloved of the Indian tribesmen. The Iroquois chiefs attempted to deceive the new governor, thinking him less acute and more pliable than the stern old count; but they were soon undeceived concerning their new Onontio. Quiet and expressionless, conciliatory in manner, he nevertheless upheld with a firm hand the dignity and honor of New France, good faith between its Indian allies, and proper subordination for the haughty Iroquois. Despite instructions from the home government to abandon if necessary the western allies, and to disregard the English claims to sovereignty over the Five Nations, Callières went on with his negotiations, neither cajoling nor yielding to the Iroquois, neither granting an inch to the English demands nor relaxing his vigilance for western interests. In the end his policy triumphed; delegation after delegation from the several Iroquois cantons came with insincere offers of peace. Callières met them with demands for the release of all prisoners and the cessation of raids into the western regions. At Mackinac was seething unrest and suspicion; the Hurons tried to desert to the Iroquois, only to find their designs discovered and their plots thwarted. At last at Montreal in September, 1700, preliminaries were drawn, belts exchanged, and the "tree of peace" between the Iroquois on one hand and the French and

THE WEST EVACUATED 265

their Indian allies on the other was firmly planted, with the surrender of hundreds of white and red prisoners as a testimonial of good faith. The famous Huron chief Le Rat (Muskrat), who was considered responsible for the massacre of Lachine, was present on behalf of the western nations, and "touched the quill" with the other chiefs.[46]

There still remained the delivery of prisoners by the western tribesmen and their ratification of the peace between New France and the Iroquois.[47] Father Enjalran, long missionary at Mackinac, and Sieur de Courtemanche, beloved of the Miami tribesmen, were sent in the autumn of 1700 to carry the news of the peace treaty to the tribes of the Great Lakes and to arrange that a delegation of the leading chiefs should come to Montreal for the final ceremonies.[48] The next summer a great concourse gathered at Mackinac and prepared for the long canoe voyage through Georgian Bay and down the Ottawa River to the gates of Montreal. Callières had had a large enclosure built upon the plain without the gates, where in state he received his Indian allies and listened to their impassioned oratory. There were gathered within the great encircling arbor of boughs chiefs from over a score of tribes—Hurons from Mackinac with their long-time allies the Ottawa of the Sable, Kiskakon, Sinago, and La Fourche clans; there were Chippewa tribesmen from Lake Superior;

[46] Blair, ii, 134-136; Charlevoix, *History of New France*, v, 110-111; *N. Y. Colon. Docs.*, ix, 697-699, 708-720. For the English attempts to thwart this peace, see H. L. Osgood, *The American Colonies in the Eighteenth Century* (New York, 1924), i, 467-471.

[47] During the latter years of the war, success had inclined to the side of the western allies. Even in 1698 and 1699, after news of peace in Europe had been received, the successful raids of the Miami and other Westerners had obstructed peace negotiations at Montreal.

[48] *Wis. Hist. Colls.*, xvi, 200-201.

Potawatomi, Sauk, Winnebago, Menominee, Foxes, Kickapoo, and Mascouten from Green Bay and Lake Michigan; Illinois and Miami from the southern end of that lake; Amikwi and Nipissing from Georgian Bay; while from the head streams of the Ottawa River came the Algonkin, Temiscaming, Cree, Gens de Terre or Inlanders; and from the eastern provinces the Abenaki and kindred tribes. All these except the Hurons spoke dialects of the Algonquian language. Opposite to these delegates of the "far Indians" stood the envoys of the Five Iroquois Nations—Agnier, Oneioute, Onontagué, Goyagouin, and Sonontouan; or as the English called them, Mohawk, Oneida, Onondaga, Cayuga, and Seneca tribesmen. Other Iroquois were also present, those of the Sault and of the Mountain—that is, the Mission Iroquois, converted by the Jesuit missionaries, who dwelt among the French at the missions of Sault St. Louis and the Three Mountains near Montreal Island.[49]

The vast concourse of natives in all their barbaric finery drew each day of the treaty negotiations large bands of spectators. The French ladies and officials came out from the towns and the neighboring manor houses. The traders, *voyageurs*, and craftsmen thronged around the improvised camp. The proceedings were carried on with dignity and decorum; nevertheless ludicrous incidents were not wanting to relieve the tedium of the occasion—as when Noro (the Porcupine), a noted Fox chief, came forward crowned with a great French wig which he gravely doffed in salute as though it were a hat. Noro's speech to the governor, however, was highly significant, freighted with warnings of fresh troubles in the West. "I now regard," he said, "the Iroquois as my brother; but I am yet at war with the

[49] *N. Y. Colon. Docs.*, ix, 722-724.

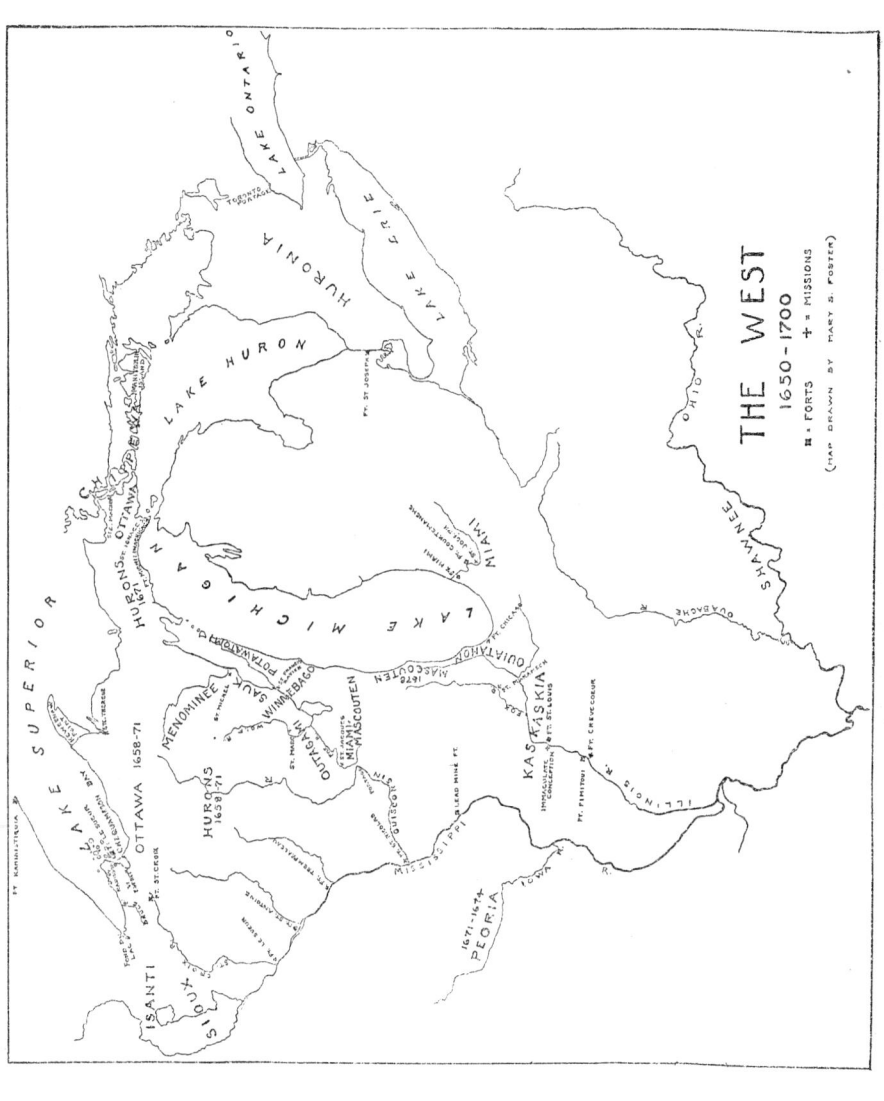

Sioux." To this the governor made no response, and the Fox chief retired with full purpose of preventing all trading expeditions to the upper Mississippi River.[50]

Day after day the negotiations continued; the western chiefs delivered all their prisoners, and received in return their own tribesmen who had been slaves among the Iroquois. The long series of Iroquois wars was at an end.[51] The conclusion of the Iroquois wars brought a breathing spell to the western country. Trade and garrison posts were not rebuilt, however, for more than a decade. The upper country was deserted. A few *coureurs de bois* yet lingered in the western villages; here and there a black-robe missionary was seen flitting through the woods to the cabin of some neophyte; but the enterprising Frenchmen of the seventeenth century, the men who explored the wilderness, mapped out empires, formed alliances with the tribesmen, opened routes of commerce, were gone. All was silence and stagnation in the Northwest. The heroic epoch when great discoveries and great adventures occurred was over. The slight veneer of civilization dropped off and Wisconsin lapsed once more into barbarism and isolation.

[50] Kellogg, "Fox Indians during the French Régime," in Wis. Hist. Soc., *Proc.*, 1907, 155.

[51] La Potherie was an eyewitness of the meeting of 1701, and gives a detailed account in his *Histoire*, iv, 193-266.

XIII. THE FIRST FOX WAR, 1701-1716

THE Iroquois menace came to an end with the peace of 1701, although these astute tribesmen attempted to play a double part and to maintain alliance with either the French or English as best suited their purposes. The Canadian rulers had, however, learned a salutary lesson, and notwithstanding the intercolonial war that began in 1702 they did not draw their western allies into the struggle, and so far as the West was concerned Queen Anne's War had little effect upon its destiny. The removal of the Iroquois danger led to a renewal of intertribal hostilities, and without garrisons or licensed traders the Northwest reverted to primitive conditions, the progress toward peace and order was checked, the rights of property were not respected, and the lives of Frenchmen were no longer safe. The anti-imperialists had temporarily brought about the ruin that Frontenac had foreseen. Nor did the plan of focusing the fur trade at Montreal succeed; the tribesmen would no longer take the long, tiresome voyage to the St. Lawrence, since they could supply themselves from the *coureurs de bois*, who swarmed in the western country, or obtain from the Iroquois English goods at a lower price than could be found at the French centers. Onanguissé, the famous chief of the Potawatomi, well expressed the feeling of most of the French allies in his speech to the governor the year after the edict of evacuation had gone forth. "Father," he said, "since we want powder, iron, and every necessary which you were formerly in the habit of sending us, what do you expect us to do? Are the majority of our women, who have but one or two beavers to send to Montreal to procure their little supplies,—are they to trust them to drunken fellows who will drink them, and bring nothing back? . . . You shall never see us again, I promise you, if the French quit us; this, Father, is the last time we shall come to talk with you."[1]

It became necessary to devise some plan to recover French dominion in the West, and to secure the frontiers of New France from utter demoralization. Instead of reëstablishing the former posts, it was determined to occupy two or three strategic points, to place considerable garrisons therein, and to concentrate French colonists around the posts, thus making a strong center of French activity in the farther West. Near these posts the Indian allies were to be settled, to be taught French customs, agriculture, and the French language, and ultimately to be incorporated into the economic unit. The straits between Lake Huron and Lake Erie were chosen for one of these sites, the mouth of the Mississippi for another, while the still existing post in Illinois was to connect the two. The plan was excellent and timely, and its partial carrying out saved French dominion in the West for over sixty years. The project was conceived by Canadian officers, who knew the West, and whose minds worked independently of the dictation of the bureaucratic officials of the home government. They were the inheritors of Frontenac's tradition, and were the imperialists of the new century. Had the French people been a colonizing race, the Mississippi valley might still be a part of their colonial empire.

The founding of Louisiana was put in charge of one of the most daring and successful of the Canadian naval officers, who during Frontenac's life was chiefly engaged in attempting to control Hudson Bay. Pierre le Moyne

[1] *Wis. Hist. Colls.*, xvi, 168.

Sieur d'Iberville sailed for the Gulf of Mexico in 1699, and there laid the foundation of the colony that received La Salle's name for the entire Mississippi valley —La Louisiane. By this movement he forestalled the English by a few months, for just as Iberville's explorers were returning down the river after a reconnaissance, they met an English frigate ascending the stream with a party of colonists on board, and warned them off from territory already claimed by the French. The same was true of the colony at Detroit. Cadillac while at Mackinac in the late seventeenth century had noted the importance of this site as a bulwark against English encroachments, and now secured permission to occupy it with a post and a colony. At the very time he was in France obtaining a royal patent, an astute English official was recommending to the governor of New York that he be allowed to obtain the Iroquois's permission to erect a fort at Detroit, a "fruitful and pleasant place," which would attract all the western Indians and become a "nursery for bushlopers."[2] Cadillac, with the cooperation of Tonty's younger brother Alphonse, came up the lakes in 1701 and laid the foundations of the present great American city of Detroit.

Meanwhile, in the Illinois, Henry de Tonty and his partner La Forest maintained their post on Lake Peoria, with subordinate forts at Le Rocher and Chicago, where Tonty's cousin, Pierre Desliette, was in charge; they also had a warehouse at Mackinac.[3] Thus at the beginning of the new century the enterprise of the French had foreseen the importance and

[2] *N. Y. Colon. Docs.*, iv, 650-651; Osgood, *American Colonies in the Eighteenth Century*, i, 473.
[3] *Mich. Pion. and Hist. Colls.*, xxxiii, 75; see also document in Chicago Historical Society, Schmidt Collection, No. 127, in which La Forest's widow makes claims for indemnity for her husband's construction of "Pimitaouy, Le Rocher, et Chicagou."

had taken possession of the keys to the interior of North America—the three great centers of modern American life: New Orleans, Detroit, and Chicago.

An important part of all the plans for the new colonies was Indian concentration. Iberville proposed a readjustment of all the Mississippi valley tribes; the Illinois were to be removed from their river to the Ohio and the Mississippi, while the more northern tribes were to be brought down to occupy the lands from which these tribesmen were removed. There were great difficulties in carrying out any such plan, but to a certain extent it was gradually accomplished. The Illinois in the early years of the century migrated in large numbers to the site now called the American Bottom, a bench of fertile land along the Mississippi below the mouth of the Illinois River, taking with them their missionaries and a number of retired traders who had settled among them. Thus they began a center of French civilization in the West that grew into considerable importance.[4] Meanwhile the Kickapoo from the Fox River valley of Wisconsin moved into the region the Illinois left unoccupied; while the Mascouten and Potawatomi gradually shifted south and southeast around the end of Lake Michigan.

Cadillac at Detroit had large plans for concentration; these were aided by the movement of the Algonquian tribes, begun at the close of the Iroquois wars, to return to their earlier habitat. The Miami had already left the vicinity of Chicago and the St. Joseph valley, and the Potawatomi had taken their place. Some of the former tribe settled on the Wabash, where

[4] Alvord, *Illinois*, 132-133. Most of the French settlers in these Illinois villages were *coureurs de bois*, who were unwilling to go back to Canada. Many of them married native women. *Wis. Hist. Colls.*, xvi, 201-202.

they were later joined by several bands of Mascouten. Other clans of the Miami went as far east as the Maumee, which takes its name from one form of the tribal appellation. Cadillac's first efforts were directed to the removal of the tribes he had formerly governed at Mackinac, the Hurons and the Ottawa. In doing this he met with determined opposition from the Jesuit missionaries, but in the end the officer was successful; the Hurons settled on the Detroit River, where they were usually spoken of as the Wyandot. Within the first few years after the founding of Detroit nearly six thousand savages were concentrated within the radius of its influence.[5] This opened opportunity for a very profitable fur trade. Cadillac organized a Company of the Colony, and wrote to the authorities at home such enthusiastic reports of the prospects of his new post, which he called the "Paris of America," that the colonial minister admonished him to confine himself to exact accounts of his colony and not to treat his reports in "the style of a romance."[6]

Cadillac's anticipations were too rosy for consummation. Such a vast aggregation of tribesmen could not long be kept at peace, and in 1706 a serious difficulty occurred. Just outside the gates of Fort Pontchartrain, as Cadillac called his new post, a Recollect missionary and a French soldier of the garrison were killed in an intertribal quarrel. At the same time trouble arose on the Illinois River. The Jesuit Father Gravier was seriously wounded, and the Chicago-Illinois portage route to the Mississippi became unsafe. As a result of these and other quarrels among the natives, some of the former residents of Mackinac returned to that vicinity,

[5] "Cadillac Papers," in *Mich. Pion. and Hist. Colls.*, xxxiii, 139.

[6] *Canadian Archives Report*, 1899, Suppl., 361, 390-391.

and that place and the Green Bay-Fox-Wisconsin route, which had been superseded by the more eastern and southern entrepôts and trade routes, became again of considerable importance. A very enterprising trader named Boisseau was operating at Green Bay at this time, and although without a license he conducted a considerable traffic.[7]

It was by the Fox-Wisconsin route that an expedition went out in the early years of the eighteenth century to try an economic experiment with the wild cattle, or buffalo, that ranged in such vast numbers on the prairies of Illinois. Charles Juchereau, an adventurous and enterprising Canadian officer, obtained a concession from the government to build a tannery on the banks of some convenient stream and to attempt to prepare buffalo skins for market. He also planned to utilize the animals' hair for weaving cloth, and to build up a profitable industry in the far West. Juchereau came west in the summer of 1702, with a company of French associates and a fleet of eight canoes conveying merchandise. On the Fox-Wisconsin waterway he encountered his first obstacle in the piracy of the Fox Indians. They had been so long left to their own devices, since the recall of Perrot, that they had adopted a profitable scheme of holding up French parties for tribute. Juchereau thought best to yield to their threats, and paid them goods worth a thousand crowns to allow his flotilla of canoes to pass.

Arrived in the Illinois he engaged a band of Mascouten to be his hunters, and took them with him to the site he chose to occupy at the mouth of the Ohio River. There he built a large establishment, sunk tanning pits, and within a few months had a great

[7] *Wis. Hist. Colls.*, xvi, 232-242; *Mich. Pion. and Hist. Colls.*, xxxiii, 262-314, 341, 370, 446-449.

pile of cured peltry stacked up on the river bank, awaiting transportation. But Juchereau had not taken into account the dangers of the climate at this low and swampy site. An epidemic of malaria broke out; Juchereau and nearly all his men died, the Indians in great fear abandoned the spot, the survivors fled to Biloxi, the leather was left to rot, and the first industrial enterprise of the Mississippi valley came to an untimely end.[8]

About the same time another business venture was undertaken by a former explorer of the Northwest. Le Sueur, when unable to renew his trading license in 1697, went to France and obtained a grant to develop a valuable mine he claimed to have discovered. He returned to America in the summer of 1700, and joined the new colony of Louisiana. Thence he set forth to ascend the Mississippi to the site of his supposed mine. He had built for his enterprise a sailing vessel with long lateen sails, like those of an Italian felucca. In this craft, with a crew of twenty men, Le Sueur mounted the great river to the entrance of the Minnesota, then called the St. Pierre. The appearance of this strange craft on the Mississippi caused great astonishment and alarm among the natives; but Le Sueur was a skillful diplomat, and won the good will of the tribes along the river. Among those of the upper stream he was much beloved. He easily obtained permission from the Sioux to build a fort on the Blue Earth River, where he had located his supposed mine. This post he called "L'Huillier," for a French official who had befriended him.[9] There he

[8] *Mich. Pion. and Hist. Colls.*, xxxiii, 175; Alvord, *Illinois*, 133-135. Juchereau's partnership contract is in Chicago Historical Society, Schmidt Collection, No. 337. It was signed May 13, 1702.
[9] *Wis. Hist. Colls.*, xvi, 177-193; Folwell, *Minnesota*, i, 40-42.

loaded his felucca with the parti-colored marls to be found in the vicinity, and with this worthless cargo floated back to Louisiana, leaving a garrison of Frenchmen to hold the fort. The winter after he left them the post was attacked by a band of Foxes, who were unwilling that their enemies the Sioux should have a place to obtain French firearms. The surprise attack found the garrison unprepared; they lost three of their number, when the survivors escaped to Illinois, and the upper Mississippi was left unoccupied by white men.[10] Le Sueur himself did not long survive the failure of his enterprise. He seems to have died shortly after his return, in the colony of Louisiana.[11]

It was evident to all New France that the incipient rebellion of the Fox tribe must be quelled. The French had no real alliance with the Sioux, despite the efforts of Perrot, Duluth, and Le Sueur. The first Sioux chief to visit the colony, who went down with Le Sueur in 1695, died before he could return, and the tribe was not legally enrolled among the number of the "children" of the French king. Therefore the Foxes played upon the situation, and took advantage of the immunity they had enjoyed since the treaty of 1701. The entire Green Bay region swarmed with *coureurs de bois*, and the prestige of the French in the West was sadly diminished by the arrogant treatment they

[10] *Wis. Hist. Colls.*, xvi, 198-200; *Mich. Pion. and Hist. Colls.*, xxxiii, 173, 175-176. The maps of this period show that some exploration in interior Wisconsin and Minnesota occurred about this time. The Franquelin map of 1708 shows Lac Vieux Desert and several rivers of northern Wisconsin; and also the Sioux tribes of the upper Mississippi. Attention was called to this map by Dr. Lawrence Martin, chief of the Map Division, Library of Congress.

[11] Le Sueur's widow wrote a letter from Fort Louis of Louisiana, applying for relief. Chicago Historical Society, Schmidt Collection, No. 173.

received from the Foxes, who considered that the white men feared them and dared not resent their exactions. In 1703 the government issued another act of amnesty for all illegal traders who would come down from the West and give themselves up. But few, however, availed themselves of the government's clemency, many going to Louisiana instead, where they were welcomed. Indeed, the accusation ran that many of the officials of both colonies profited by the acquisitions of the *coureurs de bois*.[12]

Cadillac as the ranking and most experienced officer in the West was directed to restore order and to bring the Foxes to terms. As a strong imperialist he believed in the concentration policy, and as an opponent of the Jesuits he desired to remove all western Indians from their influence. He thereupon sent in 1710 an invitation for all the tribes then resident about Green Bay to remove to Detroit. The Foxes with their kindred the Sauk, and some portions of the Kickapoo and Mascouten, determined to accept the offer and migrate to their earlier homes.[13] Sixty years before, their fathers had fled thence, a band of frightened, trembling fugitives. Now the descendants, prosperous after their long sojourn in the fertile region west of Green Bay, proud and haughty in the arrogance with which they had dominated the region, moved toward Detroit like a band of conquerors. The tribes already settled in this vicinity complained of the insolence of the newcomers, and immediately began to show a marked hostility. Just at this critical juncture, when peace in the western country depended upon the

---

[12] *Wis. Hist. Colls.*, xvi, 201, 221, 232; *Mich. Pion. and Hist. Colls.*, xxxiii, 195-196, 244, 249.

[13] *Wis. Hist. Colls.*, xvi, 293; *Mich. Pion. and Hist. Colls.*, xxxiii, 505.

THE FIRST FOX WAR 277

experience and tact of the commandant, Cadillac was removed to become the governor of the growing colony of Louisiana. He was loath to go; his enterprise at Detroit was his own, and was in its experimental stage. He had no choice, however, but to obey; and the governor of New France promised to send another veteran officer to take command at Detroit, in the person of Tonty's former partner in the Illinois, François Daupin Sieur de la Forest.[14]

This very year of the Fox migration to Detroit is signalized by the visit of the first known English colonist to journey through the region of the upper lakes. Joseph Kellogg, when a boy of twelve, was captured at the sack of Deerfield in western Massachusetts, and carried to Canada, where he remained about a year in the hands of the Indians. Finally he was ransomed by the French and lived at Montreal for the next decade, engaged in traffic and on friendly terms with the French colonists. In 1710 he joined a party of traders who were going to the upper country, and came west by the Ottawa River-Georgian Bay route. They wintered at Mackinac among the remnant of the Ottawa who had not migrated to Detroit, and the next spring set forth up Lake Michigan, and entered Illinois by the Chicago portage. They then proceeded by the Illinois River to the new settlements below its mouth, and after a profitable trade made their way back to Canada, apparently by the St. Joseph portage route to Lake Michigan. Kellogg, who seems to have been a lively, active youth with a keen power of observation, was exchanged after ten years and became one of the noted interpreters of the New England colonies. In 1721 he gave an account of his voyage in the far West

[14] Tonty retired in the early years of the eighteenth century to the colony of Louisiana, and there died September 6, 1704.

to the colonial authorities, with corrections and comments on Senex's map, probably the "Map of Louisiana and of the Mississippi," published in 1715. This geographical material was being collected for the Royal Society of London, which in 1725 published a new and revised edition of Senex's map of the world.[15] The account of Joseph Kellogg was sent to the Royal Society by the New England authorities, and there it may be found today.[16]

There is nothing remarkable about the narrative of this young New Englander. He mentioned the natural features of the country he traversed, commented on the quality of the lands and the beauty of the lakes and rivers. At his winter quarters he indulged in fishing through the ice, and hauled up "trouts" of more than fifty pounds weight. When he reached the prairies of Illinois, he "found himself in a new world, compar'd with the River of Canada. . . . The climate was so mild there was little snow, everything gay and pleasant," with pretty parroquets in the woods, which were full of fruit trees. He gave an interesting description of the French settlements in the Illinois, where "they raise excellent Wheat, very good Indian Corn, have a windmill, and have a stock of Cattle, make a very good sort of wine." The region of the Ohio Mr. Kellogg called a "noble country, vast numbers of wild Cattle that make great and open roads for many miles together. . . . Hereabouts Mr. Kellug's Company ended their trading Voyage, and so returned back to Canada."

Kellogg says nothing about unrest on the part of the

[15] Copies of both these maps are in the Wisconsin Historical Library.
[16] A somewhat incorrect version of this journal is printed in the *Kellogg Genealogy* (San Francisco, 1903), i, 60-62.

western Indians, but from other sources we learn that the year of his visit was a critical one in the annals of the western tribesmen. Cadillac had left Detroit, and his successor, La Forest, because of infirmities caused by his thirty years of service in the wilds, had not been able to take charge of his new assignment. His place was filled temporarily by Charles Regnault Sieur Dubuisson, who appears to have had but little experience and skill in dealing with the red allies of New France. Moreover, the colony itself was in the throes of a great crisis. The military operations of the intercolonial war now threatened the very existence of the French colony. A great fleet equipped in New England was on its way to conquer New France. Governor Vaudreuil, who had hitherto refrained from calling for assistance from the West, felt that the emergency justified such action. He sent messengers to Lake Superior, Green Bay, Mackinac, the Illinois, and St. Joseph, where the mass of the French savages dwelt; while other envoys summoned the tribes from the vicinity of Detroit. By early summer a concourse of western savages had reached Quebec, ready to act for their great Onontio in repelling his enemies. By the time of their arrival, however, the danger had passed; a great storm had shattered the English fleet at the mouth of the St. Lawrence, and Canada was saved.

The governor considered the time and occasion auspicious for settling the difficulties of the western tribesmen. On the plain beside Quebec he held a great council with all the western Indians, and after thanking them graciously for their prompt response to his summons, he proceeded to discuss conditions in the West. The Foxes were sternly rebuked for their attitude toward the other tribes, and warned to leave the neighborhood of Detroit and to return to their village sites in Wisconsin. "Reflect once more, Outtagamis," he urged them, "on what I have just said to you, for it is for your preservation."[17] For what perverse reason or savage whim the Foxes did not act upon the advice of the governor we do not know. He proved himself all too true a prophet of their fate. Before another year had passed, the entire band sojourning near Detroit was annihilated, and the torch of savage warfare was lighted in the West, which was not extinguished for many years.

During the winter of 1711-12, an Ottawa chief made an attack upon a band of Mascouten wintering on St. Joseph River, and the Foxes about Detroit immediately took up the quarrel and began an unexpected assault upon the villages of the allies clustered about the fort. Dubuisson unwisely espoused the cause of the Hurons and Ottawa, allowing them to take refuge within the fort and encouraging them to raid the Fox village. Thereupon the Foxes built a stockade and entrenched themselves, defying their enemies by word and deed. For nineteen days they held their own against foes who outnumbered them four to one, including even some portions of tribes as far distant as the Osage and the Missouri. We have full and dramatic reports of this siege, which has become a classic of savage warfare. Had we also the report of the Fox chieftain, what marvels of heroic defense, of mighty efforts, might we not chronicle. Even the enemies were struck with admiration at the courage of the besieged. When the first volley was felt, and the doomed Renards knew that the French were supporting the attack, the great chief mounted the rampart and called out, "What does this mean, my Father? Thou [the commandant] didst invite us to come to

[17] *Mich. Pion. and Hist. Colls.*, xxxiii, 498-506.

THE FIRST FOX WAR 281

dwell near thee; thy word [message] is even now fresh in our pouches. And yet thou declarest war against us. . . . But know that the Renard is immortal; and that if in defending myself I shed the blood of Frenchmen, my Father cannot reproach me."[18] Twice the besieged, who were being played upon by cannon from the fort, sent envoys with a white flag to ask at least a truce. Dubuisson owns that he used these embassies for his own purposes and that the Indian allies were inclined to accept the overtures. The French officer had determined upon the complete destruction of this band of savages. Within the Fox entrenchment women and children died from hunger and thirst, numbers of the warriors were mowed down by French mortars from a scaffold raised to command the enemy palisade. Finally, choosing a dark rainy night when their foes were not on guard, the Foxes made a sortie, and succeeded in escaping northeast as far as Fox Creek, now within the limits of the city of Detroit. There they were overtaken by a large band of pursuers, and a terrible slaughter ensued. Of the thousand warriors who had come at Cadillac's invitation to dwell near Detroit, very few survived. The prisoners taken were tortured to death. Dubuisson reported with pious satisfaction, "It is God who has suffered these two audacious nations [Foxes and Mascouten] to perish," and had a high mass

[18] Dubuisson wrote a long report, which was first published in pamphlet form in 1845 at Detroit, reprinted in William R. Smith, *History of Wisconsin* (Madison, 1854), iii, 315-336. Another translation appears in *Wis. Hist. Colls.*, xvi, 267-287; and in *Mich. Pion. and Hist. Colls.*, xxxiii, 537-562. This was the source used by Charlevoix and Parkman. Other reports, notably that of Léry in *Wis. Hist. Colls.*, xvi, 293-295, from which the above citation is taken, seem to sympathize with the Foxes and to blame Dubuisson. See Kellogg, "Fox Indians during French Régime," in Wis. Hist. Soc., *Proc.*, 1907, 142-188.

chanted in the chapel of his fort in honor of this conquest.

Nevertheless it was a Punic victory. From this massacre dates the series of Fox wars which brought New France to the verge of ruin, and without doubt contributed to its final overthrow. The western country suffered during the Fox wars of the eighteenth century what the colony had suffered during the Iroquois wars of the seventeenth century. Despite the slaughter on the banks of Fox Creek, there were many of the enemy tribesmen left in Wisconsin. "There still remain a great number of them near the Bay," wrote Father Marest from Mackinac. "Their brothers, the Sauk, Kickapoo, Mascouten, and Winnebago, would doubtless all unite and create terror everywhere in the West."[19] Certainly the good father was a sure prophet of misfortune. Inflamed by the passion for revenge, the remnant of the destroyed tribe haunted all the waterways and made the life of every Frenchman unsafe. Dubuisson had scattered a thousand firebrands through the forests. The enemy infested all the hunting grounds of the allied French Indians. Two years after the siege of Detroit all the tribes who had joined in the attack upon the Foxes were reported "dying of hunger in their cabins, not daring to leave them on account of their well-grounded fear that the Reynards will destroy them all, one after another."[20]

In this year 1714 La Forest, who had he been at Detroit might have avoided this disastrous war, died; and Vaudreuil sent Jacques Sabrevois, a veteran of the intercolonial wars, to take his place. The same year the governor heard that the treaty of Utrecht had been signed; and now that peace reigned between the English

[19] *Wis. Hist. Colls.*, xvi, 289.
[20] *Ibid.*, 301.

and French colonies, he was able to turn all his resources toward crushing out the rebellion in the West. He intrusted the defense of the western posts to two officers who were long identified with western affairs. Pierre Desliette, for many years in service in the Illinois, was sent thither again, and for nearly a score of years more acted on the defensive against Fox attacks in that quarter. Constant Marchand Sieur de Lignery was sent to Mackinac to restore morale in that region, where an amnesty was offered to all *coureurs de bois* who would go to his support. Lignery appears to have rebuilt the fort at Mackinac, on the south side of the straits, but a regular garrison was not sent him until later.[21] Among the Miami dwelt the veteran trader and officer Jean Baptiste Bissot Sieur de Vincennes, who had been among this tribe for many years.[22]

In the year 1714 two young scions of Canadian nobility, eager to distinguish themselves in wilderness warfare, came west to conduct a campaign against the Foxes. These were the eldest son of Claude de Ramesay, governor of Montreal, Louis Sieur de Manoir; and Gabriel François le Moyne Sieur d' Adoucourt, one of the younger sons of Baron de Longueuil.[23] These youthful officers were instructed to gather the warriors of the Miami and the Illinois tribes and await Lignery with the northern allies at Chicago; while a messenger

[21] *Wis. Hist. Colls.*, xvi, 297, 301, 306, 308, 318; *Mich. Pion. and Hist. Colls.*, xxxiii, 571. For a sketch of Lignery, see *Wis. Hist. Colls.*, v, 113-115.
[22] Indiana Historical Society, *Publications*, vii, 1-130. Vincennes is first mentioned in the West in 1698. See Kellogg, *Early Narratives*, 342.
[23] Ramesay lived in the famous chateau now used as a museum at Montreal. D'Adoucourt was a nephew of Iberville, who took his title from his mother.

was sent via Lake Superior to prevent the Sioux from granting aid or refuge to the Foxes. The plan promised well; it would seem that the malcontents must be hemmed in by the attacking Indians and forced into submission. An epidemic, however, put an end to this project; the two young officers fell prey to the malady and were forced to retire to Kaskaskia, and no check was placed on the plundering and murdering of the Foxes through the entire upper lakes region.[24] A sad fate befell the two youths who had come west with such high hopes of service. As they took their homeward way with a trading caravan that set out for Detroit via the Ohio and the Wabash rivers, they were overtaken by a wandering band of Cherokee Indians, allies of the English colonists in the Carolinas. The French party was surprised, and when fired upon by the Cherokee the young officers fell at the first volley. Some of the traders were captured and carried to the villages of the raiders, where they were redeemed by the Carolina authorities and later sent home.[25]

When the news reached Canada that these two youths from prominent colonial families had been done to death by Indians, the deed was naturally laid at the door of the Fox rebels, and popular indignation hastened preparations for their punishment. There was a general demand for a punitive expedition, and it was thought that the only man in Canada capable of tak-

[24] *Wis. Hist. Colls.*, xvi, 327-338, 341-342.

[25] The evidence for this episode has recently come to light. Compare *N. Y. Colon. Docs.*, ix, 575; *Mich. Pion. and Hist. Colls.*, xxxiii, 387; *Year Book of the City of Charleston, South Carolina*, 1895, 324-352. This last reference is the journal of an English trader in the Cherokee country. Note the entry for December 31, 1715, on page 331. Professor V. W. Crane has called my attention to this document. He also says that the ransom of the captives is mentioned in the manuscript legislative journals at Charleston for the year 1716.

THE FIRST FOX WAR 285

ing charge of such an enterprise was the veteran officer Sieur de Louvigny, who had in the preceding century been commandant at Mackinac.[26] It was not until 1716 that Louvigny was prepared to undertake the discipline of the Foxes and the pacifying of the Northwest.

Louvigny's expedition was the first army of white men to penetrate to the upper lakes and the first to invade Wisconsin's woods and waterways. The colonial government, always impecunious, planned to finance the undertaking by allowing the invaders to carry with them large stores of merchandise, and so to go at their own expense. The expedition thus became a vast trading enterprise in disguise. When the king's council heard of this project, they reversed the action of the governor and ordered all the expenses paid by the royal treasury;[27] but this order-in-council came too late to change the permissions already given. No doubt also many of the officials who were interested in the profits of the enterprise were not eager to make a change. The purpose of the expedition was openly discussed in Canada, and it was well known that the military enterprise would be subordinated to profit-making. Nicolas Perrot, then living in retirement, wrote about this time a long memoir on the history of the western country, concerned with the days when he had been in active service among these tribesmen. At its close he devoted several chapters to attempting to prove to his contemporaries that their savage allies were as treacherous as the Foxes, and that the latter by prudent management could

[26] Louvigny's term at Mackinac was from 1691 to 1694. See preceding chapter.
[27] *Wis. Hist. Colls.*, xvi, 318, 328-329, 340; *Canadian Archives Report*, 1899, Suppl., 119, 121.

easily be brought once more into the circle of French influence, and that such diplomatic measures would serve the colony far better than a military expedition.[28] "Many times have the Outaouas been known to plot against the French," he wrote. "The Miamis have slain Frenchmen, the Illinois likewise, the Saulteurs the same, as also the people of the north." And again, "If I had gone up with Monsieur de Louvigny, I would have flattered myself that I could induce the Renards to ask for peace."

But the words of the veteran explorer and apologist for the Foxes fell upon deaf ears; all the colony was interested in the Fox expedition and it was got under way with great dispatch. Louvigny left Montreal early in May with over two hundred soldiers and militia, and a large force of converted Indians from the missions. *En route* he was joined by many other white adventurers, for amnesty was offered to all *coureurs de bois* who would take part in the expedition and furnish their own boats and provisions. The expedition also carried two small cannon, and a grenade mortar for battering down any fortifications that might be raised by the hostiles. The route was by the lower lakes, in order to notify and overawe the Iroquois, who were believed to be in secret alliance with the Fox tribesmen. The former wondered at the great preparations made to conquer so small a group of rebels, for the survivors numbered scarcely five hundred warriors. At Mackinac, Louvigny halted to obtain fresh provisions and to recruit the western allies for the advance. When he left this rendezvous he had a force of eight hundred whites and savages, who proceeded in battle array

---

[28] Perrot's memoir was first published in French under the editorship of Jules Tailhan in 1864. It is translated in Blair, i, 25-272.

along the quiet shores of Green Bay and arrived without important incident at the mouth of the Fox River. Such a warlike force had never been seen in Wisconsin; one would suppose that the Foxes, as was customary in savage warfare, would flee before the face of the storm. The fact that they stood their ground and fortified themselves at their village site seems to indicate that they had an intimation of Louvigny's purpose. Their fort was in all probability located where their village had stood ever since its removal from Wolf River—that is, on the west side of Little Lake Butte des Morts.[29] They had fortified this site with a triple row of stout oak stakes, had dug a trench or moat on the inner side, from which they could fire upon the besiegers. There were within the fort five hundred fierce warriors determined to sell their lives as dearly as possible, and three thousand women, who fought as desperately as their male companions.

Louvigny carried on the siege with all the customs of the time in more civilized regions; he advanced deliberately, planted his cannon, and opened trenches toward the enemies' defenses. The small mortars which he had transported at such a cost over so many long miles made no impression on the stout stakes of the Foxes' palisade. He then determined to blow up the fortification with a mine. Already his men were suffering from the cross fire of the savages, who when three days and nights had passed sent out a white flag and asked for terms. Louvigny made a show of spurning the peace overtures, but secretly was pleased

[29] A local antiquarian believed that he found traces of the Fox fortification three-quarters of a mile west of Little Lake Butte des Morts, near Sills Creek. Wis. Hist. Soc., *Proc.*, 1899, 207-211; *Wisconsin Archeologist*, ii, 50-52. See also Deborah Martin, "Border Forts of the Great Lakes," in *Wisconsin Club Woman*, September, 1923, 151.

with his early success. He represented to his Indian allies that the Foxes expected a reinforcement of three hundred warriors, and that it would be better to end the siege before these new enemies arrived. The Foxes were preparing to make a desperate sortie, when Louvigny suddenly acquiesced in their request for a truce, and to the astonishment of all his red contingent, who thought that the Foxes were on the "brink of utter destruction," agreed to end the siege if the enemy would accept terms. These terms he later claimed were very severe; in truth, they seem to modern readers astonishingly mild. The tribesmen were to end the war, restore their prisoners, and *hunt to pay the costs of the war.* The only guarantee that Louvigny had that these terms would be fulfilled was the yielding of six hostages, among whom was the great chief Pemoussa, hero of the Detroit siege and for a long time an enemy of the French power. The Foxes and all the allies realized that the war had been ended by a promise of beaver skins, and it is doubtful whether the enemy savages had any intention of keeping the terms.

Nevertheless Louvigny returned to Quebec as a conqueror, and received a substantial reward for "ending the Fox War."[30] He was to return the next year to take back the hostages and to complete the subjugation of the rebels. But Pemoussa and one companion died of smallpox in the colony, and when in 1717 Louvigny did revisit the upper country, he did not in person trust himself in the Foxes' domain, but sent them messages by a returning hostage, which were received sullenly and had but little weight with the tribe. He forbade traders to go to the Fox villages;

---

[30] Louvigny's report is in *Wis. Hist. Colls.*, v, 78-80; the governor's commendation, in *ibid.*, 80-81. See also *ibid.*, xvi, 338-344.

but, he reported, "prohibitions of this sort have not been very well Enforced."[31] Although peace was temporarily established in the western country, and the Foxes subdued by a show of force, yet they were suspicious and wary, fearful of being again betrayed, and cherished deep in their hearts the passion for revenge. In 1719 the governor reported to the authorities in France that three Fox chiefs came to visit him and "assured me that they were all disposed to maintain peace with all the Nations."[32]

Louvigny's expedition resulted in allaying for a time the savage warfare that had raged in the West for four years, and once more opened the Fox River valley to exploitation and occupation by the French. Among the terms of the peace that were exacted of the Foxes was a definite cession of all their territory to the French crown.[33] This cession reasserted the claims made by the former ceremonies of annexation, and rendered Wisconsin more definitely a part of the French empire in America. Plans were immediately set on foot for the reoccupation and the permanent settlement of this region, acquired, as was claimed, by the conquest of French arms. Thus this expedition, which so far as military prowess was concerned proved to be a fiasco, nevertheless had important consequences for our history, reintroduced into this region the beginnings of civilization, and reopened the Fox-Wisconsin waterway to the Mississippi.

[31] *Wis. Hist. Colls.*, xvi, 347-349.
[32] *Ibid.*, 380.
[33] *Ibid.*, 346; Charlevoix, *History of New France*, v, 307.

XIV. THE REOCCUPATION OF THE POSTS, 1714-1727

THE policy of concentration of the Indian tribes had failed. The western tribesmen were not docile enough to respond to the missionary purpose, nor submissive enough to become civilized. In proud independence they maintained their native languages, religious rites, tribal customs, and intertribal enmities. They could not be molded into the nucleus for an agricultural settlement, nor did they desire to imitate the white man's ways. This has always been the kernel of the difficulty between the two races; neither would admit the superiority of the other. Historians have long lauded the French in America for their skill in dealing with the aborigines, have claimed that in this regard they far surpassed the English colonists. It is true that the French were adaptable and ingenious; if they could not control the savage by one means they tried another. But they never in North America induced any large numbers of red men to adopt French civilization, nor did they at any period keep perfect peace among the western tribesmen, whose ruling passion was war.

The treaty of Utrecht, signed in 1713, put an end to the intercolonial wars which had lasted for nearly a quarter of a century. One of the provisions of the treaty was that the subjects of both crowns—French and British—should have equal rights of trade with the natives of North America.[1] This freedom of trade was never carried into effect in the West, and never could have been with safety to the traders of either nation.

[1] William MacDonald, *Select Charters and Other Documents Illustrating American History* (New York, 1910), 232.

The French government now determined to revert to its earlier method of controlling trade and of governing the Indian tribesmen. In 1714 a beginning was made of the return to the license system; fifteen permits were issued for that year as a special grace. In 1716 the king ordered the rsëetablishment of the twenty-five licenses on a permanent basis, and granted at the same time an amnesty to all illegal traders who would come into the colony.[2]

This system involved a reoccupation of the interior posts and a restoration of commandants and garrisons. It meant a definite abandonment of the policy of concentration and civilization, and a reversion to the military and commercial occupation of the western valley which had prevailed in the seventeenth century. About the year 1712 Sieur de Lignery was sent to Mackinac to reopen that region as a fur trade center. In 1715 a garrison was forwarded to his support and a fort built on the south side of the straits, near the place now known as Old Mackinaw.[3] Mackinac had always been a rival of Detroit. Its reoccupation was a definite measure, which relegated Detroit to the status of the other western posts, and marked its relative decline as the French center of civilization on the Great Lakes. The unrivaled position of Detroit, commanding the best route to the West and serving as a barrier against English encroachments, made this post, however, of the first importance during all the rise of the French régime.

The same year that Mackinac was regarrisoned, a

[2] *Canadian Archives Report*, 1899, Suppl., 119, 121; *Wis. Hist. Colls.*, xvi, 330-331, 437. See on the utilization of the licenses, W. B. Munro, "The Coureurs de Bois," in Massachusetts Historical Society, *Proceedings*, lvii, 194-195.

[3] *Wis. Hist. Colls.*, xvi, 295, 314; *N. Y. Colon. Docs.*, ix, 860. This mainland post was occupied until 1781, when the British commandant removed the fort to the island for greater security.

post was built on the Maumee River for the Miami tribesmen, who made headquarters at this village and were kept in submission by their long-time trader Sieur de Vincennes.[4] About the same time another post for the Miami was opened on St. Joseph River, not at its mouth, where lay La Salle's old post, but near the site of the mission within the limits of the present city of Niles. A royal order in 1715 also provided for the reëstablishment of the old fort on the Illinois, with Desliette as commandant.[5]

These posts, it will be noticed, were placed to command the canoe routes and portage paths connecting the Great Lakes with the Mississippi valley. The Maumee and St. Joseph portages were the farthest east, the Illinois the farthest south. It remained to control the northern routes to the Mississippi by way of Lake Superior and the Fox-Wisconsin waterway. This latter occupation could not be undertaken until after Louvigny's expedition, hence the lasting result of this foray was the building in 1717 of a fort at the western end of Green Bay.[6]

One hundred years later the American forces advanced from Mackinac in a sailing vessel and built

[4] *N. Y. Colon. Docs.*, ix, 931. This post and village were on the site of the modern Fort Wayne. Vincennes died at this fort in 1719.

[5] *Wis. Hist. Colls.*, xvi, 333. In the Chicago Historical Society is a contract dated 1717, between Pierre Desliette, officer of the troops, and Jean B. Dupré, for trade at "Illinois pimiteouy."

[6] This fort was frequently called Fort St. François, possibly from the St. François Xavier mission. In a document (1723) in Chicago Historical Society, Schmidt Collection, No. 223, it is called "Fort St. Philippe de la baye des Puants," in honor of its first commandant. In practice it was commonly Fort La Baye. The site was probably the later site of Fort Howard. In 1909 the Green Bay Historical Society placed a tablet on a boulder in the yard of the Chicago and Northwestern Railroad, in commemoration of three posts—French, British, and American. So far as we have been able to ascertain, this post of 1717 was the first French fort built at Green Bay.

a post on the same site. We have several descriptions of the latter event with all its details. The founding of the French post we can visualize only by the aid of the imagination and the descriptions of similar contemporaneous events. For example, a fort was built on Lake Pepin a decade later, in the following fashion: Four days after the ax was laid on the first trees, the entire enclosure was finished, occupying a space of one hundred square feet. Within six weeks three log buildings for barracks and officers' quarters were completed, ranging in size from twenty-five to thirty-eight feet in length by sixteen wide.[7] In some such manner was erected the fort on Fox River, which was guarded by a small garrison of Canadian soldiers. The commandant had a house for himself, facing a large esplanade or drill ground. The missionary in charge, who was at this time Father Chardon, abandoned his mission house at De Pere and dwelt within the protection of the fort, where a special house was provided for him.[8]

It is not difficult to picture this small, rude waterside fort, built of logs from the neighboring forest, palisaded with posts cut from the surrounding trees, the merest oasis of civilization in the midst of a savage wilderness. The life lived therein was as rude as the post itself. Probably there was some form of military discipline, drill and parade, setting of guard. The chief affair of the officers was the intercourse with the savages; during the summer months they were probably around the post at all times. The commandant held formal councils with the chiefs and entertained them ceremoniously, inviting them to his own table and bestowing upon them flags and medals, indicative of their rank and of their alliance with the French govern-

[7] *Wis. Hist. Colls.*, xvii, 25-26.
[8] Charlevoix, *Journal of a Voyage* (Caxton Club edition), ii, 58, 61.

ment. By the gifts of trinkets and wearing apparel he kept the tribesmen in good humor, and received from them in return food supplies and rich furs. The food was plenty and satisfying—game of all sorts, wild rice from the marshes, Indian corn, maple sugar, and several nourishing tuber roots. If the officer enjoyed hunting, he had opportunity for this sport in rich measure. Did he care for boating, the broad bay and the wide river gave scope for his canoe or sail-rigged dugout. During the winters his Indian guests were less numerous, the tribesmen scattering to their hunting grounds in the interior. There were, however, winter sports of snowshoeing and sleighing to pass the days. Communication with the world was infrequent. Usually the commandant at La Baye could expect to hear from Montreal but once a year, when a flotilla of traders arrived bringing goods for the fur trade, letters, orders, and news from the St. Lawrence colony.

We may well ask how could a French officer, educated, fond of society, used to the pleasure of the court of France, or the lesser gayeties of the governor's court at Quebec, endure the exile at a wilderness fort a thousand miles in the interior of North America. Was he actuated merely by a sense of duty to his king, by military discipline, or by the love of the wild? All these may have been contributory motives, but the main motive was the desire for riches. Green Bay was the entrepôt to a region whence came the best and richest furs; fortunes were made there in a few years. The officers of the troops were not supposed to enter the fur trade. Indeed, there were royal ordinances forbidding such employment! These, however, were easily evaded. The authority of the commandant over the aborigines was a valuable asset. Traders were glad to enter into partnerships with French officers, and to give them a liberal share of the profits of the undertaking. The commandant, upon receiving his appointment, made a contract with the merchants of Montreal, or with some established *bourgeois* of the upper country, for a partnership in the fur trade of his post. Frequently his wife became his agent in the colony, attending to his share of the business and securing his profits. Three years was usually the term of office for a French commandant in the West. In that time most of the officers obtained a tidy fortune, which they could afterwards spend in the more congenial society of the colony.[9] Nor were they at all times without the company of the women of their families. Both Cadillac and Alphonse de Tonty had their wives with them at Detroit. In 1731 three of the Ducharme brothers—Jean, Louis, and Joseph—made a contract to transport the wife of Dutisné from Montreal to his post in Illinois.[10] Such companionship was, however, the exception rather than the rule. The Canadian army officers took their terms of service in the western country as a temporary banishment, to be considered as a profitable adventure, to be compensated later by stations in more agreeable localities. Occasionally one was found who preferred the wilderness life to all other, and who had more than the ordinary influence with the tribesmen.

The first commandant at the newly built post of La

[9] These statements are based for the most part on the business documents in the Schmidt Collection, Chicago Historical Society. Nearly every commandant at Green Bay is represented there by some contract with the traders, signed with his own hand. Several give power of attorney to their wives. Note especially No. 223, 236, 237, 239, 245, 247, 248, 250, and 252. In this valuable collection are similar papers relating to every post in the West during the French régime.

[10] Chicago Historical Society, Schmidt Collection, No. 146. For a sketch of Dutisné, see Alvord, *Illinois*, 157.

Baye was Philippe d'Amours Sieur de la Morandière.[11] He was the son of an early settler of Canada, and belonged to the *noblesse* of the colony. At this time he was thirty-seven years of age, but not yet married. He held his post at La Baye for four years, returning in 1721 to Quebec, where he married the next year and died before 1746. He was succeeded as commandant by Jacques Testard Sieur de Montigny. Captain de Montigny was one of the most distinguished officers in the Canadian army; born in 1662, he was cited for bravery in the attack on Schenectady in 1690; performed a brilliant feat of arms in Acadia in 1696; and served in Newfoundland and on the Lake Champlain frontier. By his first marriage he was a brother-in-law of his predecessor at La Baye; and by his second, a son-in-law of Louvigny. He was honored, about the time of his appointment, with the cross of the Order of St. Louis—the highest ambition of every Canadian army officer. Montigny was a brilliant and exceedingly popular officer.[12] He was accompanied on his voyage to take command of the La Baye post, by Father Charlevoix, a Jesuit who was sent by the regent to explore for routes to the western sea.

Charlevoix's purpose was not made public; ostensibly he was inspecting the mission posts of his order in the western country. He met Montigny at Mackinac, and determined to accompany him as far as Green Bay, and if possible to push beyond to the Sioux country. The traveler describes their journey in a

[11] La Morandière is indexed in *Wis. Hist. Colls.*, xxi, as Etienne Roebert Sieur de la Morandière. This is incorrect, as this latter person was a civil, not a military, officer. The D'Amours family had close relations with the West.

[12] For a sketch of this officer, see *Wis. Hist. Colls.*, xvii, 159-160. He was commandant at La Baye 1721-24, when he returned to the colony and died in 1737. See his signature on the accompanying document.

SIGNATURES OF MONTIGNY AND MARIN, 1719
From a document in the Chicago Historical Society

vivid and circumstantial manner, remarking especially upon the Menominee Indians "as the most shapely in Canada." When they arrived near the fort, the Sauk and Winnebago who dwelt close to its gates ranged themselves along the shore of the river, firing salutes of volleys from their guns. Then in an abandonment of joy they waded out to his canoe, seized Montigny, and lifted him into a large blanket of deerskins, carrying him thus ashore and to his lodgings. The next day councils began and Charlevoix learned that he would not be able to advance into the Sioux country because of the hostile attitude of the Foxes, who commanded the upper Fox River. He did, however, meet a band of Sioux at the fort, and questioned them closely concerning their knowledge of the western sea. This encounter ultimately led to the French occupation of the Sioux country.[13]

Leaving Montigny at his riverside post, Charlevoix hastened back to Mackinac in order to learn the possibility of advancing westward from Lake Superior. Two posts had been reopened since 1717 in that region. The first was at Kaministiquia, the site of Duluth's earlier fort on the northwestern shore of Lake Superior. This place was chosen in order to command the portage into the interior of the far Northwest, where the Indians gathered very rich pelts and carried them to Hudson Bay. During all the fur trade history this site has been notable; it was here that the North West Fur Company almost a century later built Fort William, the headquarters of its operations in the Northwest. In 1717 the governor sent Sieur de la Noue to begin this post.[14]

[13] *Wis. Hist. Colls.*, xvi, 410-418, a translation of a portion of Charlevoix's *Journal*. See also new edition referred to *ante*, note 8.
[14] See sketch in *Wis. Hist. Colls.*, xvi, 440; xvii, 6; Margry, vi, 504-507. See also Solon J. Buck, "The Story of the Grand Portage," in *Minnesota History Bulletin*, v, 14-16.

La Noue, who was a veteran of the colonial wars, left Montreal in July with eight canoe-loads of men and goods. He was very successful in his conduct of this far-away fort, diverting large amounts of peltry from the English at Hudson Bay. His term of service, like that of La Morandière at Green Bay, lasted four years. When Charlevoix reached Mackinac after his visit to the latter post, he found that La Noue had already passed east on his way to Canada. Hoping to learn more of western routes to the ocean, the king's messenger commandeered a swift canoe and hastened after La Noue, overtaking him somewhere in Georgian Bay. This officer told Charlevoix that Indians frequently came to his post at Kaministiquia who talked of the western sea, but that it was now too late to attempt the voyage thither for the year 1721. His successor, Captain Deschaillons,[15] had already passed up into Lake Superior. Charlevoix reluctantly returned to Mackinac, and continued his journey to Illinois and Louisiana, promising himself that he would return in 1722 and visit Kaministiquia, a promise he was never able to fulfill.[16] Kaministiquia was garrisoned throughout the French régime, and commanded at various times by very able officers. It was taken over in 1762 by a detachment of English troops, and thenceforward played an important part in fur trade history until the coming of the Canadian Pacific Railroad.

The post on the southern shore of Lake Superior was not built until 1718; in that year the reoccupation of Chequamegon Bay was ordered—the lovely landlocked opening which had been the scene of the earliest white settlements in Wisconsin, but which had since

---

[15] For sketch of this officer, see *Wis. Hist. Colls.*, xvii, 35; *Mich. Pion. and Hist. Colls.*, xxxiv, 318-320. See partnership for fur trade, Chicago Historical Society, Schmidt Collection, No. 357.

[16] Margry, vi, 498-513, 522.

the evacuation of Le Sueur's post in 1698 been abandoned to the savages and wandering *coureurs de bois*. This bay commanded all the routes into the interior along the southern shore of Lake Superior, and was the headquarters of the great Chippewa tribe whose villages almost encircled the northernmost of the Great Lakes.

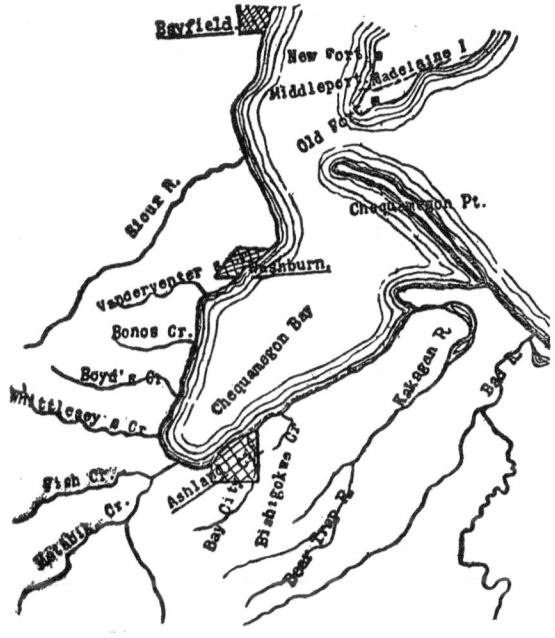

LA POINTE REGION

The Chippewa, called by the French the Saulteurs, since these tribesmen were first met by them at Sault Ste. Marie, had for over a century steadily been pushing westward and occupying the lake region of northern Wisconsin.[17] They were, from the first, loyal French allies, and their enmity with the Foxes and the Sioux was a long-standing tribal quarrel.

[17] See history of this tribe written by a half-breed, William Warren, in *Minn. Hist. Colls.*, v.

In 1718 the Fox tribe sent a submissive deputation to the governor-general, assuring him that they were desirous of keeping the peace they had signed with Louvigny in 1716, but that the French-allied Indians were threatening to attack them in revenge for their chiefs killed in the war. The governor determined to occupy Chequamegon Bay, and bring pressure to bear upon the Chippewa to keep peace.[18] He chose for this purpose one of the most distinguished officers in all Canada—Paul le Gardeur Sieur de St. Pierre, younger brother of Repentigny and Courtemanche. These officers had received by inheritance a knowledge of and love for the West, since their mother was Marguerite Nicolet, daughter of Wisconsin's first explorer. The Le Gardeur family was originally from Normandy, whence in 1636 the earliest of the Canadian family migrated and was granted a seigniory at Repentigny, a short distance below Montreal. There Paul was born in 1661, and while still a lad was involved in the Iroquois wars. Like all Canadian youths of his station, he entered the army and slowly rose through the several grades until he now had a captaincy. Frontenac in 1691 employed St. Pierre to convey his messages and orders to Mackinac. Again in 1707 he was a messenger to the western tribes. In the course of his services he came into close touch with the Missisauga tribe and their kin the Chippewa, and acquired a great influence over these powerful tribesmen. When St. Pierre went to Chequamegon he took with him his young son Jacques, then seventeen years of age. In this environment the younger St. Pierre began his training in woodcraft, which

[18] Margry, vi, 507; *N. Y. Colon. Docs.*, ix, 893; *Wis. Hist. Colls.*, xvi, 377, 380-382.

was to stand him in stead in his later western exploration and occupation.[19]

Second in command of this expedition to reoccupy Chequamegon Bay was René Godefrey Sieur de Linctot, a young officer who was to be connected with Wisconsin for many years.[20] Linctot succeeded St. Pierre when he retired in 1720, and remained at Chequamegon until 1726. These officers with their convoy left Montreal late in September.[21] Winter was approaching when they arrived at their destination, and log huts had to be quickly made ere the snows descended. Fortunately timber was at hand, and the friendly Chippewa were willing to aid in preparing for French occupation.[22] It must have appeared to officers and men as a "stern and rock bound coast," and the rigors of the winter would have appalled all but stout Canadian soldiers. Chequamegon was the last northwestern post to be reoccupied for almost a decade. The purpose for which the posts were founded is well expressed by Governor Vaudreuil in a letter to the French minister. "They were Estab-

[19] See data on Le Gardeur family, in *Recherches Historiques*, v, 233-236. See also *Mich. Pion. and Hist. Colls.*, xxxiii, 350, 362-366. The elder St. Pierre died before 1724; for Jacques, see *Wis. Hist. Colls.*, xvii, 165-166. He was the French officer who in 1753 received George Washington at Venango.

[20] See sketch in *Wis. Hist. Colls.*, xvi, 380. In 1696 he was a *sous ensign*, designated as a *joli garçon*. His lieutenancy dated from 1724, and his captaincy from 1733.

[21] In Chicago Historical Society, Schmidt Collection, No. 347, is a document signed September 26, 1718, by St. Pierre and Linctot for partnership with two Montreal merchants. Each partner had a fourth interest in the venture. Madame Linctot was to act for her husband. The contract states that St. Pierre and Linctot are on the point of departing for "Chagouamigon."

[22] The official French Fort La Pointe of the eighteenth century stood on Madeline Island at its southwestern extremity, about five hundred feet west of Cadotte's later fur trade post, known as "Old Fort." In 1925 a tablet was unveiled to mark this site of French occupation on Lake Superior from 1718 to 1759.

lished," he writes, "only in order to keep the savages attached to us; to maintain peace and union among the Nations; to keep in order the French traders who should go there with licenses to trade."[23]

Unfortunately for the tranquillity of New France, these objects were not easily attained. The Foxes were by no means submissive, or inclined to bow to French power. Temporarily humbled, they laid their plans with the deep duplicity of the savage mind; on the one hand assuring the French officers of their good will, on the other plotting a revenge for past humiliations. In truth, there were within the tribe itself two factions —one under Ouachala, leaning toward a French alliance; the other under Kiala, maintaining the old fierce barbaric impulse to free themselves from white domination. In 1720 Ouachala visited Montreal to have a conference with the governor, in which he promised to bring his tribe into the French alliance.[24] He reckoned, however, without his host; the haughty Foxes had in the intervening years forgotten the invasion of their country by a French army, and were bent upon revenge for what they considered their wrongs. Revenge is a passion dear to the Indian mind; for it he will sacrifice his own welfare and that of his tribe; revenge is to him the highest ethical demand upon his conduct. The Foxes were plotting revenge.

Complications between different groups of French colonizers played into the hands of the savages. Louisiana, founded in 1699, had become a government separate from Canada. In 1712 Louisiana had been made a private monopoly in the hands of Antoine Crozat. After the death in 1715 of the great King Louis XIV, French supremacy in Europe received a check, financial conditions in France were far from satisfactory,

[23] *Wis. Hist. Colls.*, xvi, 487.
[24] *Ibid.*, 493.

and the French nation appeared to be on the eve of bankruptcy. Crozat under these conditions was forced in 1715 to resign his charter to the government. France was temporarily saved from disaster by the financial genius of the great Scotch speculator John Law. One of the earliest of his projects was the formation of a company to exploit the French colonies overseas. The Company of the West[25] was chartered in August, 1717, and granted the monopoly of the colony of Louisiana, and the right to buy at a fixed price the beaver of Canada for twenty-five years. This company had control of the settlement and government of Louisiana, appointed all the officials, collected all the revenues, and maintained therein a full monopoly. In Canada the colonial government remained royal, the company having merely the fur trade monopoly. These arrangements portended friction, the danger of which was greatly increased when in September, 1718, the Illinois country was annexed to Louisiana and included in the company's monopoly. Illinois was, as we have seen, originally settled by Canadians; the routes thither had been from the time of Jolliet an extension of those of New France. Commercial relations were up to this time almost wholly with Montreal. Nevertheless, the Mississippi formed a highway between Illinois and Louisiana which could not be ignored. Traditionally Illinois belonged to Canada, logically to Louisiana.

The Canadian officials resented the detaching of this fertile region from their authority, all the more that they still claimed the upper Mississippi, and that both the northern and eastern boundaries of Illinois were not well defined. The Wisconsin River valley was always a part of Canada, but the Illinois officials claimed

[25] At first this was known as *La Compagnie d'Occident*, later as *La Compagnie des Indes*. It is usually called the Mississippi Company.

all the land to the Wisconsin, including the lead
mines around Galena; while the Canadian governors
thought that the Mascouten and Kickapoo country
between the Wisconsin and Illinois rivers rightfully
belonged to Canada.[26]

The Fox Indians cunningly took advantage of these
intercolonial jealousies. Their allies, the Mascouten and
Kickapoo, had long been at enmity with the Illinois
Indians. In 1719 three Fox chiefs and a Kickapoo
attended the councils at Montreal and professed a
disposition to remain at peace with all the French allies
except the Illinois, whom they accused of retaining
their prisoners and inciting raids upon the Canadian
allies.[27] The Canadian governor gave them an evasive
reply, and raids upon the Illinois were redoubled, until
the whole valley of the Illinois River became a scene
of devastation. The southern tribesmen were no match
for their barbarous opponents. They defended themselves badly, and complained to the French commandant of their woes. Father Charlevoix in 1721 had great
difficulty in passing through by the Kankakee-Illinois
route to the settlements on the Mississippi. Everywhere he saw evidences of the ravages of the merciless
Renards.[28] The next year they besieged and captured
both the village on the almost inaccessible Rocher, and
that at Peoria.[29] They grew so bold that they killed
and scalped French soldiers at the very gates of the
palisades of Kaskaskia and Fort de Chartres. The
Canadian traders even told the tribesmen that the

[26] Margry, vi, 511-512.
[27] *Wis. Hist. Colls.*, xvi, 380-381.
[28] Charlevoix, *Journal of a Voyage*, ii, 186-192. A tradition
of a great battle fought about this time between the Illinois and
Foxes on the Beaucoup tributary of the Big Muddy in Jackson
County, Illinois, was related to Draper. See Draper MSS. 6S43.
[29] *Wis. Hist. Colls.*, xvi, 429; N. D. Mereness, *Travels in the
American Colonies* (New York, 1916), 66.

Illinois Frenchmen were "other white men" whom they were not obliged to spare, thus sacrificing "their country to obtain beaver skins."[30]

Such conditions could not be borne. The Louisiana officials complained to the regent, who ordered the governor of Canada to put a stop to such outrages. Vaudreuil excused his traders and Indians, saying that the Illinois colony harbored absconding traders, and granted licenses for fur trade in Canadian territory, whence large quantities of skins were carried off. He also excused the Foxes and their allies for attacks on the Illinois Indians, since the latter had not returned the formers' prisoners and were themselves keeping up the war.[31]

Such excuses could not long avail Vaudreuil; the French ministry called him sharply to account for his lukewarmness toward the French who were murdered in Illinois. Thereupon, in 1724, the governor ordered Marchand de Lignery, commandant at Mackinac, to go to La Baye and see what might be done. Montigny had by this time been superseded at this post by Captain François Amariton, an officer who came to New France about the close of the seventeenth century. Not much is known about his career or the circumstances of his appointment. The choice of this officer was protested by the French minister on the ground that "he did not understand the Indians and was unfit for many reasons." The order to remove him, however, did not come until Amariton had had a term of three years (1724-27) at La Baye, where he seems to have held his own in the councils with the Indians.[32]

[30] *Wis. Hist. Colls.*, xvi, 460-461.
[31] *Ibid.*, 436, 438, 444-445.
[32] *Canadian Archives Report*, 1904, 58, 70, 163; *Wis. Hist. Colls.*, xvii, 18. Amariton's contract for the fur trade, signed by himself July 15, 1724, is in Chicago Historical Society, Schmidt

In August, 1724, Lignery, taking Father St. Pé from Mackinac, went to La Baye and held a council there with the Foxes, Sauk, and Winnebago on behalf of peace. Amariton and Father Chardon were likewise in the official party. The Wisconsin Indians agreed to make peace with the Chippewa and Ottawa near Lignery's post; but when Lignery approached them on the subject of the Illinois, they insisted that the latter still retained their captives. Lignery and the missionaries joined in representing to the commandant of Illinois that it was the fault of his savages that peace was not made.[33] The message was sent by a famous chief of St. Joseph, Le Chat Blanc (the White Cat). Lignery then made peace with the Foxes, leaving the Illinois question open.

Lignery's peace treaty of 1724 aroused the sharpest resentment at Kaskaskia and the other Illinois villages; their governor, Claude Charles Dutisné, complained both to Vaudreuil and to the Company of the West, and sent documents signed by all the missionaries of the Illinois to the effect that the Illinois had no Fox prisoners, that they had never acted treacherously toward the Renards, but had only defended themselves when attacked. "If the ruin of this colony is desired," he wrote to Vaudreuil, "that is the way to succeed." "We are killed everywhere by the Renards," Dutisné wrote to his superiors, "to whom Canada supplies weapons and powder. The Beaver in Their district causes the Great carnage among us; and we shall obtain no relief unless you give orders in regard to this affair."

Collection, No. 237. In 1732 the king allowed him a gratuity for his extra expenses at Green Bay, which included the rescue of an Illinois woman about to be burned at the stake. By 1733 he was dead, leaving a widow and one daughter.

[33] *Wis. Hist. Colls.*, xvi, 441-450.

Meanwhile the Illinois government, fearing that Vaudreuil would amuse the court with excuses, sent Father Beaubois with a delegation of Illinois chiefs to plead their cause at court. Among these chiefs was Chicagou, the Michigamea chief from Cahokia. His eloquence and dignity made a deep impression in France.[34] The cause of Illinois was championed by the ministers, who severely rebuked Vaudreuil for allowing a peace to be made excluding the Illinois Indians.[35] A further need for harmony in the West was the progress the Albany traders were making in securing the western trade. Despite the fact that the French agent Joncaire built a warehouse in 1720 which commanded the Niagara portage, the cheapness and quality of English goods tempted the western Indians to run the barrier and carry their furs to Albany. In 1722 the first delegation of sixteen Ottawa reached the post on the Hudson; the next year eighty western Indians arrived with a large concourse of women and children. Two years later the New York colony erected a trading post at Oswego, which was in 1726 rebuilt in permanent form, expressly for the purpose of attracting the trade of the upper Great Lakes. The French countered by erecting in the latter year a fort at Niagara, which completed their occupation of the Great Lakes route to the West.[36]

Meanwhile Governor Vaudreuil had died, before the reprimand of the French ministry had arrived in Canada. His successor, Baron de Longueuil, immediately ordered Lignery to hold another council with

[34] Alvord, *Illinois*, 162.
[35] *Canadian Archives Report*, 1904, 62, letter dated June 5, 1725.
[36] *Wraxall's Abridgment*, 140, 144; Frank H. Severance, *An Old Frontier of France* (Buffalo Historical Society, New York, 1917), i, 225-250.

the tribes at La Baye, in which peace with the Illinois Indians should be the dominant note. Lignery now realized that he had gone too far in his jealousy of the neighboring colony. June 7, 1726, he met the tribesmen at the La Baye post, and ordered the Foxes, Sauk, and Winnebago to lay down the war club now raised against the Illinois. The chiefs of these tribes replied submissively and Lignery took immediate steps to ensure their obedience. The Sioux, who from enemies had become allies of the Foxes, were detached from that alliance and made to promise not to grant them an asylum in their territory. Desliette, the veteran commandant at the Illinois, was notified to send back all the Fox prisoners, and a council was arranged for the following year to be held at either Chicago or Le Rocher to make a permanent peace among all the enemy tribesmen.[37]

The first result of this peace was the founding of a new post in the Northwest, or to speak more exactly, the reoccupation of Perrot's and Le Sueur's old posts among the Sioux. Ever since the voyage of Father Charlevoix the ministry had purposed to build a fort and establish a mission on the upper Mississippi as a basis for western exploration, and also as a profitable venture among one of the largest and most powerful Indian tribes in North America. Preparations were made on a considerable scale. Two Jesuits were chosen to begin the mission, and were furnished with mathematical instruments for purposes of observation and exploration.[38] The two missionaries chosen for this arduous task were Fathers Michel Guignas and Nicolas de Gonnor. Guignas had been for several years at Mackinac; Gonnor came up from Quebec for the expedition.

[37] *Wis. Hist. Colls.*, iii, 148-159; xvii, 1-7.
[38] *Ibid.*, xvii, 7-9.

The adventure was financed, as were all such undertakings, by the expected profits of the fur trade. A commercial company was formed in this instance, of which we possess the articles of agreement.[39] Some of the most prominent young officers and habitants were members, and to please the Montbruns, the chief promoters of the company, their uncle, La Perrière, was appointed commandant. La Perrière was the eighth son of the colonist Pierre Boucher, the first Canadian to be ennobled, whose progeny filled many of the most important offices in New France. La Perrière knew the West, having been lieutenant in Louvigny's expedition, and having before that visited the Sioux to secure their neutrality. A letter from Father Guignas gives full particulars of the expedition.[40] His is the first description of interior Wisconsin since the time of Jolliet, Perrot, Duluth, Hennepin, Lahontan, and the early Jesuits.

The expedition left Montreal June 16, 1727; five weeks were occupied in the voyage to Mackinac. The latter post was left the first of August, and after a week the Green Bay post was reached, where only two days were necessary to prepare for the perils of the journey through the country of the Foxes. Father Chardon accompanied his missionary colleagues as far as the village of these tribesmen. Three days were consumed in mounting the swift rapids of the lower Fox River; on the evening of August 14 the expedition arrived at the Winnebago village, then situated on

[39] *Wis. Hist. Colls.*, xvii, 10-14. A copy of this document with the original signature of the contracting parties is in Chicago Historical Society, Schmidt Collection, No. 381.

[40] This letter was first translated and published by Shea, *Early Voyages up and down the Mississippi* (Albany, 1861), 167-175, from a copy in St. Mary's College, Montreal. Margry also gives it, vi, 552-558. The best translation is in *Wis. Hist. Colls.*, xvii, 22-28.

Doty Island, at a point commanding the entrance to Lake Winnebago.[41]

Just when the Winnebago took possession of this noted site has not been ascertained. They were not there during the seventeenth century, since all travelers mention their presence on Green Bay or near De Pere.[42] Their numbers were so small that they had found it necessary to make close alliance with the Potawatomi and Sauk, among whom they intermarried and near whom they lived. They probably formed this village on Doty Island early in the eighteenth century. The Sioux expedition found but sixty to eighty warriors in their tribe, all "very tall and well built." Their reception of the French was gracious and enthusiastic.[43]

The next point to be reached was the village of the Foxes, "so dreaded and really very little to be dreaded."[44] These Indians ran down to the water's edge with peace calumets and gave the French a seemingly cordial welcome, dissembling their real sentiments and holding with them a friendly council. The French equipment was too formidable to attack, and it served the Foxes' purpose to let the expedition pass. Guignas noted that their tribe was a "nursery garden of children," especially of stout young boys. He said there were but two hundred men among them. This village, however, was only one of three or four, all equally populous. From the Fox village Father Chardon and the interpreter went back to La Baye;

[41] Map drawn November 10, 1730, by Chassegros de Léry, shows the location of this well-known Winnebago village. See *post*, page 314.
[42] See a contrary opinion in Wis. Hist. Soc., *Proc.*, 1906, 144-166, which I do not accept. Lahontan in 1688 found a Kickapoo village on Lake Winnebago, probably at the Doty Island site.
[43] *Wis. Hist. Colls.*, xvii, 23.
[44] For the site of this village, see *ante*, chapter xiii, note 29.

REOCCUPATION OF THE POSTS

the French expedition pressed on without guides, and found it exceedingly tiresome and annoying to thread the winding channel of the upper Fox, frequently lost in marshes and wild-rice tangles. It took a week to go from Oshkosh to the portage, which they came upon unexpectedly. "The portage," writes Guignas, "is half a league long, the half of it being only a sort of swamp full of mud." From the portage they embarked on the Ouisconsin, "a shallow river upon a bed of shifting sand," and swiftly glided down to the Mississippi, which was ascended to Lake Pepin, where they arrived September 17, after three months' voyaging from Montreal. La Perrière chose a site on the western shore of the lake two miles from the railroad station of Frontenac, Minnesota.[45] By the end of October the fort was finished and "every one found himself lodged peacefully in his own home." The post was named for the new governor Beauharnois,[46] whose fête day was celebrated with great éclat soon after the completion of the fort. Some rockets were among the goods of the company, which were set off on a fine evening, to the consternation of the natives, who thought the white men were causing the stars to drop from the sky.

The winter at Fort Beauharnois passed away peacefully. In the spring an inundation of the fort site made a temporary commotion. La Perrière, who had been ill, left in the early summer for Montreal, taking with him Father Gonnor, and leaving his nephew, Ensign Pierre de Boucherville, in command.[47] When La

[45] Folwell, *Minnesota*, i, 46.
[46] Charles de la Boische Marquis de Beauharnois was next to Frontenac the ablest and best governor of New France. His term of twenty-one years was its heyday of prosperity. See sketch in *Wis. Hist. Colls.*, xvii, 7.
[47] *Ibid.*, 36.

Perrière reached La Baye he found that Amariton had been recalled, and the command of that post had been granted to Captain François Lefebre Sieur Duplessis-Fabert, who had arrived since the building of Fort Beauharnois.[48]

The occupation of the Sioux country of the upper Mississippi marks the end of this period of French building in the Northwest.[49] A post and commandant had been promised to the Foxes during their council in 1726 with Lignery; but this promise was never kept, since the commandants at La Baye were naturally opposed to any such encroachments upon their preserves.[50] Although several temporary forts were built during the later Fox wars, yet three posts were maintained almost continuously in Wisconsin until the close of the French régime. That at La Baye was the most important and the best known; it commanded the best portage route to the Mississippi, and kept a restraining hand on the tribes about Green Bay. That on the upper Mississippi (located at several different sites) was useful in securing the Sioux trade, as the country of this tribe abounded in the best kind of beaver. This post was maintained with many vicissitudes until the outbreak of the French and Indian War. Fort La Pointe on Chequamegon Bay commanded the Lake Superior routes to the interior and to the Mississippi, and controlled the Chippewa, who were the most powerful of the northern Indians.

[48] *Wis. Hist. Colls.*, xvii, 17. In Chicago Historical Society, Schmidt Collection, No. 239, is a document signed by Duplessis-Fabert in September, 1727, then on the point of departure for his post at La Baye des Puants.

[49] This refers to the region known as the Old Northwest. The Vérendryes pushed French occupation out onto the rivers and lakes of the Canadian Northwest.

[50] *Wis. Hist. Colls.*, xvi, 467.

REOCCUPATION OF THE POSTS

It was also maintained until the military exigences of the last French war involved the withdrawal of the garrison. Of the other northwestern posts beyond the borders of Wisconsin, those of Michilimackinac, commanding the Ottawa River-Lake Huron route, and Detroit, commanding the route by the lower Great Lakes, were the most important. Those of St. Joseph, Miami, and Ouiatanon held strategic positions on the portages between the lower lakes and the Ohio. Vincennes and Illinois were in the colony of Louisiana, and were defenses against the southern tribes in alliance with the British. The later activities in the Northwest were bent toward opening the route to the western ocean that Duluth had attempted and that Charlevoix had advised. To this end a post was maintained on Lake Nipigon, and another at Kaministiquia, and thence new posts were added at important points on the great lakes of the Canadian Northwest, and out on the plains toward the "shining mountains." All these far western forts were included in the title "Post of the Sea of the West."[51] Sault Ste. Marie was not reoccupied until 1750, almost the close of the French sovereignty in America; and the same was true of the chain of posts built to hold the upper Ohio frontier against the English. Each of these far-flung wilderness forts was isolated from any real contact with the others, and while each commanded an important vantage point, they were too scattered to constitute a secure hold of so vast an extent of territory peopled by savages who had as yet attained no veneer of civilization, and who were only biding their time and opportunity to make new assaults upon French traders and soldiers in the West.

[51] *Wis. Hist. Colls.*, xviii, 185-188.

XV. THE SECOND FOX WAR, 1727-1738

WHEN was the first French settlement made in Wisconsin? This is a question easy to ask and difficult to answer. From the time when in 1668 Perrot and Baudry made their first visit to the tribal villages clustered around Green Bay, there was probably never a time when white men did not live, for part of the year at least, in what is now Wisconsin. The Jesuit mission was maintained at De Pere continuously from its inception in 1671 until the building of Fort La Baye in 1717. The upper Mississippi River posts and those on Lake Superior were garrisoned until in 1698 the edict of evacuation went into effect. Even in the period of neglect and retrogression from 1698 to 1717, *coureurs de bois* in considerable numbers lived in the Indian villages and roamed through the forest pathways. With the establishment of permanent posts, however, bringing centers of law and civilization into this region, the first real settlements began.

In 1718 a description of La Baye relates that "it is settled by the Puants [Winnebago] and folles-avoines [Menominee]; there are some French also."[1] This seems to indicate the time a permanent white settlement was begun around the French fort. Some eleven years later, in May, 1729, there was born at Mackinac a French and Ottawa half-breed who has long been designated as the "father of Wisconsin" and who is customarily spoken of as its first settler. This, as we shall see, is far from exact. Charles de Langlade did not come to reside at Green Bay until after the close of the French régime, and performed his services for the

[1] *Wis. Hist. Colls.*, xvi, 371.

French government while still living at Mackinac. None the less, as he was at a later date the most prominent of the French settlers of Green Bay, and as he left many descendants who were leaders in the community, he was long regarded as the first Frenchman to make a home in Wisconsin.[2]

Charles de Langlade's father, Augustin Mouet Sieur de Langlade, a native of Three Rivers, was the son of an officer in the regiment of Carignan. Langlade and his older brother Didace Mouet Sieur de Moras belonged to the lesser nobility of Canada, and were connected with its leading families. Didace married a daughter of Captain de Louvigny, and was an ensign in the colonial army. Augustin, who may likewise have had hopes of a military career, found that opportunities for promotion in the army were infrequent; he, therefore, like many younger sons, abandoned the army for the fur trade.[3] It was a wise policy for a French trader to ally himself with a chief's family among the natives. Augustin, on arriving at Mackinac, found there an Ottawa woman, a sister of the principal chiefs of the clan called La Fourche. This Indian woman, who was very influential in tribal councils, may have preserved even at this time some of her maidenly charm, for in her youth she was known as "La Blanche," probably for the lightness of her skin.[4] She had received "Domitelle" as a baptismal

[2] For Langlade's baptismal entry, see "Mackinac Register," in *Wis. Hist. Colls.*, xix, 3.

[3] It is to be noted that both Didace and Augustin were members of the second Sioux Company in 1731. *Wis. Hist. Colls.*, xvii, 135, 139.

[4] *Mich. Pion. and Hist. Colls.*, xxxiii, 554. It is worthy of note in consideration of the interests of the Langlades in Green Bay, that the Ottawa of La Fourche dwelt there in the later seventeenth century.

name and, when Langlade met her, was a widow, having been married by the missionary priest to Daniel Villeneuve, an early trader, to whom she had borne six children.[5] Her marriage to Langlade occurred in 1728, and their only child was Charles de Langlade, who played so important a part in early Wisconsin history.[6]

Whoever were the first settlers around the Green Bay post, their tenure of life there was very precarious. The peace which Lignery in 1726 had concluded with the Foxes was delusive. This wily tribe had no intention of keeping the treaty in good faith, nor of abandoning its cherished animosity against the Illinois tribesmen. The Foxes remained quiet and dissembled in order to consummate their designs, which involved the expulsion of the entire race of Frenchmen from their tribal lands and the formation of a vast conspiracy.

The Fox chief who built up a confederacy of hostile tribes, a precursor of Pontiac and Tecumseh, seems to have been Kiala, the leader of the anti-French party among the Foxes. He conceived of a union stretching all the way from the Abenaki of the East, embracing the Iroquois on Lake Ontario, and extending to the Sioux at the northwest and the Missouri and Oto tribes to the southwest. Had he been successful, the French both

[5] *Wis. Hist. Colls.*, vii, 124; xix, 2-3. She must have been older than Augustin de Langlade, who was born in 1703, since her son Daniel Villeneuve was baptized in 1712. However, as Indian women married very young, there may not have been as much discrepancy of ages as would seem.

[6] Charles de Langlade's grandson fixed the date of his settlement in Wisconsin as 1745. *Wis. Hist. Colls.*, iii, 199-201. It is evident that this was merely a general calculation. Documentary evidence shows that Langlade did not remove permanently from Mackinac until 1764 or 1765. He and his father undoubtedly had a trading post at La Baye before that date. The "Mackinac Register" shows that other French-Canadians were living at Green Bay earlier than the Langlades.

in Canada and in Louisiana would have been encircled by a ring of hostiles, and might have been driven from the St. Lawrence, the Great Lakes, and the Mississippi.[7] Very secretly were these alliances formed; tribe after tribe, influenced by the eloquence of the barbaric leader, responded to his appeal, and took the wampum belts indicative of war with France. It was a resurgence of barbarism against civilization, a rebellion of a brave, independent people against the demoralization of white influence and the invasion of their lands. Like barbarians, however, they were unable to plan with sufficient foresight, or to hold together their allies against the influence of the French or of intertribal rivalries. The defection of the Sioux, which was brought about by officers from Chequamegon, and by building a post on the upper Mississippi, was a setback for Kiala's plans. Meanwhile the southwestern tribes, accompanied by a band of Foxes, struck a direct but premature blow at the French power. A lieutenant and seven soldiers, sent up the Missouri River from Fort de Chartres, were attacked and all massacred.[8] It was seen how hollow was the truce that Lignery had negotiated.

Canada was reinforced in the year 1727 by the arrival of a new governor-general to take the place of Vaudreuil. The Marquis de Beauharnois was commonly reputed to be a son of Louis XIV. Certain it is that he was an able administrator, and that the years of his governorship (1727-48) were the most prosperous New France ever saw. He at once penetrated the designs of the Foxes, their connection with the Iroquois and the English; in his first report he wrote to the minister of

[7] For the sweep of this hostile confederacy and the separate tribes composing it, see Wis. Hist. Soc., *Proc.*, 1907, 166-168.

[8] Alvord, *Illinois*, 162. Until the publication of this fact, taken from the Louisiana documents, it was not known what was the immediate occasion for Lignery's expedition.

state that the Renards "have said that they would no longer suffer any French among them."[9] He determined, therefore, to be beforehand with this troublesome tribe and to strike a blow which should annihilate it. Desliette from Illinois was urging such a measure, writing that the Renards were suspicious and feared treachery, "and that the surest method would be to destroy them." Lignery, who knew the bravery and fierceness of this barbarous people, urged that it would be better to conciliate them by establishing an officer and a garrison in their country, as Ouachala had requested.[10]

Beauharnois, however, was determined to signalize the beginning of his administration with a brilliant stroke which should command the awe and admiration of all the North American savages. He reasoned that the interruption of the fur trade for a brief time would be more than compensated by later serenity in the upper country, that French lives must not go unavenged, and that the Iroquois, who inclined too strongly to the English alliance, must be overawed by a show of force.[11] The governor was too inexperienced in wilderness warfare to realize the difficulty of crushing even a single small tribe a thousand miles in the interior, so far from the base of supplies. By his energy and determination he overcame the difficulties of preparation, and sent in the summer of 1728 what seemed to be an overwhelming military force into Wisconsin. This was the second armed invasion of the region west of Green Bay, and it was planned on a more elaborate scale than that of twelve years earlier. Lignery, as the one man who best knew the region,

[9] *Wis. Hist. Colls.*, xvi, 476-477.
[10] *Ibid.*, iii, 161; xvii, 5.
[11] *Ibid.*, iii, 160-166.

THE SECOND FOX WAR 319

was chosen to command. His army, when he left Montreal, consisted of four hundred French and eight to nine hundred Indians; at Mackinac three hundred more tribesmen were recruited. This considerable army left Mackinac on August 10, and advanced in batteaux and canoes along Green Bay, taking care to arrive at the French fort during the night time. Lignery had been urged to plan a surprise, but even if it had been possible to keep the advance of such a body of warriors a secret, he was outwitted by a Potawatomi chieftain who, while professing friendship to the French, was secretly notifying the Foxes and their allies of the oncoming army.

At the Sauk village opposite Fort La Baye four enemy Indians were captured and given to the tribesmen to torture and burn—a cruelty that preyed heavily upon the mind of the Recollect chaplain of the expedition, Emanuel Crespel.[12] From the fort Lignery advanced up Fox River as far as the Winnebago village at the outlet of Lake Winnebago, whence every mortal had fled. At the Fox village on Little Lake Butte des Morts one old man and a few women who had been unable to escape were taken. From them the invaders learned that the Foxes had been gone four days; they had built a fort for defense, probably within the limits of what is now the city of Oshkosh; but having had timely notice, they had collected m than a hundred canoes for the retreat of the old men, women, and children, while the warriors followed on foot along the river bank. Lignery advanced as far as the third Fox village, situated in the marsh between

[12] *Wis. Hist. Colls.*, v, 86-91; x, 47-53. Crespel, *Voyages*, first appeared in 1742; subsequent editions were issued in French at Frankfort and Amsterdam; an English translation was published at London in 1797.

the Fox and Wolf rivers.[13] He could not persuade his soldiers to go farther. They were valiant enough only to burn the cornfields and the cabins, cut down the standing corn, and devastate the fertile fields; so that he hoped at least half of the enemy would die of hunger.

The result of this expedition was disproportionate to the effort expended, and Lignery's report is full of excuses for his mismanagement of the affair.[14] He blamed Desliettes for not marching up from Illinois and cutting off the Foxes' retreat; he blamed the *voyageurs* for their mutinous spirit, and accused the allied Indians of insubordination. Beauharnois in his report to the government blamed Lignery for tarrying at Mackinac, and for his trust in the faithless Potawatomi. The marginal comment of the ministry was: "M. De Lignery allows the Foxes to escape."[15]

This expedition had important consequences for early Wisconsin history. Some of the most prominent men in the New World served under Lignery, among whom were two sons of the late Governor Vaudreuil, one of whom was to become governor-general of Canada, while the other fixed his mind on the advantages of Wisconsin, and in process of time obtained an exclusive grant to its trade. Other participants, among whom was Augustin de Langlade, talked of the land, its beauty and fertility, until the Fox River became noted throughout the length and breadth of Canada. The immediate consequences, however, were disastrous for French interests. The Sauk refused to remain in their village at the river's mouth, so that Lignery was

[13] For the locations, see map drawn by Chaussegros de Léry, November 10, 1730, on page 314. This map has never before been published. We reproduce it from a copy of the original in the Canadian Archives.
[14] Lignery's report to Beauharnois is in *Wis. Hist. Colls.*, xvii, 31-35.
[15] *Wis. Hist. Colls.*, v, 91-95.

obliged to withdraw the garrison and to burn the French fort. He also sent a warning to the Sioux post on Lake Pepin urging the garrison there to retreat from so dangerous a situation.

About twenty soldiers and traders were then stationed at Fort Beauharnois, commanded by Ensign Boucherville, of the Boucher family; with him were his cousins, the Montbruns, and the Jesuit missionary Father Michel Guignas. Hastily holding a council of war, they decided that retreat was the only alternative to being caught between the warriors of the infuriated Foxes and those of their secret allies, the Sioux. A few of the traders preferred to take a desperate risk rather than to abandon their goods, and remained behind when Boucherville, the Montbruns, Father Guignas, and eight others set out to run the gauntlet to the Illinois. This party left the little stockade post on October 3, 1728—a time when all the forests were brilliant in autumn coloring and the high cliffs of the Mississippi wore their most glorious garb. All seemed peaceful to the *voyageurs*, as the three small canoes slipped silently down the river. A careful watch was kept for the foe; just below the mouth of the Wisconsin River traces of a Fox party were seen, and some distance below a fleet of beached canoes whose inmates had evidently retired to the interior.[16] Hope now sprang up that the French party might win through to the Illinois; the dangerous opening of the Kickapoo River (now called the Rock) was safely passed, when suddenly in the fogs of the morning, near a stream called Rivière aux Boeufs,[17] a party of Indians was descried running along the bank and paddling out in canoes to intercept the white men's passage. When the latter

[16] Probably at the mouth of the Wapsipinicon River of Iowa.
[17] Probably Iowa River, called on early maps Buffalo or Bison River. See *Iowa Journal of History and Politics*, 1916, 99.

prepared to defend themselves, the red men called out that they had no ill design, and would do no harm. Thereupon the Frenchmen surrendered to superior force. The captors proved to be a band of Mascouten and Kickapoo, Fox allies, and nearly as hostile to the whites as the Renards themselves. Although Boucherville and Father Guignas held councils with them, probably all the French would have been massacred or surrendered to the Foxes to be tortured, had not the Montbruns succeeded in escaping. This alarmed the captors, who finally, after keeping their prisoners through the winter, yielded to their importunities and agreed to abandon their alliance with the Foxes and to make a truce with the Illinois. Boucherville was conducted to Peoria, where he was able to communicate with the officers in Illinois, and by March all the captive French were permitted to leave for Fort de Chartres. There a peace was made detaching the Mascouten and Kickapoo from the Fox confederacy.[18]

Boucherville's success with these two hostile tribes neutralized Lignery's failure. The great confederacy of the Foxes began to break up. The traders who remained at Fort Beauharnois succeeded in holding the Sioux firm in the interests of the French.[19] The Abenaki were withdrawn from the alliance by their missionaries and the governor-general.[20] Even the Winnebago, who had shared with the Foxes the punishment of the French army, and had had their fields and villages ravaged, forebore revenge and promised complete submission to the will of the French officers.[21] In the

[18] Boucherville's narrative remained in manuscript until 1826, when it was printed in Michel Bibaud, *La Bibliothèque Canadienne*, from which it was translated for *Wis. Hist. Colls.*, xvii, 36-55. See list of the commandant's expenses, *ibid.*, 82-86.
[19] *N. Y. Colon. Docs.*, ix, 1017.
[20] *Ibid.*, 1014; *Wis. Hist. Colls.*, xvii, 62.
[21] *Wis. Hist. Colls.*, xvii, 89.

summer of 1729 at the annual conference at Montreal, Governor Beauharnois solicited all the western tribesmen to "destroy the Foxes, and not to suffer on this earth a demon capable of confounding or opposing our friendly alliance."[22] Urged on by the French officers, the neighboring Indians made up war parties, which hunted out the fugitive Foxes and made great havoc among them. In October, 1729, one of their hunting parties was attacked by Ottawa and Chippewa, with whom mingled a few Winnebago; this party captured and burned seventy-seven warriors of the enemy tribesmen, nearly four times as many women and children sharing the same fate.[23]

Cowed by this and other disasters, the survivors of the once haughty Fox tribe were forced to sue for their lives. A party of them approached the Sioux post and begged La Jémerais, the youth in charge, to accompany a delegation of their chiefs to the nearest post, which was the one on St. Joseph River. There the embassy promised the commandant that some of their chiefs would go to Montreal to beg for peace when La Jémerais went down; but at the last moment their hearts misgave them, and they refused to put themselves in the power of their numerous enemies.[24] Beauharnois thereupon determined to send a French officer among the allies to complete the work of subjugation. The one chosen for this mission was Paul de la Marque Sieur Marin, who was for the next quarter-century to be the leading personage in northwestern history.[25]

[22] *Wis. Hist. Colls.*, iii, 105; xvii, 62-64.
[23] *Ibid.*, v, 104.
[24] *Ibid.*, xvii, 65-68.
[25] *Ibid.*, v, 116-117; xvii, 315. From documents in the Chicago Historical Society we learn that Paul Marin was an officer resident in Montreal as early as 1719; he was then interested in western trade. See page 296 for document with his signature.

Despite his accomplishments and his success in practically ending the Fox wars, Marin remains a shadowy, legendary figure in western history. He belonged to the class of gentlemen, since he held a commission in the colonial army, and rose therein to the rank of captain; he served in several colonial wars, died on the Ohio frontier, and was buried above Pittsburgh. In Wisconsin history his name was the synonym of "terror," and the strategem by which he subdued the Foxes was long recounted by the older *voyageurs*.[26] In the summer of 1729 he left Montreal and came as far as the Menominee village, where he established headquarters in a deserted fort, which he repaired and in which he wintered. Early the succeeding spring he had a serious encounter with a band of Foxes on Little Lake Butte des Morts, whither they had returned to besiege the treacherous Winnebago. Marin relieved the Winnebago fort, and the Foxes after five days of grim fighting stole off in the night time, leaving in their haste even the mats with which they built their cabins.[27]

In their desperation the Foxes now sought a desperate remedy. Surrounded on every side by former allies now turned enemies, they resolved to abandon their homeland and to seek a refuge among the Iroquois, who had long solicited their alliance and had offered them an asylum. During the early summer of 1730 they sent a messenger to the Seneca, with two redstone

---

[26] *Wis. Hist. Colls.*, iii, 208-211; historians have never been able to localize this incident in time or place.

[27] See Marin's long narrative of this campaign, in *Wis. Hist. Colls.*, xvii, 88-100. See also the Winnebago tradition, in Wis. Hist. Soc., *Proc.*, 1914, 192-207. With regard to the post in the Menominee country, this account of Marin is our only knowledge of it. It was doubtless a trader's post subsidiary to Fort La Baye.

THE FRENCH POST NEAR TREMPEALEAU
From an idealized sketch by Mrs. Hattie M. Pierce

axes in token of their desire to come to live among them. Joncaire, the French agent among the Seneca, secured possession of these tokens and sent them to Montreal, at the same time terrifying the Iroquois with threats of vengeance should they listen to the Foxes' proposal.[28] Notwithstanding this miscarriage of their embassy, the Foxes received secret advices that they would be welcomed by the Iroquois, when they at once prepared for the great trek from Wisconsin to the shores of Lake Ontario.

It would seem that at this time the Foxes were living somewhere in southern Wisconsin, and began their migration by advancing toward the old battle ground of Le Rocher on the Illinois; there a party of Illinois was encountered from whom the Foxes took a victim in the person of the son of the great Cahokia chief. They had planned to go through the country of the Ouiatanon Indians dwelling on the Wabash near the present Lafayette, Indiana. With this tribe they had a secret understanding, not only for permission to pass through their lands, but for aid and provisioning *en route*.

The first news of their march was carried to the French commandants by their late allies the Kickapoo and Mascouten, through whose country they were obliged to pass. The sixth of August the latter sent runners to Coulon de Villiers, then in command of the post of St. Joseph, to say that the Foxes were passing into the Iroquois country. Villiers at once notified

[28] *Wis. Hist. Colls.*, xvii, 119; *Wraxall's Abridgment*, 181; *N. Y. Colon. Docs.*, v, 911-912. The English agents rebuked the Seneca for not taking advantage of this offer of reinforcements. There is no indication, however, that the project arose with the English. The redstone weapons were a token of the Foxes' desire to return to aboriginal weapons and no longer to be dependent upon French iron.

Deschaillons at Detroit, and Des Noyelles at the Miami post. Meanwhile St. Ange, who upon the death of Desliette in 1729 had succeeded to the leadership in Illinois, gathered a body of French and Peoria Indians and pursued the Foxes. When the Foxes' scouts warned them that they were being hemmed in by hostile bands, they stopped and erected on the prairie between the Illinois and the Wabash, a fort strong enough to stand a great siege, with covered passageways leading to the water of a small creek.[29]

St. Ange's contingent was the first to overtake the enemy, coming in sight of their fort on August 10; Villiers came up on the seventeenth, and his force was soon augmented to eight hundred French and Indians. Vincennes was hastily summoned from the post bearing his name, and brought up a contingent of Piankeshaw which swelled the numbers of the besiegers to fourteen hundred. St. Ange and Vincennes camped on the southeast, Villiers and Des Noyelles on the northeast of the Fox fort.

For twenty-three days this devoted tribe made an heroic defense of their prairie fort. The endurance of this siege would have been impossible had not many of the besiegers secretly sympathized with the sufferers and surreptitiously supplied them with provisions. They even tried to induce the French commandants to spare the lives of the unhappy victims, but all to no purpose. Finally the end came; the night of September 9 proved stormy, and the besieging Indians in conse-

[29] The site of this fort, and of the great siege, is a vexed question. See *Wis. Hist. Colls.*, xvii, 129, note; Alvord, *Illinois*, 164, note. All French accounts place it from one hundred and twenty to one hundred and fifty miles south-southeast of Le Rocher. Léry says the little stream was near the Macoupin; more probably it was an eastern branch of the Kaskaskia, as the Macoupin is southwest of Le Rocher.

quence refused to stand guard; the Foxes, under cover of the storm and darkness, issued from their fort and fled toward the southwest. The crying of their little children betrayed them; with dawn the pursuit was organized, and the Foxes, burdened with their families, were soon overtaken. Then the peaceful prairies of Illinois were the scene of a horrible butchery; one by one the fleeing savages were caught and struck down with bullet or tomahawk, amid the war whoops of the victors and the heartless glee of the French, until from two to three hundred brave foemen, with as many women and children, were massacred. Four or five hundred more were captured and scattered among the victors; the few who escaped fled back to their old haunts in Wisconsin, and nursed their hope of vengeance through the long winter months.[30] Villiers sent his eldest son to carry the news of the victory to Canada; then the colonial engineer drew a map of the location from the description of the younger Villiers.[31] The war with the Foxes seemed to have come to a victorious end; the prisoners were parceled out as slaves among the French allies, some of them even finding their way to servitude in the St. Lawrence valley itself.[32] Beauharnois wrote to his superiors in France that "Tranquility for so many years disturbed in the upper country, will now reign, and Enable us to continue our Establishments there."[33]

[30] *Wis. Hist. Colls.*, xvii, 100-102, 109-119, 129-130.

[31] *Ibid.*, 120. The messenger was Nicolas Villiers, Jr. The map made by Léry is in the Canadian Archives; a tracing of it may be seen in Illinois State Historical Society, *Transactions*, 1908, 254.

[32] In 1731 a merchant of Montreal sold an Indian slave to a customer, guaranteeing that this slave was not a Renard, and that in case the governor-general should claim him as a Renard the buyer should be reimbursed for his purchase. Chicago Historical Society, Schmidt Collection, No. 162.

[33] *Wis. Hist. Colls.*, xvii, 140.

The next summer the governor had reason again to congratulate himself on the successful extermination of this troublesome tribe. Two of the Fox chiefs came down with Villiers to beg for the lives of the few remnants of their tribe, while all the other tribes showed by their submissive spirit the impression produced by the fate of the Foxes. He was confirmed in his "opinion as to the necessity that existed of destroying a nation as wicked as it was pernicious to the colony."[34]

Beauharnois, however, counted without his host; he did not yet know anything of Indian politics. Later in his career he wrote: "You may imagine, Monseigneur, that the Savages have their policy as we have Ours, and they are not greatly pleased at seeing a nation destroyed, for Fear that their turn may come. They manifest Much ardor towards the French and act quite differently."[35] This, however, was after he had learned the lessons of the Fox wars. Supposing all to be well in the West, the governor-general determined to restore the two posts destroyed after Lignery's fiasco. In the summer of 1731 he sent Villiers to rebuild the fort at Green Bay. Villiers was also rewarded by a promotion in army rank, and a commission for his eldest son. The Sioux fort was likewise restored under the auspices of a second company of traders,[36] and Linctot, formerly at Chequamegon, was sent to command what proved to be a post of the greatest danger. Linctot on his outward voyage mounted the Mississippi only as far as Mount Trempealeau, and there on the site of Perrot's old wintering post he built a fort which was maintained for five years, and which has

[34] *Wis. Hist. Colls.*, xvii, 145; *Bulletin des Recherches Historiques*, xii, 170.
[35] *Wis. Hist. Colls.*, xvii, 256.
[36] *Ibid.*, 135-141.

THE SECOND FOX WAR

left to posterity the only remains yet discovered of a French post in Wisconsin.[37]

Meanwhile reprisals still continued upon the wretched remnants of the Foxes that had gathered on the banks of the Wisconsin River in a village composed of nearly fifty cabins.[38] The chiefs who had gone with Villiers to Montreal had been promised by the governor-general that he would spare the lives of the remaining members of their tribe, on condition that four principal chiefs should come to adjust the matter the succeeding year. Not waiting to determine whether the Foxes would keep their promise, Beauharnois secretly connived at the departure of a large war party of mission Indians, who went overland part of the way on snowshoes in order "to eat up the Renard." This party fell upon the Wisconsin River village in the dead of winter, and although the Foxes defended themselves bravely, they were again decimated, over three hundred being killed or captured. This devoted tribe recognized the treachery of the governor-general and the falsity of his promises, crying out in their despair, "It is our Father Onontio, who has caused us to be killed." The few who escaped the carnage fled to an outlying village of their people on the Mississippi.[39] Beauharnois, reporting this massacre to the king, hypocritically as-

[37] Wis. Hist. Soc., *Proc.*, 1915, 111-123; six fireplaces were uncovered at this site, and the remains of a blacksmith's forge, where an attempt had been made to produce iron from local ores. See the probable appearance of this Trempealeau post, in the accompanying sketch made by Mrs. H. M. Pierce, of Trempealeau.

[38] This village would seem to be the one Carver mentioned in 1766 as deserted thirty years before. It stood five miles above the mouth of the Wisconsin. *Wis. Hist. Colls.*, vi, 225.

[39] This is the first definite mention of an Indian village at Prairie du Chien. The seventeenth-century French post, Fort St. Nicolas, may have been on the prairie or below it. The town takes its name from a Fox chief, called by the French Le Chien.

serted, first, that he had not sent out the party of mission Indians, who went to settle old scores; second, that the Foxes had not kept their word, and sent in their chiefs as promised—this, months before the time appointed for the coming of the hostages.[40] It seemed apparent to every one that the Foxes were to be utterly exterminated; the governor-general willed it, the allied Indians were enraged against them; the few poor fugitives were tracked out on every side. In the autumn of 1732 a band from Detroit composed of Hurons, Ottawa, and Potawatomi found some fifty warriors entrenched in a fort on Fox River of Illinois. There the attackers were unsuccessful, and after two attempts to storm the stronghold retreated, after obtaining a vague promise of future surrender.[41]

By the early summer of 1733, however, the Foxes themselves gave up all hope. Then the great chief Kiala, who had so long animated their courage against the French and who had built up the confederacy now in ruins, determined to sacrifice himself for his people. With great heaviness of spirit, weighed down by a sense of failure and of the doom of the red men, he with three other chiefs approached La Baye and begged for mercy at the hands of Villiers. But fifty warriors were left of the entire tribe, ten of these being mere lads. Villiers was rejoiced; he felt assured that hereafter he would be known as the conqueror of the Foxes. He started at once with Kiala and the other hostages to report to the governor-general the end of the Fox wars. Trade would now revive, and the French might pass in safety from Canada to Illinois and the upper Mis-

[40] *Wis. Hist. Colls.*, xvii, 148-169.
[41] This appears to have been the affair at Maramech. See references *ante*, 248, note 10; also *Wis. Hist. Colls.*, xvii, 172-174.

sissippi along the convenient Fox-Wisconsin waterway.[42]

Villiers, upon bringing down the Fox hostages, was received with honor at Montreal; he was promoted to a captaincy and sent back to La Baye with instructions to show no mercy to the surviving Foxes, but to exterminate the whole tribe without even taking any of the warriors prisoners. The women and children were to be transported to the colony to be scattered among the mission Indians as slaves, or perchance like the great chief Kiala to be sent to the islands of the West Indies, there to die of hard labor in tropic heats.[43] In triumph Villiers returned to his post, with several of his sons and sons-in-law in his company. All portended the annihilation of the Foxes and the complete submission of the Wisconsin tribes. "The result," writes Beauharnois, "has not fulfilled our expectations." With overweening confidence and foolhardy rashness Villiers acted as though in command of a war expedition; he brought with him from Mackinac sixty French and two hundred allied tribesmen, boasting loudly of what he intended to do. The Sauk were seriously alarmed; they had permitted the few fugitive Foxes to take refuge in their village; now their French "father" demanded the surrender, without conditions, of these poor refugees. The Sauk temporized and parleyed, loath to break the bond of

[42] In Chicago Historical Society, Schmidt Collection, No. 252, is a contract dated June 9, 1732, between Didace Mouet de Moras and Jacques le Gardeur de Courtemanche for trade at La Baye des Puants "as well with the French as with the savages." This may have meant supplies for the garrison. It indicates, however, something of a settlement around the post.

[43] Instructions for Villiers are in *Wis. Hist. Colls.*, xvii, 182-183; see the fate of Kiala, *ibid.*, 210; see also *Canadian Archives Report*, 1905, i, p. xix.

hospitality with their persecuted kinsmen. Villiers haughtily advanced in person to the gate of the palisaded village and attempted to force an entrance. A chance shot struck down his young son at his side; in wrath the French fired blindly, when a twelve-year-old Sauk lad, taking careful aim at the commandant's breast, fired, and Villiers dropped dead.[44]

Then ensued a scene of the wildest confusion; after a brief battle at the gates of the village all the savages fled and took their stand at Little Butte des Morts, whither the French, led by Villiers's eldest son, followed and battled with them for an entire day. The French[45] as well as the Indians lost heavily; since the close of the intercolonial wars there had been no such list of fatalities among the French officers. The Villiers, Le Gardeur, Ailleboust, Duplessis, and other well-known families mourned the loss of their youth. Besides losing Villiers the father, and the young son killed at his side, Louis, later "le grand Villiers," who opposed Washington at Fort Necessity, was wounded at the battle of Butte des Morts.[46]

This clash at Green Bay with its fatalities on both sides led to certain important changes in the situation. The Sauk now definitely abandoned the region and never again had a permanent village in that location. They also definitely espoused the cause of the Foxes, and the two tribes became united, almost amalgamated.

[44] This lad became a renowned chief by the name of Blackbird. *Wis. Hist. Colls.*, iii, 206.

[45] Augustin Grignon said that his grandfather Charles de Langlade was in this battle, which is obviously impossible since he was but four years old; no doubt Augustin de Langlade was present. Grignon also said that two of his father's uncles were killed in this skirmish. *Wis. Hist. Colls.*, iii, 206. See also *ibid.*, viii, 207-208.

[46] Beauharnois's accounts are in *Wis. Hist. Colls.*, xvii, 188-191, 200-204. It is believed that the great mound at Butte des Morts was erected to cover the tribesmen slain in this battle.

Several other tribes, secretly pleased with the brave resistance of the Foxes, sent them back their captives; so that their numbers again became formidable and menacing to the French authority. The newly allied Sauk and Foxes built a fort on the Wapsipinicon River in Iowa and there awaited the future action of the French.

Beauharnois was much exasperated at the failure of his plan to exterminate the Foxes, who had seemed wholly within his power. His first task was to preserve the French posts in the upper country. Pierre Hertel Sieur de Montcourt was transferred from Crown Point to La Baye, and deputed to hold that post at all hazards.[47] Linctot, at his post on the Mississippi, was in constant peril; he managed, however, to maintain himself and his garrison by the aid of friendly Sioux, although one of his men had a narrow escape from massacre by a band of enraged Foxes.[48]

When in the summer of 1734 the delegates from the allied tribes visited the governor-general, he found that they could not be persuaded to attack the Foxes unless a party of French placed themselves at their head. For all their protestations of loyalty Beauharnois realized that French prestige in the West had received a severe blow, and that a punitive expedition was necessary. He thereupon issued a call for volunteers, when eighty-four soldiers, officers, and habitants with two hundred mission Indians agreed to undertake a foray.

[47] Montcourt was son of the famous François Hertel of the Iroquois wars, who was ennobled for his services. Pierre was born in 1687; married in 1721 Thérèse Judith d' Ailleboust de Périgny. He was an ensign in rank. His term of service at La Baye is known by a document in the Chicago Historical Society, Schmidt Collection, No. 245, which consists of an agreement, June 7, 1734, to supply Pierre Hertel Sieur de Montcourt, commanding for the king at the post of La Baye des Puants, with merchandise. He died in 1739.

[48] *Wis. Hist. Colls.*, xvii, 151-152, 207.

Des Noyelles, who had taken part in the Fox defeat in 1730, was chosen to command. This third armed French incursion into the West went overland, instead of by water like the previous ones. Des Noyelles left the colony in the autumn, and winter had already begun when the post among the Ouiatanon was reached. Here he expected to obtain guides who would lead him in the direction of the villages of the Renards. But the Kickapoo guides, secretly sympathizing with their former allies, led him astray; part of his army of mission Iroquois deserted; finally on March 12, after crossing the Mississippi, the invading force came in sight of the Fox fort on the Wapsipinicon, only to find it abandoned. A reconnoitre showed a trail leading toward the Des Moines River; thither Des Noyelles hastened, wading icy streams *en route*, and finally arrived on the eastern bank of a broad impassable river full of floating ice. At length a jam of logs and driftwood was found on which the army crossed, only to find that their prey had again escaped. After several days of starving, when the invaders broke into small bands to hunt for food, and one band was worsted by an unexpected attack of the enemy, Des Noyelles found the tribesmen he sought fully entrenched on an island. Futile attacks and useless parleying followed. The Kickapoo withdrew from Des Noyelles's party to a small eminence, prepared to take the part of whichever side should prove the stronger. Skirmishing followed in which several of the French were killed, including one or more of the officers. Hunger pressed upon the invaders until they ate their moccasins. The chances for the French and their allies to defeat the Foxes dwindled away. Des Noyelles and his party abandoned the enterprise, and made their way as best they might to the nearest French settlements at the Illinois.⁴⁹

French prestige now touched its lowest point in the estimation of the western Indians. Céloron at Mackinac had been unable to induce the Indians of that post to reinforce Des Noyelles; the Indians of the Illinois were supine; only the Sioux kept faith with the French, influenced by their friendship for Linctot and for his successor, Sieur de St. Pierre. Linctot's position at Trempealeau was so perilous that it was reported in the winter of 1735 that he and Father Guignas had been taken and burned by the savages.⁵⁰ Anxiety on their behalf was relieved by Linctot's arrival during the following summer at Montreal, with a fine consignment of furs and the news of the Sioux's powerful protection. He had left the missionary and six men to hold the post during his absence.⁵¹ Beauharnois at once sent thither a relief party under St. Pierre,⁵² which successfully reached the Trempealeau fort, and the following spring removed the post twenty-five leagues higher up the river. There St. Pierre was able to maintain himself less than eighteen months, doing in the meantime an excellent trade for the furs of the Sioux.⁵³

⁴⁹ Des Noyelles's account is in *Wis. Hist. Colls.*, xvii, 221-229; Beauharnois's report, *ibid.*, 216-221; that of the Jesuit chaplain for the Indians, in *ibid.*, 215-216; that of the intendant Hocquart, in *ibid.*, 230-233.

⁵⁰ *Jes. Rel.*, lxviii, 255.

⁵¹ *Ibid.*, 251, 281; *Wis. Hist. Colls.*, xvii, 230, 274.

⁵² For a sketch of this officer, see *ante*, chapter xiv, note 19. See also Margry, vi, 572-573.

⁵³ Wis. Hist. Soc., *Proc.*, 1915, 121-122. It has usually been assumed that St. Pierre rebuilt Fort Beauharnois near Frontenac, Minnesota. In view of Carver's notice of St. Pierre's post, only thirty years after its occupancy, on the east side of Lake Pepin, it would seem to have been in Wisconsin, near the earlier Fort St. Antoine. See *Wis. Hist. Colls.*, ix, 286; x, 372; xviii, 283.

It was of supreme importance for the French of the West to keep the Sioux on friendly terms with their commandants. This great tribe with its many divisions commanded the key to the richest fur trade country then known. The French post on the Mississippi had been founded with the design of advancing thence to the western sea; none of its commandants during the ten years of its maintainence (1727-37) was ever in a condition to undertake western exploration; because of the Fox wars, their situation was at all times precarious. These officers, however, performed an important function by keeping the great Sioux tribe neutral, if not entirely friendly. Meanwhile from Lake Superior an enthusiastic French explorer was making every effort to cross the continent to the western ocean. Pierre Gautier de Varennes Sieur de la Vérendrye, a native of Three Rivers, had in 1726 been given command of a small post on the shore of Lake Nipigon, where his imagination was inflamed by the tales of his Indian visitors of a great salt water in the West. One in especial from the head of Lake Superior drew for him a map of a western-flowing river which he was determined to discover.[54] La Vérendrye carried this map to the colony and persuaded the governor to give him permission for a western expedition. Beauharnois, bound by instructions to incur no expense, could permit the officer to undertake the discovery only at his own cost, granting him, however, the monopoly of the fur trade of the region he might explore. In 1731 La Vérendrye with his three eldest sons and his nephew La Jémerais, formerly at the Sioux post on the Mississippi, left Montreal for the farther West. During the next season they built Fort St. Pierre on Rainy Lake; and the same year pushed on to the Lake of the Woods,

[54] For a copy of this map of the Indian Ochagach, see *Wis. Hist. Colls.*, xvii, 102.

where Fort St. Charles was erected on the northernmost point of what is now Minnesota. Thence Jean de la Vérendrye voyaged over the waters and portages to the foot of Lake Winnipeg, where in 1734 he built Fort Maurepas.

All this time La Vérendrye and his party were on good terms with the neighboring natives, chiefly Chippewa and Cree. These tribes, however, were the hereditary enemies of the Sioux, and in 1736 the latter tribe took a fearful revenge upon the French for their friendship with the Chippewa. Jean de la Vérendrye with Father Aulneau and a party of nineteen *voyageurs* left Fort St. Charles early in June to bring up provisions from Lake Superior. Only a short distance from the fort they landed for a noonday rest on an island, since named Massacre, where June 6 they were suddenly attacked by several hundred Sioux on the warpath, and cruelly murdered.[55] This tragedy made it impossible for St. Pierre to maintain his post on the upper Mississippi. Early in September the Sioux began to display to the French the trophies of their horrid deed; then they devastated the tiny garden of the French missionary, wreaked their ill humor on the Winnebago camped around the fort—in brief, showed every hostile disposition without actually venturing an attack. Finally, May 30, 1737, St. Pierre, Father Guignas, and the men of the garrison determined to retreat while yet the way was open. The Sioux could no longer be counted among the allies of the white men.[56]

Meanwhile this same disastrous year of 1736

[55] *Wis. Hist. Colls.*, xvii, 261-262; Lawrence J. Burpee, "Lake of the Woods Tragedy," in Can. Roy. Soc., *Proc.*, 1903, sec. ii, 15-28; also in *Pathfinders of the Great Plains* (Toronto, 1914), 20-43; Reverend Francis Schaefer, "Fort St. Charles," in *Acta et Dicta* (St. Paul, 1909), ii, 114-133. The site of Fort St. Charles with the skeletons of the massacred men was found in 1909.

[56] *Wis. Hist. Colls.*, xvii, 269-274.

brought an even greater tragedy to the French settlements of the central West. For several years the tribes east of the Mississippi and south of the Ohio had been in rebellion against the French authority. When the allied tribes of the western country were weary of harassing the Foxes, they were urged to send out war parties against the Chickasaw to the south, who were in firm alliance with British traders in the Carolinas. In 1736 Bienville, governor of Louisiana, was prepared to strike; he assembled an army on the lower Mississippi, and ordered Dartaguiette, governor of the Illinois, to advance to his succor. Vincennes also joined Dartaguiette with a contingent from his fort on the Wabash. The junction of the two wings of the army over so wide a territory was not easy to effect. Dartaguiette arrived at the rendezvous prematurely, was deceived by his guides, attacked a Chickasaw stronghold, and was repulsed. In the retreat he and most of his officers were captured; they were taken to the Chickasaw village, where on Palm Sunday, March 25, seventeen perished at the stake, including the commandants of the two posts, the Jesuit chaplain Antoine Senat, Pierre St. Ange, and other French officers.[57]

The problem was no longer merely one of the Fox enmity. Aboriginal hatred for the Frenchman had broadened until it embraced many tribes. The empire of France in the West was slipping from its grasp. Therefore when the chiefs from the upper country assembled at Montreal in 1737 and asked mercy for the Sauk and Foxes, Beauharnois was in no situation to refuse. "The position of affairs," he wrote to his superior, "does not permit me, Monseigneur, to hesitate for a moment to grant them what they urgently

[57] *Wis. Hist. Colls.*, xvii, 259; Alvord, *Illinois*, 176-179; Indiana Historical Society, *Publications*, vii, 102.

asked of me."[58] The governor graciously accorded what he dared not deny. He welcomed the recalcitrant tribes among the number of the allies, and sent Marin to establish order among the late hostiles, and to urge them to return to their former homes in Green Bay. This they consistently refused to do; "stained with French blood" was the earth at this place. In reality it was too near their former enemies. They felt safer on the vast plains west of the Mississippi. Marin then built a fort in the new territory they were then occupying,[59] and in 1740 persuaded their chiefs to accompany him to Montreal.[60]

Green Bay was almost deserted by the tribesmen. Only the Menominee remained near the French post, the commandant of which in 1737 was Lieutenant de la Martinière,[61] with Joseph Tonty Desliettes second in command.[62] The Potawatomi had by this time moved south and east around the shore of Lake Michigan and were under the charge of the post at St. Joseph. The Mascouten had united with the Ouiatonon at their post on the Wabash. The Kickapoo were on lower Rock River and in eastern Illinois. Gradually the Winnebago who had dwelt around the French post on the Mississippi moved back to their old village site on Menasha Island. The fort at La Baye became important chiefly for keeping open the communication between the Great Lakes and the Mississippi.

It seems to have been at this time that the French settlement began to grow. Trade quickly revived

[58] *Wis. Hist. Colls.*, xvii, 267, 275-276.
[59] *Ibid.*, ix, 286.
[60] *Ibid.*, xvii, 329-330.
[61] See sketch in *ibid.*, 276.
[62] *Ibid.*, 322. In Chicago Historical Society, Schmidt Collection, No. 248, is a document of May 28, 1738, in which Ensign Joseph Tonty Sieur Desliettes, second in command at La Baye des Puants, gives his wife, Louise Dubuisson, his power of attorney.

with the pacification of the interior tribes. Marin was in 1739 transferred from Rock River to the La Baye post. There he prospered and built up a considerable fortune. Marin is to be considered as the pacificator of the Fox tribe. It was his policy of conciliation that succeeded in ending the Fox wars, after the policy of terrorism had failed. When in 1739 a French expedition came down the Ohio to punish the Chickasaw for the massacre of Vincennes and Dartaguiette, the Foxes could hardly be persuaded that they were not to be the victims of French wrath. The same summer Marin brought to Montreal two Sioux and a Winnebago chief to ask pardon of the governor. In 1740 delegations from all the western tribes accompanied Marin to Canada and made conciliatory and humble speeches to the governor-general.[63] The Fox wars were ended. Their results were not, however, without permanent effect on the French régime in the Northwest. Because of this long series of wars, the western trade routes were shifted to the eastward. Had the Fox-Wisconsin and the Chicago-Illinois waterways never been blocked, the St. Joseph-Wabash and the Maumee-Wabash might not have been developed with the resulting conflict with the English traders. Had the Fox Indians proved docile to French dictation, French sovereignty in the West might never have been shaken, and the French imperial system might have been developed and maintained. The resistance of one fierce, barbarous people, secretly dreaded yet admired by the other tribes, undermined French influence in the upper Mississippi valley, and hastened the changes that brought it to an end.

[63] *Wis. Hist. Colls.*, xvii, 338, 339, 404, 416.

XVI. EARLY MINING IN THE NORTHWEST

THE first miners in the region of Wisconsin were the Indians. Archeologists have found clear evidence that an aboriginal mining industry of large proportions was located on the shores of Lake Superior. The belief that the American Indians did not utilize metals was abandoned years ago because of the proof afforded by the great number of copper implements and ornaments that have been found in Wisconsin. Our earlier scientists were astonished to find these prehistoric copper artifacts in such numbers upon our soil.[1] Later search has resulted in more and more coming to light. Over twenty years ago a count was made and thirteen thousand copper pieces had been recovered from Wisconsin mounds and village sites.[2] The chief collector of copper artifacts in Wisconsin expressed his belief that the copper articles manufactured by the North American Indians amounted to millions.[3]

Copper implements and ornaments are likewise found in Ohio mounds,[4] and in sites along the Atlantic

[1] *Wis. Hist. Colls.*, viii, 152-173. In 1876 an exhibit at the Centennial Exposition of prehistoric coppers from Wisconsin attracted marked attention from archeologists, notably from Schleimann, the excavator of Troy. See his letters thereon, in *Wisconsin Journal of Education*, vi, 379-380, 384-386.
[2] *Wisconsin Archeologist*, iii, 50.
[3] *Ibid.*, i, No. 3, p. 11. H. E. Hamilton, of Two Rivers, in 1919 bequeathed his collection of artifacts, containing 1745 pieces of copper, to the Wisconsin Historical Museum.
[4] Recent exploration of Ohio mounds, such as the Tremper Mound and those of Fort Ancient and Mound City, have resulted in the recovery of a large number of copper ornaments of beautiful workmanship. *Ohio Archeological and Historical Quarterly*, xxxi, 433-525.

coast plain as far south as Georgia and Florida. The manufacture of these metallic articles was formerly attributed to a pre-Indian race called the mound builders, who were thought to have been of a higher culture than the aborigines found by whites on the discovery of the western continent. Now that the theory of the mound builders as a separate race has been abandoned, it is freely admitted that the prehistoric Indians had sufficient skill to have been the manufacturers of the copper artifacts found in the mounds. None of these show signs of casting or of melting by fire. Modern Indians have not lost the art of fashioning copper without smelting. Plates as thin as those used in the making of ornaments may be beaten out and shaped with stones, and the edges of the metal hardened in the process. Indeed, it is probable that the prehistoric miners and artificers considered the copper nuggets only as a peculiar kind of stone.

The source of the prehistoric copper is not difficult to find. The glacial drift brought down into the northern Mississippi and Ohio valleys many small pieces of copper, which were seized upon by the Indian workers; but the chief source of their supply was the Lake Superior deposits. As early as 1848, when agents of the Minnesota Mining Company were prospecting in the northern peninsula of Michigan, they found hundreds of abandoned diggings along the copper lode. As mining in this region progressed, prehistoric workings were located over a range one hundred miles long and from three to five miles wide in Ontonagon, Houghton, and Keweenaw counties; these were soon discovered to have been opened on the richest parts of the lode, and the early prospectors profited by the

EARLY MINING IN THE NORTHWEST 343

sagacity of their remote predecessors.[5] On the north shore of Lake Superior, also, Indian mines have been discovered, and the prehistoric workings on Isle Royale are the most extensive yet found. Numberless pits have been seen from which copper was taken, and excavations of another type seem to have been used by the prehistoric miners as dwellings.[6] William H. Holmes, one of our leading archeologists, is convinced that the Lake Superior mines were worked by Indians for hundreds of years.[7]

The methods employed by these primitive miners are shown by the remains that have been found. Stone hammers were evidently used, and with these copper masses were pounded until flakes were broken off. They cared little for large pieces of metal, since these were too refractory for their methods of transportation and manufacture. Evidences of the use of fire abound, but heat was used, not to melt the metal, but to loosen the rock strata in which it was embedded. After fires were built, water was dashed upon the heated rocks to crack them. In some of the deeper pits ladders have been found and wooden props on which small masses of metal were raised. Immense numbers of

[5] "Report on the Geology and Topography of a Portion of the Lake Superior Land District of the State of Michigan," in *United States Executive Documents*, 31st Congress, 1st session, No. 69, p. 158-163; *Wisconsin Archeologist*, iii, 54; vi, 232-241. See also Edward H. Kraus, "Some Unusual Specimens of Float Copper," in *American Mineralogist*, ix, No. 2, p. 23-26. This article describes a chief's head in copper, discovered in 1923 in Houghton County, Michigan, now in the museum of the state university.

[6] *Wisconsin Archeologist*, x, 73-100; W. P. Ferguson, "Michigan's Most Ancient Industry: The Prehistoric Mines and Miners of Isle Royale," in *Michigan History Magazine*, vii, 155-170. On the north-shore mines, see *Canadian Journal*, new series, i, 225.

[7] *American Anthropologist*, iii, 684-696.

broken stone hammers and axes lie around these old workings, and everything testifies to the indefatigable industry of these primitive miners.

No studies have yet been made of the tribal affinities of these first miners on Lake Superior. Some archeologists hold that the region about this great lake was the primitive home of the great Siouan race,[8] and that therefore the early miners must have belonged to this stock. Radisson, the first observer of the Lake Superior peoples, noted that some of his Siouan visitors wore in their ears crescents and stars of copper polished until it shone.[9] On the other hand, few copper artifacts have been found on prehistoric Siouan sites, and even the Wisconsin Winnebago acquired the copper artifacts they had by intertribal trade, and not by manufacture. So few metallic remains have been found in Winnebago graves and village sites, that their recent historian definitely asserts that members of this tribe were never copper makers.[10]

On the other hand, evidence is fast accumulating that the greater number of copper artifacts are to be found on Algonquian sites. In Wisconsin the richest finds of prehistoric copper have been made along the Lake Michigan littoral, on sites associated with the Menominee and Potawatomi villages of historic times. The Georgia and Ohio mounds in which copper ornaments have been found are thought to have been the burial places of Algonquian peoples. Most of the early explorers along the Atlantic coast found the aborigines they met supplied with copper ornaments, and these tribes were nearly all of the Algonquian stock. It

[8] See references *ante*, chapter v, note 16.
[9] *Wis. Hist. Colls.*, xi, 86.
[10] Paul Radin, "The Winnebago Tribe," in Bureau of Ethnology, *Thirty-seventh Annual Report*, 85-87.

seems then reasonable to suppose that the ancient miners of Lake Superior were the ancestors of the historic Algonquian tribes, all the more since the original home of this great race is thought to have been northwest of the Great Lakes, and that from this region they migrated east and south. Whether we can ever identify these primitive miners any more closely than to say that they were probably Algonquian is doubtful. The great branch of that race which now occupies the lands around Lake Superior—the Chippewa—was not there when the whites first came west. One tribe of the Chippewa was met at the Sault (hence their French name, Saulteurs), but they had come from farther east, and the whole trend of their migratory movement seems to have been a counter one from that of the primitive Algonquian. Moreover, the Chippewa knew nothing of mining methods. They were in possession of many copper nuggets, which they regarded as sacred and cherished "as household gods";[11] but although they acted as purveyors of the metal, they denied all knowledge of the ancient mines, declaring that these had existed before they came to Lake Superior.[12]

Certain natural facts gave an impetus to the primitive use of Lake Superior copper; one was its color, which made it highly prized, for when polished it glowed almost like gold. "Red copper" it was always called by the first explorers. The second fact was its purity. Because of these qualities its use was widespread, and it early came to the notice of European adventurers. Fish, furs, and metals were the first

[11] Kellogg, *Early Narratives*, 105, 113; *Minn. Hist. Colls.*, v, 98-99.
[12] Benjamin G. Armstrong, *Early Life among the Indians* (Ashland, Wis., 1892), 151.

resources of the New World to be sought and exploited. Mines were especially in demand because of the riches Spain had acquired in Central and South America. So the discoverers of the St. Lawrence were alert for evidences of mineral wealth, and Cartier in 1535 was told by the savages something about the copper of the upper lakes. One of the chiefs that he carried off to France made him a present of "a great knife of red copper that came from the Saguenay"—that indefinite region which lay in the far north.[13] Champlain on his first visit to Canada in 1603 was told that the Hurons wore bracelets of copper brought from a mine in the far north. These, he heard, were of "very fine copper."[14] Lescarbot, one of Champlain's contemporaries, wrote that the people beyond the Saguenay had much gold and red copper.[15] Sagard, who was the earliest author to visit the western country, wrote of the Hurons: "Their treasures consist principally in quantities of pelts of different animals terrestrial and amphibious. There are also mines of copper which should not be slighted . . . about eighty or one hundred leagues from the Huron country there is a mine of red Copper, of which the Interpreter showed me an ingot on his return from a voyage he made to that country."[16] This may indicate that Etienne Brulé was the first white man to see the Lake Superior copper mines.[17]

A quarter of a century then elapsed in which we find no mention of copper mines. In 1653 Father Bressani, an Italian Jesuit, when describing the resources of America wrote: "There is a Copper ore,

[13] *Ante*, chapter ii, note 6.
[14] H. P. Biggar, *Champlain's Voyages* (Toronto, 1922), i, 164.
[15] Grant and Biggar, *Lescarbot's Works* (Toronto, 1911), ii, 145.
[16] Sagard, *Le Grand Voyage*, 236.
[17] *Ante*, chapter iv, note 23.

which is very pure, and which has no need of passing through the fire; but it is in places far distant and hard to reach, which render its transportation almost impossible. We have seen it in the hands of the Barbarians, but no one has visited the place."[18] Five years later a savage at the mouth of the Saguenay River presented to his missionary a copper ingot.[19]

The first western traders were watchful for signs of copper among the savages. The traders in Lake Superior from 1660 to 1663 carried to the colony news of heavy deposits. From their information, Pierre Boucher wrote in his *History of Canada* in 1664: "In Lake Superior there is a large island, about fifty leagues around, in which there is a fine mine of red copper; there are also found in several places large pieces of this metal in a pure state. . . . They [the traders] have told me that they saw an ingot of pure Copper, weighing according to their estimate more than eight hundred pounds, which lay along the shore; they say that the savages when passing by, make a fire above this, after which they cut off pieces with their axes; one of the traders tried to do the same, and broke his hatchet in pieces"[20]—thus showing the superiority of stone over iron tools for primitive copper mining.

Father Allouez, who in 1665 made a voyage to Lake Superior, received instructions to investigate the possibility of utilizing the copper deposits. He found the natives very averse to talking about the metal, asserting that their manitous would be angry if they revealed the secret of the copper mines. Allouez, however, persisted and gained the tribesmen's con-

[18] *Jes. Rel.*, xxxviii, 243.
[19] *Ibid.*, xlv, 219-221.
[20] Author's translation from Can. Roy. Soc., *Proc.*, 1896, i, 167.

fidence sufficiently to obtain several large samples of copper ore and some information of the places from which they were procured. This information he carried to his superior, who made a careful report of the several sites Allouez had discovered. In this report mines are mentioned on the north shore of the lake, and especially those on Isle Royale; the McCargo's Cove excavations are noted with accuracy. On the south shore he reported masses of copper west of Chequamegon Bay, and several slabs and irregular rocks of metallic origin located around the bay. These the missionary thought were probably washed by the ice and the waves from the northern shore. The large deposit on Ontonagon River, however, seemed to be of a different character, and to promise a considerable deposit that might be worked as a mine. He also noted appearances of mines on the Keweenaw peninsula, and had been assured that many deposits existed in the interior.[21] Thus within a decade after Lake Superior was first visited by Frenchmen, the main deposits of copper were known.

It was another matter to utilize this knowledge and to make the mines profitable to the colony. Talon, who was always on the alert for benefits to Canada, acting on the report made by the missionaries, sent Jean Peré as his confidential agent to Lake Superior to verify the report, and to determine whether it was practicable to open the mines and transport the ore. Peré had himself found on a trading voyage to the northern lake what he thought was a rich copper mine, and readily undertook Talon's commission. He went out in 1667, and when he did not return the following year, Talon sent Louis Jolliet to carry to him

[21] *Jes. Rel.*, liv, 153-167; reprinted in *Wis. Hist. Colls.*, xvi, 72-76.

supplies and to learn of his success. Jolliet was not able to find Peré because of tribal war raging in Lake Superior; he did, however, on his homeward journey discover a deep waterway, by which he thought the product of the mines might be transported.[22] Acting on Jolliet's report, Talon sent in 1670 an expedition to assert French sovereignty over the far Northwest, and to explore further for copper.[23] The leader of this expedition did not succeed in finding Peré or any mines; his account of the difficulties of transportation was very discouraging, and Talon's recall to France put an end for a decade to any attempt to develop the mines.[24]

Duluth, whose whole interest was in exploration and not in exploitation, did not make any attempt to open mines along his route. His brother La Tourette, however, in the summer of 1687 brought to the colony a large copper ingot, and the governor was preparing to make further inquiries when the exigencies of the Iroquois wars stopped all prospecting in the far West.[25] Lahontan, who about this time was at Mackinac, wrote: "Upon that lake [Superior] we find Copper Mines, the Mettal of which is so fine and plentiful that there is not a seventh part lost from the Oar."[26] Le Sueur, while an enterprising trader, also kept a sharp lookout for profitable mines, and claimed to have located copper in several places. When in 1698 all traders were recalled to the colony, Le Sueur went

[22] *Ante*, chapter vii; *N. Y. Colon. Docs.*, ix, 63, 70, 789.
[23] *Ante*, chapter ix, note 16; *N. Y. Colon. Docs.*, ix, 803.
[24] Margry, i, 94-96. In the Clements Library at the University of Michigan is a copy of the Jesuit map of Lake Superior 1670-71, on which is a legend stating that St. Lusson explored as far as the Ontonagon River.
[25] *N. Y. Colon. Docs.*, ix, 344; Margry, vi, 52.
[26] Thwaites, *Lahontan*, i, 316.

to Paris and endeavored to obtain permission to exploit the mines he had discovered. The intendant of New France at that era was not in favor of these distant operations, and wrote of Le Sueur, "The only mines that he seeks in those regions are mines of beaver skins."[27]

By 1710 the intendant of that time had a wider vision of opportunity for New France; he made a report of the resources of the colony in which he says: "It is almost certain that there are copper mines on the borders of this lake [Superior] and in the islands within its extent. There are found in the sands pieces of this metal, which the savages make into daggers for their own use. Verdigris rolls from the crevices and clefts of the rocks along the shores, and into the rivers which fall into the lake. They claim that the island Minong [Royale] and small islets in the lake are entirely of copper. Among the pebbles of this lake are pieces of a lovely green color which crush easily."[28] After the presentation of this report the ministry declared that the discovery of these mines was an object of great importance.[29] The Fox wars, however, closed these northern regions to French enterprise for two decades longer.

It was not until the eighteenth century was well established that another attempt was made to prospect for copper in the Northwest. Governor Vaudreuil in 1722 tried to attract attention to the mineral resources of Canada, and obtained permission to send three canoes to explore for copper mines in Lake

[27] *Wis. Hist. Colls.*, xvi, 174; see also 178, 184. Le Sueur's contract for men to go with him to search for mines and to be gone five years is dated September 23, 1698. Chicago Historical Society, Schmidt Collection, No. 165.

[28] Margry, vi, 11-12 (the author's translation).

[29] *N. Y. Colon. Docs.*, ix, 865.

Superior, especially on the river Ontonagon.³⁰ The attention of all France was then centered on the riches to be obtained in the rival colony of Louisiana, and nothing apparently came of Vaudreuil's proposal. Five or six more years went by; then at last a veteran officer of New France at the post of La Pointe on Chequamegon Bay had the opportunity of opening these northern mines.

Louis Denis Sieur de la Ronde was born in France about 1670; at a very early age he entered the French navy, and was junior officer on the ship that in 1689 carried James II to Ireland in his vain attempt to recapture his crown. Two years later La Ronde came to America for a cruise along the New England coast. By 1693 he had attained the rank of lieutenant and was sent with Iberville to Hudson Bay to recapture the forts therein for the French. La Ronde also accompanied his chief on the expedition that began the colony of Louisiana, but he soon returned to Canada and was stationed there for several years. In 1723 he visited Boston on a diplomatic mission; and four years later was assigned to the command of the post at Chequamegon.³¹ At this time he ranked as captain in the Marine, which was the department in control of the colonies. The contract made by him when in 1727 he left the St. Lawrence to adventure to the distant post of La Pointe is extant.³²

La Ronde found his new post one of great interest, despite the isolation and the severities of the climate. Among the reports the Indians brought him were

³⁰ *Canadian Archives Report*, 1904, 39.
³¹ *Wis. Hist. Colls.*, xvii, 299-305. Parkman, in *A Half-Century of Conflict* (Boston, 1892), i, 151, states that La Ronde had lived some time in Boston and spoke English.
³² Chicago Historical Society, Schmidt Collection, No. 349.

those of a floating island of copper, which no mortals could approach since it was guarded by spirits who would strike any intruder dead. La Ronde also secured specimens of copper ore and sent them to the colony by some of the officers who had been on Lignery's futile expedition of 1728. Among these was the younger St. Pierre, whose father had formerly been commandant at the La Pointe post, and with whom La Ronde formed a partnership for copper mining. La Ronde's specimens were sent to France for assaying, and while waiting for the result he and his partner made a proposal to build ships for the transportation of the ore, which would be too heavy to carry in the ordinary craft—the birch-bark canoe.[33]

It is characteristic of the delays incident to the government of Canada, that even after the samples of ore had been successfully assayed, and the mines had been proved to contain riches, it was not until 1733 that permission was received to operate them, and it was not until 1734 that La Ronde and St. Pierre could begin prospecting in earnest.[34] When, however, the proper preliminaries had been arranged, the enterprise developed rapidly and more real mining progress was made in the ensuing ten years than in all the preceding years of French occupation.

One of the earliest measures taken was the building of a bark to navigate the great lake. The shipyard was at Sault Ste. Marie, and the difficulties to be overcome must have equaled or exceeded those of La Salle's party when nearly half a century earlier they built the *Griffon* at Niagara. La Ronde's little vessel was of twenty-five tons burden, and carried two or more sails; it was of immense use in transporting men

---

[33] *Wis. Hist. Colls.*, xvii, 86, 87, 105, 165.
[34] *Ibid.*, 176, 187, 305.

and provisions to the fort at La Pointe, and in skirting the coast to prospect for mines. Without this small craft all of La Ronde's efforts would doubtless have been useless.

The search for suitable places to mine centered around the Ontonagon River, on whose banks lay the large copper mass which was in the early nineteenth century transported to Washington and placed as a specimen in the museum of the Smithsonian Institution. La Ronde, while not able to detach this copper rock *en masse*, did succeed in obtaining from the vicinity several very promising samples of ore, which in 1736 he carried in person to Canada to be assayed. The only person in Quebec who had any expert knowledge of minerals was one Chambellan, a gold and silver smith, who was suggested as an expert to visit Lake Superior. La Ronde, however, had other plans and wrote to the colonial minister at Paris asking for some miners of established reputation to be sent out. The government acquiesced, and in 1737 sent two experts of German origin, named John Adam Forster, father and son.

Meanwhile La Ronde's men had already begun operations, employing the methods that the Indians had used before them. One of these operators, named Corbin, sent to the governor some articles he had made from nodules of copper "by hammering it while cold just as it came from the mine." He also stated that he had seen a great mass of copper rock, lying on the bottom of the lake, "which must weigh 8,000 to 10,000 pounds."[35] The Forsters were sent up to Mackinac by the first canoes that left for that place in the spring of 1738, and going on to Sault Ste. Marie expected to find La Ronde awaiting them. He was at this precise

[35] *Wis. Hist. Colls.*, xvii,237-240.

moment beating eastward in his sailing craft, against the spring gales of the lake, and arrived at the Sault only to find that his long-desired experts had gone with a trader named Guillory in an attempt to locate mines. There was nothing to do but to await their return, which La Ronde did with such patience as he could muster. When they came he found to his dismay that they had not visited the right places, and had no favorable report to make. They were unwilling to prolong their stay in the Northwest, since their contract expired early in 1739 and they could not reach Europe by that time if they remained longer on Lake Superior. La Ronde, however, was urgent, and by dint of persuasion and offers of pecuniary increase, obtained the consent of the Forsters to return along the southern shore of the lake and to inspect the sites he had already explored. They accompanied him to La Pointe, and thence under the guidance of the younger La Ronde visited the copper exposed on Ontonagon River, and found evidences of four mines which they pronounced very promising, eastward from La Pointe. One of these was on the Ontonagon, one at the mouth of Black River, and two on the cliffs that faced one another at the mouth of Ste. Anne River— probably the one we now know as Iron River. Of one of these mines they wrote: "One could never see a mine, apparently finer, and it is certain that if one wished to start in the business and invest money there, a great return of copper might be hoped for."[36]

La Ronde was jubilant; he saw in perspective all his plans justified, he himself on the road to wealth, and hailed as a benefactor of the entire colony. He determined to conduct the Forsters in person to Quebec,

[36] La Ronde's account is in *Wis. Hist. Colls.*, xvii, 306-311; the Forsters' report is in *ibid.*, 262-263, 314-315.

receive the governor's congratulations, and then to arrange for working the mines. At the Sault he engaged twelve *voyageurs* to begin an establishment on the Ste. Anne River, there to build a fort, a forge, and a smelting furnace. He planned to transport his ore by the Toronto portage, and to have for that purpose a vessel of eighty tons built on Lake Huron; he also expected to transport cattle and horses to Lake Superior from Detroit, and to begin an agricultural settlement at the mines.[37] Most of these well-laid plans were never carried out; so far as we know the vessel for Lake Huron was never built, nor were cattle transported from Detroit, nor was a permanent settlement made. He did, however, begin mining operations and take out considerable ore, and La Ronde may well be known, not only as the first practical miner on Lake Superior, but as the first to open that region to civilization. He had at La Pointe a fort with a garrison, horses, and probably a mill, also a dock, and some beginnings of agriculture—all this on the present Madeline Island, then called St. Michel.[38] It was during this period also that the name "Apostle Islands" was first given to the group at the mouth of Chequamegon Bay.[39]

In the colony La Ronde's return with the mining experts and their favorable report was received with enthusiasm; hopes of great profits spread throughout

[37] *Wis. Hist. Colls.*, xvii, 311-314.

[38] For the site of Fort La Pointe, see *ante*, chapter xiv, note 22. The name "Isle St. Michel" was applied to Madeline Island for over a century, from the time of the Franquelin map of 1688 to the date of McKenney's *Tour of the Lakes* in 1826. The name cannot have been given for Michel Cadotte, as asserted in *Wis. Hist. Colls.*, xi, 372.

[39] The name "Apostle Islands" was thought to have originated with Jonathan Carver in 1768. *Wis. Hist. Colls.*, xiii, 402. The name, however, appears on several French maps before the time of Carver.

Canada, and the governor recommended to the ministry in France that La Ronde be given the command at Chequamegon for three more years, and a monopoly of its fur trade in order to enable him to continue his mining ventures. Enough was realized from the ore already transported to pay the expenses of the Forsters, and to reimburse the royal treasury for its advances.[40] All promised well for a rapid growth. But the blight which fell upon so many promising ventures in the West swept away the beginnings of Lake Superior mining—that is, trouble with the natives, due to the impossibility of keeping at peace tribes whose greatest glory and honor depended upon war.

The Sioux-Chippewa war was a struggle lasting for over a century, and while at times subdued by the ability of French officers, like Duluth, Le Sueur, and La Ronde, it smouldered under the surface at all times, and in 1739 broke out with renewed virulence. In that year an attack by a party of wandering Sioux upon some French allies near the Wisconsin portage had disastrous consequences in Lake Superior. By the summer of 1740 the Chippewa bands from the Sault, from La Pointe, and at many of the intervening points were on the warpath, and Lake Superior became dangerous for any white voyagers. In vain the younger La Ronde at his fort at La Pointe tried to halt the hostilities. His influence was not potent enough to allay the wrath of tribesmen against hereditary enemies, and to brush aside their determination to drive the Sioux from the lakes and streams of northern Wisconsin. It was about this time that the places in the interior of Wisconsin where the Chippewa still dwell—

---

[40] *Canadian Archives Report*, 1904, 290.

at Lac du Flambeau and Lac Court Oreilles—were wrested from the Sioux.[41]

Meanwhile, Sieur de la Ronde at Quebec was making every effort to continue his plans for developing his copper mines. He trusted to his great influence with the Lake Superior Chippewa to stop their warfare and to establish tranquillity in the Northwest. Leaving the colony, he had arrived at Mackinac and was about to start for the Sault, when he was overtaken by a mortal illness, and returned to Quebec only to die.[42] His eldest son, Philippe, succeeded him in command at La Pointe, and his widow was granted for several years the lease of this profitable fur trade post in reward for her husband's services to New France.[43] If among these services were the discovery and operation of the copper mines of the far North, neither the colony nor the La Ronde family profited thereby. The fur trade was a more certain means of enrichment than copper, and again it was a question whether "mines of beaver skins" or those of metal were to make Canada prosper.

Tradition of the rich mines of copper in the inaccessible Northwest persisted throughout all the French régime. In 1749 Peter Kalm, the Swedish traveler, said that he saw on the St. Lawrence a "piece of native copper from the Upper Lake." "They find it there," he continued, "almost quite pure so that it does not want [need] melting." It was found, he was told, only at the outlets of rivers; thus the true source was to be

[41] *Wis. Hist. Colls.*, xvii, 360, 361; *Minn. Hist. Colls.*, v, 190-193.

[42] *Wis. Hist. Colls.*, xvii, 426; *Canadian Archives Report*, 1905, i, 10. The great-grandson of La Ronde was a Wisconsin pioneer in the early nineteenth century, and married into the Winnebago tribe. *Wis. Hist. Colls.*, vii, 345.

[43] *Ibid.*, xvii, 361, 433, 444.

sought on the northern shore.[44] Thenceforward until the close of French sovereignty in North America there were no more attempts to profit by La Ronde's beginnings, nor to utilize the copper deposits as a source of gain. When, however, the British took possession of the western posts, they heard from French officers and traders of the rich mines awaiting development adjacent to their new stations. In 1765 Sir William Johnson reported that a certain Canadian (probably La Ronde) had taken considerable ore from the mines in Lake Superior. Three years later a company was formed, in which Johnson, although professing himself skeptical concerning the possibility of success, finally decided to take a part. Three British traders in Lake Superior—Alexander Henry, Henry Bostwick, and one Baxter—were the active partners, and even royalty deigned to invest in this promising enterprise. Prospects were made in several places, and in 1771 an establishment was formed on the Ontonagon River, and a number of miners wintered at this place. The following spring, at the first attempt to mine, a landslide from a cliff buried three of the miners. This so discouraged the proprietors that this region was abandoned and operations transferred to the northeast shore. There workings were no more successful than on the Ontonagon, and before the American Revolution the enterprise was relinquished and the royal charter that had been prepared was never issued.[45]

Lead, another metal found in abundance in Wisconsin, was known to prehistoric Indians, but was

[44] Kalm, *Travels into North America* (London, 1772), ii, 330, 399-400.
[45] *Wis. Hist. Colls.*, xi, 37-38; xviii, 293-295, 311; James Bain, *Travels and Adventures of Alexander Henry* (Boston, 1901), 225-229; *United States Senate Documents*, Serial 551, p. 381-385.

little prized. Galena has been found in mounds as far east as Ohio. But, considering the abundance of that ore and the ease with which it could be obtained, astonishingly few leaden artifacts have been found antedating historic times. It was occasionally used for net-bobs, for boatstones, and ornaments, such as beads. A few pipes, some turtle effigies, and a cone comprise the entire series of prehistoric leaden implements found in Wisconsin.[46] Even its use to inlay catlinite pipes dates from historic times. The fact is that not until the use of firearms became common did the tribesmen come to covet lead; after they had many times exchanged beaver skins for pouches of leaden bullets, the idea occurred to them that they might obtain these articles on their own land, and save their beaver skins for other purchases.

The French, always alert for indications of mineral wealth, discerned signs of mines in southwest Wisconsin at a very early date. Radisson says that he heard of lead mines in the West, but his report is too vague to be reliable. Marquette thought he saw in 1673 traces of an iron mine on the south bank of the Wisconsin River. Tonty reported lead mines near the Mississippi, which were so rich that only a third part became refuse.[47] It was Nicolas Perrot, however, who was the real discoverer of the lead mines, and it was due to his popularity with the Indians that the secret of the mines was made known to him. About 1690 a chief of the Miami presented Perrot with some lead, which he said came from "a very rich lead mine, which he had found on the banks of a stream which empties into the Missisipi." The chief would reveal

[46] *Ohio Archeological and Historical Quarterly*, xxxi, 557; *Wisconsin Archeologist*, iv, 89; ix, 14.
[47] *Wis. Hist. Colls.*, xi, 93; Kellogg, *Early Narratives*, 236, 302.

its locality to his white friend if the latter would build a fort in the vicinity. Perrot affected to be uninterested, while secretly much pleased; finally after many solicitations he followed his guide and built a fort near the mine, somewhere below the mouth of the Wisconsin.[48] The exact site is not known; from Perrot's description of its rocky crevices it is supposed that the lode he worked was at the present Dubuque, and that his fort was on the eastern bank near Dunleith, Illinois.[49]

Perrot's post at this place did not long exist, but it is believed that he taught the Indians some crude mining methods, which they used for many years. Perrot says that he taught them to cut out the ore from the rocks, and that by melting it was reduced one-half.[50] Later, when the Indians worked a deep mine, they learned to use an inclined plane, by which they carried down wood, built fires, poured water on the heated rocks, and dug out the mineral with all sorts of implements, such as buck horns, hoes, old gun-barrels, and the like. Most of the labor was performed by the squaws, who drew out the ore thus extracted in birch-bark "mococks," and then placed it in a crude furnace built of logs, set fire to the whole, and as the lead melted and ran down, scraped out a place large enough for it to settle and form the large flat pieces, known as "plats," in which it was transported. Each of these bars weighed from thirty to seventy pounds, and hundreds of tons of lead were made by these crude methods.[51]

[48] Blair, ii, 59, 66, 74; *Wis. Hist. Colls.*, x, 330-333; xvi, 143-152.
[49] Penicaut in 1700 mentions Perrot's mines, and Delisle's maps of the eighteenth century place lead mines near both Galena and Dubuque.
[50] Blair, ii, 74.
[51] *Wis. Hist. Colls.*, ii, 132, 228; vi, 281-282; *Iowa Historical Record*, v, 350. See also description of the Indian lead furnaces, in W. R. Smith, *History of Wisconsin*, iii, 353-354.

From Perrot's time throughout the entire French régime, the lead mines were worked more or less constantly both by Indians and by white *voyageurs*, who used the product to supplement the fur trade. When Le Sueur in 1700 ascended the Mississippi in his sailing vessel, he stopped long enough to take out a supply for his proposed fort, probably from Wisconsin mines.[52] Had he but continued operations in this region, instead of mounting to the Blue Earth River, he might have made his enterprise a success, and have supplied Louisiana with lead.

With the lead in the mines of southwestern Wisconsin and northwestern Illinois is always found a trace of silver. This excited the hopes of the French for greater profits than could be obtained from lead. In 1720 Philippe François Renault, a Parisian banker, was appointed director general of the mines of the Illinois country, and came thither with a force of workmen and negro slaves to develop and work the hoped-for silver mines. He found that there was more profit to be obtained from lead, and opened several very good mines in Missouri, in northwestern Illinois, and in Iowa. By 1725 he was obtaining profit from his investment; but the dangers to his operations caused by the Fox wars lessened both the profits and the enlargement of his mining ventures. In 1744 he sold his holdings, returned his patent to the government, and went back to France.[53]

The Fox hostilities were a constant detriment to the progress of lead mining. In 1733 the governor of Illinois wrote in answer to an inquiry, that his district pro-

[52] *Wis. Hist. Colls.*, xvi, 181. Dr. Thwaites thought that this mine might have been at Snake Diggings, now Potosi. *Wis. Hist. Colls.*, xiii, 274.

[53] Alvord, *Illinois*, 154, 159, 209; N. D. Mereness, *Travels in the American Colonies*, 70.

duced only enough lead for its own use, and had none for export to Louisiana. After Renault's surrender of his monopoly, and the close of the Fox wars, mining increased to a considerable extent. In 1747 the lead mines of Illinois, Iowa, Missouri, and Wisconsin were examined by an expert from Portugal. He found several new localities that promised good returns, especially in the region north of Rock River.

Major de Gruis, a French officer stationed at Kaskaskia, also investigated the mines, and in 1734 sent a memoir to France describing the several locations where lead was found and the Indian method of extraction. Some years later the same officer claimed to have discovered a copper mine, to which the shortest route was the La Baye portage. We do not know just where his proposed mine was situated, but he wrote that vessels could be loaded at it and proceed down the Mississippi, so the inference is that his copper mine was in the vicinity of the lead mines. Major de Gruis did not obtain the concessions for which he asked, and thereafter his mining reports cease to appear.[54]

Interest in the mines continued to exist throughout the entire period of French occupation. In 1748 the governor of Louisiana wrote of the Illinois lead mines: "The yield has not been of any great value so far, although it is asserted that they are very rich and can be rendered productive with hardly any expense." This optimism was not shared by the minister in France, who the same year wrote to the governor-general of Canada: "Everybody knows that the hopes that had been raised with regard to mines [in the

---

[54] *Wis. Hist. Colls.*, xiii, 276; xviii, 98; *History of Grant County* (Chicago, 1881), 393-394; unpublished MSS. in the Illinois Historical Survey, at Urbana.

Illinois] have vanished, since the whole thing is reduced to getting a little from those of lead."[55]

With the outbreak of the French and Indian War the demand for lead increased, and a consequent activity developed in the Illinois and Wisconsin mines. These have never ceased to be worked from Perrot's time to the present, and it is an evidence of the richness of the deposits that they were not exhausted by the wasteful methods of the Indian miners. Lead became a useful adjunct of the fur trade, and in the case of certain tribes mining almost took the place of hunting. After the departure of French officers from the West, the Indians guarded the secret of the mines carefully, and only revealed their sites under duress, or to favored French traders like Dubuque, who was the largest lead miner of the British and Spanish period. He obtained his first knowledge of the mines from the Indians with whom he traded, and after settling on the site of the city which now bears his name, he obtained a Spanish grant to the region, with the privilege of mining. Dubuque was the last of the French operators in this region, and he never made a fortune in mining, for when he died his property was heavily mortgaged to St. Louis merchants.

Thus while the French discoverers and explorers were keenly interested in mining operations and revealed the two great deposits of metal—copper and lead—in the Northwest, the difficulties of transportation and of scientific operation hindered them from utilizing these metals to any large extent, and made of early mining a promise rather than a performance.

[55] *Wis. Hist. Colls.*, xvii, 514; xviii, 15.

XVII. CHANGES IN FUR TRADE METHODS, 1738–1759

THE fur trade was the main reason for the presence of the French in the West. The zest for discovery and the desire to carry French sovereignty across the continent never died out during the period of French occupation of North America; the zeal for conversion of the heathen in the western world was an active, if declining, motive during the eighteenth century; the hope of finding rich mineral wealth lured some Frenchmen to the shores of Lake Superior, and to the waters of the upper Mississippi. But without the fur trade all these visits would have been occasional, and would not have resulted in peopling the West. Canada was founded as an agricultural colony, and the first care of the early governors was to develop land cultivation. Farms had to be hewn from the encompassing forest, and the work of preparing the soil was slow and arduous. To aid in its growth the feudal institutions of old France were transported to the New World, and the territory along the banks of the St. Lawrence was early parceled out into seigniories, over each of which presided a seignior who was responsible for the workers on the land. The fur trade, on the other hand, developed without fostering on the part of the authorities. Everywhere about the small clearings lived the red men, who coveted the white men's goods and were willing to give in exchange the fur robes that they wore. Exchange was mutual and inevitable, and at first its terms were fixed by the civilized man. The tribesman, ignorant of values except as expressing wants, traded his superb furs for a trinket or a glass

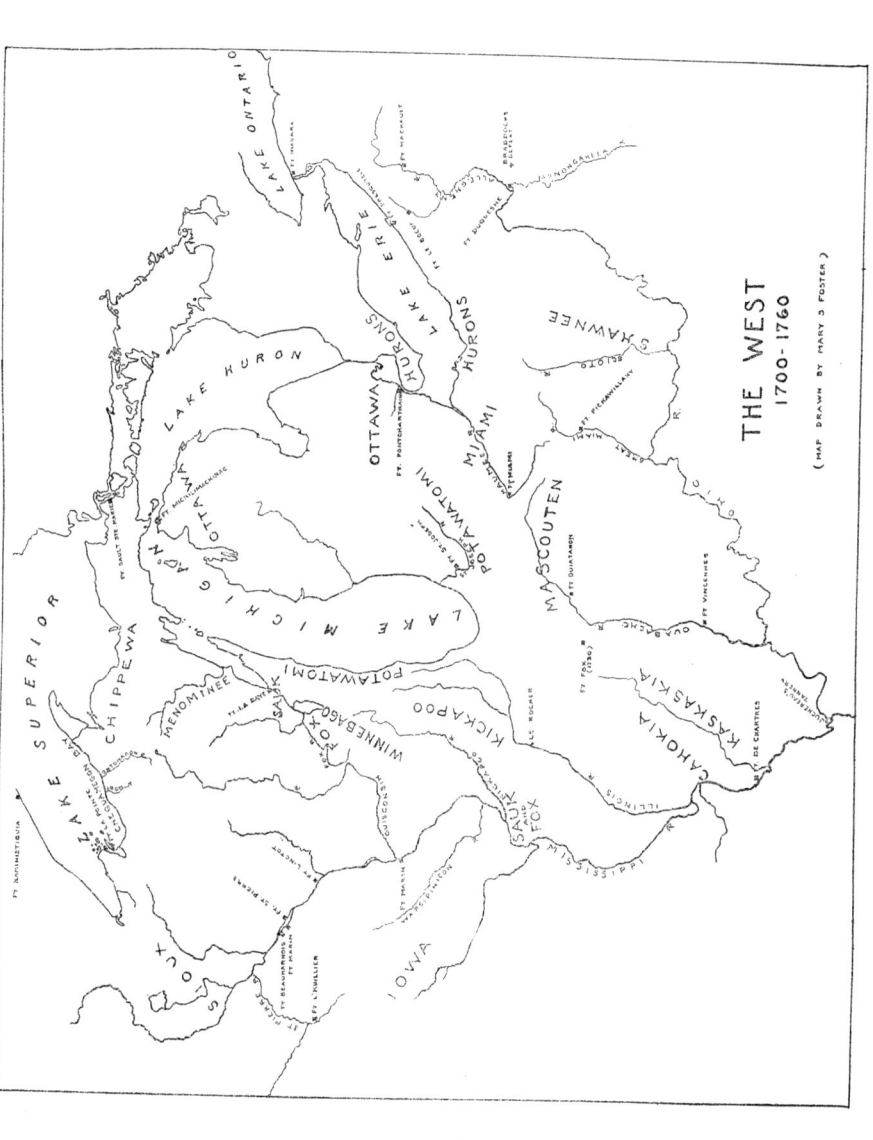

CHANGES IN FUR TRADE METHODS 365

of fire water. He very soon, however, became aware of the differences in values, and under competitive bidding for his wares grew careful to obtain more for his exchange.

This primitive traffic about the homes of the habitants was merely a by-product of agriculture. But when the missionaries and the explorers had made the Canadians aware of the great opportunities for Indian trade in the West, when that vast region filled with fur-bearing animals and savages expert in their capture became known, the fur trade took on new aspects. The distances to these newly discovered regions made the journey thither one of danger and adventure; the lure of the wilderness and the prospects of gain led the youth of the Canadian colonists to abandon the dull life of the cultivator for the care-free life of the woods trader and the excitement of trafficking with the red men. At first the task of the traders was to induce the western Indians to visit Montreal, and we have already seen what the great fur fair there meant to the colony, and what distress and dearth came to pass when the yearly flotillas were kept from coming by the dangers of the Iroquois wars. But as the years passed, and more and more goods were taken in canoes to the western posts and carried to the Indian villages, the red men ceased to visit the colony with their wares, and the methods of the trade necessarily changed.

With the traders following their customers into these remote places, abuses crept into the system. The forest knew no law but the rule of the strongest or the craftiest. The woods were filled with young Canadians who had broken away from all the restraints of civilization and tended toward the savage level. The colonial authorities had to establish regulations to keep Canada from being depopulated, and at the same time to exert control over the traders in the wilderness. Two measures were resorted to to supervise the trade: the building of posts in the heart of the fur trade country, garrisoned by troops with some degree of discipline and officers of the gentleman class; and the granting of licenses for visits to the upper country, and the prohibition of any Frenchmen to go without such a license (called by the French a congé). The commandant at these woodland posts had full authority over the traders in his vicinity; he assigned them to the places where they might trade, he controlled their relations with the red men and protected the latter from extortion, and he had also authority to order the traders away from their trading grounds in case of intertribal quarrels or danger, and even in extreme necessity to commandeer their goods for the public service. By the license system the colonial authorities obtained reputable traders, who gave bonds for their own conduct and that of their employees, who were expected to treat the Indians justly and to obey all the edicts concerning the trade. The number of licenses was limited, usually to twenty-five, and the proceeds of their sale were devoted to the poor of the colony. The competition for these congés was exceedingly keen, and their holders would often sell them in fractions, as one license permitted four canoes' worth of goods to be carried to the West. They were transferable also, and this fact lessened the degree of control exercised.

Neither of these means of control was sufficient to cure the evils that crept into the fur trade. The commandants connived at every means to increase the profits, and usually accepted the office expecting to enrich themselves in a brief term of service. The licensed traders also were but a few of those who trafficked in the wilderness. The ¡Canadian youth had grown too fond of the life of the woods to abandon it at the behest of authority; thence arose the custom of slipping off into the woods without a license, of living for years in the Indian villages, and of becoming almost savages themselves. The governors and ministers fulminated in vain against these *coureurs de bois*. From time to time edicts of amnesty were issued which brought many back to the colony; a considerable share of these *voyageurs*, however, elected to live permanently in the Indian country, and it was from this class that the French residents of the West were largely recruited.[1]

The actual methods by which the trade was carried on were as follows: Indian trade goods were nearly all exported from France, where a particular type of manufacture grew up in order to supply the forest commerce and to cater to the desires of the red men.[2] Merchants in the colony, largely settled at Montreal, received consignments of these goods and supplied the holders of licenses either on shares or on credit. Nor were the merchants without interest in the illegal traders, who could usually obtain on credit an outfit for forest ranging. The goods were carefully baled in packages for transport, each weighing about ninety pounds —the amount a *voyageur* could carry around the portages. The value of the goods in a canoe varied from $1600 to $1900. The craft was propelled by five men, one of whom was frequently the proprietor, and carried

[1] W. B. Munro has a very interesting paper on "The Coureurs de bois," in Massachusetts Historical Society, *Proceedings*, lvii, 192-212 (January, 1924), in which he uses the term synonymously with trader, and includes such well known Westerners as Nicolet, Jolliet, Perrot, Duluth, the Tonty brothers, Langlade, and many others. As we understand it, these licensed traders and explorers would indignantly have repudiated the ascription of *coureur de bois*, which to the Canadian authorities indicated an outlaw.

[2] Kalm, *Travels*, ii, 391-395, enumerates the goods used for the Indian trade.

in addition to the cargo the food supply and luggage of the men.[3]

Three routes were in use during the eighteenth century for canoes going to the upper country. The Ottawa River route, with portages to Georgian Bay, was the oldest and the one most used; it was also the most difficult. The Great Lakes route was used for the more southern fur trade regions, and after the founding of Detroit became popular; its chief obstructions were the upper St. Lawrence rapids and the falls at Niagara. The third route avoided the latter obstacle by going through the Toronto portage to Georgian Bay, but this had the longest land carriage and was comparatively little used.

The holder of the license, in addition to the initial outlay for goods, had to furnish the canoe, the *voyageurs*, provisions, tents, and all supplies necessary for life for many months in a wilderness. The proprietor was called the *bourgeois*, and upon him rested the responsibility for the successful trip and for the comfort, often the lives, of his employees. These latter were recruited from the peasant and small proprietor class of the colony, and usually required from the *bourgeois* an advance for their outfit. They signed a contract, called an "engagement," which was in fact a sort of apprenticeship document, in which they promised to obey their employer, seek his advantage at all times, do no trading on their own behalf, and be governed in all matters by their superior's demands.[4] This contract

[3] A memoir of 1784 by Marbois is published in the *American Historical Review*, xxix, 725-740, concerning the North American fur trade; while relating to later times, this article gives facts and figures for the trade as it existed in the French régime.

[4] Typical engagement contracts are published in *Wis. Hist. Colls.*, xix, 292, 343. The manuscripts on the fur trade in the Wisconsin Historical Society abound in these contracts, which

furnished the basis of whatever law there was to be found in the fur trade country.

The *engagés* were divided into two classes. Those who engaged merely for the voyage, going and returning the same season, were known as *mangeurs de lard*—a term of contempt, loosely equivalent to the later American term "tenderfoot." Those who remained for a year or more in the fur trade country were called *hivernants*, winterers. They were the seasoned employees, who spent the winters either in the small log posts of the traders or in the Indian villages. Frequently they were called upon for a *drouine*; that was a short trading trip with a limited amount of goods to some point where the tribesmen were thought to have brought in a number of skins.[5] These *hivernants* were masters of woodcraft, usually versed in one or more Indian languages, familiar with the manners and customs of some one tribe—in short, adepts at wilderness life. They knew how to make and mend canoes, guide them in rough water and adown swift rapids, negotiate a portage carrying heavy packages and the craft itself; they knew how to make camp and how to utilize the gifts of the forest; they knew how to hunt and trap, how to pack and bale furs, how to judge their qualities, and how to allot to the Indian their value and no more. Their fare was simple and portable; pemmican, dried peas, wild rice, and game constituted

---

became so completely stereotyped that blanks were printed to be filled out with names and dates.

[5] *Wis. Hist. Colls.*, xix, 200. The life of a fur trade winterer at an interior post is illustrated by the two journals published in *Wis. Hist. Colls.*—that of Malhiot at Lac du Flambeau, in xix, 163-233; that of Curot on Yellow River in the northwestern part of the state, in xx, 396-471. Although these accounts were written in the early nineteenth century, conditions differed little from those of the French trade in the early eighteenth century.

their food. As a rule they were illiterate, signing with a mark, care-free and merry in temper, usually in debt to their *bourgeois* for clothing, tobacco, and beverages. Visits to the colony were infrequent. When too old or too frail for the hard work of the fur trade, they usually settled near some fort, took an Indian woman for a wife, and lived to a tranquil old age.

Between the *bourgeois* and the *voyageur* classes was the *commis*, or clerk, usually a young man of good family in training for the position of *bourgeois*. Throughout the entire fur trade régime this system persisted. The sovereignty changed, and the chief traders became in turn British and American, but they were always dependent upon the French-Canadian *engagés*, recruited from the habitants, among whom the type first developed.[6]

The entire fur trade system rested upon credit. The *bourgeois* took his goods from the merchants on credit, gave credits for outfits to his *engagés*, who in turn gave out his goods on credit to the Indians. They received credits of weapons, traps, ammunition, blankets—without which they would not, and in most cases could not, hunt. When he brought in his furs the tribesman frequently received nothing for them but a remission of his credits. The temptation was great for the primitive man to carry his goods to another trader, and obtain goods in return. The *hivernants* were expected to prevent this change of traders, and it should be remarked that most of the Indians had a strong sense of responsibility to their traders, and of honor in paying their debts. The entire system, however, was wasteful and expensive and led to many abuses.

[6] *Wis. Hist. Colls.*, xix, p. xii-xiv, 138-145.

When the traders brought their peltry to Montreal they were not permitted to sell it in open market. The entire output of the colony was leased or "farmed" to some commercial company, such as the Company of the Indies, which had received monopoly rights in France. All furs must be brought to their storehouses and sold at a price fixed by these farmers, supported by the law.[7] This system put the French traders at a disadvantage compared with the English, whose market was free. *Coureurs de bois* carried their peltry to the English merchants, and were a constant menace to the legitimate French fur trade.

The beginning of a second French colony in the heart of the continent tended to demoralize the fur trade and to encourage illegal trading. With the possibility of escape to Louisiana, where new colonists were welcomed and "no questions asked," the system of Canadian supervision broke down. Constant complaints came from the merchants of Montreal that their creditors, after trading in the western country, took their furs down the Mississippi to Louisiana, and evaded the payment of their debts. On the other hand, the authorities of Louisiana complained of Canadian encroachments upon the hunting grounds that belonged to their colony. In truth the boundaries between the two colonies were never defined. Illinois was annexed to the province of Louisiana after its cession in 1731 to the crown. Just how far Illinois extended northward was never legally determined. The governors of Louisiana claimed the headwaters of the Mississippi, but this claim was never admitted either by the French government or by the Canadian authorities, who cited the fact that this region had been discovered by men from the older colony, and that it

[7] See prices as listed in Kalm, *Travels*, ii, 391.

had always been considered a part of the upper country. In practice the upper lead mines near Galena and beyond were regarded as a part of Canada, while farther east the Ouiatanon post on the Wabash, near the modern Lafayette, was garrisoned and officered from Canada, and Vincennes lower down on the same river was administered by Louisiana. Approximately, then, the boundary between Illinois and what is now Wisconsin was believed to run near the fortieth parallel of latitude, and to reach the Mississippi at the mouth of Rock River, although occasionally an enthusiastic Louisianian attempted to stretch the northern boundary of Illinois to the Wisconsin River.[8] In 1748 the question was seriously discussed whether it would not be best to have the administration of Illinois attached to Canada, and the governors of both colonies were called upon for an opinion. Vaudreuil of Louisiana insisted that since the natural outlet of Illinois must always be the Mississippi, it would be a mistake to attach it to the northern colony. La Galissonière, then governor-general of Canada, replied that while Illinois was originally an extension of his colony, and its Indian trade was a part of the Canadian system, yet it was not very advantageous since its chief furs were buffalo hides, and since the heat of the country spoiled the furs before they could be exported. Illinois, therefore, would yield no revenue for a long time;

[8] Vaudreuil's report on boundaries and on the importance of Illinois to Louisiana is in an unpublished memoir in the Colonial Archives at Paris, C13A29-83. He claimed as the northern boundary of Louisiana a line from the Wabash where the Vermillion enters, to Le Rocher on the Illinois River, and thence to the mouth of Wisconsin River. The authorities of Canada, he stated, claimed Rock River for the boundary. See also on this matter, *Wis. Hist. Colls.*, xviii, 452; Vaugondy's map of "La Nouvelle France," 1755; and Alvord and Carter, *The Critical Period*, (*Illinois Historical Collections*, x), 145.

but as a source of provision supply and as a barrier to English advance it should be maintained, whether connected with Canada or Louisiana was immaterial.[9] As a result of this discussion Illinois remained a part of Louisiana; but when Vaudreuil, then governor of Canada, was defending his colony, he utilized the Illinois as though it belonged to his own province.

The seventeenth century fur trade of the French defeated its own objects by excess of zeal and unwise exploitation. When in the next century the posts were reëstablished in the West, the trade became systemized, and except for the difficulties due to the Fox wars, flourished greatly. The period after the close of the Fox wars was the best regulated period of the French fur trade, and the most prosperous the colony had known since its inception. The harvests along the St. Lawrence grew larger each year, and in 1741 the exports for the first time exceeded the imports. The officers at the interior posts were among the best men of the colony, and far-seeing enough to forbid methods that in the end would ruin the wilderness traffic. The Indians were dealt with firmly and justly, and bowed to the white men, whom they revered. The custom of giving presents, however, to express the generosity of the higher race, and to render the red men loyal to the French overlordship, grew to unwise proportions and, added to the expenses that were incurred in closing the Fox wars and harmonizing the intertribal quarrels, caused considerable dissatisfaction to the home ministry. In 1741, notwithstanding the general prosperity of the colony, the government revenues showed a serious deficit. The next year the ministry ordered drastic remedies with regard to the western posts. In order to reduce their expenses and

[9] *Wis. Hist. Colls.*, xvii, 493-498, 513-518; xviii, 14-17.

increase the colony's revenue, an edict of April 20 of that year suspended all the licenses for the western trade and ordered that the posts be auctioned off to the highest bidder for monopoly exploitation.

This decree caused the greatest consternation in Canada, since its prosperity was bound up with the yearly returns of the western posts. The Montreal merchants, however, received the order with satisfaction; it would enable them to do away with the middlemen in the trade and to exploit the posts without hindrance. The governor protested to the ministry that the traders would be ruined. He prophesied that goods would become scarcer and that prices would soar, to the deep dissatisfaction of the natives and their ultimate alienation. All this opposition was ignored in France, and the officials of the colony had no option but to enforce the decree. The post at Green Bay was one of those chosen for the initiation of this experiment. Its commandant at this time was Sieur Marin, who had put an end to the Fox wars. He was ordered to retire, having in some way incurred the displeasure of the ministry, although his merits were proclaimed by the governor.[10] His place was taken by Lusignan, an officer of great ability, cultivated and intelligent, distinguished for courtesy and integrity.[11] At the same time the trade of La Baye was put up at auction and bid in by a large Montreal firm headed by the Ailleboust family, who had some years previously formed a company to exploit the upper Mississippi post.[12] Lusignan came to his command in 1743 and

[10] *Wis. Hist. Colls.*, xvii, 439-440. Joachim Sacquepée, who is mentioned as at La Baye in 1742 (*ibid.*, 425), was not a commandant, but an agent of Marin.

[11] Kalm, *Travels*, ii, 183, 210.

[12] *Wis. Hist. Colls.*, xvii, 435. Joseph d'Ailleboust Sieur de Coulonge was a partner of Augustin de Langlade in the Sioux Company in 1731.

remained three years. For a man of his culture and acquirements life at Green Bay must have been a species of exile from all for which he cared. To make his situation worse, the traders to whom the Montreal merchant sublet his privilege for eighty-one hundred livres were men of low standards and sordid aims. Lusignan did all he could to combat their influence with the Indians, and his example for the small group of French clustered around his fort must have been elevating. Probably he occupied himself in part with scientific research, as he had done in other places in Canada.

Notwithstanding the commandant's efforts and example, the result of the leasing system with its monopoly of the fur trade was what the governor had foretold. The savages were alienated by the exorbitant prices asked for the goods, and disappointed at the assortment brought to them. All Lusignan's efforts for the advantage of the colony and the post were neutralized by the bad conduct of the lessees. *Coureurs de bois* took advantage of the situation to draw the Indians within their influence. The monopolists of the post, in absolute disregard of colonial regulations, entered into dealings with these illegal traders and sold them goods. The commandant was without a garrison and unable to check these lawless proceedings.[13] The chief offender was Etienne Augé, who had been a *voyageur*, and had by his ill-gotten gains succeeded in becoming one of the lessees of La Baye. Lusignan reported his misconduct, and was ordered to send the disturber of the peace to Montreal. Before these orders were put into effect, Augé was killed by a Menominee Indian in a quarrel in which he himself was the aggressor.[14]

[13] *Wis. Hist. Colls.*, xvii, 443, 449.
[14] *Ibid.*, xvii, 445-446; xviii, 6-7; *N. Y. Colon. Docs.*, x, 37. Another person named Augé was at La Baye later. *Wis. Hist. Colls.*, xix, 20.

It is easy to imagine the scandal which all this caused at Green Bay; but once Augé's evil influence was removed, Lusignan succeeded in pacifying the tribesmen and in bringing about a truce between the Sioux and the Chippewa, which was a great relief for the French traders in the interior. Affairs at the settlement also were adjusted and all might have been well, despite the changed system of conducting the trade, had not a disastrous fire occurred which destroyed a large amount of the peltry stored at the fort. These small log forts, situated in forest clearings, were in constant danger from fire; the *voyageurs* all smoked, and a careless tinder sufficed to start a serious fire. La Baye was burned twice within a decade, the fire of 1756 proving even more destructive than that of 1746.[15]

The leasing system was continued for several years, and its proceeds were used for defending Canada in the new colonial war that began in 1744, after thirty years of peace. This disaster increased the evils of the monopoly fur trade in the West. The English fleets scoured the seas and captured the French merchantmen with trade goods. These grew so scarce that by 1745 the governor offered licenses free, and no one would accept them. He was forced to solicit the traders as a personal favor to carry to the West what goods they could secure, in order to retain the good will of the Indian tribes. When in 1746 the lease of La Baye fell in, no one would bid for its trade privilege, and the commandant at Mackinac allowed two private traders to go from his post to Green Bay for the small payment of one thousand francs each.[16] It is believed that one of these traders was Augustin de Langlade, and that from this event dates his close connection with

[15] *N. Y. Colon. Docs.*, x, 37-38; *Wis. Hist. Colls.*, xviii, 165.
[16] *Wis. Hist. Colls.*, xvii, 447, 449-451.

the settlement at Green Bay, although he had long been associated with the fur trade on the upper Mississippi among the Sioux. It was, no doubt, at this time that the elder Langlade built a warehouse and perhaps a dwelling at Green Bay, and he may have spent a considerable portion of the year at this place, while retaining his family residence at Mackinac until after the close of the French régime.[17] In this same year Lusignan's appointment expired, and he took with him to Montreal a contingent of western Indians prepared to go to war, if desired, for their French allies.[18] The governor thanked his red friends for their zeal in his behalf, and sent them back to their homes with renewed faith in the French cause.

The next year affairs for the fur trade were somewhat more favorable. The scarcity of goods was in part compensated for by the high prices offered for furs. La Baye, including the trade of the Menominee, Winnebago, Foxes, and Sauk, and also of the Sioux, was bought in by three Montreal merchants, and then sublet to a company of experienced traders. The terms of these leases tell us much about this method of conducting the trade. The Montreal outfitters were to pay the government five thousand livres per year for their monopoly, as long as the war lasted; in case it ceased before the expiration of the lease, the price would be raised to six thousand francs; while if the French ships should fail to bring goods, the price would drop to three thousand. The lessees could send as many canoes loaded with goods to their post as they chose, and the commandant was bound to give them his support. They were required to transport the commandant and his personal belongings to his post,

[17] *Wis. Hist. Colls.*, iii, 199; xviii, 130, note 68.
[18] *N. Y. Colon. Docs.*, x, 34, 36-38.

and to make him an allowance of goods with which to purchase his food. They also had to pay for the presents that it was necessary to give to maintain the tribesmen in their alliance. The lessees also had to pay an interpreter, and they were entitled to the profits made by the post blacksmith.[19]

The new commandant who went up this year to replace Lusignan was Jean Jarret Sieur de Verchères, an elderly, reliable officer who had for several years commanded in the West. He was Canadian born, and a brother of the well-known heroine Madeleine de Verchères, who in the Iroquois wars so bravely defended her father's fort. Jean had been one of the defenders also, and had grown up in the colonial atmosphere of caution with regard to the tribesmen. He had less cultivation than Lusignan; nevertheless he was a trusted and able officer, and his long experience with Indians was a valuable asset for his success at his new post. Verchères had need of all his resources, for the year 1747 was a critical one everywhere in the West. Beauharnois left Canada in that year, and the new governor, Count de la Galissonière, was wholly inexperienced in dealing with Indians. The fur trade was completely demoralized; goods could not be had, the lessees of the posts prayed to be released from their contracts, licenses offered free found no takers, and the Indians were sullen and rebellious. The post at Mackinac was attacked, and the commandant destined for La Baye was obliged to stop *en route* and aid in its defense. Reports then reached him that the tribes at the Bay were still loyal and eager to receive a French "father" among them. But shortly after his arrival at his post he found that all the surrounding tribesmen were plotting to destroy the fort.[20] We have no details

[19] *Wis. Hist. Colls.*, xvii, 451-455; xviii, 7-10.
[20] *Ibid.*, xvii, 462-465; xviii, 62, 64.

of the manner in which Verchères broke up this formidable conspiracy, which was in fact a part of a larger revolt that threatened all the French posts in the West. But the opportune ending of the intercolonial war in 1748 made it possible to subdue the western conspiracy and to restore tranquillity to the posts.

After the treaty of Aix la Chapelle the license system was restored, and none of the posts were leased except those of Lake Superior for which the contracts had already been made. Licenses sold now for six hundred francs per canoe. New posts were built at Toronto, at Sault Ste. Marie, and on the upper Mississippi. The first of these was designed to guard the portage to Georgian Bay, and to prevent furs being carried to the British post at Oswego on the other side of Lake Ontario; the Sault post was designed to check the traffic to Hudson Bay, and also to be a supply depot, raising provisions for northwestern traders. It was erected into a seigniory like the grants on the St. Lawrence. The building of the Mississippi post was a last attempt to control the great Sioux tribe and to increase the returns from the entrepôt at Green Bay. Marin was sent out to establish this last post, and hoped to take thence a substantial fortune.

It was Marin who persuaded the governor, Marquis de la Jonquière, when he arrived in Canada in 1749, to restore the license system, assuring him that it offered opportunities for enrichment that the leasing of posts did not present. La Jonquière was notably avaricious, and he readily listened to Marin's scheme for controlling the Wisconsin trade. Marin's son was sent to command at La Pointe, where he could keep the Chippewa quiet, while Marin himself built a fort among the Sioux, whose hinterland was the richest beaver territory in the West. The commandant at

La Baye was to be a mere tool of the ring. They found an agent in a poor youth named Pierre Mathurin Sieur Millon. The governor was to take care that no one obtained a license for this region except those whom Marin should designate. Marin counted on his personal prestige with the western Indians as one of his chief assets.

The plan succeeded admirably. La Jonquière called the traders together and impressed them with his desire to further their interests. He assigned Marin a garrison of soldiers, and made him a liberal allowance for Indian presents. Eight licenses were taken out, and with all his equipment Marin started June 1, 1750, for the West. His return was hailed with rejoicing by the tribesmen; he passed through Green Bay and the Fox-Wisconsin waterway, mounted the Mississippi, and built a post as had been planned. This last French post on the upper Mississippi was maintained for six years under the successive commands of Marin and his son. It was apparently located on the west side of Lake Pepin, near the present Frontenac, Minnesota, not far from the former Fort Beauharnois.[21]

At Green Bay, Sieur Millon met with a tragic fate while boating on the river below his post; his canoe was overturned and he was drowned. Four days later the overturned craft was found, but the officer's body was not discovered until next spring. A gentleman cadet, Charles Porcheron Sieur de Combre, took charge of the post during the winter, which was a troubled one, as many rumors of foul play for the late commandant were about. When Millon's body was found, however, it was plainly seen that his death had been an accident, and the excitement subsided. Sieur Millon was suc-

[21] *Ante*, chapter xiv, note 45; E. D. Neill, in Macalester College, *Contributions* (St. Paul, 1890), first series, 214, 218.

CHANGES IN FUR TRADE METHODS 381

ceeded in his post by Villebon, whom the governor thought "very fit for the position." Villebon kept his command for a brief term, being supplanted in 1752 by the younger Marin.[22]

These years of the first part of the fifties were peaceful and profitable ones. Trade flourished to an astonishing extent. The profits of the ring formed by Marin and the governor rose to one hundred and fifty thousand francs per year, due to Marin's skillful management of the Indians and traders. He brought about a peace between all the tribes of the West; but as for the fur-bearing animals, they were exploited to a dangerous degree, on the principle "after us the deluge."[23] For three years the partners enjoyed this prosperity and orgy of profit-making; then La Jonquière suddenly died, and the new governor, Marquis Duquesne, had other favorites. Marin was recalled in 1753, and hurried to the upper Ohio frontier. There he died late in the same year, leaving his successor, St. Pierre, to receive the young ambassador from the Virginia colony, Major George Washington. Marin's son was allowed to retain the upper Mississippi post three years longer, but the combination of fur traders was broken and the profits passed into other hands.

La Jonquière and Marin instituted a system which persisted throughout the remainder of the French régime, and which by favoritism, corruption, and undue profits hastened the downfall of New France. "Formerly," says Bougainville in 1757, "the posts were auctioned off. . . . To-day the governor general disposes of them for the benefit of his favorites with the approbation of the court. The most important are the Sea of the West, the post of La Baye, Saint-Joseph,

[22] *Wis. Hist. Colls.*, xviii, 65-66.
[23] *Ibid.*, 63, 80, 192.

the Nipigons, and Michilimackinac."[24] La Baye under this régime was granted as a perquisite to the new governor's brother, François Arnaud Marquis de Rigaud; both of these noblemen were the sons of the former Governor Vaudreuil, and the younger Vaudreuil had been governor of the province of Louisiana. When transferred to his native colony, he lost no time in planning to enrich himself and all his family. He had been a member of the expedition which in 1728 had invaded Wisconsin, and had evidently been impressed with the accounts he had heard of the riches of the fur empire in La Baye's hinterland. He had also heard of the spoils obtained by Marin and his confederates. His first move was to obtain the grant of La Baye for two years for his brother Rigaud; the lease was twice renewed, the last time (in 1759) for life. The first year the profits were three hundred and twelve thousand francs.[25]

Rigaud never visited Green Bay in person, but made contracts with traders for the working of the post. In 1758 he contracted with Jacques Giasson and Ignace Hubert to gather the furs for a one-third interest in the profits.[26] He likewise had something to say about the choice of the commandant, and after the recall of Joseph Marin, who left the post in 1756, Vaudreuil sent his nephew, Hubert Couterot, to become what proved to be the last French commandant at La Baye. Green Bay now fell upon evil days. Its former commandants had been men of high reputation, ability, courage, and honor. All of them had been gentlemen

[24] *Wis. Hist. Colls.*, xviii, 192.
[25] *Ibid.*, 127, 132, 156, 164, 183-184, 193. The final grant was made the basis of an English claim in 1766 to Green Bay. *Ibid.*, 274-275.
[26] *Ibid.*, 197-199.

with ideals of soldierly conduct in the face of danger. Couterot, who had not been bred in Canada, and had had no experience of wilderness life, was a craven, and his influence with the tribesmen was less than nothing. They despised him for his personal effeminacy and as the agent of corrupt dealings. The Menominee, who had been the stanchest in their devotion to French interests, and whose village lay next to the post, now rose in revolt. They planned to kill the commandant, pillage the traders, and make themselves masters of the fort. When the insurrection began, eleven Frenchmen were killed and the warehouse plundered. Couterot, although "inept with fear," managed to save his own life.[27] Thus low had French prestige descended at La Baye under the rule of monopoly and favoritism. The following year the Menominee went down to offer expiation for their crime, and two of the guilty were put to death in the governor's presence, "the first event of this kind on the part of the Indians since Europeans have lived in the country."[28] Couterot, however, continued his dishonest practices. He forged certificates to an immense amount in the interest of his uncle, which his other uncle the governor countersigned, and thus depleted the royal treasury in New France at the very moment when all its resources were needed for defense.[29] Thus Wisconsin and its posts must be held to have contributed to the corruption and venality that were the ultimate cause of the overthrow of French sovereignty in North America.

We have confined ourselves in this chapter largely to the events at the Green Bay post as typical of the

[27] *Wis. Hist. Colls.*, xviii, 203-205.
[28] *Ibid.*, 211; but see Duluth's action described *ante*, chapter xii. See Pierre Grignon's recollections of this matter, Wis. MSS. 54B106.
[29] *Wis. Hist. Colls.*, xviii, 206.

demoralization that occurred during the latter period of the fur trade in the French régime. The situation at the other posts was similar, if not so flagrant as that at La Baye. At La Pointe, where the La Rondes were supplanted by the Marins in 1749, the post became merely subsidiary to the one on the upper Mississippi. The growth of the trade in interior Wisconsin was considerable; traders followed the Chippewa to their new locations on the headwaters of the Wisconsin and Chippewa rivers. Probably several inland posts were built in this period, but we have no record of them. The last French commandant at our most northern outpost was Sieur de Beaubassin, and the last lessee was Sieur St. Luc. The latter paid the royal treasury eight thousand francs for the fur trade monopoly at La Pointe; he also paid the commandant's salary of three thousand francs, and the wages of an interpreter.[30] La Pointe was thus maintained under the leasing system until the withdrawal of the commandant and garrison during the last critical years of the French and Indian War. It is instructive to note the condition into which the Indians declined when French traders no longer visited them. The first British traders on the site of La Pointe found the Chippewa in a desperate plight, naked and starving, having lost the arts of primitive life and of fending for themselves during their century of dependence upon the French traders.[31]

The great evil of the fur trade was not only that it debased the natives, but that it debauched the civilized men who took part in it. The wilderness knew no law but that of the strongest and craftiest; the pressure of competition was tremendous; all was condoned for the sake of profits. Life was hard in the

[30] *Wis. Hist. Colls.*, xviii, 191.
[31] *Ibid.*, 277; Bain, *Alexander Henry*, 187-188.

interior, and there was no pressure of public opinion to induce decent living. The white traders often fell below the standards of their red customers, and especially the illegal traders threw off all restraints. When the rulers of the colony were given over to fraud and dishonesty, it was not to be expected that the rank and file should be disinterested. Only at the posts was a civilized life possible, and in the little clearings where the retired traders dwelt we find some semblance of gentle living.

XVIII. THE FRENCH RESIDENTS OF WISCONSIN

ONE of the most eminent of Wisconsin historians has given this title to his narrative: *Wisconsin: The Americanization of a French Settlement.*[1] It is the object of the present volume to describe how there came to be a French settlement in Wisconsin, its origins, vicissitudes, changes, and destiny. We have seen that it was the result of the fur trade, and that aside from the officers and garrison that were sent for temporary occupation, all the settlers were present or past traders. The unit of settlement was the military post, and around the forts were clustered all the permanent French dwellers in Wisconsin. The French forts were located at strategic places, to control either the water routes or some important tribe. The chief post of the Northwest was at Mackinac. That place was to the early inhabitants of Wisconsin a metropolis and an entrepôt. A visit to Mackinac was an event of importance. The fort at this place during the first three-quarters of the eighteenth century was on the southern side of the straits, at what is now called Old Mackinaw. Its commandant ranked all the other French officers in the Northwest, and its garrison was the strongest on the upper lakes. Its population varied with the season. In summer it was at its height, being the rendezvous of all the traders in the West, and visited by merchants from the colony; in winter the number of inhabitants dwindled, but there were residents the year round, including the clerks and

[1] Reuben Gold Thwaites, in the volume published in the American Commonwealth Series (Boston, 1908).

agents of the principal merchant dealers in provision supplies, unemployed *voyageurs*, and those retired for age or infirmities. At Mackinac was a permanent missionary, who cared for the spiritual welfare of the entire Northwest, christened and married the western Frenchmen who came thither from places hundreds of miles distant. He also said mass for the outgoing companies of traders, heard their confessions when they returned to this place, and exercised supervision over the small number of savages who had accepted the white men's faith.[2] At Mackinac also was a royal notary, who placed the official seal upon all contracts, from a *voyageur's* engagement to a contract of marriage. The last French notary was François Louis Cardin, who in the British period held the office also of justice of the peace; but in the French era all judicial functions rested in the commandant, whose decisions the notary merely registered.[3]

The largest settlement in Wisconsin was around Fort La Baye, and occupied both sides of the Fox River from near its mouth up the stream for two or three miles. At the Fox-Wisconsin portage a few Frenchmen dwelt, employed in transporting canoes and goods from one stream to another.[4] How large the French settlement was on the Prairie du Chien, just above the mouth of the Wisconsin, we do not know. Some think the white settlement was not begun until after the French period, but in all probability

[2] See entries in the register of the priests at Mackinac, printed in *Wis. Hist. Colls.*, xviii, 469-513; xix, 1-162. See also letter of Father Gibault, written from Mackinac in 1768, in *Illinois Catholic Historical Review*, iv, 197-198.

[3] *Wis. Hist. Colls.*, xviii, 140, note 83.

[4] The earliest French settler at Portage whose name we know was one Pinneshon, who was said to be a deserter from the garrison in Illinois. *Wis. Hist. Colls.*, xviii, 282, note 95.

there were some permanent dwellers before 1761. The upper Mississippi forts also seem to have had no permanent group of French settlers such as made homes at La Baye. At Chequamegon Bay there was the nucleus of a French village, but this did not survive the evacuation of the post in the last years of the French régime, its dwellers retiring either to the Sault or to Mackinac.

If what we have described were the extent of the French settlement in Wisconsin, it could hardly be dignified by the name of settlement, so little knowledge have we of the number or the permanence of the French residents of this region during the period of French sovereignty. But from this small group developed during the succeeding seventy-five years a considerable Canadian-French population, homogeneous in character, and similar in type to the earlier settlers, and clearly an outgrowth of the occupancy of Wisconsin by the French. It was this relic of the French régime that the American immigrants found upon their arrival in Wisconsin, and it is the habits and manners of these settlers that we propose to describe irrespective of the date of their advent in Wisconsin.

The economic basis of the French colony in Wisconsin was the trade with the natives, who were an ever-present factor in the life of the community. Indeed, it is difficult to speak of the French without including some at least of the Indians, since intermarriage was so frequent and affinities so close, that the aborigines played an important part in the life of the settlement. Near Green Bay was a Menominee village with which relations were very intimate, while Prairie du Chien was the resort of several tribes who kept in touch with the village people. Yet there was no real commingling of the two races, each of which main-

THE TANK COTTAGE, GREEN BAY, IN 1906

tained its exclusiveness, the half-breeds gravitating to one or the other race according to education and environment.

In addition to the fur trade there was a beginning of agriculture, especially at the two settlements of Green Bay and Prairie du Chien. Farming was first begun to supply the traders and as a means of individual support; its products never were used for export, except during wars or in distant trading operations. The farms were opened like those of Canada, in long strips back from the river front. As far as was ever ascertained there were no legal titles, but each cultivator occupied as much land as he could use, and after a few seasons custom confirmed him in his occupancy. When in 1820 the United States sent a commissioner to examine these land claims, he found farms from four arpents to a little more than half a mile in breadth.[5] In depth these farms had no limit but the activity of the farmer; in reality they did not extend more than a half-mile back from the river; and it was estimated in 1831 that the area of cultivation in the Green Bay settlement did not exceed two thousand five hundred acres.[6]

Their farming implements were very primitive, being local adaptations of those in use in Canada. An early American pioneer thus describes the method of preparing the land for crops: "Most of them had teams of native oxen, and a kind of implement claimed to be a plow, with which they broke the soil. This plow went on wheels, one of which was twice the size of the other, the larger one going in the furrow, the smaller one going on the land. The plow beam was fourteen feet

[5] *American State Papers: Public Lands*, iv, 852-865. An arpent is an old French measure equal to 192.5 feet.
[6] *Wis. Hist. Colls.*, xv, 403.

in length; the chip, on which the share was fastened, was four feet long, and altogether, when in motion was drawn by six or eight bulls, it was a formidable object, and answered well the end of its construction. The furrows were nearly two feet in width, but quite shallow. The style of plowing was what is known as 'back furrowing,' and only two each way, to a land, forming ridges about eight feet wide, with a dead furrow between, which ensured thorough drainage. The breaking was commonly done in June; then leaving it till the next spring, when as soon as the farmer could get at it, it was thoroughly harrowed, and if for wheat, the seed put in without waiting for warm weather.

"These bull-teams were a curiosity to a raw American. The animals were unblemished—the yoke was a straight stick of hickory, worked off smooth, and bound to the bulls' necks just back of the horns, with a strip of raw hide, to which stick was fastened the pole of the cart, on which rested the plow beam."[7]

The extreme fertility of the virgin soil made good crops a certainty. The grains raised were wheat, oats, rye, and barley. Indian corn or maize was common and much hay was made. Vegetables were produced in great abundance—potatoes, peas, cabbages, melons, onions, and squashes. The householders were very careful about their gardens, and one of the frequent requests in their letters is for good garden seeds.

The citation above speaks of "native oxen," but that does not mean that they were indigenous. The first cattle may have been brought from Canada, but more probably were obtained from Detroit, where they were imported at the foundation of the post. Horses were a common possession, bred from farm

[7] *Wis. Hist. Colls.*, vii, 218-219.

horses imported with the cattle, crossed frequently with Indian ponies. Cows and hogs were also numerous, the latter running at large.[8]

The houses were of two kinds, all built of logs, but in quite a different fashion from that of the early American settlers. The simpler houses were built of upright posts planted in the ground, and grooved at the sides, then filled in with small timber or poles, and the whole plastered over with clay and whitewashed; the roofs were usually of bark, and sometimes the entire house was covered with bark. The use of whitewash made the villages appear gay and clean. The better sort of dwellings were built of squared logs, either oak or pine, laid horizontally. These were carefully hewn with the ax, the corners neatly dovetailed, and frequently a second story was added with huge beams to support it. Carpenters were sometimes imported from Canada in order to build edifices for the gentry. They frequently made the furniture of the houses, and employed considerable skill, carving the cupboards and chests, and even the woodwork of the interior of the house.[9] The oldest house now standing in Wisconsin was one built at Green Bay during the latter part of the eighteenth century. This was not built of logs but of sawed timbers, probably prepared by hand with a whip-saw. It was at a later time boarded over. The Green Bay Historical Society has preserved this old house for the benefit of future generations. It has a great chimney of rubble, and originally its small windows were protected by

[8] See list of animals furnished for provisions to the British in the War of 1812, *Wis. Hist. Colls.*, xii, 126-131.
[9] *Ibid.*, ii, 119; Wis. Hist. Soc., *Proc.*, 1912, 181-182.

heavy wooden shutters. It is an eloquent survival of the old French days in our commonwealth.[10]

As we have indicated, the settlers were divided into classes, based on the sharp distinctions in the fur trade. The *bourgeois*, or chief trader, became the aristocrat of the settlement, where his former *voyageurs* rendered him the same honor and obedience that he was accorded when at the head of a trading expedition. He lived the life of an ancient patriarch, surrounded by dependents for whose welfare he held himself responsible. The Indians also, his former customers, hung about his residence, expecting doles of food and clothing. Several of the leading men of the Green Bay settlement impoverished themselves because of the great number of those who depended upon their bounty, and because they had not the heart to refuse aid to the indolent and unfortunate. There was much poverty in the French settlements, but no actual suffering or starvation.

One of the servants employed by every one of the gentry was a hunter. Frequently he was an Indian or a half-breed, and an expert with the gun. His duty was to keep his master's table supplied with the products of the chase—venison and other game, for deer were plentiful in the forests, and wild fowl abounded in the wild-rice stretches on the rivers and marshes. This hunter frequently had a small lodge near the gateway of the garden; his duties sometimes included supplying firewood for the great hearths built into every room of the larger houses. Domestic servants were usually half-breeds or Indians. There was a species of Indian

[10] Wis. Hist. Soc., *Proc.*, 1908, 120-121. The wood in this old cottage is still in an excellent state of preservation. The picture herein given was taken before the removal of this building from its original site. See *ibid.*, 1906, 46.

slavery in Canada and in the West. These slaves were called "panis," because the earlier ones were captured from the Pawnee and kindred tribes in the far West. As a rule they were kindly treated, were members of the household; occasionally one such slave would escape to the woods, but he was usually returned to his master by the tribesmen, they themselves holding captives in bondage.

Food was abundant and varied, and some of the better class of inhabitants were almost epicures. All the early travelers speak of the great variety of game, fish, and vegetables, and the skill with which they were prepared for the table. "It would be impossible," says one of the first Americans at Green Bay, "to do justice to the courses of the dinner; suffice it to say that for variety or rarity of dishes, it equalled any of a similar character in more civilized climes. The dishes were largely made up of game. There was venison, bear meat, and porcupine; a dozen varieties of the feathered tribes from the waters, as geese and ducks; and of fishes, an almost endless list, headed by that king of all the fish tribe, the sturgeon."[11] Wine was made from wild grapes, and a kind of beer was brewed in the larger settlements. Good wines were also imported from Canada and France, and brought forth to grace every social occasion. There was a great deal of drinking among all classes, but one observer reports that it was considered a disgrace to be drunk. Excessive indulgence, however, was condoned, and proved to be the ruin of some of the more promising young men of the upper class.

The dress of the common people was nondescript, and portions of it, like that of the Indians, were frequently made of deer skin; the rest of the costume was

[11] *Wis. Hist. Colls.*, vii, 263-264.

fashioned from stuffs procured from the traders. The ordinary habitant wore a cotton or calico shirt, deerskin *culottes*, fastened by a bright sash, a colored neckerchief, and a cap, either of an animal's skin or of parti-colored cloth. The universal footwear was moccasins made by Indian women. In winter, or on a journey, the useful *capot* was utilized—a kind of cape of heavy material, with a hood to be drawn over the head in storms. The gentry dressed very differently. In the earlier times they were usually in uniform. Later, when settled on the land, they imported fine costumes of silks and velvets, and on festal occasions, and when on visits to Mackinac or Montreal, appeared like gentlemen of fashion. The women, as a rule, were less well supplied, and since many of them were of Indian origin, they dressed more like the natives, usually cherishing some pieces of finery brought them as presents.

Traveling was almost entirely by water, in the birch-bark canoe or stouter Mackinac boat. When land carriage was desired, it was on horseback, as there were no wagons or carriages, and the common carts were without springs. In winter the French *traine*, a kind of carriole, was used, drawn by one horse or a tandem team. There were practically no roads, except Indian trails. Contact with the outer world was to be had only in summer; when once frozen in for the winter, the communities were isolated and had to be self-sufficing. Then the social season began. Among the amusements horse racing was very popular; races were usually run on long stretches of ice. Boxing and wrestling were common, especially among the lower classes. Dancing was a universal pastime, and the fiddler was one of the most popular members of the community. Balls were conducted with much dignity and propriety, older persons being present and insisting on deportment and decorum. Politeness and good breeding were the rule, and all rudeness of manners was frowned upon and considered a disgrace. The feasts and festivals of the Catholic church were observed. Christmas was an especially merry season; presents, however, were reserved for the New Year. Lent was also kept with some strictness, especially in the matter of abstinence from meat.

The happiest time in the year was one that combined both work and pleasure; that was the sugar-making season. Almost every family owned or appropriated a sugar bush—a grove of maples near the settlement. When the time came early in spring to begin collecting the sweet sap, the whole community entered upon a prolonged picnic, moved out into cabins built for the purpose, and spent several weeks in the woods. It was a time of hard work and much gayety. The actual preparation of the stores of maple sugar, which were to last the household a year and which were frequently an object of sale, involved considerable labor, and much care for cleanliness (the Indian methods were so unclean that the better class of French would not use sugar made by the natives). Feasting and merriment helped to lighten the labors of the sugar camp. There was frequent visiting from one camp to another, and much sport over the turning of *crêpes*, as the French called the pancakes made to be eaten with the syrup.[12]

Courtship often took place at these sugar camps. Marriage was early on the part of the women, and the families were large. Here was one of the flaws in the civilization of the western French settlers. In the early days, when there were no women of their own race in the country, Frenchmen were wont to mate with the Indian women, and adopted the Indian habit of easy

[12] *Wis. Hist. Colls.*, xiv, 28-33.

divorce. Moreover, there were no priests to give religious sanction to the union, which often became one of mere convenience. Most of the gentry took occasion on visits to Mackinac to take along at some time their Indian women and their children, and to have the ceremonies of marriage and christening performed all at the same time. The finer natures among the Frenchmen remained monogamous and true to the mother of their children. As for the Indian women so circumstanced, they were not only models of conduct, but frequently grew into beautiful, dignified matrons, fit consorts for their educated white husbands, excellent housekeepers, able managers of servants, respected and revered by their families and their community. The chief drawback to this condition was the swarm of Indian relatives that claimed kinship and consideration, and made the homes of the white men not far removed from the wigwam.[13]

The lack of religious instruction and an opportunity for education were the most serious drawbacks to residence in the western country. There were no priests nearer than Mackinac, and their duties were too arduous to enable them to travel to the western settlements. As for education, there were only two possible means by which the children could acquire it— by having a private tutor, or by being sent from home. Both methods were employed. Jacques Porlier, one of the most influential of the French settlers of Green Bay, came there when but eighteen years of age to be a tutor to the younger Grignon children, the grandsons of Charles de Langlade. Pierre and Charles, the two oldest Grignon sons, were educated at Montreal.

[13] See entries in the Mackinac register—for example, those recording the marriage and the baptism of the Grignons—in *Wis. Hist. Colls.*, xviii, 493; xix, 88-91.

Porlier in his turn sent his son and daughter, children of a half-breed mother, to be educated among their relatives in Canada. Marguerite, the daughter, never returned to her native village, marrying in Canada and making her permanent home there. When, however, she first left her parents and family to live with aunts who were strangers to her, not only was the little girl desperately homesick, and filled her epistles with prayers to be allowed to go home, but her aunts found her a little savage in demeanor, and complained in their letters of the difficulty of taming her.[14]

Men such as Porlier, educated and well-mannered, were of great importance to the Wisconsin French. He insisted upon care in the use of the language by his pupils, children, and dependents, and it was remarked by no less a visitor than the Prince de Joinville, that the French spoken at Green Bay was remarkable for purity and excellence of accent. The example of the courtesy and charm of manner of this worthy gentleman, who became in later days a judge and who then acted as magistrate for the settlement, had a restraining and elevating influence upon the young half-breeds who were growing up in Wisconsin, and made them emulous of the name and attributes of a French gentleman.

The patriarchal life at Green Bay, an oasis of civilization in the midst of barbarism, was lived under three flags, and was subjected to three modes of governance. During the French régime proper all government was in the hands of the military officers, who had discretionary jurisdiction in all matters relating to the French traders as well as to the Indian allies. All disputes

[14] Many of the letters that passed between Porlier and his sisters and daughter are in the manuscripts in the Wisconsin Historical Library.

between the two races, or between the different classes of traders, were settled by the commandants. If any reference to law was required, the code used was the *coutume de Paris*, which governed all of New France. The only check upon the commandant, aside from this somewhat shadowy code, was the detailed report he was obliged to make to his superior officer, the governor, who could recall him for misconduct. In truth, the term of the commandant had usually expired before an order for his recall could become effective. The result was that the rule of the chief officer of the post was arbitrary, and the inhabitants became accustomed to autocratic government. In fact the French never became interested in self-government, and after the opening of the American epoch could hardly be induced to vote, and when they did, voted from the personal standpoint, giving their voice always for one of the leaders of the community, irrespective of his qualifications or candidacy.[15]

Under the British, conditions changed only in so far that the chief trader acted as magistrate or ruler, while a kind of traders' code developed, unwritten but powerful, according to which life in the Indian country was regulated and misdeeds punished. As far as it had any legal foundation this code was based upon the sacredness of contract, and rested upon the engagement bonds made by the *voyageurs* when entering the employ of the *bourgeois* or of one of the great companies. There were always magistrates at Mackinac before whom offenders might be brought, and at Green Bay a retired trader by the name of Charles Reaume held some kind of commission of magistracy. Many are the amusing stories told of the manner in which Judge Reaume exercised his authority, which seemed purely

[15] *Wis. Hist. Colls.*, ii, 141.

arbitrary and dependent upon his personal will.[16] Nevertheless it is probable that substantial justice was done by the seeming autocrat; he knew his community and all the persons with whom he had to deal, and his primitive methods were suited to the primitive conditions under which the French lived.

The climate of Green Bay and of the other parts of central Wisconsin was held by French writers to be excellent; nevertheless, the health of Wisconsin residents was not good. The traders were usually worn by the hardships of their wintering in the Indian villages and by the long journeys in tiny craft, where a cramped position was a necessity. Although they were much in the open the *bourgeois* took little exercise, and when settled on the land lived a somewhat indolent life, eating and drinking heartily. The result was that they complained of many ailments, and only a few lived to a "good old age." There were no physicians in the settlements except those connected with the posts. These usually were permitted to engage in general practice and to alleviate the sufferings of the settlers. Many of the Indian women had considerable empirical skill with herbs and medicinal poultices, and they were often called upon to serve as midwives. In Prairie du Chien was a notable woman of this sort, who had some negro antecedents and probably came there from the Illinois.[17]

Relations with the Indians were of vital concern to the French dwellers in their territory. Two of the functionaries of each settlement were there because of the Indian needs—the blacksmith and the interpreter. The first of these tradesmen came west at a very early day, since the Indians, once having discarded their native implements and weapons for the white

[16] *Wis. Hist. Colls.*, i, 59-61; ii, 87-90, 105-107.
[17] *Ibid.*, ii, 125-126.

men's, had no knowledge or skill in repairing these. The Jesuit missionaries at De Pere had a blacksmith attached to the mission, as a means of winning the tribesmen's favor. When the posts were reëstablished early in the eighteenth century, a smith was sent to every fort. The earliest smith of whom we have the name was François Campeau, who accompanied the Sioux expedition of 1727 and helped to build Fort Beauharnois. He appears to have lived in the West for several years, and may have been the artificer with Linctot at Trempealeau, the products of whose forge have been found.[18] The blacksmith at Mackinac for many years was a son of Madame Augustin de Langlade by her first husband, Villeneuve. The first smith we have record of at La Baye was Charles Personne *dit* La Fond, who was married at Mackinac in 1747 to Susanne Reaume, of Green Bay.[19] Another sister of the Reaume family married about this same time Jean Baptiste Jourdain, from whom descended Joseph Jourdain, the blacksmith in the early nineteenth century.[20] Thus these two families of Jourdain and Reaume are known to have been among the earliest French at La Baye.

The founder of the Reaume family in Wisconsin was Pierre, an early interpreter, who was in the West before 1718.[21] Indeed, several of the early explorers, such as Perrot and Duluth, were utilized as interpreters. The interpreter was an official at every post, and his salary was paid by the government. His influence with the natives was great, and he usually had opportunity to profit by the fur trade, although he was

[18] *Wis. Hist. Colls.*, xvii, 135; Wis. Hist. Soc., *Proc.*, 1915, 114.
[19] *Wis. Hist. Coll.;* xviii, 474; xix, 25.
[20] *Ibid.*, xviii, 473; xix, 20.
[21] *Ibid.*, xvi, 377.

JOSEPH JOURDAIN

not supposed to use his influence for that purpose. In later years nearly all the interpreters were half-breeds, who knew their mother's language as well as their father's. Scions of the Grignon and Porlier families were so employed by the Americans in their dealings with Wisconsin Indians; and at Portage, the Winnebago half-breed Pierre Pauquette was a valued and trusty interpreter.

The social status of these functionaries was between the aristocrats and the common people, for on trading voyages they ate with the *voyageurs*, but had trusted duties connected with the *bourgeois*. When Indian negotiations took place at the forts, or when delegations of Indians came to visit the commandant, both the blacksmith and the interpreter were of great importance. It was they who detected any incipient dissatisfaction among the tribesmen that might lead to hostilities. A skillful interpreter could often allay misunderstandings with the natives, without appeal to the officers. An evil-minded interpreter, bent upon mischief, could arouse feelings of distrust that might have disastrous consequences.

For the little groups of French in the Indian country were never allowed to throw off all guard. They were always so much in the minority that the whims and prejudices of the natives had seriously to be considered. An Indian uprising was as much feared by the French of Wisconsin as a slave insurrection was dreaded by the Southerners before the Civil War. Ordinarily the tribesmen were satisfied with their yearly presents, and with doles of food when they appeared at the French houses. When their women were mistresses of the house, it increased their demands but lessened the dangers of an unexpected attack. They were always fond of the half-breeds of their tribes, and at Indian treaties provided a liberal share of either land or annuity for these relatives. After the uprising of the Menominee in 1758 the French of Green Bay always lived on good terms with their Indian neighbors, and were never molested. This was due in large measure to the half-breed descendants of Claude Carron, an early trader with this tribe.[22] At Prairie du Chien the danger from hostiles was greater, and was manifested at several times, notably in what was known as the Winnebago War of 1827. While on the whole the relations of the French in the West with the tribesmen were stronger and safer than those of either British or Americans, the tradition that the French understood the management of the North American aborigines better than other European peoples seems to have been somewhat overstressed.

The French of Wisconsin maintained close relations with Canada during all their sojourn in the West. Montreal was their metropolis, and a visit to that place was the ambition of every resident. Social and business contacts were cherished, and the arrival of the yearly messages from the St. Lawrence was the event of the season. All luxury goods were imported from the Canadian merchants, and craftsmen were sent for, to build homes and improve conditions at the western villages. All the leaders of the western communities came originally from Canada, and their civilization was an adaptation of that of the St. Lawrence valley.[23] Communication was also maintained with the other French settlements in the West—those of Detroit and the Illinois, and later with St. Louis.

[22] Wis. MSS. 54B106, in Wisconsin Historical Library.
[23] In *Wis. Hist. Colls.*, ii, 122, is a list of the principal French pioneers of Prairie du Chien; and *ibid.*, viii, 242, the same for Green Bay.

Merchants going through Green Bay from the Mississippi River settlements, to and from Mackinac or Canada, were cordially, even lavishly, entertained; in some cases marriages occurred between the youth of the different French settlements, and close intimacies were maintained. Next to Mackinac the Green Bay settlement seems to have been the center of western activities, due to its situation on the chief trade route, and also to the high character and fine hospitality of its principal men. The social life at this place was most enjoyable. All travelers speak of the genuine cordiality with which they were received and of the lively interest the community exercised in making their stay pleasant. It was typical French hospitality, merry and gay, good-tempered and untiring, yet not coarse or rude, or lacking the elements of a well-mannered group.

These were the main features of the life in the French settlements in Wisconsin and the Northwest —isolated communities as they were, with lands cleared from the surrounding forests, the rivers running past their doors their only means of communication. Their little villages with the clean white houses, their green fields, and their horses and cattle, made a pleasing picture to the eye; and the cordial hospitality of their homes made an enduring memory for the mind of the visitor. Because of their French traditions they maintained somewhat more grace of life and manner than the average American pioneer; but their constant contact with the savages, and their commingling with the lower race, tended to coarsen and degrade the lives of the youth and to drag them down to the level of their mothers' people. The lack of educational opportunities was a serious drawback, and the few educated men of the communities had to bear the burdens of keeping up the standard of living. The moral and religious traditions were maintained with difficulty; drinking habits were especially prevalent, and the gay and mercurial temperament of the average *voyageur* led to an irresponsibility of conduct that told heavily against progress.

Progressive these French settlements never were in the American sense of the word; planted in a distant region, the residuum of the fur trade, with little contact with the larger world, they tended to a static rather than to a developing condition. They, however, kept burning the torch of civilization in the far West for over a century, and proved to be a link in the history of the West that cannot be ignored. In several cases these small French western settlements became the nucleii of new American centers and the bases of their social life. In Detroit and St. Louis strong traces still exist of the early French founders, and many of the leading families derive descent from French pioneers. In Wisconsin the French element has had a smaller share in social history, due to the accident of location rather than to any inherent difference in the nature of the social group. The French of Michigan and Missouri grew wealthy by the enhancement in value of their lands placed in the midst of a great American city. The French of Green Bay and Prairie du Chien had no such good fortune. Unused to competitive methods of business, they stayed in the fur trade long after it ceased to be profitable, and lost their lands for the most part by mortgages to John Jacob Astor and the other magnates of the great fur companies. Thus the Wisconsin French sank rather than rose in the social scale; many of their children, in default of profitable occupations, joined the Indian tribe to which they belonged by affinity, and removed with the tribesmen to reservations. Others remained in the settlements, affiliated with the Americans, and lost their distinctive characteristics as Frenchmen. Thus the influence of the French inhabitants of Wisconsin has not been lasting. None the less they did preserve in early Wisconsin some of the charm of gracious living that characterizes French people in every part of the world, and their institutions and mode of life made an impression on the first Americans that has never been effaced.

Nor should it be forgotten that the founder of Wisconsin's largest city was a Frenchman—Solomon Juneau—and that his post at Milwaukee was a direct outgrowth of the French settlement at Green Bay. Several of our other large communities find their first history in trading posts of French origin, notably Sheboygan and Manitowoc; while the first trader known to have visited the site of Madison was Oliver Armel, an immigrant directly from old France, without intermediary Canadian ancestors. Fond du Lac, Oshkosh, Appleton, and the other Fox River cities had their beginnings in French trading posts and settlers; while the upper Wisconsin River was first peopled by men of French origin from Green Bay. The French residents of Wisconsin, few in number and small in influence, must be remembered when counting the origins of civilization in the Northwest; and had the armies of New France not been defeated on the Plains of Abraham, there might have grown up in the Mississippi valley a culture as notable, if not as strenuous, as that which has superseded the beginnings of the French settlement of Wisconsin.

XIX. INTERCOLONIAL RIVALRY FOR THE WESTERN TRADE, 1741-1752

SO MUCH has been written about the French and British rivalry in the fur trade, and the disastrous consequences to the power of the former in the New World, that it would seem superfluous to discuss it here, were it not for the fact that the object of this rivalry was the western trade. In reaching out hands to control the country about the Great Lakes and the headwaters of the Mississippi, the English were encroaching upon territory that the French had exploited for nearly a century and considered theirs by inviolable right. It was in this region that the French had built up their system of alliances with the native tribes on which their trade rested; it was here that they dreaded invasion or defection, since should these alliances once be broken and the country thrown open to free trade, the entire system of control would be destroyed and the somewhat precarious grasp of the French upon the western Indians would be lost. By the methods which we have already described the fur trade rested upon exclusive national rights, and once the traders of another nation secured a foothold in the preëmpted region, the nationals of the first were no longer safe in property or life. The first impulse of the tribesmen upon entering into a new alliance was to murder all the traders of their former friendship and to confiscate all their goods. This hostile attitude of mind grew out of the Indian custom of regarding as enemies all beyond the bonds of clan or tribe; it was fostered by both French and British during the intercolonial wars, and in time of peace it served to bar all but the traders of one nationality from the Indian country.

The French, having control of the great routes to the West—the St. Lawrence valley, the Great Lakes, and after the founding of Louisiana, the Mississippi—had been able to keep the western country as a fur trade preserve. This region, however, was open to penetration from the east by several routes, each of which played its part in the rivalry for the western trade. The earliest invading route was that of the Mohawk valley and the country of the Iroquois, which was utilized in the seventeenth century by Dutch and English successively. We have seen how this route was closed by the watchfulness of the French officers and by the neutrality of the Iroquois, who refused to become the exclusive allies of either of the rival powers. After the founding of Detroit, and later of the post at Niagara, the French successfully guarded for many years the trade routes to the upper lakes.

The next peril to French interests in Indian trade came from the southern English colonies. The Atlantic coast line trends sharply to the southwest, and the distance from the coast dwellers to the Appalachian mountain barrier is much less in Virginia and the Carolinas than in New York or Pennsylvania. The fur traders are usually the pioneers of the pioneers, and in Virginia they began as early as 1670 to cross the mountain barrier to the interior Indian towns. Gabriel Arthur, an indentured servant of James Needham, was captured in 1673 after his master's death at the hands of a treacherous Indian, and carried far to the westward. Rescued and adopted by a Cherokee chief, Arthur traveled to the Spanish outposts in Florida, and probably as far north as the Ohio. His principal achievement was to obtain for his employer, Colonel

Abraham Wood, the alliance of the powerful Cherokee tribe, which thereafter was English in its sympathies.[1] After these early ventures Virginia traders were not as enterprising as the more southern English colonists in securing the trade with the great tribes of the eastern Mississippi valley. We have seen how the Carolina traders, in the last decade of the seventeenth century, were led over the mountains by a French deserter and found their way even to the Mississippi, and claimed to have approached the Great Lakes.[2] During the first decade of the eighteenth century the Carolinians made good progress in forming alliances with the interior tribes and in breaking down the system of French friendship with the lower Mississippi natives.[3] Checked for a time at the close of Queen Anne's War, in the succeeding years the Carolina traders were so enterprising as to endanger the very existence of the colony of Louisiana; and after the massacre at Natchez in 1729 and the disastrous defeat of Dartiguette in 1736,[4] the French officers at the northern posts constantly urged their allied tribesmen to make reprisals upon these southern tribes in the English interest.[5]

There remained the third route into the Mississippi valley, the easiest to penetrate, but the most remote from the English settlements—the Ohio valley. It was not until traders from Pennsylvania, combined with those from the back counties of Maryland and Virginia, found their way into the heart of the French territory

[1] Alvord and Bidgood, *First Explorations of the Trans-Allegheny Region*, 210-226.
[2] *Ante*, chapter xii.
[3] Verner W. Crane, "The Southern Frontier in Queen Anne's War," in *American Historical Review*, xxiv, 379-395.
[4] *Ante*, chapter xv.
[5] These southern tribes are called in French documents, Têtes Plats (Flatheads). *Wis. Hist. Colls.*, xvii, 250.

and tampered with some of their most reliable allies, that the French realized the English were threatening to break their monopoly of western trade and drive them from the most valuable fur trade regions.

The habitat of the western tribes had gradually shifted eastward during the first half of the eighteenth century, due in part to the concentration policy of the French, in part to the Fox wars, and chiefly to the innate desire of the tribesmen to seek the earlier homes from which they had been driven nearly a century before. The French allies by the end of the first quarter of the century occupied the territory west and north of the Wabash and the Maumee rivers; and the trade routes in use followed the St. Joseph-Wabash and the Maumee-Wabash waterways, along which were clustered the great tribe of the Miami, with its kindred the Mascouten-Kickapoo and its large branches the Ouiatanon and the Piankeshaw, containing at least ten thousand warriors and hunters. Around Detroit the Ottawa and Hurons yet retained their villages, the latter being partially Christianized and having missionaries among them. East of this Wabash-Maumee line the territory had been long unoccupied, due to the terror awakened by the terrible Iroquois raids in that region when the Erie and their kindred were destroyed in the seventeenth century. The Iroquois claimed this region by right of conquest, and refused permission for any tribes to occupy it unless dependents of their confederacy. Such were the Delawares, who began moving from the Susquehanna to the upper Ohio after 1725. Stragglers from the cantons of the Six Nations (who in the West were called Mingoes) came also to settle in this game-filled region, and to attract to their villages wanderers from many other tribes. Among others the Shawnee began moving into the region south of Lake Erie in considerable numbers—some from the south, whither they had ranged after leaving the Illinois; some from Pennsylvania and Maryland—all of them familiar with English traders. The French made efforts to bring the Shawnee back into the circle of the allied tribes, and their chiefs promised again and again to settle on the Wabash or near Detroit; but the rank and file of the tribe preferred the English alliance and never came within the French sphere of influence.

All these tribes which now occupied the rich region between the Wabash and the Allegheny, well called "the debatable land," had long been supplied by English traders. As they moved westward their traders followed them, notably those from Pennsylvania, where the frontier had been augmented by recent immigrants of German and Scotch-Irish stock. The latter especially adapted themselves to the Indian trade, and from their homes in the mountain valleys of Pennsylvania and Virginia made their way westward into the Ohio valley. Notable among the more recent immigrants who led the way into this newly populated fur trade region were Conrad Weiser and George Croghan.

Weiser was a German pietist, belonging to one of the sects that flocked into Pennsylvania in the early eighteenth century. For a time after his migration he lived in the Mohawk valley, and there was adopted into the Iroquois tribe of that name. Because of that circumstance, his great facility with Indian languages, and also because of his trustworthy and faithful character, he was as early as 1731 appointed official interpreter for Pennsylvania. He had much influence with the tribesmen in alliance with the province, and gradually his fame extended to the "far Indians," who ventured to visit the English colony. Weiser was the interpreter at the important treaty of Lancaster in 1744, when officials from Pennsylvania, Maryland, and Virginia met delegates of the Six Nations and secured from them some kind of cession of trans-Allegheny lands. He was from that time forward on the watch for opportunity to form alliances with the Indians in that vast region, and to enlarge the market for the Pennsylvania traders.[6]

Chief of these traders and most active in extending the trade of that province into French territory was George Croghan, an Irishman who emigrated to America in 1741 and settled on the frontier not far from Harrisburg.[7] Croghan immediately entered the Indian trade, and his enterprising nature led him far afield. From his home at the eastern end of the great trail, he sent his pack-horse trains into the West and established trading posts far in advance of those of any previous British trader.[8] Croghan had organizing ability, as well as popularity with both his white employees and his red customers. He was personally brave and fearless, and his adventurous disposition led him to attempt greater expansion than any other Pennsylvanian had done. His opportunity came in the intercolonial war that commenced in 1744. As we have seen, the French were unable during that period to furnish their allies with the goods they needed, because

---

[6] R. G. Thwaites, editor, *Early Western Travels* (Cleveland, 1904), i, 17-20.

[7] *Ibid.*, 47-52. The best account of Croghan's trading activities is that of Albert T. Volwiler, *George Croghan and the Westward Movement* (Cleveland, 1925), chapters i-iii.

[8] Mr. Volwiler calls attention to the importance to the British traders, of the pack-horse, which took "the place the canoe occupied among the *Coureurs de bois.*"

the English fleet swept the seas and captured French merchantmen bringing Indian trade goods. Croghan, on the other hand, not only had a full supply of goods, but was able to exchange them for furs at a much higher price than the French had ever given. He sent his employees out toward Lake Erie and attracted thither the tribesmen from the settled villages around Detroit. His activities were largely responsible for the defection of the Hurons under the renegade chief Nicolas, which culminated in a revolt that involved all the allies in the West and almost destroyed French sovereignty over the fur trade regions.[9]

Nicolas, whose Huron name was Orontony, had been in the habit of hunting in the neighborhood of Sandusky, and about 1740 built a permanent village at that place, where he attracted a large portion of his tribe. A short distance eastward on the Cuyahoga River stood a village of Mingoes, with whom Croghan sent his men to trade. Nicolas took advantage of their presence to induce some of these traders to visit his village, and was delighted with the good bargains he made for his peltry. Croghan, on his part, was glad to open trade with a new and vigorous tribe, and the affair quickly had momentous consequences.[10] As early as 1743 the commandant at Detroit sounded the alarm, and was ordered to discipline the seceding Hurons. This order could not be complied with; and when the war opened the secession not only involved all the Huron tribe, but gradually swept in all the allies around the Great Lakes. The timely closing of the war in 1748 and the vigorous action of the governor-general in dispatching troops to Detroit and

[9] For the La Baye Indians' share in this revolt, see *ante*, chapter xvii; for the general revolt, *Wis. Hist. Colls.*, xvii, 456-469.
[10] Hanna, *Wilderness Trail*, i, 321-329.

RIVALRY FOR WESTERN TRADE 413

Mackinac saved the day for the time being, and checked the disaffection of the lakes Indians.[11]

Meanwhile Croghan had been tampering with the important tribe of the Miami and inducing a large number to secede from the French. The Miami were very friendly with the Shawnee, whose principal village was now at the mouth of Scioto River.[12] In 1748 a delegation of the Miami (whom the English called Twigtwee) Indians accompanied the Shawnee to Lancaster, and with the assistance of Weiser made a treaty of alliance with the province of Pennsylvania. This group of seceders was led by a chief whom the French called La Demoiselle, and who was after this incident known as Old Briton. He and his band removed from the village on the Maumee and built a new habitation on what has since been called the Great Miami River, near the site of the present Ohio town of Piqua. To this village was given the name of Pickawillany. For four years this advance post for English trade was maintained at the threshold of the French preserve, and its occupancy brought on a state of war between the traders of the two nations. The English flocked thither in surprising numbers; in 1750 there were "upwards of fifty Traders, including servants, lodging in cabins that belonged to the Miamis Indians."[13] Pennsylvania licenses were issued for a small sum, and Croghan having shown the way, other firms sent out their employees into this debatable land where trade with the Indian malcontents was so profitable. Although the new Indian town was fully eight hundred miles from Philadelphia and seven hundred from the province's frontier, neither distance nor danger daunted

[11] *Wis. Hist. Colls.*, xvii, 505-512.
[12] *Ibid.*, xviii, 4, 11, 20.
[13] Hanna, *Wilderness Trail*, ii, 270.

the enterprising traders, most of whom were Irish or Scotch and habituated to following the wilderness trails. The French were not slow to perceive the danger of this disaffection of the powerful tribe of the Miami, affiliated with all their allies and reverenced by them as superior in culture and ability.[14] Among the Miami the chiefs had extraordinary powers and were more influential than in any other of the western tribes.[15] This fact may partly account for the success of La Demoiselle's movement, and it increased the anxieties of the French officials. It was decided to take strong measures to bring back the revolted Miami to their former village, and to submission to their French "fathers." At the same time the English were to be warned off from the Ohio valley, and impressed with the ability of the French to make good their claims. The governor-general sent in 1749 a military expedition to overawe the recalcitrants and to impress the English traders. The leader chosen was Pierre Joseph Sieur de Céloron, former commandant at Mackinac and Detroit, and leader also of the expedition which ten years earlier had gone down the Ohio to join Bienville against the southern tribes.[16] In 1749 there were detailed for his command twenty regulars, nearly two hundred Canadian militia, and a few of the domiciled Indians of the mission stations. The expedition left Montreal June 15, and advanced up the St. Lawrence River, over the Niagara portage, and along Lake Erie, until the route to Chautauqua Lake was reached; thence it moved southward toward the heads of the

---

[14] Marquette thought the Miami "the most civil, the most liberal, and the most shapely" of the Indians he met on Fox River. Kellogg, *Early Narratives*, 233.

[15] *Ibid.*, 88.

[16] For a sketch of this officer, see *Wis. Hist. Colls.*, xvii, 207; xviii, 28.

Allegheny, which was entered at the site of Warren, Pennsylvania. Céloron had been supplied with inscribed leaden plates, which he was to use to assert the French ownership to the territory of the Ohio valley. Instead of erecting these plates and the shields with the arms of France upon a pole, as had been done in previous assertions of sovereignty, Céloron, uncertain of the temper of the neighboring tribesmen, buried his plates in the soil at the mouths of several of the Ohio tributaries.[17] He was surprised to see how the Indian population had increased since his voyage over this same route a decade earlier; villages of many tribes were strung along the banks of the Allegheny, all supplied by British traders. Some of the far western French allies were found dwelling in these villages, notably a band of Foxes from Wisconsin. At every stop Céloron interviewed the tribesmen, attempted to win them back to the French allegiance, and sent off the English traders with letters to the governors of their respective colonies.[18] He encountered no serious opposition, although he received no cordial welcome, until he came near the Scioto village on the site of the present Portsmouth, Ohio. Upon the imminent approach of the French, great excitement awoke in this village, and the envoys sent in advance by Céloron received rough treatment and were nearly burned by the infuriated tribesmen. An Iroquois savage rescued them, and upon their return to the expedition the officers decided that there was nothing to do but to advance. They camped opposite the village, threw up an embankment to fortify their camp, and awaited the

[17] Several of these plates have been disinterred and preserved. See *Wis. Hist. Colls.*, xviii, 44.

[18] He had orders to pillage the traders' goods, but was not strong enough to do this in the face of the hostile attitude of the Indians.

expected reinforcement from Detroit. A messenger at last came in, bringing the ill news that the Detroit Indians refused to march. After vain advice to the "Republic of Scioto" to abandon this village and return to their former homes, Céloron passed on down the river, to attempt the principal object of his journey—the recovery of the Miami of Pickawillany. The voyage up the Great Miami was a difficult one; it was late summer and the streams were low. Finally they arrived at La Demoiselle's village, where the French officer found only two *engagés* of the English traders, whom he sent away. His council with the chief and his braves was most unsatisfactory; the Frenchman intended to break up the newly-formed village, and to induce all its occupants to go back to their old home on the banks of the Maumee. This he could not persuade the savages to do. They replied humbly and in their customary submissive language that they would go back after the hunting the next spring; but, as one of the chiefs at the old village told Céloron upon his arrival, "I hope I am mistaken, but I am sufficiently attached to the interests of the French to say that La Demoiselle lies."

The expedition was not only a failure, but the advantage of the British traders was thereby increased. As Céloron significantly wrote: "The Indians in council made a conciliatory reply, with which the governor of New France would be satisfied if one could believe in their sincerity; but it is to their interest to trade with the English, whose goods are so much cheaper than those of the French."[19] The reverberations of the French failure were heard throughout all the upper

---

[19] Céloron's journal is translated and printed in *Wis. Hist. Colls.*, xviii, 26-58. His chaplain's account is in *Jes. Rel.*, lxix, 151-199.

country. The French allies grew restless, and even the faithful Illinois conspired against the monopoly of their masters.[20] Croghan planned for larger trading caravans, and many more customers were seduced from the French villages. La Demoiselle sent his envoys to all the western tribes inviting them to come and trade with the British. His village grew rapidly; by the end of 1750 there were over four hundred families settled at Pickawillany, and the village on the Maumee was almost deserted. Even into the far West the disaffection spread, and French traders were killed on the upper Mississippi by the Sioux and on the Des Moines by the Iowa.

Meanwhile Croghan persuaded the governor of Pennsylvania to send him with a considerable present on a diplomatic mission to the western Indians. He was confident of success and hoped to win over the other bands of Miami and all their allies to the British interest. He left the province in the autumn and proceeded first to his trading post on the Muskingum, where he was joined by Christopher Gist, a Virginia agent, who was out looking for Ohio valley land. While at this western outpost, Croghan and his associates received the bad news that the French were making vigorous reprisals and that they had captured three English traders, among whom were two of Croghan's employees. They had also offered a reward for the scalps of Croghan and his interpreter, and had built a post at Sandusky in order to reclaim the Hurons. As Nicolas died about this time, the French hoped that the seceders of his tribe would go back to their former allegiance. Croghan and Gist, notwithstanding this setback, went on their way and arrived at Pick-

[20] Alvord, *Illinois*, 234-235; *Wis. Hist. Colls.*, xviii, 58-60, 69, 90-94.

awillany early in February. There they were received with great honors. The English colors were erected over the chief's house, and councils were held to reaffirm the alliance with the British and to draw new branches of the Miami therein. Delegates came from the Ouiatanon and Piankeshaw of the Wabash, and in solemn conclave they pledged their trade and interest to the new alliance.

While these affairs were proceeding, a delegation of Ottawa made its appearance, bearing the French colors and asking a hearing. Old Briton told them that they "were always differing with the French" themselves, and in the council which followed hurled defiance at the French Indians, and assured them that he would take the road to the English and would die rather than go back to the French.[21] All this betokened trouble and an open breach between the traders of the two nations and their groups of customers. The French officers at Fort Miami and Detroit were in despair; every day western tribesmen deserted to Pickawillany and brought into that village their families and possessions. Even the northern tribes were taking their furs past Sault Ste. Marie to the English at Hudson Bay. Céloron was sent to command at Detroit, with strict orders to arouse the allies who remained faithful to attack Pickawillany. A declaration of war was sounded in a time of international peace.

In the summer after Croghan's visit to the Miami, a second expedition was sent out from Montreal to recapture the rebels and bring them back within the French sphere of influence. This party was well officered by Sieur de Bellestre, later the last French commandant at Detroit, and the Chevalier de Lon-

[21] William M. Darlington, *Christopher Gist's Journals* (Pittsburgh, 1893), 37-53.

gueuil, who had extensive trading interests in the West.[22] They were accompanied solely by Indian troops, a band of Algonkin and Nipissing from the settlements. They went out by the route of the lower lakes and recuperated at Detroit before attempting the path to Pickawillany. This expedition met with unexpected resistance on the part of the western allies of the French. The Ottawa tribesmen near Detroit would not permit the raiders to pass through their territory, saying that the Miami had intermarried with them and that they would not consent to an attack upon their relations. Bellestre tried to spirit up Céloron to raise a small force for him, but the latter after his own experience two years previously thought it was impractical. Bellestre finally left Detroit with only seventeen Nipissing, and pushed on to the revolted post; but he could do nothing with so small a force, and after his tribesmen had killed and scalped two stragglers, retreated to the French territories.[23]

This affair had evil consequences for the aggressors. The commandant at the Ouiatanon post (near the present Lafayette, Indiana) was warned to protect himself "from the storm which is ready to burst on the French"; soldiers were killed and scalped at the very gates of Fort Vincennes and Fort Miami; the commandant at Detroit wrote that the West was "menaced with a general conspiracy." The governor-general at Quebec was much concerned. "What shall the savages think?" he wrote. "Shall not the English turn this to account to more and more bribe these nations? These overwhelming thoughts have caused me an incomprehensible grief."[24]

[22] For these two officers, see *Wis. Hist. Colls.*, xvii, 459, and xviii, 22.
[23] *Ibid.*, xviii, 104-108; Hanna, *Wilderness Trail*, ii, 282-285.
[24] *Wilderness Trail*, ii, 285.

Suddenly in the midst of their perplexity and dread, the sky cleared for the French and the whole offending settlement of the Miami was swept out of existence. This was effected by a young Westerner, hardly more than a boy, unskilled in military methods, but thoroughly acquainted with the Indians, among whom he had lived all his life and to whom he was attached by the bonds of consanguinity. This was Charles de Langlade, of Mackinac and La Baye. Born in the Indian country, from boyhood he had been familiar with frequent alarms and witness to excursions against rebellious tribesmen. In 1739, if tradition relates correctly, when only ten years of age he was in the party from Mackinac that joined Céloron's expedition to punish the massacre of Dartiguette. At that winter camp on the lower Mississippi the boy Langlade had seen and known many French officers, and had learned something of camp life and military discipline. An evident talent for warfare and the influence of powerful relatives procured him a cadetship in the colonial army by the time he was twenty-one. Burning to distinguish himself by some effort in behalf of his country, he had heard with shame of the several defeats at the post of Pickawillany, and longed to retrieve French honor and turn back the English invaders of the French preserve. His influence with his own tribe was great; although this same tribe—the Ottawa—had turned aside Bellestre's Indians, Langlade by some means succeeded in changing their minds, and in enlisting a force of two hundred and forty savages, keen for French honor and fired by the enthusiasm of their youthful leader.

By what savage rites young Langlade played upon his allies' minds we do not know. At a later time when attempting to raise a force among reluctant Indians, he resorted to the wild excitement of a dog feast to appeal to their savage bravery, and by this means succeeded.[25] By some such legerdemain he aroused the martial vigor of his followers, and with the consent of the commandant at Detroit marched against Pickawillany. The journal of this expedition has unfortunately been lost; we know of it only by the results reported, and by the accounts of the English traders. According to these latter sources it was a wild and horrid raid. The surprise was complete; although the village was well fortified, there was no water to withstand a siege, and all but twenty of the warriors were away hunting. The savages of the attacking party fell upon some women in their cornfields, who escaped and gave the alarm; several of the English traders were about, and their houses were for the most part without the fort. Three of them barricaded themselves in a log house, which the besiegers at once attacked, when the defenders showed the white feather and surrendered without firing a shot. This circumstance revealed to the French leaders the weakness of the defense within the fort, and at a parley which took place late in the afternoon of the fatal day, June 21, a surrender was arranged. Langlade agreed to spare the tribesmen and to save the English traders' lives if they were surrendered. This promise was only partially kept; in all probability the youthful leader could not control the savages, whose passions when once aroused were avid for blood. All but one of the white men were saved, and after a prison term in France were ultimately sent back to Pennsylvania; fourteen of the Miami and Shawnee were killed, among them Old Briton, who had instigated the revolt. His body was bar-

---

[25] *Wis. Hist. Colls.*, iii, 230-231.

barously cooked and eaten.[26] The raiders secured a vast amount of plundered goods, estimated as worth three thousand pounds; Croghan claimed that a third of this loss was his.[27]

This act of war in time of peace had a profound influence on the affairs of both colonies. From this time forward until the latter years of the French and Indian War the French controlled both the fur trade and the occupancy of the Ohio valley. The English fortunes declined. Most of the Miami returned to the Maumee; the site of Pickawillany became a desert. The valiant youth from Mackinac was pensioned by his government and entered the colonial army, in which he received the commission of ensign in 1755, and that of lieutenant in 1760.[28] From this event the intercolonial rivalry entered upon a new phase. The French again had control of the West, and the fortunes of its later rivalry were wrought out on the New York and Pennsylvania frontiers, and determined by the arbitrament of war.

[26] Such cannibalism was rare among the aborigines; it took place only when it was desired to instill the virtues of the victim into the partaker. Old Briton had a reputation for bravery.

[27] The sources for this raid are enumerated in *Wis. Hist. Colls.*, xviii, 128-130.

[28] The latter commission signed by the king is in the possession of the Misses Martin, of Green Bay, and is deposited in the museum at that place. See facsimile in *Wis. Hist. Colls.*, vii, 146. For the commission of 1755, see *ibid.*, xviii, 149.

XX. THE END OF THE FRENCH RÉGIME IN THE NORTHWEST, 1752-1761

THE English penetration of the Ohio valley came to an abrupt end with the capture of Pickawillany. Croghan and several of the English traders were ruined. The revolting tribes, aghast at the punishment meted out to their colleagues, hastened to make their peace with their French officers and to resume trade with the French merchants on the old terms. The Miami, Hurons, and most of the Shawnee became once more obedient, resumed their former alliances, and hopes rose high for a complete submission in the West. The year of this victory, La Jonquière died and a more enterprising governor-general came to take his place. Marquis Duquesne seized the opportunity to recover the entire Ohio valley, and to protect it not merely by buried plates and claims of discovery, but by actual occupation of strategic places with forts and garrisons. In this movement he utilized the services of western officers, accustomed to wilderness methods and adept in the control of Indians.

We do not intend to recount here the familiar story of the fortifying of the Allegheny and the building of the Ohio posts, but only to note the share the western officers and forces had in this enterprise, and its effect on conditions in the West. Duquesne recalled the elder Marin from La Baye, and put him in charge of the advance expedition. His commands in Wisconsin were conferred on his son, who for three years longer had charge of the posts on the upper Mississippi and at Fort La Baye. Marin senior was at Niagara early in April, 1753, and after consultation with his engineers concluded to adopt the route from Presqu'isle (now

Erie) to French Creek, and built at the terminals of this route the two forts of Presqu'isle and Le Boeuf. Marin's advance may well be called the silk-stocking campaign, since we read that bales of velvets, damasks, silk stockings, and such goods were furnished, while food was scarce and many of the soldiers died of scurvy. Marin himself fell victim to improper food and late in October died at Fort Le Boeuf, while the corruptionists at Quebec made their unrighteous profits. Duquesne sent another western veteran to replace Marin, in Le Gardeur de St. Pierre, Marin's predecessor on the upper Mississippi, now just returned from his fort on the far reaches of the Saskatchewan River, a link in the "Post of the Sea of the West."

St. Pierre was the officer whom Major George Washington met when he came to Fort Le Boeuf with the message of the governor of Virginia, and whom he described as "an elderly gentleman, and has much the Air of a Soldier."[1] Before replying to the English summons to retire from the Ohio, St. Pierre sent for his kinsman then in command at Presqu'isle, Captain de Repentigny,[2] son of the officer of that name killed at La Baye in 1733, and brother of the founder of the new post at Sault Ste. Marie. The Frenchmen replied to the English summons that they had no permission to retreat and must maintain at all hazards their Ohio posts. The next spring they continued the advance, and after driving from the forks of the Allegheny and Monongahela the Virginia officer who had begun a post there, built a strong fortification which was called Duquesne. Its commandant was the Sieur de Contre-

---

[1] Worthington C. Ford, editor, *Writings of George Washington* (New York, 1889), i, 27.
[2] Washington speaks of him as "Riparti." For a sketch of this officer, see *Wis. Hist. Colls.*, xviii, 68.

coeur,[3] who had been second in command in Céloron's expedition; while among his officers were Louis Coulon Sieur de Villiers and his brother Jumonville, sons of the commandant killed at La Baye two decades earlier. Thus it may be seen how large a share the western French officers had in this undeclared war on the Ohio frontier.

The advance of Washington to enforce the Virginia demands, and the death of Jumonville in a skirmish, were the instigating causes of the determined effort on the part of the British to drive the French from the upper Ohio. General Braddock with two full regiments of regulars sailed from the British Isles early in January, 1755—as "troops of defense," the British ambassador at Paris declared. All these military operations were reported throughout the West and caused much excitement. A few of the tribesmen took part in the earlier campaigns; Miami were with Marin in 1753, and Hurons were among the defenders of Duquesne the following year. It was not, however, until the approach of Braddock that all the forces of the West were summoned to the Ohio, and that the disguised state of warfare took on a poignant character. The summer of 1755 saw the first of the series of large detachments of Indian auxiliaries leave the upper country and hasten to the aid of their French patrons.

The southern contingent, comprising the Miami, Mascouten, Kickapoo, and Ouiatanon, was led by the younger Lignery; while the tribesmen from Mackinac, including Ottawa, Chippewa, Menominee, Winnebago, Potawatomi, and Hurons, were under the charge of the young half-breed Ottawa, for whom a commission in the colonial army had just been issued—Charles de Langlade. His grandson stated that Pontiac was with Lang-

[3] *Wis. Hist. Colls.*, xviii, 49.

lade on this occasion; and that among his subordinates were such well-known traders as Pierre le Duc Sieur de Souligny and Philippe de Rocheblave, father of the British officer captured in 1778 by George Rogers Clark.[4] The western Indians arrived at Fort Duquesne early in July. Already scouts were coming in with reports of the redoubtable British army pouring through the forest and advancing with irresistible strength upon the French outpost. The situation for the French was very grave. Contrecoeur called a council, and the younger and more daring of his officers advised a sortie and an attack to create confusion in the ranks of the invaders. No one imagined it could be more than a mere temporary check for the seasoned English veterans advancing so confidently toward their post. Dumas, Beaujeu, Lignery, and Langlade were designated to encourage the tribesmen, who shrank from a conflict with the cannon in Braddock's train. "I," exclaimed Beaujeu, "am determined to go out against the enemy. I am certain of victory. What! will you suffer your father to go alone?" Fired by such appeals, six hundred of the tribesmen in full war panoply of paint and feathers, brandishing the tomahawk and scalping knife, and well armed with French rifles, rushed to the fray. Seventy regulars and one hundred and fifty Canadians accompanied them, and stood out to meet the vanguard of the English advance. Braddock's redcoats had already crossed the last creek intercepting their path, and were within seven miles of the fort which was their goal. The general ordered an advance with all standards flying and with the drums and Scottish bagpipes animating the march. The first faint efforts of the French had no effect, the Canadian militia broke and ran; Beaujeu, rallying his forces, was mortally

[4] *Wis. Hist. Colls.*, iii, 212-213.

wounded. Langlade then begged permission of Dumas to lead his savages around the advancing column, and at a little ravine it was about to enter, to attack from all sides. It was a desperate expedient, but the movement was well executed. The tribesmen spread through the forest and silently took their stand behind trunks of trees, each one singling out a redcoat for deliberate aim. At the signal, their war whoops rang out through the quiet noonday, and at the first volley hundreds of the English fell. The forest became a slaughter pen; on every hand shots came from invisible assailants; bravery was useless. The colonials, accustomed to Indian warfare, sought the shelter of trees, but Braddock drove his men forward with the flat of his sword. Huddled together and firing aimlessly, they killed their own men; while incessantly came the mysterious volleys from the woods, mowing down men and horses alike. The artillery was useless, firing only into the trees and crashing down branches upon friend and foe. Unhorsed steeds careered wildly across the battle field, adding to the confusion. Braddock had four horses shot from under him; Washington, his aide, was mounted on a third charger. Braddock at last gave the signal for retreat, falling mortally wounded at the same moment. The rout was complete. The English fled in terror before the savages, whose hideous yells carried fear to the stoutest heart. Braddock's force was annihilated. The fugitives were no longer an army, but a mob, fleeing for miles back toward the settlements, regardless of their fallen comrades. The French were themselves surprised at the result of their sortie. They made no attempt to follow the fleeing foe, and the Indians could not be withdrawn from the rich plunder left in the abandoned camp. Langlade had won his spurs, and although as a subordinate his name does not appear in contemporary reports, he was known for many years, among both French and British officers, as the victor of the Monongahela.[5]

The news of this great victory spread throughout the western world, and was confirmed by the articles from the camp that were brought home as trophies. For years, gold and silver coins, garments of broadcloth and velvet, chased and engraved weapons, and even books and letters were to be found in savage villages and in squalid hunting camps—the loot of Braddock's army. Captain Morris, an English officer, saw in 1763 upon the Maumee one of Braddock's horses, and found a copy of Shakespere's works in possession of a savage in the same vicinity.[6]

War was now formally declared between the two powers, and the final struggle of both nations for the New World was at hand. Canada had learned the value of Indian auxiliaries, and from this time forward no important campaign was planned without calling for help from the West. All through the winter succeeding Braddock's defeat, Indians in the control of French partisans raided the frontiers of Pennsylvania and Virginia, the war whoop became a familiar sound, and hundreds of innocent families fell victim to savage raids. Then began that hatred of the Indians which characterized the British backwoodsmen, and that spirit of vengeance toward all members of the race. Washington, who had charge of the defense, wrote soon after the battle, "I tremble at the consequences this defeat may have upon our back settlers." And by spring he reported to the governor, "Not an hour,

[5] Langlade's share in Braddock's defeat is recognized by historians on the basis of the authorities cited in *Wis. Hist. Colls.*, iii, 212-214; vii, 130-135.

[6] Thwaites, *Early Western Travels*, i, 311-312.

BRADDOCK'S DEFEAT, JULY 9, 1755

nay, scarcely a minute passes that does not produce fresh alarms, and melancholy accounts. So that I am distracted what to do."[7] By the summer of 1756 large contingents of western Indians were again in motion toward the frontiers. The northern group numbered over seven hundred, officered by Langlade from Mackinac, the Chevalier de Repentigny from the Sault, and by Beaubassin, who came with his Chippewa from La Pointe. Joseph Marin also brought sixty Menominee and Winnebago from La Baye. At this time the post on the upper Mississippi was abandoned, and after this time Marin never returned to the West, where he and his father had so long dominated.

The forces from the West were in this year divided: Langlade again rendezvoused at Fort Duquesne, while Marin was sent to reinforce the French general-in-chief, the Marquis de Montcalm, who was preparing to capture Oswego. At the latter place early in July Marin distinguished himself in an action that intercepted the English reinforcements and paved the way for Montcalm's victory of August 14, which made a tremendous sensation among the Westerners. This was the English fort to which they had carried their furs when seeking the advantage of English prices and the English alliance. It had also been under the protection of the Iroquois, and its fall seemed to predict complete victory for New France. Langlade, for his part, was ordered out against Fort Cumberland, Washington's outpost on the Virginian frontier. Langlade's success in this action, however, was slight; he did not attack the fort, but merely intercepted a paymaster's convoy. His orders were to "do all in his power to prevent them [Indians] from inflicting cruelties upon those

[7] Ford, *Writings of Washington*, i, 175, 252.

who may fall into their hands."[8] This humane injunction it was out of Langlade's power to obey. He probably received it with wonder that any one who employed the savages in warfare could suppose it were possible to restrain them from their customary cruelties. All the training of the Indian youth inculcated the doctrine that every member of the enemy tribe or race was equally guilty, and that the only rational mode of making war was to attack unexpectedly and unmercifully. The idea of non-combatants was foreign to the Indians' ethical code. Age or sex was never a reason for sparing an enemy; the infliction of harm on the whole community was the basis of the Indians' warlike activities. Langlade, accustomed from childhood to such ideas, was callous to the suffering caused; while the French officers more recently from Europe were horrified by the savages' cruelty. The conduct of the western Indians in all the intercolonial wars, and especially in this final one, has always been a reproach upon the humanity and honor of the French officers. The burden of the guilt rests upon the authorities—who, knowing the impossibility of restraining the savages, nevertheless employed them—rather than upon the subordinate leaders, who were expected to secure certain results. Such humane orders as those given to Langlade were impossible of execution as long as the Indians outnumbered the French and were by them urged out upon the warpath.

It was not until the following season, however, that reproach fell anew upon Langlade's braves. Montcalm after the capture of Oswego removed to the Lake Champlain frontier, which the English had so strongly fortified that there was need of all the resources of New France to make headway. The western Indians

[8] *Wis. Hist. Colls.*, viii, 213.

were summoned for a winter campaign—a startling command to the savages. Nevertheless, five hundred Ottawa and Potawatomi, at the behest of the new governor-general, the Marquis de Vaudreuil, canoed down the St. Lawrence, and met their new Onontio in council at Montreal. Langlade accompanied these tribesmen, his fame as a successful partisan being known to all the colony. Vaudreuil also was well acquainted with affairs in the upper country. His father had been governor-general in the earlier part of the century, while he himself had been in Lignery's expedition of 1728 to Wisconsin, and his brother was now the concessionaire of the post of La Baye. The western Indians gave him good greeting and assured him of their devotion to the French cause. In their hyperbolical mode of speaking their chief said, "Father, we are famished; give us fresh meat. We wish to eat the English."[9]

Vaudreuil sent these fierce barbarians to the aid of Montcalm, who employed them to skirmish and to intercept the convoys of provisions sent to the English fort. The familiarity of the Indians with snowshoes and their ability to track the enemy in the woods made their services of especial value, all the more that the English had enrolled their frontiersmen in a company of rangers, led by the famous partisan Robert Rogers. Langlade defeated Rogers' Rangers in a skirmish on January 21, 1757, and wounded their leader. These two brave officers were to meet at Mackinac before a decade should pass, under other auspices than now, for Rogers was to be commandant at that place and Langlade an officer in the British service. Marin also distinguished himself on this winter campaign; but the real crisis did not arrive

[9] *N. Y. Colon. Docs.*, x, 500, 512.

until the summer, when the fort called by the English William Henry was besieged and captured. Over a thousand warriors from the upper country came to Lake Champlain to participate in the siege. Their coming embarrassed, rather than encouraged, the general, who had seen enough of the savages' mode of warfare the preceding winter. The summer contingent was especially insubordinate, and its own officers had difficulty in its control. Marin and Langlade are both mentioned in the dispatches, the former for his "rare audacity," the latter for his humanity. In one of the skirmishes an Indian was wounded, whom Langlade refused to abandon, and brought off in the face of personal peril.[10]

It is well to have an incident of this kind to relieve the horror invoked by the Westerners' conduct after the surrender. It was these far Indians who were responsible for the massacre of the unarmed English soldiers and their families—a deed execrated by French and British alike.[11] The Indians were sent back to their homes under a cloud of disapproval from their commanders, and it was soon found that a more dread nemesis pursued them. The smallpox had been rife in the English ranks, and the victims now took revenge upon the victors. An epidemic of such virulence and proportions had never been known at Mackinac, and the priest's register presents a dismal list of burials through all the autumn and winter of 1757-58.[12] Langlade's reward for his services on this campaign was a commission as second in command of the post at Mackinac, where his superior was Louis Liénard

[10] *N. Y. Colon. Docs.*, x, 569-570, 574, 579.
[11] Both Montcalm's and Vaudreuil's reports are in *ibid.*, 616, 618.
[12] *Wis. Hist. Colls.*, xix, 152-158.

Beaujeu-Villemond, brother of the officer killed at the battle of the Monongahela.

The siege of Fort William Henry with its consequent decimation of the western tribesmen by smallpox marked a turning-point in the war. As if in punishment for broken faith and for Indian atrocities, the fortunes of New France, up to this time in the ascendant, began to wane. The capture of the Lake Champlain post was the last great success of the colonial army. The next year the English recaptured the forks of the Ohio and changed the name of the fort from Duquesne to Pitt. This event had an immense effect upon the traders and tribesmen of the West. The post had been built for their protection, had been successfully defended by them in 1755, and now that it was in the hands of the enemy, the nearer tribesmen went back to the British alliance. The Shawnee, Delawares, and Mingoes came in first; two days after Fort Pitt was occupied Croghan was there, sending messengers to his former customers, the Miami and Hurons. These latter tribes were strongly inclined to return to the British alliance, and much alarm was felt at Detroit, bereft at this time of an able and popular French commandant. Even the faithful Potawatomi could no longer be trusted, and were plotting the murder of their Canadian traders. All these defections were known in Wisconsin and were the inciting cause of the Menominee revolt, when over a score of French were murdered and an attack was made upon the La Baye post.[13] A premonition of French disaster seemed to run like a shudder through the western world, and to foreshadow the downfall of the power that had reigned for one hundred years.

[13] Post's journals, in Thwaites, *Early Western Travels*, i, 177-291; Hanna, *Wilderness Trail*, ii, 20; *Wis. Hist. Colls.*, xviii, 203-205.

The western officers who had carried on the contest for the French supremacy were succumbing to wounds and disease. St. Pierre was killed in 1755; Villiers died soon after the capture of Fort William Henry. Lignery and Marin were yet active on the Ohio frontier, where the former had brilliantly sustained French prestige in the face of an overwhelming force of English. Both of these officers after aiding in the defense of Fort Niagara were captured when it fell, July 24, 1759; and Lignery died in captivity, of his wounds.

In the summer of 1759 the northwestern partisans were called upon once more, when Langlade, Chevalier de Repentigny, and Beaubassin gathered from the regions around Lakes Superior and Michigan twelve hundred tribesmen for the defense of Quebec. At this time the last French garrison on Lake Superior, at La Pointe, was withdrawn; the other Lake Superior posts and those of the Sea of the West had been abandoned earlier in the war. Now only Detroit, Michilimackinac, and La Baye flew the flag of France and remained to guard the Northwest.

When Langlade and Repentigny reached the French camp before Quebec, they found Montcalm engaged in his final struggle with the invading English forces. On July 25 these two officers were called out with their savage auxiliaries to defend the crossing near the Falls of Montmorency. Langlade saw an opportunity to create terror in the ranks of the English by a surprise like the one he had employed at Braddock's defeat; the English soldiers had a great horror of savage warfare, and might easily have been ambushed and defeated. But the higher officers were too timid to give the permission, and the chosen moment passed never to return. Montcalm himself had a strong reluctance to let loose upon an honorable enemy the savages whose actions at Fort William Henry he only too well remembered.[14] He kept his western auxiliaries for scouting and provisioning until the fatal day on the Plains of Abraham. Then they were stationed on the flanks of Wolfe's army, and did effective service until the fall of their commander and the flight of the French army into Quebec. Langlade often in after years recounted the events of that decisive battle. He mentioned his Menominee comrades; and his friend La Rose delighted to tell of Langlade's intrepidity and coolness, when in the midst of conflict he would stop to light his pipe. After the battle he was among those who thought Quebec might be defended, and upon its capitulation left for his western home with a sad heart.[15]

The doom of New France was now at hand; with the loss of Montcalm and the fall of the capital little hope remained of saving the colony. Throughout the long winter of 1759-60, the defenders of Canada maintained a guerrilla warfare and harassed the British army shut up in Quebec; and at the brilliant victory of Ste. Foy on April 27, 1760, animated the hopes of the French that the invaders might be expelled. In that battle a French trader was killed who had left in Wisconsin an Indian family famous in the annals of the West. This was Joseph des Caris, whose Indian widow, known as Glory-of-the-Morning, was herself a great chieftess and the founder of the Decorah family of Winnebago chiefs.[16]

The victory of Ste. Foy was made of no effect by the arrival soon afterwards of a strong British fleet, with

[14] *Wis. Hist. Colls.*, vii, 139-144.
[15] *Ibid.*, iii, 217-218.
[16] *Ibid.*, 286; v, 297; vi, 224; xviii, 422. See also William Ellery Leonard's drama entitled "Glory of the Morning," based on historic facts, and admirably illustrating the relations between the Frenchmen and their Indian consorts.

reinforcements. Whereupon Vaudreuil retired to Montreal and called all the forces of Canada to fight one more campaign for the control of North America, against the converging troops of the English advancing from Quebec, Lake Ontario, and Lake Champlain. For the last time Langlade in the summer of 1760 led his savage allies to the support of the French. During the winter months he had received word of his promotion, and he now ranked as lieutenant in the colonial troops. His contingent did not arrive until the middle of August, when Vaudreuil wrote that he was sending Langlade and his savages to the support of Bourlamaque.[17] But all to no avail; Montreal was doomed. Vaudreuil sent Langlade off a few days before the capitulation on September 8, probably that the tribesmen should not be involved in the surrender. Somewhere *en route* he was overtaken by a messenger with a letter from the governor announcing the inevitable end, and explaining the terms granted by the victorious English. All the upper country was included in the surrender. The troops were to lay down their arms and not serve again during the war. The citizens of Mackinac and the other western posts were to be left in possession of their property, and to have free trade with all subjects of Great Britain; they were secured in the exercise of their religion; and might migrate to French territory or remain subjects of the English king, according to their wish. They were henceforth to be governed by the common law of England, rather than by the *coutume de Paris*. The governor closed his note with the polite wish that he might soon see Langlade in France.[18]

[17] H. R. Casgrain, *Collection des Manuscrits du Maréchal de Lévis* (Montreal, 1895), viii, 208.
[18] *Wis. Hist. Colls.*, viii, 215-217.

France, however, was a strange land to Langlade and to most of the Canadian-born. All their attachment and interests clung to the land of their childhood; it was easier to renounce allegiance to a monarch never seen, than to abandon the only homes they had known. For the Westerners the change of sovereignties was doubly easy. Their chief interests lay in the trade with the natives, and in developing the wilderness. Loyal as they had always been to the interests of France, they saw with great sadness the departure of the garrisons; while at the same time they realized that the change would advantage the fur trade. The Langlades and most of the French traders in the Northwest elected to remain under the British rule.

The commandant at Mackinac, however, decided otherwise. Immediately on Langlade's arrival with the news of the capitulation, Beaujeu made preparations for departure in order to avoid the humiliation of surrendering the garrison and post to a British officer. The way through the land to the Mississippi was yet open. Beaujeu, after denuding the fort, started with all his forces for the Illinois. Since this province was part of Louisiana, it was hoped it would not be included in the capitulation. Arrived at La Baye, Couterot and his garrison joined in the retreat, making up a force of four officers, two cadets, forty-eight soldiers, and seventy-eight militia. This was the last French expedition to pass along the Fox-Wisconsin waterway, and we may imagine that the late autumn landscape along their route fell in with the melancholy of their spirits at the abandonment of this lovely land. The season was cold, and before the Illinois settlements could be reached the ice in the Mississippi stopped their retreat. There was nothing to do but to winter among the Indians at the mouth of Rock River, in the village where Marin had once commanded, and where a few years later the chief Black Hawk would be born. It was a strange fatality that the last winter of the French in the Northwest was spent among the Sauk Indians who had made the original grant of the land upon which the post of La Baye stood.[19] Slowly spring crept over the western land; at the first release of the boats from the ice-bound river, Beaujeu and his men hastened on to Fort de Chartres. Their arrival made a welcome addition to the garrison at that place, which resisted for four more years the surrender of that fort to the English.[20]

Thus quietly and without the dramatic pomp and ceremony with which they took possession in 1671 and 1689, the French departed from the northwestern posts. Langlade, who was left in charge at Mackinac, heard with some chagrin that his late enemy Major Robert Rogers, accompanied by trader Croghan, whose plans he had thwarted at Pickawillany, was advancing upon Detroit. That post surrendered November 29, 1760, and its garrison was transported to Philadelphia. British detachments went out from Detroit and took over the forts at Miami and Ouiatanon, while Rogers in person started for Mackinac. But the early winter interfered with his arrangements, and cold and ice forced the ranger to return to Detroit. Thus for one more season the fleurs-de-lis floated over the northern lakes.

Langlade expected to be visited by a British force early the next spring, but it was not until September

[19] *Wis. Hist. Colls.*, xviii, 221-222.
[20] Alvord, *Illinois*, 242. Beaujeu later reached France, but in after years returned to his manor on the St. Lawrence, and there died about 1802. He and Langlade no doubt often met on the latter's journeys to Canada.

that Lieutenant William Leslie arrived at Mackinac with a detachment of three hundred men. English traders had been there before the military, and found themselves in great peril, since the Indians claimed they were still at war. Langlade and the few militia he had gathered at the fort made a formal surrender, and the tribesmen were awed by force into outward submission. From Mackinac the British passed on to La Baye, where they arrived October 12. They found no one to welcome them, the Indians being away hunting and the French traders having moved off to avoid seeing the enemy take possession. The fort was in a bad condition, the stockade ready to fall, the houses unroofed, and the wood of the whole place rotting away.[21] Such were the conditions caused by the neglect of the concessionaire in his haste to enrich himself.

It is well known that New France fell, not for lack of military prowess, but because of corruption and graft. The exploitation of the western posts and the venality of the fur traders contributed to this downfall. The protection of the fur trade had induced the war in America, and its best avenues of approach—by the Ohio and the Great Lakes—were now in the hands of the British. This was, however, but a temporary occupation; the future depended upon the treaty of peace. A considerable party in England desired to return Canada to France in exchange for Guadeloupe in the West Indies. Then negotiations centered on the territory south of the Ohio, and the tentatives for peace were broken off. France drew Spain into the contest; and the last two years, 1761 and 1762, were more disastrous to the Latin nations than the former had been. The treaty as finally signed in 1763 ceded to England all of Canada, as well as the Ohio valley, and

[21] *Wis. Hist. Colls.*, i, 25-26; xviii, 237.

Louisiana east of the Mississippi except for the island of New Orleans. With the cession to Spain as compensation for its losses in Florida, of Louisiana west of the great river, France was stripped of all its continental possessions in North America.[22]

Wisconsin had been the keystone of the arch of the French empire in the New World. With one end resting upon Quebec and one on New Orleans, Wisconsin was the connecting link between the Great Lakes and the great river, and was central in all plans for French civilization in America. From the time its shores were visited by Champlain's messenger Nicolet, until the signing of the final treaty relinquishing French sovereignty, one hundred and thirty-nine years had passed, during which Wisconsin had been made known to the world by French explorers, had been occupied by French officers and soldiers, had been peopled by French residents. Its aborigines had been subdued and brought into dependence upon French merchants. Its resources of fur-bearing animals and minerals had been exploited. A beginning had been made for a French culture in the heart of America. Now all was at an end. France has always proved to be daring in discovery, heroic in exploration, successful in subduing inferior tribesmen. But permanent colonization does not attract many Frenchmen from home. The population of the French colonies in America was but a fraction of that of the smaller English provinces. To hold the great interior valleys of America with the French who could be persuaded to settle there was an impossible task. So the French in Wisconsin gave way before the English, as the Indians in their turn had yielded to the white man.

[22] C. W. Alvord, *The Mississippi Valley in British Politics* (Cleveland, 1917), i, 45-75.

French Wisconsin has played an insignificant part in the development of our commonwealth. Its population has merged indistinguishably with the American. Its forts have fallen and disappeared until hardly their sites are known; its heroes are remembered only by name. Yet France has left traces upon our map that are ineradicable. Fourteen of our seventy-one counties bear French names—Calumet, Eau Claire, Fond du Lac, Juneau, La Crosse, Lafayette, Langlade, Marinette, Marquette, Pepin, Portage, Racine, St. Croix, and Trempealeau. Among our lakes are the Buttes des Morts, Court Oreilles, Flambeau, and Vieux Desert. The French rivers, in addition to those that have given their names to counties, are the Aux Plein, Baraboo, Bois Brulé, Eau Galle, Montreal, Platte, and Prairie. Of our larger cities, Racine, Superior, La Crosse, Eau Claire, Marinette, and Fond du Lac have French titles. Among the smaller places, Baraboo, De Pere, Juneau, Prairie du Sac, St. Croix Falls, Tomah, and Trempealeau recall memories of traders, missionaries, and chiefs.

As long as heroism is prized and memories of brave men remain, the names of the French explorers and exploiters of Wisconsin will be remembered; and the history of Wisconsin will be embellished with the records of Nicolet, Radisson, Perrot, Jolliet, Marquette, Duluth, Tonty, Louvigny, Lignery, and Langlade. And as long as men wish to recall the past and the development of great ideals, so long will the French projects for expansion in North America fascinate the imagination and enlarge the mind. The greatness of the Mississippi valley, its resources for feeding the nations, its influence on migration and commerce, its potentiality as the home of a unified civilization, were first recognized by Frenchmen. Unable to occupy and people this imperial valley, the French renounced it and left it as a legacy to the forces of a more expansive nation, which has opened its boundaries to all of Europe. Pierre Radisson, the first Frenchman to enter this great valley, saw its possibilities as the home for Europe's disinherited, and wrote in his journal: "The country was so pleasant, so beautifull and fruitfull that it grieved me to see that the world could not discover such inticing countrys to live in. This I say because that the Europeans fight for a rock in the sea against one another, or for a sterill land and horrid country, that the people sent here or there by the changement of the aire ingenders sicknesse and dies thereof. Contrarywise those kingdoms [in the Mississippi valley] are so delicious and under so temperat a climat, plentifull of all things, the earth bringing foorth its fruit twice a yeare, the people live long and lusty and wise in their way. What conquest would that bee att litle or no cost; what laborinth of pleasure should millions of people have, instead that millions complaine of misery and poverty!"[23]

[23] Kellogg, *Early Narratives*, 47.

INDEX

INDEX

ABENAKI Indians, in La Salle's colony, 219; at peace treaty, 266; join Foxes, 316; withdraw, 322.
Acadia, officers in, 183, 253, 296.
Accault, Michel, explores Mississippi, 212-214.
Achirigouan Indians, habitat, 68.
Acta et Dicta, 337.
Adoucourt, Gabriel François le Moyne d', in West, 283; killed, 284.
Africa, Jesuits in, 143.
Agnier Indians, French name for Mohawk, 266.
Agriculture, in French settlements, 389-391.
Ailleboust family, western merchants, 374; losses, 332.
Aix la Chapelle, treaty of, 379.
Alabama, Spanish in, 27.
Alarcón, Hernando de, explorations, 29-30.
Albanel, Charles, Jesuit missionary, 170.
Albany (N. Y.), traders from, 85, 90, 182, 202-204, 230-231, 243, 254, 255, 307; Radisson at, 105; raids near, 248.
Alexander, Sir William, "Our Encouragement to Colonies," 78.
Algonkin Indians, Nicolet among, 66; at peace treaty, 266; on expedition, 419.
Algonquian Indians, geographical names of, 248; habitat, 52, 56, 57, 85, 89, 91, 271, 345; tribes belonging to, 69, 71, 266; attacked, 87, 222; take refuge in Wisconsin, 84, 88, 93-94, 100, 122, 154, 221; missions for, 90, 91, 159; youth among, 61; refugees among, 92; intertribal relations, 132; La Salle assembles, 219, 223-224; as copper miners, 344-345.
Algonquin Lake, in glacial epoch, 32.
Allegheny Mountains, as a boundary, 33, 411; Indians of, 72.
Allegheny River, Indians on, 410, 415; French expeditions, 415, 423-424.
Allouez, Claude, Jesuit missionary, at Three Rivers, 152; goes west, 120, 152; rescues captives, 132; on Chequamegon Bay, 141, 153-156; circles Lake Superior, 154; takes copper to colony, 131, 155, 347-348; at the Sault, 156, 157, 184, 188; Green Bay missions, 134, 158-166; Illinois mission, 170-171; Miami mission, 234; ambition, 192; death, 168; cited, 128, 135.
Allumette Island, on Ottawa River, 53, 54, 57, 79; Indians on, 66-68.
Alton (Ill.), cliffs near, 196.
Alvord, Clarence W., opinions, 196; *The Illinois Country,* 70, 166, 206, 217, 250, 261, 271, 274, 295, 307, 317, 326, 338, 361, 417, 438; *Mississippi Valley in British Politics,* 440: and Bidgood, *First Explorations of Trans-Allegheny Region,* 180, 231, 257, 408; and Carter, *Critical Period,* 372.
Amariton, François, commandant at La Baye, 305-306; recalled, 312.
America, origin of name, 4; continental character, 13, 15.
American Anthropologist, 343.
American Bottom, in Illinois, settled, 271.
American Geographical Society, publications, 3.
American Historical Review, 196, 368, 408.
American Mineralogist, 343.
American Scenic and Historic Society of New York, publications cited, 10, 43.
American State Papers: Public Lands, 389.
Amikouek (Beaver) Indians, habitat, 68; defeat the Iroquois, 117; St. Lusson among, 184; at Sault ceremony, 186; at peace treaty, 266.
Andastes Indians, habitat, 57; visited, 58; destroyed by the Iroquois, 222.
André, Louis, Jesuit missionary, 162; on Green Bay, 163-165, 170; at Sault ceremony, 188; characterized, 162, 169-170; letters, 170.
Angoulême Lac, first name of St. Peter's Lake, 18.
Anticosti Island, ceded to Jolliet, 201.
Apalache, Indian village, 25.

445

Apostle Islands, when named, 355; on map, 299.
Appleton, fur trade post at, 405.
Arctic Ocean, outlet to, 36.
Arizona, explorations in, 29.
Arkansas, Spanish in, 28; French concession, 256.
Arkansas River, mouth of, 28; Jolliet reaches, 196-197.
Armand, ——, merchant, 121.
Armel, Oliver, at Madison, 405.
Armstrong, Benjamin G., *Early Life among the Indians*, 345.
Arpent, defined, 389.
Arthur, Gabriel, visits the West, 407-408.
Artois (France), Le Sueur's birthplace, 251.
Ashland *Press*, cited, 109.
Asia, America a part of, 4, 6, 13, 24; Jesuits in, 143.
Assiniboin Indians, at Sault ceremony, 186; intertribal relations, 211; French among, 225, 226, 237, 261.
Astor, John Jacob, owns Green Bay lands, 404.
Augé, Etienne, lessee of La Baye, 375; killed, 375-376.
Aulneau, Jean Pierre, Jesuit, killed, 337.
Aux Boeufs River. See Iowa River.
Aux Plein River, a French name, 441.
Avery, E. M., *History of the United States*, illustrations, 3.
Ayllon, Lucas Vasques de, explorations, 5.

BADIN, F. V., priest, 233.
Bain, James, *Travels of Henry*, 358, 384.
Balboa, Vasco Nuñez de, discovers the Pacific, 2, 4.
Ballin, Albert, artist, 81.
Baraboo, a French name, 441.
Baraboo River, a French name, 441.
Batiscan (Canada), resident, 115.
Baudry, Toussaint, Perrot's partner, 123, 127, 130, 131, 135, 159, 314; later life, 136.
Baugy, Chevalier de, in Illinois, 228, 256; *Journal*, 236.
Baxter, ——, miner, 358.
Baxter, James P., *A Memoir of Jacques Cartier*, cited, 16, 19, 22, 23, 24, 38, 41, 42.
Beaubassin, Pierre Joseph Hertel de, at La Pointe, 384; leads Indians, 429; recalled, 434.

Beaubois, Nicolas de, Jesuit missionary, 307.
Beauchamp, William M., "A History of the New York Iroquois," 84.
Beaucoup River, Indian battle on, 304.
Beauharnois, Charles de la Boische de, governor of New France, 311, 317-318; policy, 328, 329, 333, 336; choice of officers, 335; recalled, 378; reports, 320, 327, 330, 331, 332, 335; speeches, 323, 338-339.
Beaujeu, Daniel Liénard de, at Braddock's defeat, 426; killed, 427; brother, 433.
Beaujeu-Villemond, Louis Liénard, commandant at Mackinac, 432-433; evacuates the West, 437-438; in France, 438.
Beauvais, René le Gardeur de, captured, 227, 228.
Beaver, used as food, 74, 81, 239; types of furs, 130, 258; plethora of, 257.
Beaver Indians. See Amikouek.
Belle Isle Strait, discovered, 16.
Bellecourt *dit* Columbier, Jean François Pouteret, in Lake Superior, 115-118.
Bellegarde, ——, with Duluth, 209.
Bellestre, Marie François Picoté, commandant at Detroit, 418; expedition fails, 419-420; sketch, 419.
Bellomont, Richard, earl, governor of New York, 263.
Belmont, Abbé de, *Histoire du Canada*, 229, 236.
Berlin, Indians near, 129.
Beverly swamp, location, 133.
Bibaud, Michel, *La Bibliothèque Canadienne*, 322.
Bienville, Jean Baptiste le Moyne de, governor of Louisiana, 338, 414.
Big Butte des Morts. See Butte des Morts.
Big Muddy River, in Illinois, 304.
Big Stone Lake, Duluth's men visit, 211.
Biggar, H. P., *Champlain's Voyages*, 346; "Charles V and the Discovery of Canada," 20; *Early Trading Companies*, 54; "Precursors of Cartier," 8; *Voyages of Jacques Cartier*, 16, 22, 38.
Biloxi, capital of Louisiana, 274.
Black Hawk, birthplace, 438.
Black River, Lake Superior tributary, 354.
Black River, Mississippi tributary,

INDEX 447

Indians at source, 99, 116, 149-151, 153.
Blackbird, Sauk chief, 332.
Blacksmiths, importance of, 399-401.
Blaeu, Willem J., map, 43.
Blair, E. H., *Indian Tribes of the Upper Mississippi*, 84, 95, 96, 98, 99, 115, 117, 120, 124, 126, 128, 130, 135, 136, 146, 148, 150, 158, 161, 181, 184, 186, 189, 190, 203, 204, 214, 229, 230, 231, 232, 233, 234, 236, 241, 246, 247, 248, 250, 251, 253, 265, 360; "Perrot's Memoir" in, 286.
Block Island, earliest name, 12.
Blue Earth River, post on, 274, 275; mining operations, 361.
Bodleian Library (Oxford), manuscripts in, 104.
Bois Brulé River, a French name, 441. See also Brule River.
Boisguillot, ——, French officer, 241; signature, 252.
Boisseau, ——, western trader, 273.
Boisseau, Jean, "Description de la Nouvelle France," 87.
Bolton, H. E. and Marshall, T. M., *Colonization of North America*, 40.
Bonneault, André, Jesuit missionary, 171.
Boston (Mass.), French envoys at, 351.
Bostwick, Henry, miner, 358.
Boucher, Pierre, *Histoire du Canada*, 118, 347.
Boucher family, descendants, 309, 321.
Boucherville, Pierre de, at Fort Beauharnois, 311, 321; reaches Illinois, 322; narrative, 322.
Bougainville, Louis Antoine de, cited, 381-382.
Bourgeois, fur trade term, 368, 370, 398; in settlements, 392, 401; mode of life, 399.
Bourlamaque, François Charles de, in French and Indian War, 436.
Bourne, E. G., *Narratives of De Soto*, 27; *Spain in America*, 5, 25, 27; *Voyages of Champlain*, 47, 48, 62.
Braddock, Gen. Edward, defeated, 425-428; picture of, 428.
Brébeuf, Jean, Jesuit missionary, 79, 86; martyred, 92.
Brereton, John, *Briefe and True Relation*, 41.
Bressani, Francisco, Jesuit missionary, cited, 346-347.
Brinton, Daniel G., ethnologist, 72.
Bristol (England), port, 2.

Brittany, pilots from, 8; voyagers, 9, 34, 37-38.
Broshar, Helen, "The Albany Traders," 203, 231, 255.
Brouage (France), home of Champlain, 44-45.
Brower, J. V., opinions, 110; *Minnesota*, 108.
Brown, Alexander, *Genesis of United States*, 51.
Brown, Charles E., works cited, 74.
Brown University Library, maps, 35.
Bruce Peninsula, Indians of, 56, 70, 87.
Brulé, Etienne, with Algonquian Indians, 51-52; accompanies Champlain, 54; explorations, 58-60, 88, 346; treachery, 62; death, 63.
Brule River, on portage route, 212, 252. See also Bois Brulé.
Buck, Solon J., "Story of Grand Portage," 297.
Buffalo, range in Wisconsin, 112-113, 129; attempt to utilize, 273-274.
Buffalo (N. Y.) Historical Society, *Publications*, 307.
Bulletin des Recherches Historiques, 202, 219, 301, 328.
Burpee, Lawrence J., "Lake of the Woods Tragedy," 337; *Pathfinders of the Great Plains*, 337.
Butte des Morts, village near, 205.
Butte des Morts Lake, village on, 287, 319; fighting on, 324, 332; mound, 332; a French name, 441.
Butterfield, C. W., *Jean Nicolet*, 82.

CABEZA de Vaca, Alvar Nuñez, explorations, 25-27.
Cabot, John, explorations, 2, 8.
Cabot, Sebastian, map, 23, 29.
Cabrillo, Juan, explorations, 15.
Cachetière, Robert, Lake Superior trader, 121-122.
Cadillac, Antoine La Mothe de, Indian policy, 176, 271, 272; commands at Mackinac, 254, 259, 270; recalled, 260, 277, 279; founds Detroit, 270, 295; invites Foxes, 276-277, 280-281; "Memoir," 254; "Papers," 272.
Cadiz, Spanish port, 45.
Cadotte, Michel, on Madeline Island, 252, 301, 355.
Cahokia, Illinois village, 307.
Cahokia Indians, chief's son, 325.
California, missions in, 143; distance to, 210.

California Bay, explorers on, 29; charter to explore, 78; land route to, 196.
Callières, Louis Hector, count de, governor of New France, 264-267.
Calumet, uses of, 123, 126, 130, 185, 187, 310.
Calumet County, a French name, 441.
Cambrai, treaty of, 15.
Campbell, Henry C., "Father Ménard," 148; "Radisson," 108.
Campeau, François, blacksmith, 400.
Canada, origin of term, 18; discovered, 24; population in 1653, 97; in 1665, 119; in 1670, 180; government reorganized, 118-119; claims Illinois, 303, 372; rivalry with Louisiana, 304-308, 371-372; boundary, 303-304, 371-373; agriculture in, 364, 373.
Canada Geographical Survey, *Museum Bulletin*, 74.
Canada Royal Society, *Proceedings*, 52, 108, 115, 118, 119, 122, 183, 188, 236, 238, 337, 347.
Canadian Archives, research in, 202; map, 327; *Publications*, 8, 16; *Reports*, 23, 122, 198, 224, 225, 238, 251, 257, 272, 285, 291, 305, 307, 331, 351, 356, 357, 358.
Canadian-French population of Wisconsin, 387-405.
Canadian Journal, 343.
Canadian Pacific Railroad, station, 298.
Canerio, Nicolay de, chart, 3.
Cantino, Alberto, map, 3.
Cap-de-la-Madeleine, resident, 115.
Cape Breton Island, discovered, 8.
Cape Cod Bay, explored by French, 49.
Cape Rouge River, Cartier on, 21.
Cárdenas, Garcia López de, explorer, 29.
Cardin, François Louis, notary, 387.
Carignan-Salières regiment, arrives in Canada, 119; officer of, 202.
Carron, Claude, descendants, 402.
Cartier, Jacques, discovers the St. Lawrence, 16-20, 55; third voyage, 20-22, 24, 38, 41; maps and documents, 22, 23, 36, 37, 38, 41, 47; meets Thevet, 42; sees copper, 346; cited, 54.
Carver, Jonathan, cited, 329, 335; geographical names, 355.
Casgrain, H. R., *Collection des Manuscrits*, 436.
Casson, François Dollier de, Sulpitian missionary, 133-135, 161.
Cattle, in Canada, 121; on Lake Superior, 355; at Green Bay, 390-391, Cayuga Creek, vessel built in, 213-214, Cayuga Indians, in war time, 249; at peace treaty, 266.
Céloron, Pierre Joseph, commandant at Mackinac, 335; leads Ohio expedition, 414-416, 420, 425; buries plates, 415; commandant at Detroit, 418, 419; journal, 416.
Centennial Exposition, Wisconsin coppers at, 341.
Central America, Spanish in, 346.
Chabot, Philippe, French admiral, 16, 20.
Chaleur Bay, discovered, 16.
Chambellan, ——, goldsmith, 353.
Champlain, Samuel de, explorations, 43, 346; early life, 44-45; voyage of 1603, 46-49; explores New England, 49-50; settles Quebec, 50; voyage of 1609, 50-51; Indian policy, 51-53; fur trade policy, 101; voyage of 1615, 54-55, 57-58; later life, 59-64; patron of Nicolet, 65, 66, 76-78; character, 46-47, 66; death, 83; cited, 85; maps, 53, 62, 75, 87; illustrated, 62; manuscripts, 45-46; illustrated, 46; *Des Sauvages*, 47.
Champlain Lake, on early maps, 35, 51; discovery of, 43, 50; officers on, 296; in French and Indian War, 430-433, 436.
Channing, Prof. Edward, cited, 4.
Chardon, Jean Baptiste, Jesuit missionary, 171, 293, 306, 309-310.
Charles I, of England, 62.
Charles II, of England, 119.
Charles V, of Spain, 8, 13, 15, 20.
Charleston (S. C.), French trader at, 256; *Year Book*, 284.
Charlevoix, Pierre F. X. de, visits West, 296-298, 304, 308, 313; sources used, 281; on missions, 172; *History of New France*, 122, 150, 214, 251, 263, 265, 289; *Journal Historique*, 172, 293, 297, 304.
Charron, Father ——, cited, 109.
Chartier, Martin, deserts to English, 255.
Chastes, Aymar de, colonizer, 46, 49.
Chateau de Ramesay, at Montreal, 283.
Chaudron, Guillaume, early trader, 63.
Chautauqua Lake, on portage route, 414.
Chauvin, Pierre, merchant, 46.
Chenaux Islands, on map, 135.

INDEX

Chequamegon Bay, Radisson visits, 109-111; Ottawa Indians on, 110, 115, 116, 147, 149, 186; traders, 115-118, 123, 127, 147-148, 151; missionaries, 95, 120, 132, 141, 148-149, 153-156, 158, 188, 193, 348; abandoned, 163, 165, 209; Le Sueur's post on, 252; French official fort, 298-302, 312-313, 317, 351-357, 384; evacuated, 388; settlers on, 388; British traders, 384; islands of, 355; copper near, 348; map of, 299. See also Fort La Pointe and Madeline Island.
Cherbourg, French port, 65.
Cherokee Indians, band, 196; trade with, 256; hostilities of, 284; English relations with, 407-408.
Cheveux Relevés. See Ottawa Indians.
Chicago, Indian massacre at, 136, 160, 234; Marquette winters at, 167, 168; Indians at, 205, 271; French fort at, 223-224, 228, 230, 250, 270, 271; rendezvous, 283; council at, 309.
Chicago and Northwestern Railway, at Green Bay, 292.
Chicago Historical Society, documents, 123, 152, 216, 224, 260, 270, 274, 275, 292, 298, 301, 305, 309, 312, 323, 327, 331, 339, 350, 351; documents described, 259; *Reports*, 168.
Chicago-Illinois portage route, in glacial epoch, 32; Nicolet's version of, 82; first crossed, 197; described, 199; Tonty at, 217; St. Cosme, 262; Indian troubles near, 272, 340; route via, 277.
Chicago Lake, glacial epoch, 32.
Chicagou, Illinois chief, 307.
Chickasaw Bluff, on the Mississippi, 28.
Chickasaw Indians, band, 196; trade with, 256; massacre French, 338; punished, 340.
Chippewa Indians, origin of name, 91; early habitat, 57, 68; migrations, 71, 345; at the Sault, 89, 186; Nicolet visits, 79; meet Radisson, 108; defeat the Iroquois, 98, 117, 132; mission for, 154, 156; Duluth among, 209, 226; relations with Sioux, 210, 252, 299, 337, 356; intertribal relations, 306, 323; French allies, 337, 379, 429; fur trade with, 384; post among, 300, 301, 312; murder French, 226, 286; at peace treaty, 265; Braddock's defeat, 425-426; history of, 299, 345.
Chippewa River, Ménard on, 150; fort near, 232; traders on headwaters, 384.
Chouart. See Groseilliers.

Chouskouabika, Indian village on Green Bay, 164.
Christino Indians. See Cree Indians.
Clark, Col. George Rogers, captures Illinois, 426.
Clements Library, University of Michigan, map, 198, 349.
Colbert, Jean Baptiste, French minister, 118, 119, 121, 180, 182; geographical names given for, 195, 198, 201, 220; map drawn for, 198.
Colden, Cadwallader, *History of the Five Nations*, 229.
Collection de Manuscrits de la Nouvelle France, 82, 85, 257.
Colorado River, grand cañon discovered, 29-30.
Columbus, Bartholomew, map, 4.
Columbus, Christopher, discoveries, 1-3, 9.
Columbus, Ferdinand, map, 7.
Combre, Charles Porcheron de, commands at Green Bay, 380.
Company of New France, founded, 61; interpreter for, 76; purchases furs, 102; charter revoked, 118, 181.
Company of the Colony, founded, 102; dissolved, 103; organized at Detroit, 272.
Company of the West, formed, 303; complaint to, 306.
Company of West Indies, organized, 119; fur trade monopoly, 371.
Condé, Henri, prince de, Huguenot leader, 44-45.
Congress of Americanists, *Proceedings*, 73.
Congressional Library, maps, 36, 92, 275.
Conibaz Lake, explained, 42.
Connolley, W. E., cited, 55.
Conseil Souverain, *Jugements*, 115, 117, 122, 225, 251.
Contrecoeur, Claude Pierre Pécaudy de, at Fort Duquesne, 424-426.
Copper, Indian traditions of, 352; first seen by French, 19, 346-349; situation of mines, 59, 75, 342-343; Indian artifacts, 74, 341-342, 344-346; reported by traders, 117, 118, 347; samples taken to Canada, 131; Indian miners of, 341-346; mining methods, 343-344; exploring for, 346-351; La Ronde's mines, 352-358; British mines, 358; on Mississippi, 362.
Coronado, Francisco Vasques de, explorations, 29-30.

Cortereal brothers, explorations, 2, 8.
Cortes, Hernando, explorations, 5.
Cosa. See La Cosa.
Coulonge, Joseph d'Aillebout de, in Sioux Company, 374.
Courcelles, Daniel de Rémy de, governor of New France, 121, 181; invades Iroquois territory, 182; recalled, 191.
Coureurs de bois, origin of, 366-367; increase of, 268; Jesuits oppose, 174, 259; edicts against, 202-204, 260; join Duluth, 209; Duluth proscribed as, 216-217; Le Sueur, 252; at Green Bay, 239, 275, 314, 375; settle in West, 271, 367; relation to English, 371; amnesty for, 219, 276, 283, 286, 291, 367.
Court Oreilles Lac, origin of name, 99; Indians on, 110, 115, 147-148; Ménard, 150; Chippewa on, 357; French name for, 441.
Courtemanche, Augustin le Gardeur de Repentigny de, in the West, 249, 250, 265; defeats Iroquois, 250; recalled, 260; brother, 300.
Courtemanche, Jacques le Gardeur de, contract, 331.
Couterot, Hubert, last commandant at La Baye, 382-383; characterized, 383; evacuates post, 437.
Coutume de Paris, used, 398; superseded, 436.
Couture, Jean, deserts to English, 256-257.
Coxe, Dr. Daniel, English adventurer, 257.
Crane, Verner W., aid acknowledged, 284; "The Tennessee River as the Road to Carolina," 256; "Southern Frontier in Queen Anne's War," 408.
Cree (Christino) Indians, language affinities, 71; described, 108; rendezvous with, 110; mission for, 154; at Sault ceremony, 186; French among, 225, 337; at peace treaty, 266.
Creek Indians, village, 25.
Crespel, Emanuel, Recollect chaplain, 319; *Voyages*, 319.
Creuxius, Francis, map, 92, 114.
Croghan, George, Pennsylvania trader, 411-413, 417-418; loss at Pickawillany, 422, 423; at Fort Pitt, 433; Detroit, 438.
Crozat, Antoine, owns Louisiana, 302; resigns charter, 303.

Cuba, early name for, 1.
Curot, Michel, fur trade journal, 369.
Curtis, Edward S., *North American Indians*, 73.
Cuyahoga River, Indians on, 412.

DABLON, Claude, Jesuit missionary, 158, 163; visits Wisconsin, 162; superior, 163, 169, 191; at Sault ceremony, 188; letter for, 199.
Daillon, La Roche, Recollect missionary, 60.
Dakota Indians. See Sioux.
D'Amours family, in the West, 296.
Daniel, Antoine, Jesuit martyr, 92.
Darlington, William M., *Christopher Gist's Journals*, 418.
Dartaguiette, Pierre, murdered, 338, 340, 408; avenged, 420.
Daughters of American Revolution, erect tablet, 194.
Davenport, Harbert, "The Expedition of Narvaez," 26.
David, Claude, on Lake Superior, 115-118; sketch, 115.
Decorah family, Winnebago chiefs, 435.
De Costa, B. F., article cited, 13.
Deerfield (Mass.), captured, 277.
Delamer, Marguerite, Nicolet's mother, 65.
Delaware, coast explored, 11.
Delaware Indians, migrations, 409; English allies, 433.
Delisle, Guillaume, maps, 360.
Deming, Edwin W., artist, 81.
Denonville, Jacques Brisay, marquis, governor of New France, 230; orders, 232, 241; expedition, 234-236, 239; relations with Iroquois, 244.
De Pere, a French name, 441; Indians, 310; mission, 163-167, 170, 171, 314; chapel, 169, 170, 171; blacksmith, 400; ostensorium, 232-233; Marquette at, 197, 199; Tonty seeks refuge at, 217-218; Duluth at, 225; Perrot, 227, 232, 235; peltry stored at, 235; burned, 236; abandoned, 176, 293.
Dépôt des Cartes, at Paris, 198.
Des Caris, Joseph, killed, 435.
Desceliers, Pierre, map, 23.
Deschaillons, Jean B. St. Ours, at Kaministiquia, 298; at Detroit, 326.
Desliens, Nicolas, map, 23.

INDEX 451

Desliettes, Joseph Tonty, at La Baye, 339.
Desliettes, Pierre, at Chicago, 270; commandant in Illinois, 283, 292, 308, 318; blamed, 320; successor, 326.
Des Moines River, Indians on, 196; hostilities, 334, 417.
Des Noyelles, Nicolas Joseph Fleurimont, attacks Foxes, 326-327, 334-335; report, 335.
Des Plaines River, portage to, 82. See also Chicago-Illinois portage.
Desroches, Jean, Montreal merchant, 123.
Detroit, route to, 284, 313; founded, 269-271, 368, 407; Indian tribes near, 272, 276, 279, 330, 409, 410, 412, 416; commandants, 277, 279, 282, 412, 418; French women at, 295; settlement, 402, 404; domestic animals, 390-391; troops at, 412; Foxes attacked at, 280-282, 288; expeditions at, 419, 421; declines in importance, 291; in French and Indian War, 433, 434; surrenders to English, 438.
Detroit River, first mention of, 48; Indians near, 69, 70, 272; first traversed, 132, 134; Tonty on, 214; Duluth's post on, 231, 235, 236, 238-239.
Dieppe, French port, 8-10, 12, 61, 191; governor, 46.
Dollard (Daulac), Adam, defends the Long Sault, 109, 111, 114.
Dollier de Casson. See Casson.
Dongan, Thomas, governor of New York, 229; cited, 230.
Door County, Indian villages in, 125; voyage along, 262.
Dorsey, George A., "Siouan Sociology," 72.
Doty Island, village on, 310, 339.
Douniol, Charles, *Relations Inédits*, 199.
Drake, Sir Francis, map, 33; raids on Spanish, 39.
Draper, Lyman C., map drawn for, 232; tradition narrated to, 304.
Draper Manuscripts, cited, 304.
Dreuillettes, Gabriel, Jesuit missionary, 141, 162; at Sault ceremony, 188.
Drouine, term explained, 369.
Dubuisson, Charles Regnault, at Detroit, 279; leads attack on Fox Indians, 280-282; report, 281.
Dubuisson, Louise, married, 339.
Dubuque, Julien, lead miner, 363.

Dubuque (Ia.), lead mines near, 248, 360.
Ducharme brothers, contract, 295.
Duchesneau, Jacques, intendant, 204.
Du Creux. See Creuxius.
Duluth (Dulhut), Daniel Greysolon, early life, 208; comes West, 210; among the Sioux, 189, 210-212, 225, 275; missionary with, 172; comrades, 209, 214; purposes, 224-225, 257, 313, 349; rescues Hennepin, 212-213, 216, 221, 238; proscribed, 216, 219; returns to Canada, 216-217, 237, 274; in Lake Superior, 225-226, 230, 237; leads Indians to war, 229, 230, 235, 236; fort at Detroit, 231, 235, 236; punishes Indians, 226, 383; cousin, 214, 218; acts as interpreter, 400; adventures, 441; last days, 238, 246; successor, 252; characterized, 207, 216, 217, 221, 238; signature, 202.
Duluth (Minn.), origin of name, 238; council at, 209.
Duluth Lake, glacial epoch, 32.
Dumas, ———, at Braddock's defeat, 426-427.
Dunleith (Ill.), fort near, 360.
Duplessis-Fabert, François Lefebre, commandant at La Baye, 312.
Duplessis family, losses, 332.
Dupré, Jean B., contract, 292.
Duquesne, Ange, marquis, governor of Canada, 381, 423, 424.
Dutch, in Albany, 85, 90, 105, 182; war with France, 179; in western fur trade, 230-231, 234, 245, 255, 407.
Dutisné, Claude Charles, commandant in Illinois, 295, 306.
Du Verney, ———, early trader, 63.
Dwellings, how built, 391-392.

EAU CLAIRE, a French name, 441.
Eau Claire County, a French name, 441.
Eau Galle River, a French name, 441.
Edits et Ordonnances Royaux, 119, 202, 204, 219.
Effigy mounds, work of Winnebago, 73-74.
English, early discoveries, 2, 3, 8, 14, 33; privateers capture Canada, 61-62, 76, 78; return colony to French, 62, 86; French desert to, 111; subsidized by French, 179; revolution among, 243; in Hudson Bay, 225, 237; approach Great Lakes, 180, 257; intercolonial wars, 222, 243-244, 248-250,

268, 279, 282-283, 376-379, 408, 411-412; peace with, 263, 282, 290, 379, 412, 439-440; rivalry in fur trade, 202, 221, 222, 230-231, 234-235, 241, 243, 254-257, 268, 307, 313, 371, 406-422; relations with Indians, 263, 338; first in West, 277-278; attempt colonies, 270; claim to Green Bay, 382, 398-399; copper mining, 358.

Enjalran, Father Jean, wounded, 235; at Mackinac, 265.

Erie (Pa.), site, 423-424.

Erie Indians, habitat, 56; lake named for, 87; destroyed by the Iroquois, 222, 409.

Erie Lake, first sight of, 40; early mention, 48; Indians near, 56-57, 410; discovery of, 86-87; voyage on, 132-134, 206, 414; war party on, 229-230, 235; English traders near, 412; statue of, 31, 32.

Espíritu Santo, early name for Mississippi, 5, 25, 28.

FAFFART, ——, with Duluth, 209.
Farrand, Livingston, ethnologist, 72.
Ferguson, W. P., "Michigan's Most Ancient Industry," 343.
Fischer, Prof. Joseph, discovers maps, 4.
Fish Creek, on Chequamegon Bay, 148, 153; on map, 299.
Five Nations. See Iroquois.
Flambeau, Lac du, a French name, 441; Chippewa on, 357; French traders, 369.
Flathead Indians. See Têtes Plats.
Florida, mounds in, 342; discovered, 3, 5, 6, 7, 14, 24, 25; explored, 27; French colony in, 33, 34, 35; Spanish in, 256, 407; ceded to English, 440.
Florin, Jean, pirate, 14.
Folwell, W. W., *History of Minnesota*, 110, 172, 210, 211, 252, 274.
Fond du Lac, fur trade post at, 405; a French name, 441.
Fond du Lac County, a French name, 441.
Fond du Lac of Lake Superior, council at, 209, 211.
Ford, Worthington C., *Writings of George Washington*, 424, 429.
Forlani, Paulo, chart, 35.
Forster, John Adam, mining expert, 353-355; paid, 356.

Forster, John Adam Jr., on Lake Superior, 353-355; expenses, 356.
Fort Ancient, in Ohio, 341.
Fort Beauharnois, built, 311-312; abandoned, 321; traders at, 322; not rebuilt, 335; post near, 380; blacksmith at, 400.
Fort Crêvecoeur, built, 215, 216; destroyed, 217.
Fort Cumberland, Langlade attacks, 429-430.
Fort de Chartres, in Illinois, 304; soldiers from killed, 317; treaty at, 322; French officers, 438.
Fort Dover (Ontario), missionaries winter at, 134.
Fort Duquesne, built, 424; defense of, 425-426, 429; captured, 433.
Fort Frontenac, planned, 202; built, 192, 204; La Salle at, 197, 206, 216, 255; Randin, 201-202; Denonville, 235; Duluth, 238.
Fort Howard, site, 292; built, 293.
Fort Kaministiquia, built, 226; Duluth at, 237; importance of, 313.
Fort La Baye, built, 292-293, 314; subsidiary post, 324; importance of, 312, 339, 381; treaty at, 305, 306, 308; visited, 309, 318; burned, 320-321, 376; rebuilt, 328; leased, 374-378, 381; exploited, 379-383; granted, 382-385, 431; commandants, 294, 297, 305, 312, 330, 333, 339, 374-375, 378, 380-382, 423, 429; commandant killed at, 332, 425; drowned, 380; interpreter, 378; blacksmith, 378; plots against, 378-379, 383, 433; settlement at, 387-405; in French and Indian War, 434; evacuated, 437; English occupy, 439. See also Green Bay.
Fort La Pointe, site, 301, 355; built, 298-301; commandants, 300, 301, 351, 357, 379, 384, 429; importance, 312; developed, 351-357; exploited, 384; settlers at, 388; evacuated, 313, 384, 388, 434.
Fort La Tourette, built, 226; fur trade at, 237.
Fort Le Boeuf (Venango), built, 424; Washington at, 301.
Fort L'Huillier, built, 274; abandoned, 275.
Fort Louis, in Louisiana, 275.
Fort Marin (on lower Mississippi), site, 339; officers at, 438.
Fort Marin (on upper Mississippi),

INDEX 453

built, 379-380; abandoned, 381, 429.
Fort Maurepas, built, 337.
Fort Miami, built, 292; importance, 313; commandants, 326, 418; surrenders to English, 438.
Fort Michilimackinac. See Mackinac.
Fort Orange. See Albany.
Fort Ouiatanon, importance, 313; expedition at, 334; tribesmen, 339; belongs to Canada, 372; revolt at, 419; surrenders to English, 438.
Fort Pitt, named, 433.
Fort Pontchartrain, at Detroit, 272. See also Detroit.
Fort Presqu'isle, built, 424; officer at, 424.
Fort St. Antoine, site, 335; named, 231; built, 232; besieged, 233; garrison, 235, 240; ceremony at, 241-242, 251; abandoned, 248; map of site, 242.
Fort St. Charles, massacre at, 337.
Fort St. Croix, built, 225.
Fort St. François. See Fort La Baye.
Fort St. Ignace, at Mackinac, 222. See also Mackinac.
Fort St. Joseph (on St. Clair River), Duluth's post, 231, 235; Lahontan at, 236, 238-239.
Fort St. Joseph (on St. Joseph River), established, 292; importance, 313, 381; Foxes sue for peace at, 323; commandant, 325; Indians at, 339; summoned from, 279, 306.
Fort St. Louis, on Illinois River, 222; built, 223; besieged, 228; confederacy around, 255; sketch, 224.
Fort St. Nicolas, built, 232; commandant, 241; location, 329.
Fort St. Philippe. See Fort La Baye.
Fort St. Pierre, on Rainy Lake, 336.
Fort St. Pierre, on upper Mississippi, 335; abandoned, 337.
Fort Trempealeau, built by Perrot, 232; rebuilt by Linctot, 328, 333, 400; removed, 335; pictured, 328. See also Trempealeau.
Fort Venango. See Fort Le Boeuf.
Fort Vincennes. See Vincennes.
Fort Wayne, French post at, 292.
Fort William, on Lake Superior, 297.
Fort William Henry, captured, 432-435.
Fox, George R., cited, 60, 127.
Fox Creek, at Detroit, 281, 282.
Fox Indians, early habitat, 57, 70, 87-88, 95; refuge in Wisconsin, 94, 99; met by whites, 127-128; villages, 127, 205, 262, 287, 310, 319-320, 329; visit Montreal, 136, 181, 279-280, 339-340; mission for, 141, 154, 160, 164, 165; at Sault ceremony, 185, 186; hunting parties, 215, 227; intertribal relations, 136, 181-182, 262, 299, 331-333; on war parties, 229, 235; at peace treaty, 266-267; Perrot's methods with, 246-247, 275; hostilities with, 176, 233, 237, 261, 273, 275-289, 298, 333, 350; remove to Detroit, 276-277; defeated at Detroit, 280-282, 288; Louvigny's expedition against, 285-289; Lignery's expedition, 318-320; ask peace, 300, 302, 323, 328, 329, 380; plot vengeance, 302; attack Illinois, 304-308; form confederacy, 316-317, 322; attacked by French allies, 323-324, 329, 330, 334-335; retreat eastward, 324-325; defeated, 325-327; reprisals on, 328-331; unite with Sauk, 332; abandon Green Bay, 332-333, 339; site of fort, 287; ask for post, 312, 318; visited, 309-310; cede territory, 289; fur trade with, 377; on the Allegheny, 415; map of villages, 314.
Fox River, discovered, 82; early name for, 160, 205; Indians on, 95, 99, 127, 129, 130, 164, 192, 204, 205, 239, 271, 414; missionaries on, 160-162; idol overthrown in, 162, 200; voyage on, 185, 193-194; hostilities on, 225, 298; described, 239-240, 311; taken possession of, 241-242; expeditions on, 287-289, 309, 319-320; post on, 293; settlement, 387; map of, 314.
Fox River of Illinois, early name for, 262; Indians on, 205; fort, 248; portage to, 262; hostilities on, 330.
Fox-Wisconsin waterway, first voyages on, 194-195, 213; Jolliet on, 192-195; Duluth on, 213, 225, 237; Lahontan, 240; closed, 261, 340; reopened, 273, 289, 292, 331; voyages on, 287-288, 319, 380; last French expedition, 437. See also Portage.
Francis I, of France, explorations, 8-14, 15, 22; at war, 13, 20; prisoner, 13; land occupied for, 19.
Franciscan missionaries, in New Spain, 143. See also Recollect missionaries.
Francy Roy, French settlement, 22.
Franquelin, Jean Baptiste, obtains information, 236, 237; map of 1681, 199; map of 1684, 248; map of 1688, frontispiece; referred to, 211, 225,

226, 228, 232, 355; characterized, 237, 248; map of 1708, 275.
French, earliest explorations, 8-14; extent of exploration, 33; discover the St. Lawrence, 15-22, 32; colonization, 33, 35; support missions, 142-144; annex the West, 179-190; residents in Wisconsin, 386-405.
French and Indian War, expeditions, 425-436.
French-Canadians. See Canadian-French.
French Creek, forts on, 424.
French River, route via, 54.
French ships, pictured, 20, 176.
Frontenac, Louis Buade, count de, appointed governor, 191-192; recalled, 220, 223; reappointed, 244; returns, 245; relation to Jolliet, 198, 201; plans for West, 201-202, 204, 207, 219, 223, 268-269; relations with Duluth, 202, 209, 216, 217, 238; in Iroquois war, 246, 250, 251, 253; policy, 248-250, 253, 260; holds Indian council, 263; officers, 300; death, 238, 264; geographical names in honor of, 195, 198, 210, 220.
Frontenac (Minn.), fort at, 311, 335, 380.
Fur trade, beginnings, 9, 34, 46, 47, 101, 364-365; early, 56, 85, 97; fleets from West, 98-99, 103, 126, 250-251; at Montreal, 101-103, 126, 135-136, 268, 365, 367; on Lake Superior, 114-118, 120, 123, 302; around Green Bay, 127-130, 294-295, 374-383; with Sioux, 335-336; regulated, 202-204, 220, 257-258, 291; contracts for, 123, 309; effect on tribesmen, 137-138, 222, 386; English rivalry for, 192, 221, 230-231, 243, 250, 307, 373, 406-422; in war time, 250-251, 376-379, 411-412; freedom of, 290-291, 406; methods, 367-371, 411; changes, 364-385; engagements, 368-369, 398; credits, 370-374; leasing system, 374-378, 381, 384; exploitation, 379-385; evils of, 384-385; decline of, 404. See also Licenses and *Coureurs de bois*.

GAGNON, Ernest, *Louis Jolliet*, 192.
Galena (Ill.), lead mines near, 304, 360, 372.
Galinée, René de Bréhant de, Sulpitian missionary, 134, 161; map, 131, 134, 135; cited, 161-162.
Garnier, Charles, Jesuit missionary, 87.
Gaspé Bay, Cartier at, 16; Indians on, 55.
Gastaldi, Jacopo, map, 35.
Gaudais-Dupont, Louis, royal commissioner, 119.
Gens de Terre Indians, at peace treaty, 266.
George Lake, on map, 51.
Georgia, Spanish in, 27; copper artifacts, 342, 344.
Georgian Bay, discovery of, 54; Indians on, 55, 56, 57, 68, 69, 79, 90, 92, 266; route via, 60, 86, 96, 131, 265, 277, 298; devastated, 93; St. Lusson on, 184; portage to, 368, 379.
Germans, as mining experts, 353; as traders, 410.
Giasson, Jacques, fur trader, 382.
Gibault, Father Pierre, visits Mackinac, 387.
Gilbert, Sir Humphrey, explorer, 36, 37, 41; colony, 44.
Girouard, Judge Désiré, "L'Expedition du Marquis de Denonville," 236.
Gist, Christopher, explorer, 417-418.
Glacial age, in Wisconsin, 31-32.
Glareanus, Henricus, *De principiis*, 4.
Glory-of-the-Morning, Winnebago chieftess, 435.
Gomara, Francisco López de, Spanish historian, 17, 34.
Gómez, Estévan, explorations, 6, 7, 8, 35.
Gonner, Nicolas de, Jesuit missionary, 172, 308, 311.
Goyagouin Indians, French name for Cayuga, 266.
Grand Cañon of the Colorado, first seen, 29-30.
Grant, W. L., *Voyages of Champlain*, 47, 52, 58; and Biggar, *Lescarbot's Works*, 346.
Grant County History, 362.
Gravier, Jacques, Jesuit missionary, 272.
Great Lakes, first mentioned, 18, 24; conjectures concerning, 31-43, 76, 78, 82, 194-195; discovery of, 44-64, 78-80, 83; described, 91; new routes in, 131-132, 191, 197, 313; first circuit, 135, 159; annexed to France, 179-190; shipping on, 182, 214, 352-354; fur trade on, 243, 257, 259, 307, 368, 406-422; routes from, 292; on maps,

INDEX 455

92, 199, 206; maps of, 42, 52, 62, 92, 150; allegorical fountain, 31; picture of, 32. See also the several lakes: Erie, Huron, Michigan, Ontario, and Superior.
Great Miami River, English fort on, 413; French expedition, 416.
Great Salt Lake, rumor of, 210, 211.
Green Bay, French names for, 124, 135, 241; entrance, 135, 261, 262; islands of, 95; route via, 273, 380; described, 314; Indians on, 71, 72, 73, 93, 229, 266; Indian villages near, 96, 121, 133, 141, 156, 159, 205; remove from, 276, 279; Nicolet visits, 80-83, 94-95, 159; Radisson, 109; Perrot, 123-130, 203, 227, 231, 237, 240, 246-248; La Salle, 214; Duluth, 237; Lahontan, 239-240; Charlevoix, 296-298; missionaries, 159-165, 169-172, 177; trade center, 121, 127, 219, 294, 314, 331, 379; annexed to France, 241; French post on, 171, 292-293, 374; hostilities on, 275-276, 282-289, 318-320; deserted, 339; commandants, 295-297, 328; drowned, 380; French settlers at, 314-315, 339-340, 376-377, 387-405, 420; land titles, 389, 404; Indian grant of, 438; revolt at, 383, 402, 412; French evacuate, 437. See also Fort La Baye.
Green Bay (city), first church at, 233; Tank cottage, 392.
Green Bay Historical Society, erects marker, 292; preserves Tank cottage, 391.
Green Lake County, Indian village in, 129.
Grenoble, ———, French explorer, 59, 60, 88.
Griffon, La Salle's vessel, 213-215, 352.
Grignon, Misses ———, cited, 164.
Grignon, Augustin, cited, 332, 425-426.
Grignon, Charles, education, 396.
Grignon, Pierre, recollections, 383.
Grignon, Pierre Jr., education, 396.
Grignon family, at Green Bay, 233; baptisms, 396; act as interpreters, 401.
Groseilliers, Madame ———, receipt, 152.
Groseilliers, Médart Chouart de, with the missionaries, 90, 107; western voyages, 104, 105, 107, 108-111, 114; journal lost, 108; later life, 111-112.
Gruis, Major ——— de, miner, 362.
Guadeloupe, exchange for Canada, 439.

Guérin, Jean, Jesuit *donné*, 115, 117; death, 152.
Guignas, Michel, Jesuit missionary, 172, 308; retreats, 321-322, 337; reported burned, 335; letter, 309-311.
Guillory, ———, Lake Superior trader, 354.

HAKLUYT, Richard, activities, 37-40, 43; *Divers Voyages*, 38, 39; map in, 7, 13, 29, 35, 36, 40, 41, 42, 43; reproduced, 42; *Principall Navigations*, 22, 38, 40, 41; *Discourse on Western Planting*, 37-38.
Hakluyt Society, *Publications*, 33, 46.
Hale, Horatio, ethnologist, 72.
Hall, E. H., "Henry Hudson," 43, 51.
Hamilton, H. E., archeologist, 341.
Handbook of North American Indians, 69, 73, 84.
Hanna, Charles A., *Wilderness Trail*, 206, 217, 255, 412, 413, 419, 433.
Hantsch and Schmidt, *Kartographische Denkmäler*, 23.
Harper's Magazine, 238.
Harrisburg (Pa.), trader at, 411.
Harrisse, Henry, opinions, 14, 35; *Notes on New France*, 198, 199, 201; *Terre Neuve*, 8, 41.
Harvard University Library, maps, 150, 200.
Havre, French port, 49.
Hawkins, Sir John, slaver, 39.
Hayes, Edward, discoverer, 41.
Hennepin, Louis, Recollect missionary, among the Sioux, 210, 213; comes West, 214; rescued by Duluth, 212-213, 216; *New Discovery*, 195, 205, 212, 214; writings, 164, 211; map, 210. See also Thwaites, R. G.
Henry IV, of France, 43, 44-46, 65; grants, 49-50; assassinated, 52, 66.
Henry VIII, of England, 8, 13.
Henry, Alexander, miner, 358.
Hertel, François, French partisan, 333.
Hispanic Society of America, maps, 3, 33, 43.
Hochelaga, Indian village, 18, 24, 38, 41, 55.
Hocquart, Gilles, intendant, 335.
Hodge, Frederick W., *Spanish Explorers*, 25, 29, 30.
Holmes, William H., archeologist, 343; *Anniversary Volume*, 71.
Honduras, coast, 3.
Horses, in Canada, 121; at Detroit, 355; at Green Bay, 390-391.

456 THE FRENCH RÉGIME

Houghton County (Mich.), copper in 342, 343.
Houghton Point, on Chequamegon Bay, 110.
Hubert, Ignace, fur trader, 382.
Hudson, Henry, discoveries, 43, 51, 53.
Hudson Bay, on map, 53; forts on, 111; missionaries, 158, 170; rivalry for, 191, 269, 351; fur trade at, 225, 297, 298, 379, 418.
Hudson River, Spanish on, 6; route via, 35; discovered, 43; on map, 51, 52; becomes English, 182; post on, 307.
Hudson's Bay Fur Company, founded, 111; French rivalry with, 237.
Hudson's Strait, ice bound, 53.
Hughes, Thomas, *History of the Society of Jesus in North America*, 144.
Huguenots, in America, 33, 34; religious wars, 34, 44-45; expelled from France, 143, 258.
Huron Indians, village on St. Lawrence, 16; in Huronia, 52, 346; described, 55-57; missionaries with, 54, 79, 84, 85, 91, 144, 176; Champlain, 55-58; intertribal relations, 57, 84; trade fleets, 61-63; allies, 69, 70; accompany Nicolet, 79-82; destroyed by Iroquois, 89, 92-93, 103, 144, 222; at Lorette, 93.
Huron Indians of West, village, 96; repel Iroquois, 98; flight westward, 99, 145, 209; as traders, 114; migrations, 115, 116, 153, 163; missions for, 145-153, 164, 165, 409; message for, 186; at peace treaty, 265; intertribal relations, 163, 164, 264, 265; remove to Detroit, 272, 280, 330, 409; trade with English, 412, 417, 433; return to French alliance, 423, 425. See also Petun Hurons and Wyandot.
Huron Island, on Green Bay, 95.
Huron Lake, first knowledge of, 19, 38; early descriptions, 48, 91, 134; first visited, 54-55; early names for, 54; exploration of, 57, 58; on map, 62, 87, 135; Indians on, 69, 88, 100, 117; route via, 131, 184, 313; war party on, 235; missions on, 162; taken possession of, 188; shipping on, 355; statue of, 31, 32.
Huronia, described, 56; white men in, 58-64, 346; Nicolet, 79, 82; missions to, 86-88, 91; destroyed, 92-93, 144, 145; shown on map, 92.

IBERVILLE, Pierre le Moyne d', founds Louisiana, 72, 269-270; Indian policy, 271; nephew, 283-284; officers, 351.
Illinois, boundary, 303-304, 372; buffalo in, 273; Indians, 70, 220, 335, 339; mining in, 361-363; Radisson, 109; Jolliet, 197, 206; La Salle, 213-216, 219, 224; Tonty, 217, 224, 228, 249, 260, 261; Charlevoix, 298; Indian hostilities in, 217-221, 223, 228, 279, 304-308, 325-327; colony in, 269, 271, 273-275, 277, 330, 402; described, 278; annexed to Louisiana, 303, 313, 371-373, 437; commandants, 283, 320, 326; officers in, 322, 335, 438; in French and Indian War, 437-438. See also Fort St. Louis and Fort de Chartres.
Illinois Catholic Historical Review, 167, 195, 387.
Illinois Historical Collections, 372.
Illinois Historical Survey, manuscripts, 362.
Illinois Indians, habitat, 70; intertribal relations, 230, 283, 304, 322; hostilities with Winnebago, 88; Foxes, 304-307, 316, 325-327; with the Iroquois, 98, 224, 250; with the French, 286; migrations, 99, 161, 162, 193, 219, 271; message for, 127, 186; missions for, 141, 154, 158, 166-168, 192; effect of, 176; language, 196; woman rescued, 306; on war party, 235; at peace treaty, 266, 308; visit France, 307; revolt, 417.
Illinois Park Commissioners, *Report*, 224.
Illinois River, Indians on, 167, 271, 304; Jolliet and Marquette, 197; La Salle, 215, 217; fort on, 222, 223, 270, 292; route via, 277, 292; disturbance on, 272; hostilities, 304, 325; on boundary, 372.
Illinois State Historical Society, *Transactions*, 196, 327.
Illustrations:
French ship of sixteenth century, 20.
Fountain of the Great Lakes, 32.
Champlain's manuscript, 46.
Winnebago village, 74.
Landfall of Nicolet, 80.
Perrot's contract 1667, 124.
French ship of seventeenth century, 178.
Jolliet and Marquette at Portage, 194.
Duluth's signature, 202.

INDEX

The Perrot ostensorium, 232.
Le Sueur's signature, 252.
Montigny's and Marin's signatures, 296.
French post near Trempealeau, 328.
Tank cottage at Green Bay, 392.
Joseph Jourdain, 400.
Braddock's defeat, 428.
Indiana Historical Society, *Publications*, 283, 338.
Indians, stocks, 70-73; as mound builders, 73-74; peculiar customs, 42, 74-75, 113; feasts, 81, 88-89, 420-421; cannibalism, 422; dress, 187; music and dances, 239; war customs, 430; treatment of captives, 245, 246; justice among, 226; first white contact, 127-128; effect of, 137-138; Jesuit plans for, 173-178; relation to French, 294, 373, 383, 392, 396, 399, 401-402; duplicity, 328; English relations, 290; mining methods, 341-346, 358-360. See also the several tribes and Fur trade.
Ingram, David, narrative, 38-40.
Interpreters, importance of, 399-401; for English, 410-411.
Iowa, Indians in, 99, 141, 333; first white man, 104, 196; French invasion of, 334-335; mining in, 361-363; celebrations in, 195.
Iowa Historical Record, 360.
Iowa Indians, affinities, 73; asylum among, 99; alliance with, 232; kill traders, 417.
Iowa Journal of History and Politics, 196, 200, 321.
Iowa River, Indians on, 196; early name for, 321.
Iron River, mines on, 354; establishment, 355.
Irondequoit Bay, expedition on, 235.
Iroquet, Algonquian chief, 52.
Iroquoian linguistic stock, tribes, 55-57, 196.
Iroquois Indians (Five Nations), tribes composing confederacy, 266; habitat, 55, 57, 107; villages, 133; enmity of, 84-100, 102-103, 106, 111, 114, 117, 221-242, 244-250, 253; capture Radisson, 104-105; missions for, 106, 108, 133, 144, 146, 155, 158, 176; hostilities on Ottawa River, 119, 120, 246; relations with western tribes, 132, 157, 160, 164, 166, 181, 204, 205, 244-250, 286, 316, 317, 324, 409; raid Illinois, 217, 219, 221-223, 228, 234;
territory invaded, 222-223, 227-230, 234-236, 260; peace with, 60, 67, 105, 121, 124, 129, 136, 159, 182, 229, 263-267; treaty with English, 411; intercolonial policy, 268, 318; interpreter among, 255, 410. See also Cayuga, Mohawk, Oneida, Onondaga, and Seneca.
Iroquois of the missions, expeditions, 333-335.
Iroquois Point, on Lake Superior, 117.
Isanti Sioux, origin of name, 110; Duluth visits, 210, 211.
Italians, as navigators, 9, 14.
Ivry, battle of, 45.
Izatys, Sioux village, 210.

JACKSON County (Ill.), battle in, 304.
Jacksonport, Indian village near, 125.
Jaillot, C. H. A., map, 226.
James I, of England, 51.
James II, of England, 351.
James Bay, visited, 111.
Jameson, J. F., *Narratives of New Netherland*, 85.
Jansenists, in France, 173.
Japan, on early globes, 1.
Jean Alphonse, *Cosmographie*, 23, 24.
Jesuit Archives, at Paris, 199.
Jesuit Relations, described, 139-140; prepared, 141-142; popularity, 145; suppressed, 140, 164, 172; unpublished, 169; value, 177-178. For citations, see Thwaites, R. G.
Jesuits, in Spanish colonies, 143; arrive in New France, 60; missions for Hurons, 86-88, 150-152; for Northwest, 106, 114-115, 146-178, 308-312; popularity, 142-145; as traders, 117, 152, 203; as envoys, 120; as martyrs, 92-93, 97, 152, 168; servants, 122, 247, 251; killed, 205, 219; at Sault Ste. Marie, 131-134, 187-189; oppose Sulpitians, 134; favor Nicolet, 76; oppose La Salle, 215-216; oppose Cadillac, 272, 276; policy, 234, 258-259; rivalry, 192; decline of, 173-176; claim discovery, 199-201; services for settlers, 177, 387; map of Lake Superior, 154, 163, 349. See also Missions.
Jogues, Isaac, Jesuit missionary, 89; captured, 89-90; martyred, 92.
John Carter Brown Library, maps, 4, 6, 198, 200, 201; manuscripts, 46.
Johnson, Sir William, report on mines, 358.

Joinville, François d'Orleans, prince de, at Green Bay, 397.
Jolliet, Adrien, on Lake Superior, 115-118, 121; brother, 131; not at Sault ceremony, 188; sketch, 115.
Jolliet, Louis, born in Canada, 115; visits West, 131-132, 155, 157, 348, 349; return route, 132-134, 349; sends traders to Green Bay, 133, 135, 159; at Sault ceremony, 188; voyage of discovery, 191-198, 441; later life, 201; maps, 197, 198, 199, 200; journals lost, 198, 199; letters, 199; illustration of, 194.
Jolliet, Zacherie, trader, 225; messenger, 245.
Joncaire, Louis Thomas, at Niagara, 307; among Seneca, 325.
Jones, Father Arthur E., cited, 56, 86, 194.
Jourdain, Jean Baptiste, married, 400.
Jourdain, Joseph, blacksmith, 400; picture, 400.
Journal of American Folk Lore, 73.
Juchereau, Charles, tannery in West, 273-274; signature, 252.
Judaeis, Cornelius, *Speculum Orbis*, 42.
Jumonville, Joseph Coulon de Villiers de, killed, 425.
Jump River, voyage on, 150.
Juneau, Solomon, at Milwaukee, 405.
Juneau, a French name, 441.
Juneau County, a French name, 441.

KALAMAZOO River, in Michigan, 248.
Kalm, Peter, *Travels into North America*, 357-358, 367, 371, 374.
Kaministiquia, Duluth at, 226, 237, 297; reoccupied, 297-298, 313. See also Fort Kaministiquia.
Kanabec County (Minn.), site in, 110.
Kankakee River, portage route, 215, 304.
Kaskaskia, Illinois settlement, 284; hostilities at, 304, 306; officer, 362.
Kaskaskia Indians, village, 167, 168, 197; Tonty among, 217.
Kaskaskia River, branches, 326.
Kathio. See Izatys.
Kellogg, Joseph, visits the West, 277-278.
Kellogg, Louise P., *Early Narratives of the Northwest*, 66, 70, 80, 83, 89, 106-108, 113, 134, 135, 162, 167, 184, 189, 193-195, 199, 200, 210, 213, 214, 216, 218, 228, 230, 236, 238, 261, 283, 345, 359, 414, 442; "First Missionary in Wisconsin," 148; "First Traders in Wisconsin," 108; "Fox Indians during French Régime," 128, 267, 281; "Marquette's Authentic Map," 193, 200; "Wisconsin Anabasis," 218.
Kellogg family, *Genealogy*, 278.
Kentucky, Indians of, 70.
Kewaunee, Indian village near, 125, 215, 262.
Keweenaw Bay, Ménard on, 147-148; Indian murder at, 226.
Keweenaw County, copper in, 342.
Keweenaw Point, portaged, 109, 148-149; mines on, 348.
Kiala, Fox chief, 302; conspiracy of, 316-317; surrenders, 330; fate, 331.
Kickapoo Indians, early habitat, 57; village, 310; affiliations, 70; take refuge in Wisconsin, 94, 99, 161; message for, 127; migrations, 219, 271, 276, 304, 339, 409; on war party, 235, 425; kill missionary, 218; hostilities, 232, 282, 304; detached from Foxes, 322, 325; act as guides, 334; not at Sault ceremony, 185; at peace treaty, 266; characterized, 194.
Kickapoo River. See Rock River.
King George's War, effect on fur trade, 376-378, 411-412; close of, 379, 412.
King William's War, and the West, 243-244.
Kirke brothers, English privateers, 61.
Kiskakon Indians, join the Ottawa, 69; Christianized, 156, 158, 165; remove Marquette's remains, 168; at peace treaty, 265.
Knife Lake, in Minnesota, 110.
Knights of Columbus, erect tablet, 195.
Kraus, Edward H., "Some Specimens of Float Copper," 343.

LA BARRE, Antoine Lefebre de, governor of New France, 220, 223, 239; agents, 228; expedition against Iroquois, 227-230; treachery, 230, 253; recalled, 230; patron of Perrot, 231, 233.
Labrador, discovered, 6, 14.
La Chaise, Père, king's confessor, 259.
Lachine Rapids, location, 18, 38, 47; on map, 23; trading at, 53; massacre near, 244, 265.
La Cosa, Juan de, chart, 2, 3.
La Crosse, a French name, 441.
La Crosse County, a French name, 441.
La Dauphine, Verrazano's ship, 10-12.
La Demoiselle, Huron chief, 413; goes

INDEX   459

over to English, 414, 416; sends envoys west, 417; speech to Ottawa, 418; killed, 421-422.
La Durantaye, Olivier Morel de, western officer, 221, 222, 227, 228, 230, 231; leads expedition, 229, 235; returns to Canada, 236.
Lafayette (Ind.), Indians near, 325; post, 372, 419.
Lafayette County, a French name, 441.
Laflêche family, in Canada, 115.
La Fond, Charles Personne *dit*, at Green Bay, 400.
La Fontaine, Marion *dit*, leads English, 230.
La Forest, François Daupin de, in Illinois, 249; partner of Tonty, 261, 270; commandant of Detroit, 277, 279; death, 282; widow, 270.
La Galissonière, Michel R. Barin, count de, governor of New France, 372, 378.
Lahontan, Louis Armand, baron de, comes West, 236; voyage, 239-240, 310; report on copper, 349; characterized, 238-239; *Voyages*, 226; editions, 240. See also Thwaites, R. G.
La Jémerais, Christophe Dufros de, at Fort Beauharnois, 323; in far West, 336.
La Jonquière, Pierre Jacques de Taffanel, marquis de, governor of Canada, 379-380; profits, 380-381; death, 381, 423.
Lalement, Gabriel, Jesuit martyr, 92.
La Martinière, Claude A. Berman de, at La Baye, 339.
La Montagne, ——, early trader, 63.
La Morandière, Philippe d'Amours de, commandant at Green Bay, 296.
Lancaster (Pa.), Indian treaty at, 411, 413.
Langlade, Augustin Mouet de, marriage, 315-316; out with Lignery, 320; at battle of Butte de Morts, 332; partner, 374; settles at Green Bay, 376-377.
Langlade, Charles de, ancestors, 119, 315; birth, 314, 316; baptism, 315; boyhood, 420; traditions concerning, 332; adventures, 441; descendants, 396; captures Pickawillany, 420-422; commissioned, 422, 432, 436; at Braddock's defeat, 425-428; in French and Indian War, 429-432; humanity, 432; at siege of Quebec, 434-435; at Montreal, 436; remains at Mackinac, 437-439; in British service, 438.
Langlade, Domitelle, married, 315-316; son, 400.
Langlade County, a French name, 441.
La Noue, Zacherie Robutel de, at Kaministiquia, 297-298.
Laon (France), Marquette's birthplace, 132, 156.
La Perrière, René Boucher de, in Wisconsin, 309; builds fort, 311; returns to Canada, 311-312.
La Pointe region, map of, 299. See also Chequamegon Bay and Fort La Pointe.
La Potherie, Bacqueville de, at peace treaty, 266; *Histoire*, 124, 126, 128, 130, 135, 136, 206, 258.
Largilliers, Jacques, accompanies Marquette, 167-168; at the Sault, 188; on Mississippi expedition, 193.
La Ribourde, Gabriel de, Recollect missionary, 215; death, 218.
La Roche, Marquis de, explorer, 44, 46.
La Rochelle, merchants of, 121.
La Ronde, John T., in Wisconsin, 357.
La Ronde, Louis Denis de, early life, 351; at La Pointe, 351-358; explores for copper, 352; builds ship, 352-353; uses experts, 353-355; death, 357; cited, 354.
La Ronde, Philippe Louis Denis de, accompanies mining experts, 354; at La Pointe, 356; succeeds to command, 357; successor, 384.
La Rose, Amable le Gere *dit*, in French and Indian War, 435.
La Rue, —— de, with Duluth, 209.
La Salle, Robert Cavelier de, early life, 133; hostility to Jesuits, 216; Indian policy, 176, 219, 222, 224, 255; at Fort Frontenac, 197, 206; relations with Frontenac, 202, 204; in France, 204, 207; rejoins Tonty, 219; Tonty seeks, 230, 256; voyages, 189, 206, 213-216, 220; sends out Hennepin, 212, 213, 216; defends Illinois, 222-224; characterized, 213, 216, 224; death, 224; letter, 224.
Lassay, Marquis de, squire for, 208.
La Toupine, Pierre Moreau *dit*, western trader, 189.
La Tourette, Claude Greysolon de, comes to New France, 208; in the West, 225, 226, 237; brings copper, 349.

460 THE FRENCH RÉGIME

Lauson, Jean de, governor of New France, 103, 194, 106-108.
Laval, François de, bishop of Canada, 199.
Laverdière, C. H., *Œuvres de Champlain*, 46, 47, 62, 67.
La Vérendrye, Jean, massacred, 337.
La Vérendrye, Pierre Gautier de Varennes de, explorer, 336-337.
La Vérendrye family, explorers, 312, 336-337.
La Vigne, Paul, with Duluth, 209.
Law, John, forms company, 303.
Leacock, Stephen, *Mariner of St. Malo*, 19.
Lead mines, discovered by Perrot, 122, 248, 359-360; Indians use, 358-359; mining methods, 360-361; in Illinois and Missouri, 361-363; in Canada, 372.
Leau, Monsieur de, Breton, 38.
Le Borgne, Indian chief, 66.
Le Brochet, Indian chief, 148, 151.
Le Caron, Father ——, goes to Huronia, 54, 59.
Le Chat Blanc, messenger, 306.
Le Chien, Fox chief, 329.
Le Clercq, Chrétien, *First Establishment of the Faith*, 60, 67, 214, 262.
Leeman, Indians near, 127.
Le Gardeur family, origin, 300, 301; losses, 332.
Le Maistre, ——, with Duluth, 209.
Le Mercure Français, 76.
Le Moyne, Jacques, map, 35; described lake, 49.
Lenox globe, described, 1; pictured, 2.
Leonard, William Ellery, "Glory of the Morning," 435.
Le Picard, Antoine du Gay Auguel, among Sioux, 212, 213.
Le Rat, Huron chief, 265.
Le Rocher, on Illinois River, 167, 326; fort at, 270; captured, 304; council at, 309; hostilities near, 325; on boundary, 372.
Léry, Chaussegros de, cited, 281, 326; maps, 310, 320, 327; reproduced, 314.
Lescarbot, Marc, notes copper, 346; *History of New France*, 49.
Leslie, Lieut. William, at Mackinac, 439.
L'Espèrance, Pierre Levasseur *dit*, on Lake Superior, 115-118; with Ménard, 149-151; sketch, 115.
Le Sueur, Pierre, trader, 225, 257; early life, 251-252; sent West, 252; recalled,

260; ascends the Mississippi, 274, 361; discovers mines, 349-350; post, 299, 308; death, 275; signature, 252.
Lewis, Theodore H., edits document, 28.
Licenses, for fur trade, 203, 204, 225; prices, 379; revoked, 257, 374; regranted, 291, 379-380; rivalry in, 305; system of, 366.
Lignery, Constant Marchand de, at Mackinac, 283, 291; makes peace treaties, 305-306, 308-309, 316, 317; expedition against Foxes, 318-320, 328, 352, 382, 431; report, 320; adventures, 441; sketch, 283.
Lignery, François Marchand de, at Braddock's defeat, 425-426; captured, 434.
Linctot, Madame—de, power of attorney, 301.
Linctot, René Godefroy de, at La Pointe, 301; on the upper Mississippi, 328, 333, 335, 400; post pictured, 328.
Lionne, Hugues de, French minister, 180.
Lok, Michael, map, 13.
London Company, colonizes, 43.
Long River, Lahontan describes, 240.
Long Sault, defense of, 109, 114.
Longueuil, Charles le Moyne, baron de, governor of New France, 307; son, 283.
Longueuil, Paul Joseph le Moyne, chevalier de, at Detroit, 418-419.
Lorette, mission village, 92.
Louis XIII, of France, 62, 66.
Louis XIV, of France, 118, 119, 180, 191; European wars, 179, 243-244; annexation in name of, 188, 210, 241; on war expedition, 194; western policy, 259; signs treaty, 263; death, 302; son, 317.
Louise of Savoy, French regent, 9; names given for, 12; arranges peace, 15.
Louisiana, named, 220; founded, 269-270, 302, 351; early settlers, 274, 275, 276; governor, 277, 338, 362; Charlevoix visits, 298; rivalry with, 302-306, 371-372; speculation in, 302-303, 351; boundary, 303-304, 371-372; posts in, 313; tragedy in, 338, 408; cessions of, 440.
Louisiana Historical Quarterly, 261.
Louvigny, Louis de la Porte de, sent West, 245-246; commands at Mackinac 249, 285; expedition of 1716, 285-289, 300; effect of, 292; sons-in-

INDEX 461

law, 296. 315; officers, 309; adventures, 441; sketch, 246.
Louvois, François Letellier, marquis de, French minister, 180.
Lowery, Woodbury, *Spanish Settlements*, 15, 25, 27.
Lusignan, Paul Louis Dazenard de, commandant at La Baye, 374-376; retires, 377; successor, 378.
Lyons (France), Duluth's home, 208.

MACALESTER College, *Contributions*, 380.
McCargo's Cove, on Isle Royale, 348.
MacDonald, William, *Select Charters*, 290.
McGee, W. J., ethnologist, 72.
McGregory, Major Patrick, English trader, 234; arrested, 235, 254.
McIlvaine, Caroline, aid acknowledged, 123.
McIlwain, Charles H., *Wraxall's Abridgment*, 229, 255, 263, 307, 325.
McKenney, Thomas L., *Tour of the Lakes*, 305.
Mackenzie, Sir Alexander, explorer, 209.
Mackinac, mission at, 156, 163, 165, 172, 176, 245, 259, 282, 387; Indians at, 272; importance of, 313, 382, 386, 403; fort at, 222, 227, 249, 283, 386; rebuilt, 291; warehouse, 270; commandants, 249, 254, 260, 270, 283, 285, 305, 335, 431; Tonty at, 218, 219; Duluth, 213, 216, 225; St. Cosme, 261; Charlevoix, 298; Langlade, 314-316, 377, 420, 422; amnesty proclaimed at, 219; unrest at, 244-246, 249, 264, 378; expeditions at, 226-227, 229-230, 235, 236, 250, 265, 279, 288, 309, 319, 320, 331, 425; English traders at, 230-231, 234, 277; English remove from, 376-377; troops at, 413; magistrates, 387, 398, 400; smallpox at, 432; in French and Indian War, 434; evacuated, 437; English occupy, 439; visited, 395-396; described, 254.
Mackinac Island, Nicolet passes, 79; on map, 135; mission at, 156, 163; fort on, 291.
"Mackinac Register," cited, 315, 316; described, 387; entries, 396, 432.
Mackinac Straits, described, 91; crossed, 94, 95; mission on, 163, 165, 172, 176, 245, 259, 282, 387; letter from, 216.
McLellan, William, "A Gentleman of the Royal Guard," 238; "Death of Dulhut," 238.

Macoupin River, in Illinois, 326.
Madeline Island, post on, 252, 301, 355; early names for, 355; map of, 299.
Madison, fur trader at, 405.
Maestricht, captured, 194.
Magellan, Fernao de, voyage around the world, 1, 9.
Mahican Indians, in La Salle's colony, 219, 255.
Maine, Cadillac in, 254.
Maine Historical Society, *Collections*, 37, 254.
Maintenon, Madame de, interest in missions, 259.
Malhiot, François V., fur trade journal, 369.
Manitoba, first white man, 104.
Manitoulin Island, Indians on, 69, 90, 93, 184; St. Lusson, 184, 188.
Manitoumie maps, described, 200; name on, 220.
Manitowoc, fur trade post at, 405.
Manitowoc River, mission on, 262.
Manoir, Louis Ramesay de, in West, 283; killed, 284.
Mantet, Nicolas d'Ailleboust de, at Chicago, 250; recalled, 260.
Maple sugar, at feast, 240; making described, 395.
Maps:
    Franquelin 1688, frontispiece.
    Lenox globe, 2.
    Franciscus Monachus, 6.
    Great Lakes 1600, 42.
    North America 1610, 52.
    Champlain 1632, 62.
    Sanson d'Abbeville 1650, 92.
    Great Lakes 1680, 150.
    Hennepin 1683, 210.
    Site of Fort St. Antoine, 242.
    West 1650-1700, 266.
    La Pointe region, 299.
    Fox country 1730, 314.
    West 1700-1760, 364.
"Maramech," location, 248, 330.
Marameg Indians, band of Chippewa, 186.
Marbois, François Barbé de, French minister, 368.
Marest, Joseph, Jesuit missionary, 172, 241; cited, 282.
Margry, Pierre, *Découvertes et Etablissements des Français*, 99, 168, 184, 189, 192, 198, 199, 201, 203, 205, 209, 210, 213, 214, 216, 224-228, 233, 242, 248-250, 254, 256, 258, 259, 298, 300, 304, 309, 335, 349, 350.

Marguerite of Savoy, names given for, 12.

Marin, Joseph, at La Pointe, 379, 383; on upper Mississippi, 380-381; at La Baye, 381, 423; recalled, 382; in French and Indian War, 429, 431-432; captured, 434.

Marin, Paul de la Marque, early life, 323; in Wisconsin, 324, 339, 438; ends Fox wars, 340, 374; commandant at La Baye, 374; on upper Mississippi, 379-380; profits in trade, 379-382; recalled, 381, 423; on Ohio frontier, 423-425; death, 381, 424; signature, 296.

Marinette, Indians at, 125; a French name, 441.

Marinette County, a French name, 441.

Marquette, Jacques, at the Sault, 132, 156-158; on Chequamegon Bay, 158, 188; removal to Mackinac, 163, 164; Illinois mission, 166-168; voyage of discovery, 191-197, 441; death, 168, 200; letter, 196; mentions mines, 359; journals, 199-200; cited, 414; maps, 154, 193, 200; illustration of, 194.

Marquette County, a French name, 441.

Marquette University, at Milwaukee, 168.

Martin, Deborah B., "Border Forts of the Great Lakes," 227, 240, 287; owns Langlade commission, 422.

Martin, Dr. Lawrence, aid acknowledged, 275.

Mary, queen of England, 263.

Maryland, French Indians in, 255; traders from, 408; Indians from, 410; Indian treaty for, 411.

Mascouten Indians, meaning of name, 57; affiliations, 69-70; early habitat, 95; refuge in Wisconsin, 94, 99, 241; village, 129, 162, 192; mission for, 160-161, 164, 165, 168; Perrot visits, 127, 130, 253; Jolliet, 193, 194; found near Milwaukee, 167, 262; not at Sault ceremony, 185, 186; migrations, 168, 176, 205, 215, 219, 271, 272, 276, 304, 339, 409; with Juchereau, 273; hostilities, 233, 280-282, 304; detached from Foxes, 322, 325; on war party, 235, 425; at peace treaty, 266; characterized, 194.

Massachusetts Historical Society, *Proceedings*, 291, 367.

Massacre Island, in Lake of the Woods, 337.

Mattawan River, route via, 54.

Maugras, Jacques, western trader, 189.

Maumee River, origin of name, 272; fort on, 292; portage route, 340, 409; Indian village on, 413, 416, 417, 422; English officer visits, 428. See also Fort Miami.

Mazarin, Cardinal, death, 118.

Mazza, Giovanni B., map, 40.

Méchingan, native village, 96, 97; named St. Michel, 141.

Membré, Zenobius, with La Salle, 214; at De Pere, 218; narrative, 214, 262.

Ménard, René, Jesuit missionary, 115, 117; in Northwest, 146-150; lost, 116, 150-152; death marked on map, 150.

Menasha, landmark at, 81; Indian village, 339. See also Doty Island.

Menominee (Mich.), Indians at, 125.

Menominee Indians, early history, 71, 95; food, 74, 124; village, 124-125, 159, 314, 344; described, 297; intertribal relations, 125, 126; mission for, 161, 164, 165, 176; fur trade with, 377; fort for, 324; at Sault ceremony, 185, 186; allies of French, 126, 339, 388; revolt, 205, 219, 375, 383, 402, 433; on war parties, 229, 235, 425-426, 429, 435; at peace treaty, 266.

Menominee River, Indians of, 72; fishing in, 124, 164; villages on, 125.

Mercator, Gerardus, maps, 29, 35-36.

Mercator, Rumoldus, map, 40.

Mère de l'Incarnation, *Lettres*, 90, 109, 155, 183, 259.

Mereness, N. D., *Travels in the American Colonies*, 304, 361.

Meskousing. See Wisconsin River.

Mexico, conquered by Spanish, 5; shore line, 15; Spanish in, 28, 39; missionaries, 143, 176.

Mexico City, on maps, 7.

Mexico Gulf, explored, 3, 15; on maps, 4, 5, 7, 24-25; early voyage on, 26; Mississippi's outlet, 197; French on, 270.

Mézy, Augustin de Saffrey de, governor of New France, 119.

Miami Indians, clans, 248; chieftainship, 130, 166, 185, 414; habitat, 70; migrations, 99, 168, 176, 204, 205, 215, 219, 271, 272, 409; village on Fox River, 129, 161, 162, 194; mission for, 160-161, 164-166, 168; Perrot among, 130, 248; Vincennes, 283; post for, 292; not at Sault ceremony, 185; intertribal relations, 230, 234, 250, 265, 283, 413, 419; show lead

INDEX 463

mine, 359; on war party, 234, 235; at peace treaty, 266; hostilities, 286; English alliance, 255, 413-414, 416-418, 420, 433; defeated, 421-422; return to French alliance, 422, 423, 425; characterized, 194, 414; place names for, 272.

Michelson, Truman, "Linguistic Classification of Algonquian Tribes," 69.

Michigamea Indians, Jolliet meets, 196; chief of, 307.

Michigan, Indians of, 57, 69, 70, 87-89, 95; upper peninsula, 71, 342; flight from, 93, 94, 154; missions in, 168; French settlements, 402. See also Detroit, Mackinac, and Sault Ste. Marie.

Michigan History Magazine, 343.

Michigan Lake, discovered, 57, 76-80; Indians on, 87, 88, 93, 94, 97, 100, 176, 204, 266, 339, 434; Indian villages, 121, 125, 271, 344; described, 91; explored, 197, 206; early visit to, 112; voyages on, 167, 168, 197, 215, 218, 261-262, 277; on map, 114; allegorical statue, 31, 32.

Michigan Pioneer and Historical Collections, 168, 250, 254, 270, 272, 273, 274, 275, 276-280, 281, 283, 284, 298, 301, 315.

Michilimackinac. See Mackinac.

Mille Lac, Sioux village on, 210, 211; Hennepin at, 213.

Millon, Pierre Mathurin, commandant at La Baye, 380; drowned, 380; successor, 381.

Milwaukee, Marquette at, 167; Tonty, 218; Juneau, 405.

Milwaukee River, first mentioned, 262; Indians on, 205; St. Cosme visits, 262.

Mingo Indians, in the West, 409, 412; English allies, 433.

Mining. See Copper and Lead.

Minisink (N. Y.), Indians at, 255.

Minnesota, first white man in, 104, 110, 211; forts in, 211, 274-275, 311, 335-337, 380; explorations, 275.

Minnesota Historical Collections, 108, 299, 345, 357.

Minnesota History Bulletin, 297.

Minnesota Mining Company, operations, 342.

Minnesota River, taken possession of, 242; early name, 251; Le Sueur on, 274, 275.

Minong Island. See Royale Isle.

Missions, Recollect, 54, 59-60; Jesuit, 60, 76, 139-178, 259; Seminary, 261-262; among the Hurons, 54, 59, 60, 79, 84, 86-88; destroyed, 92-93, 95; for the West, 114-115, 139-178, 308-312, 314; colonies, 266; at Mackinac, 386; map of, 266. See also Jesuits and Recollects.

Missisauga Indians, habitat, 68; officer among, 300.

Mississippi, Spanish in, 27.

Mississippi Company. See Company of the West.

Mississippi River, Indians on, 72, 73, 89, 99, 196, 271, 417; villages, 329; discovery, 5, 24-28, 37, 104, 109, 191-197; early mention of, 81, 82, 109, 154, 157-158, 161, 162; several names for, 195; fur trade on, 243, 246-247, 256, 267, 407, 408; French posts, 308-314, 328-329, 333, 335-337, 379-380, 388, 423; Duluth on, 212, 224-225; Hennepin, 213, 216; Tonty, 230; La Salle, 220, 223; Perrot, 231-233, 244, 248; Le Sueur, 252, 274, 275; missions on, 261-262; colony, 269-270, 303; voyages on, 274-275, 321, 361; taken possession of, 189, 242; importance of headwaters, 371, 406; outlet for Illinois, 372; on maps, 199-200, 242.

Mississippi valley, French names for, 195, 220, 270; colony in, 269; economic experiments, 273-275; routes to, 292; French domination of, 340, 441-442.

Mississippi Valley Historical Review, 203, 231, 255, 256.

Missouri, lead mines in, 361-363; French settlements, 404.

Missouri Indians, affinities, 73; intertribal relations, 280, 316.

Missouri River, Indians on, 72, 73; mouth discovered, 196; raid on, 317.

Mobile River, early name for, 25.

Mohawk Indians, at peace treaty, 266; adopt trader, 410.

Mohawk River, drainage, 32; fur trade route, 407; settlers on, 410.

Molineaux, Emerich, engraves map, 41-43, 50.

Monachus, Franciscus, *De Orbis*, map, 6; reference to, 15.

Monongahela River, forks of, 424; French victory on, 428.

Monsoni Indians, at Sault ceremony, 186.

Monsoupelia Indians, identified, 196.

464 THE FRENCH RÉGIME

Montbrun brothers, fur traders, 309; retreat from Mississippi, 321-322.
Montcalm, Marquis de, in French and Indian War, 429-432; at siege of Quebec, 434; death, 435; report, 432.
Montcourt, Pierre Hertel, commandant at La Baye, 333.
Montigny, François Jolliet, missionary, 261.
Montigny, Jacques Testard de, commandant at Green Bay, 296-297; successor, 305; signature, 296.
Montmagny, Charles Hualt de, governor of New France, 85.
Montmorency Falls, battle of, 434-435.
Montreal, rapids near, 197-198; site, 18; Champlain visits, 47; founded, 90; Sulpitians at, 122, 123, 133; in Iroquois wars, 97, 105; fur trade at, 101-102, 114, 117, 126, 135-136, 146, 157, 184, 202, 205, 243, 251, 268, 303, 335, 365; merchants, 123, 208, 295, 367, 371, 374, 375, 377; in war times, 277, 436; councils at, 223, 244, 253, 264-267, 304, 323, 338-340, 431; news from, 294; visits to, 261, 396, 402; expeditions leave, 414, 418.
Montreal Island, stream along, 59; massacre on, 244.
Montreal River, a French name, 441.
Monts, Pierre du Gaust de, colonizer, 49-50.
Mooney, James, ethnologist, 72.
Moose, hunting of, 184.
Morales, Pedro, narrative, 39-40.
Moras, Didace Mouet de, marriage, 315; contract for trade, 331.
Morris, Capt. Thomas, on the Maumee, 428.
Mound builders, known to be Indians, 342.
Mound City, in Ohio, 341.
Mounds, of Indian origin, 73-74, 341-342; copper in, 344-345.
Mount Desert Island, explored, 49.
Mount Trempealeau, described, 232; post at, 328; pictured, 328. See also Trempealeau.
Munro, W. B., "Coureurs de Bois," 291; criticized, 367.
Muskingum River, trading post on, 417.

Nadouessis Indians. See Sioux Indians.
Nafrechoux, Isaac, Montreal merchant, 123.

Nantes, Edict of, issued, 44; revoked, 143, 258.
Narvaez, Panfilo de, explorations, 25-26.
Natchez, massacre at, 408.
Navarre, king of. See Henry IV.
Needham, James, Virginia trader, 407.
Neill, E. D., cited, 380.
Neutral Indians, habitat, 56, 57; intertribal relations, 57, 70; missionary among, 60, 86-87; hostilities, 87, 89; destroyed by Iroquois, 93, 222.
Neville, Arthur C., aid acknowledged, 159; cited, 163.
New Brunswick, discovery of, 39, 40.
New England, on early maps, 7; explored by French, 49, 351; in intercolonial wars, 248, 279; interpreter for, 277, 278.
New Mexico, explorations in, 29; missionaries, 143.
New Netherland, taken by English, 119.
New Orleans, French claim, 271; ceded to Spain, 440.
New York, becomes English, 119, 182; in intercolonial wars, 248-250; colonial governors, 228-230, 241, 263, 270.
New York City, harbor formed, 32; named, 11-12; on maps, 35, 50.
New York Colonial Documents. See O'Callaghan.
New York Historical Society, owns globe, 13.
New York Museum of American Indians, visited, 71.
New York Public Library, aid acknowledged, 1; owns map, 87.
New York State Museum, *Bulletin*, 84.
Newfoundland, fishing off, 16, 34, 65; harbors, 17, 21; colonized, 44; officers in, 296; maps of, 7, 8, 14.
Newport (R. I.), earliest name, 12.
Newton, Stanley, *The Story of Sault Ste. Marie*, 157.
Niagara Falls, in glacial epoch, 32; first mentioned, 47; as an obstruction, 368; portage at, 414; on map, 62.
Niagara River, Indians on, 56, 57; early name for, 87; discovery of, 86-87; expedition on, 229, 235; post on, 236, 307, 407, 423; captured, 434.
Nicolas, Louis, Jesuit missionary, 155, 156.
Nicolas, Huron chief, 412; death, 417.
Nicolet, Jean, early life, 65-68; western voyage, 75-83, 440, 441; landfall, 81; Indians met, 94-95; death, 77; suc-

INDEX   465

cessor, 122; descendants, 249, 300; landfall pictured, 80.
Nicolet, Marguerite, children, 300.
Nikikoek (Otter) Indians, habitat, 68.
Niles (Mich.), Jesuit mission at, 168; fort, 292.
Nipigon Lake, route via, 96; Indians near, 154; fort on, 226, 237, 313, 336, 382; on map, 114.
Nipissing Indians, and Champlain, 57; mission for, 59, 154; Nicolet among, 68, 75-76, 79; migration, 96; interpreter for, 115; defeat of Iroquois, 117; at Sault ceremony, 186; at peace treaty, 266; on expedition, 419.
Nipissing Lake, in glacial epoch, 32; route via, 19, 54; Indians on, 57, 61.
Noel, Jacques, explorer, 38; letter, 40-41.
Noquet Indians, habitat, 71, 95; at Sault ceremony, 186.
Normandin, Mathurin, Lake Superior trader, 121-122.
Normandy, voyagers from, 34, 46, 65.
Noro, Fox chief, speech, 266-267.
North America, coast explored, 3-14; on maps, 15; maps of, 6, 52, 92.
North Carolina, discovered, 10-11; Spanish in, 27; traders, 284, 338, 408.
North Dakota, first white men in, 104, 211.
North West Fur Company, post, 297.
Northwest Passage, search for, 36, 38.
Notary public, importance of, 387.
Nouvel, Henri, Jesuit missionary, 163, 164; at De Pere, 171.
Nova Albion, on map, 33.
Nova Scotia, colonized, 50. See also Acadia.
Nuttall, Zelia, *New Light on Drake*, 33.

O'CALLAGHAN, E. B., editor, 182; *New York Colonial Documents*, 119, 182, 184, 186, 190-192, 198, 201-204, 211, 216, 223, 231, 236, 237, 241, 242, 245, 246, 248-251, 253-255, 257, 259, 261, 265, 266, 270, 284, 291, 292, 300, 322, 325, 349, 375-377, 431, 432.
Ochagach, draws map, 336.
Oconto River, Indian village on, 125; trail along, 127.
Ohio, mounds in, 341-342, 344, 359; Indian villages, 410-413.
Ohio Archeological and Historical Quarterly, 341, 359.
Ohio River, on line of migration, 72-73; Indians on, 271; portages to, 313; mouth discovered, 196; was La Salle on, 206; route via, 256, 284; expeditions on, 340, 414-416; English on, 255, 407; colony at mouth, 273-274; posts on, 313; officers, 381.
Ohio valley, struggle for, 255, 408-422; recovered by French, 423-424; land agent in, 417; ceded to English, 439.
Old Briton. See La Demoiselle.
Old Mackinaw, fort at, 291, 386. See also Mackinac.
Onanguissé, Potawatomi chief, speech, 268-269.
Oneida (Oneioute) Indians, at peace treaty, 266.
Onondaga Indians, French among, 105; at peace treaty, 266.
Ontario Archeological Report, 55.
Ontario Archives, *Report*, 56, 86.
Ontario Historical Society, *Papers and Records*, 52, 134.
Ontario Lake, early names for, 55; salt springs near, 48-49; Indians on, 107, 316; Indian account of, 47-48; early mention of, 19, 38, 40; discovered, 55; portage to, 131; missions on, 133; French travelers on, 131-132; expeditions on, 182, 229, 235; fort on, 192, 201, 379; vessels, 182; in French and Indian War, 436; on maps, 35, 41, 51, 53, 62, 87; statue of, 31, 32.
Ontonagon County, copper in, 342.
Ontonagon River, copper on, 348, 349, 351, 353; mine found, 354, 358.
Orignal. See Moose.
Orleans Island, named, 17.
Orontony. See Nicolas.
Ortelius, Abraham, maps, 29, 35, 37, 40; *Theatrum Orbis*, 36.
Osage Indians, intertribal relations, 280.
Osgood, H. L., *American Colonies in the Eighteenth Century*, 265, 270.
Oshawa-Lake Simcoe route, 131.
Oshkosh, site of, 311, 319; fur trade post at, 405.
Ossauamigonong. See Suamico.
Ostensorium, presented by Perrot, 171, 232-233; LaBarre orders, 231; buried, 236; picture of, 232.
Oswego (N. Y.), fur trade post at, 307, 379; captured, 429-430.
Otchagras, name for Winnebago, 95.
Oto Indians, affinities, 73; join Fox confederacy, 316.
Ottawa country, voyages to, 123, 131, 133; fur trade in, 260.
Ottawa Indians, clans, 69, 186, 265;

early habitat, 57, 69, 79; migrations, 93, 95, 96, 99, 110, 115, 149, 153, 163, 209; missions for, 90, 95, 141, 152-178; repel Iroquois, 98, 103, 117; intertribal relations, 75, 76, 163, 280, 306; trade fleets, 103-104, 106-107, 114, 116, 117, 120, 123, 146, 154, 155; monopoly broken, 122, 126, 155; in war party, 229, 323, 431; at peace treaty, 265; remove to Detroit, 272, 277, 409; hostilities, 285, 330; visit Albany, 307; attack English, 418, 420-422; oppose expedition, 419; at Braddock's defeat, 425-426; halfbreeds, 314-316.
Ottawa Lake. See Court Oreilles.
Ottawa of the Fork, habitat, 69, 186, 265; chiefs, 315.
Ottawa River, in glacial epoch, 32; sources, 19, 36; Indians on, 52-53, 56, 57, 61, 266; first mentioned, 18; route via, 54, 60, 66, 86, 96, 98, 113, 126, 131, 134, 147, 153, 156, 209, 265, 277, 313; described, 368; Iroquois hostilities on, 102, 106, 111, 117, 146, 246; fur trade fleet, 250; on map, 53.
Ouachala, Fox chief, 302, 318.
Ouestatimong, Fox village, 127.
Ouiatanon Indians, habitat, 205, 409; intertribal relations, 325; Mascouten join, 339; post among, 334; English alliance, 418; on war party, 425.
Ouisconsin, French form of Wisconsin, 195.
Outagami Indians. See Fox Indians.
Outagamie County, Indians in, 127.
Ozark Mountains, on map, 28.

PACIFIC Ocean, discovered, 2; sought, 48-49, 209, 224; first overland trip to, 209.
Pack horses, in fur trade, 411.
Paltsits, Victor H., aid acknowledged, 1.
Pamlico Sound, coasted, 11.
Panama Isthmus, crossed, 5.
Paouitagouing Indians. See Chippewa.
Papal bull of 1493, 2.
Paris, colonial archives at, 372.
Paris, treaty of, terms, 439-440.
Parkman, Francis, sources used, 281; *Count Frontenac*, 229, 235, 252, 263; *Half-Century of Conflict*, 351; *La Salle and the Great West*, 219; *Old Régime*, 114; *Pioneers of France*, 33; Map No. 4, 150.
Parkman Club Papers, 108, 148, 232.
Patrick papers, cited, 164.

Patron, Jacques, Montreal merchant, 208.
Pauquette, Pierre, at Portage, 401.
Pawnee Indians, slaves captured among, 393.
Pekitanoui River, name for Missouri River, 196.
Pelée Island, in the Mississippi, 99; post on, 252.
Pemoussa, Fox hostage, 288.
Penetanguishene Bay, mission in, 92, 93.
Penicaut, ——, narrative, 360.
Pennsylvania, traders from, 408-422; frontiers raided, 428.
Penobscot River, Champlain on, 49.
Pensaukee River, village on, 164; missionary, 165.
Peoria Indians, Jolliet meets, 196; return to Illinois, 197; attack Foxes, 326-327.
Peoria Lake, fort on, 215, 250, 270; Indian village, 304; officers at, 322.
Pepin brothers, with Duluth, 209.
Pepin County, fort in, 232; a French name, 441.
Pepin Lake, origin of name, 209; French posts on, 172, 232, 240, 293, 311-312, 321, 335, 380, 429; map of portion, 242.
Peré, Jean, trader, 121; explores route, 131; in Lake Superior, 132, 155, 226; finds copper mine, 348-349.
Père Marquette River, origin of name, 168.
Périgny, Thérèse Judith d'Ailleboust de, married, 333.
Perrot, Nicolas, Indian name for, 185, 246; first trading voyage, 120, 314; at Green Bay, 122-131, 135-136, 159, 237, 240, 246-247; at ceremony of annexation, 183-190; in fur trade, 203, 236, 250, 257; a western officer, 222, 225, 227; commission, 231; at Trempealeau, 231-232; at Fort St. Antoine, 172, 189, 232-233, 251, 308; leads Indians to war, 229, 234, 235; summoned to Montreal, 244; returns West, 246; on upper Mississippi, 172, 189, 231-234, 241-242, 248; at lead mines, 248, 359-361; presents ostensorium, 171, 232-233; furs burned, 236; takes possession, 241-242; acts as interpreter, 181, 400; Indian policy, 253, 275; departs from West, 260, 273; characterized, 122, 221, 441; writes memoir, 95, 285, 286; journals, 124; cited, 253; signature, 124; map

INDEX 467

of post, 242; Trempealeau post pictured, 328. See also Blair, E. H.
Perrot State Park, at Trempealeau, 232.
Peter Martyr, *De Orbe Novo*, 40.
Petun Huron Indians, habitat, 56, 70; missions for, 87; attacked by Iroquois, 92-93; flee West, 93, 95; chief's title, 149. See also Hurons of West.
Philadelphia (Pa.), traders from, 413.
Philip III, of Spain, 51.
Philippine Islands, discovered, 9.
Piankeshaw Indians, on the Wabash, 409; English alliance, 418.
Piasa monsters, paintings of, 196.
Pickawillany, built, 413; Céloron visits, 416; enlarges, 417, 418; English visit, 418; French attack, 419; capture, 420-423, 438.
Pierce, Mrs. H. M., artist, 328, 329.
Pierson, Philippe, Jesuit missionary, 164; goes to Sioux, 172, 225.
Pigafetta, Antonio, visits French court, 9, 10.
Pijart, Pierre, Jesuit missionary, 87.
Pike River, Marquette at, 167.
Pineda, Alonzo de, explorations, 5, 7, 24-25.
Pinneshon, ——, at Portage, 387.
Piqua (O.), site, 413.
Pistakee River. See Fox River of Illinois.
Pittsburgh, French officers near, 324; French post at, 424. See also Fort Duquesne and Fort Pitt.
Plains of Abraham, battle on, 404, 435.
Plancius, Petrus, *Orbis Terrarum*, 42.
Platte River, a French name, 441.
Plymouth (Mass.), harbor, 49.
Plymouth Company, colonizes, 43.
Pointe aux Trembles (Canada), resident, 136.
Ponce de Leon, Juan, explorations, 5, 7.
Poncet, Antoine, Jesuit missionary, 105.
Pontgravé, François de, in North America, 46-50, 62.
Pontiac, precursor, 316; at Braddock's defeat, 425.
Porcupine, Fox chief. See Noro.
Porlier, Jacques, tutor, 396; characterized, 397.
Porlier, Marguerite, in Canada, 397.
Porlier family, as interpreters, 401.
Portage, Jolliet and Marquette at, 194; Perrot, 248; Indian attack at, 356; route via, 362; described, 311; first settlers at, 387, 401.

Portage County, a French name, 441.
Portage Lake, on Keweenaw Point, 148.
Porter, Peter A., opinions cited, 200.
Porteret, Pierre, accompanies Marquette, 167-168; at the Sault, 188; on Mississippi expedition, 193.
Portsmouth (O.), site, 415.
Portuguese, early discoveries, 2, 3, 6, 14; reports, 10; maps, 20, 23; mining experts, 362.
Possession, acts of taking, 16, 19, 58, 183-190, 210, 220, 241-242, 415.
Post, Christian F., journals, 433.
Potawatomi Indians, meaning of name, 57, 69; intertribal relations, 310; migrations, 70, 87, 94, 95, 176, 271, 339; villages, 123, 125, 135, 215, 218, 262, 344; use of canoes, 130; missions for, 133, 134, 141, 154, 159, 160, 165, 169, 171; fur trade with, 127, 129, 135-136; first visit to Montreal, 123, 126, 156; allies of French, 181, 319, 330; at Sault ceremony, 185, 186; repulse Iroquois, 96-98; on war parties, 235, 425, 431; at peace treaty, 266; chief, 268-269; revolt of, 433; characterized, 124.
Potawatomi Islands, on Green Bay, 95; *Griffon* at, 214.
Potosi, mines at, 361.
Poulain, Guillaume, Recollect missionary, 59.
Prairie du Chien, Fox village at, 329; French fort, 232, 241, 329; settlement, 387-388, 399, 404; farming at, 389; hostilities, 402; celebration, 195.
Prairie du Sac, a French name, 441.
Prairie Island. See Pelée Island.
Prairie River, a French name, 441.
Presqu'isle. See Erie (Pa.).
Prince Society, *Publications*, 78, 104.
Puans (Puant) Indians. See Winnebago.

QUADUS, Mathias, *Novi Orbis*, 42.
Quapaw Indians, Jolliet among, 196-197.
Quebec, Indian village at, 18; climate, 49; founded, 50; Champlain at, 53, 58, 60, 63, 66, 101; Nicolet, 82; mission village near, 92; mission headquarters, 139, 155, 162; governor at, 198; besieged, 248-249, 434-436; relieved, 279; council at, 260; assayers in, 353, 355.

Quebec Literary and Historical Society, *Transactions*, 229.
Queen Anne's War, effect on West, 268, 279, 408; ended, 282-283.

RACINE, a French name, 441.
Racine County, a French name, 441.
Radin, Paul, "Social Organization of the Winnebago," 74; "The Winnebago Tribe," 344.
Radisson, Marguerite, married, 104.
Radisson, Pierre-Esprit, journeys dated, 104-108; itinerary, 108-111; at Three Rivers, 107, 152; mentions copper, 344; lead, 359; later career, 111-112; journals found, 104, 113; value of, 112-113; adventures, 441: cited, 442.
Rainy Lake, post on, 336.
Raleigh, Sir Walter, interest in exploration, 37.
Ramesay, Claude de, governor of Montreal, 283.
Ramusio, Giovanni B., *Delle Navigationi et Viaggi*, 16, 35.
Randin, Hugues, visits Lake Superior, 201-202, 208, 209; map, 201.
Ranjel, Rodrigo, De Soto's secretary, 27.
Raudin. See Randin.
Raymbault, Charles, Jesuit missionary, 89.
Reaume, Charles, Green Bay judge, 398-399.
Reaume, Pierre, interpreter, 400.
Reaume, Susanne, married, 400.
Recollects, as missionaries, 54; among the Hurons, 59-60; retire from Canada, 86; with La Salle, 210-215, 218; at Detroit, 272; as chaplain, 319.
Red Banks, Winnebago habitat, 81.
Renards Indians. See Fox Indians.
Renault, Philippe François, miner, 361; surrenders monopoly, 362.
Repentigny, Lieut. —— de, killed at La Baye, 424.
Repentigny, Louis le Gardeur de, at Sault Ste. Marie, 424, 429; in French and Indian War, 434.
Repentigny, Pierre Jean le Gardeur de, at Presqu'isle, 424.
Repentigny, seigniory of, 300.
Ribero, Diego, map, 7-8.
Richelieu, Cardinal, plans for New France, 60-61, 90; letter to, 82, 85.
Richelieu River, discovered, 50.
Richer, Jean, interpreter, 115.

Rigaud, François Arnaud, marquis de grant of La Baye, 382-383, 431.
Robertson, James A., *Magellan's Voyage*, 9.
Roberval, Jean F. de la Rocque de, explorer, 20-23.
Rocheblave, Philippe de, at Braddock's defeat, 426.
Rocheblave, Pierre de, captured by Clark, 426.
Rochemonteix, Camille de, *Les Jesuits et La Nouvelle France*, 199.
Rocher. See Le Rocher.
Rock River, Indians of, 72-73, 339; early name for, 321; post on, 340; mines near, 362; mouth, 372; officers winter at, 437-438.
Rocky Mountains, French reach, 33.
Rogers, Robert, Langlade defeats, 431; Detroit surrenders to, 438.
Root River, Marquette at, 167; portage route, 262.
Rosaccio, Giuseppe, *Il Monde*, 40.
Roseboom, Capt. Johannes, trades to West, 230-231, 234; arrested, 235, 254.
Roseboom, John, *Genealogy*, 231.
Royal Mount, at Montreal, 18, 21, 47.
Royal Society of London, owns manuscript, 278.
Royale Isle, copper mines on, 60, 343, 347, 348, 350.
Ruysch, Johann, map, 8.
Ryswick, treaty of, 363.

SABLE Ottawa Indians, at peace treaty, 265.
Sabrevois, Jacques, commands at Detroit, 282.
Sacquepée, Joachim, fur trader, 374.
Sagard-Théodat, Gabriel, Recollect missionary, 59, 60; works cited, 59, 63, 68, 75, 346.
Saginaw Bay, Indians on, 57, 70.
Saguenay, supposed island of, 19, 20, 23; copper in, 346; sea of, 37.
Saguenay River, sources, 19, 23, 97; mission on, 141, 347.
St. Ange, Pierre, murdered, 338.
St. Ange, Robert Jean Groston de, commandant at Illinois, 326-327.
Ste. Anne River. See Iron River.
St. Augustine (Fla.), founded, 33; sacked, 39.
St. Charles River, Cartier on, 19.
St. Clair Lake, first voyage on, 134.

INDEX 469

St. Clair River, French post on, 231, 235, 236, 238.
St. Cosme, Jean François Buisson de, missionary, 261; voyage, 261-262.
St. Croix County, a French name, 441.
St. Croix Falls, a French name, 441.
St. Croix River, on portage route, 212; post on, 225, 252; taken possession of, 242.
St. Esprit Bay. See Chequamegon Bay.
St. Esprit mission, location, 90; Marquette at, 158.
Ste. Foy, battle of, 435.
St. François Xavier mission, founded, 159; transferred, 163; permanent site, 163; progress of, 163-167, 170-171; chapel for, 169, 170, 171; Marquette at, 197; Hennepin, 216; Membré, 218; Tonty, 219; Lahontan, 239-240; ostensorium presented to, 232-233; burned, 236; hostilities at, 246-247; fort named for, 292; closed, 176.
St. Germain, treaty of, 62.
St. Germain-en-Laye, Duluth's birthplace, 208.
St. Ignace mission, at Mackinac, 163, 164, 165, 168, 171, 172; expedition outfitted at, 191, 193, 200; Duluth at, 216, 218, 226; declines, 176. See also Mackinac.
St. Ignace Point, Nicolet passes, 80; mission at, 163, 171; post at, 249.
St. Jacques mission, on upper Fox River, 161, 166, 171.
St. John's River, in Florida, 33.
St. Joseph County (Ind.), portage in, 215.
St. Joseph mission, site, 168, 169; progress, 171, 172.
St. Joseph River, Indians on, 204, 271; mission, 168; La Salle visits, 215; raid on, 228; post, 250, 292; portage route, 277, 292, 340, 409; Indians summoned from, 279, 306. See also Fort St. Joseph.
St. Julien, French vessel, 45.
St. Lawrence Gulf, explored, 16, 17, 34; on maps, 23, 35, 36.
St. Lawrence River, in glacial period, 32; sources, 40-41, 47-49, 55, 65, 83; rapids in, 368; island, 201; origin of name, 17, 34; discovered, 17-18, 346; explored, 21-22, 34, 38, 52, 60; Indians on, 52, 55-57, 93; fur trade, 103, 118, 155, 250-251; colonized, 50, 63, 144; voyages on, 182, 414; English, 279.

St. Louis (Mo.), French at, 402, 404.
St. Luc, La Corne de, lessee of La Pointe, 384.
St. Lusson, François Daumont de, pageant of, 183-190, 349; sketch, 183.
St. Malo, French port, 16, 17, 20, 22, 38; letter from, 40.
St. Marc, mission for Foxes, 141, 160.
Ste. Marie, in Huronia, 91, 92. See also Sault Ste. Marie.
St. Mary's College, at Montreal, 309.
St. Maurice River, route via, 97.
St. Michel mission, named, 96, 141.
St. Michel Archange, Menominee mission, 161.
St. Michel Archange, Sioux mission, 172.
St. Michel Island. See Madeline Island.
St. Pé, Jean Baptiste, Jesuit missionary, 306.
St. Pierre, Jacques le Gardeur de, at La Pointe, 300-301; on upper Mississippi, 335; abandons post, 337; partner of La Ronde, 352; receives Washington, 381, 424; killed, 434; sketch, 301.
St. Pierre, Paul le Gardeur de, at La Pointe, 300-301, 352; death, 301.
St. Pierre River, named, 251. See also Minnesota River.
St. Sulpice Library, in Paris, 199.
Ste. Thérèse Bay. See Keweenaw.
San Domingo, early name for, 1; Spanish territory, 5.
Sandusky, Indians at, 412; French post, 417.
San Miguel, Spanish colony, 5.
Sanson d'Abbeville, Nicolas, map, 92, 134; reproduction of, 92.
Saskatchewan River, French post on, 424.
Sastaretsy, title of Huron chief, 149.
Sauk Indians, early habitat, 57, 69-70, 95; refugees in Wisconsin, 94, 99, 124; intertribal relations, 127, 282, 306, 310; mission for, 154, 159, 165, 166, 172; at Sault ceremony, 185, 186; on war party, 229; at peace treaty, 266, 308; remove to Detroit, 276; return to Green Bay, 297, 320, 331-332; villages, 319, 331-332; kill Villiers, 332; unite with Foxes, 332-333; fur trade with, 377; grant land at Green Bay, 438; characterized, 125.
Sauk and Fox Indians, fort, 333, 334; mercy for, 338-339.
Sault au Recollect, origin of name, 59.

470   THE FRENCH RÉGIME

Sault de Gaston, early name for Sault Ste. Marie, 59, 60, 62.
Sault St. Louis, at Montreal, 197-198; Mission Indians at, 266.
Sault Ste. Marie, named, 60, 89; Indians at, 68-69, 70, 87, 95, 98, 299, 345, 356; Indian battle at, 117; first visit to, 88-89; Radisson at, 109, 111; Jolliet, 131, 197; Duluth, 209, 226; mission at, 131, 134-135, 153, 156-158, 170, 252; described, 161-162; burned, 165, 198; traders at, 136; ceremony of taking possession, 184-190, 241; reoccupied, 313, 379; post at, 379, 418, 424, 429; shipyard at, 352; miners, 353-354; story of, 157.
Saulteur Indians. See Chippewa Indians.
Schaefer, Rev. Francis, "Fort St. Charles," 337.
Schafer, Joseph, *History of the Pacific Northwest*, 15.
Schenectady (N. Y.), in colonial wars, 296.
Schliemann, Heinrich, archeologist, 341.
Schoolcraft, Henry R., *Indian Tribes*, 74.
Scioto River, Indian village on, 413, 415; republic of, 416.
Scotch-Irish, as traders, 410-411, 414.
Scull, Gideon D., *Voyages of Peter Esprit Radisson*, 104, 106, 114.
Seigneley, Jean Baptiste Colbert de, minister, 241.
Seminary missions, in the West, 261-262.
Senat, Antoine, murdered, 338.
Seneca Indians, habitat, 56; territory invaded, 234-236; abandon home, 249; at peace treaty, 266; relations with Foxes, 324-325.
Seneffe, battle of, 208, 212.
Senex, John, maps, 278.
Severance, Frank H., *An Old Frontier of France*, 307.
Shakespere, William, mentions map, 41; works found among Indians, 428.
Shawano Lake, route via, 127.
Shawnee Indians, early habitat, 70; visit Marquette, 157; in La Salle's colony, 219, 255; on war party, 235; migrations, 255-256, 409-410; village, 413; at Pickawillany, 421; French allies, 423; English, 433.
Shea, John G., editor, 60, 122; *Discovery and Exploration*, 200; *Early Voyages up and down the Mississippi*, 309.

Sheboygan, fur trade post at, 405.
Ships. See French ships.
Shore's Landing, on Chequamegon Bay, 109.
Sills Creek, Indian village near, 287.
Silver, mining for, 361.
Silvy, Antoine, Jesuit missionary, 168, 170-171.
Simancas archives, map from, 51; reproduced, 52.
Simcoe County (Ontario), Indians in, 52.
Simcoe Lake, location, 56; on portage route, 131.
Sinago Indians, join the Ottawa, 69; at peace treaty, 265.
Siouan linguistic stock, 100; tribes of, 72, 99; migrations, 72-73, 344.
Sioux Indians, first mention of, 89; intertribal relations, 99, 116, 160, 163, 185, 210, 211, 233, 252, 262, 267, 275, 284, 299, 308, 316, 321, 356, 376; Radisson among, 110, 113, 344; Perrot, 122, 232, 240-242, 248; Duluth, 209-213, 225, 237; missions for, 154, 158, 172, 176; country annexed, 189, 241-242, 251; fur trade with, 248, 251, 312, 335-336, 377; French alliance with, 252, 275, 317, 322, 333, 335, 336, 340; posts among, 232, 252, 308-312, 321, 323, 328, 379, 400; company for trade, 315, 328, 374; Charlevoix meets, 296-298; massacre French, 337, 417; driven out by Chippewa, 356-357.
Sisseton Sioux Indians, habitat, 211.
Sixte le Tac, *Histoire*, 58.
Skinner, Alanson, *Culture of Menomini*, 71; *The Mascoutens*, 69.
Slavery, among Indians, 327, 331; among Canadian-French, 392-393.
Smallpox, among the Indians, 162; in Canada, 211, 288; at Fort William Henry, 432, 433; carried to Mackinac, 432.
Smith, William R., *History of Wisconsin*, 281, 360.
Smithsonian Institution, Lake Superior copper in, 353.
Société des Missions Etrangères, in the West, 261-262.
Sonontouan Indians, French name for Seneca, 266.
Soto, Hernando de, explorations, 26-29, 72.
Souligny, Pierre le Duc, at Braddock's defeat, 426.

INDEX   471

South America, on early maps, 1, 2; outlined, 15; Jesuits in, 143, 175, 176; mines in, 346.
South Bend (Ind.), portage near, 215.
South Carolina, fur traders in, 256, 284, 338, 408.
South Dakota, first white man, 104, 211.
South Dakota Historical Collections, 211.
South Sea, interpretation of term, 158. See also Pacific Ocean.
Southwestern Historical Quarterly, 26.
Spanish, explore America, 2-8, 14, 15, 24-30, 346; colonization, 33, 45; international relations with, 20, 39, 45, 51, 197; trade with, 256; in French and Indian War, 439; cede Florida, 440; early maps, 23, 28.
Stadacona, Indian village, 18, 20, 21, 55.
Starved Rock. See La Rocher.
Stevenson, E. L., *Maps Illustrating Early Discovery*, etc., 3, 5, 7-9, 12, 13, 23.
Steward, J. F., *Lost Maramech and Earliest Chicago*, 248.
Stickney, Gardner P., "Nicolas Perrot," 232.
Sturgeon Bay, portage, 167; Tonty at, 218.
Suamico, Indian village at, 164.
Sugar. See Maple sugar.
Sulpitian missionaries, servants, 122-123; mission party, 133-134, 136, 159, 161, 206.
Sulte, Benjamin, opinions cited, 78, 108, 109; *Histoire des Canadiens Français*, 56; "La Baye Verte et le Lac Superieur en 1665," 122; "Le Régiment de Carignan," 119; "Les Français dans l'Ouest en 1671," 183, 188; "Pierre Boucher et Son Livre," 118; "Valley of the Ottawa," 52.
Superior, site, 110; a French name, 441.
Superior Lake, copper in, 19, 74, 117-118, 131, 155, 183, 189, 341-358; route to, 131, 299; first heard of, 52, 59, 89, 91; explored, 57, 59-60; Indians in, 71, 73, 120, 279; missions, 90, 147-150; Nicolet sees, 79, 88; Radisson on, 109-112, 344; traders, 114-118, 120, 121, 123; Randin visits, 201-202, 208-209; Duluth, 209, 211, 225, 226, 237, 238, 244; Le Sueur, 251, 252, 299; taken possession of, 188; voyages on, 96, 153, 284, 292; French posts, 237, 297-298, 312-314, 336, 379, 434; shipping on, 352-354; maps of, 62, 92, 114, 154, 163, 336, 349; "Report on Geology of," 343; ideal statue of, 31, 32.
Susquehanna River, discovered, 58; Indians on, 409.
Sweden, subsidized by France, 179.

TADOUAC Lake, on early map, 41, 43.
Tadoussac, fur trade mart, 46, 47, 101, 113, 114; cold at, 49; English fleet, 62; mission at, 170.
Taft, Lorado, sculptor, 31.
Tailhan, Jules, edits Perrot's memoir, 123, 286.
Talon, Jean, intendant, 121; interest in exploration, 131, 181-183, 189-190, 191, 348; recalled, 349; report, 186; orders, 202; successor, 204.
Tampa Bay, Spanish explorers on, 25, 27.
Tank cottage, at Green Bay, 391-392; pictured, 392.
Taylor, F. B., cited, 32.
Taylor County, streams in, 150.
Tecle, Corneille, Lake Superior trader, 121-122.
Tecumseh, precursor, 316.
Temiscaming Indians, at peace treaty, 266.
Tennessee, Indians of, 70.
Tennessee River, route via, 256.
Têtes Plats Indians, in the South, 408.
Tetinchoua, Miami chief, 185.
Teton Sioux Indians, habitat, 211.
Texas, missions in, 143; La Salle's death in, 224, 256.
Thévenot, Melchisédech, *Recueil de Voyages*, 200.
Thevet, André, cited, 42.
Thomas, Cyrus, "Primary Indian Migrations," 73.
Thorne, Robert, early map, 7.
Three Mountains, mission colony at, 266.
Three Rivers (Canada), built, 101; fur trade at, 52, 97, 113, 290; Nicolet at, 76-77, 82, 83; Groseilliers, 107, 112; residents, 115, 152, 156, 336.
Thwaites, Reuben G., opinions, 361; *Early Western Travels*, 411, 428, 433; *Father Marquette*, 158; *Hennepin's New Discovery*, 205; *Jesuit Relations*, described, 140; cited, 52, 67, 68, 79, 81, 86-92, 95, 97, 103, 105-107, 109, 114, 116, 117, 120, 122, 126, 128, 130, 141, 146-149, 152-155, 158, 161-171, 181, 182, 184, 186, 189, 198-200, 205,

219, 223, 224, 245, 259, 335, 347, 348, 416; *Lahontan's New Voyages*, 226, 229, 236, 239, 240, 349; "Story of Mackinac," 163; *Wisconsin*, 148, 386.
Tinawatawa, Iroquois village, 133.
Tionnotates Indians. See Petun Hurons.
Tomah, a French name, 441.
Tonquin, destroyed, 214.
Tonty, Alphonse de, at Mackinac, 260; cession for, 261; at Detroit, 270, 295.
Tonty, Henry de, La Salle's lieutenant, 214, 215, 219, 230, 231, 256; in Illinois, 217; retreats through Wisconsin, 217-218; descent of Mississippi, 220, 223, 230, 256; leads war party, 235, 250; defends Illinois, 223-224, 228, 249; finds mines, 359; Indian policy, 221-222, 224, 255; retains concession, 260; cedes seigniory, 261; later life, 261, 270; relatives, 214, 218, 224; men, 256; death, 277; narrative, 214, 228; characterized, 216, 221, 441; signature, 214.
Tonty, Joseph. See Desliettes.
Toronto, portage route, 231, 368; La Ronde uses, 355; fort on, 379.
Tracy, Alexandre Prouville, marquis de, governor of New France, 119, 121.
Trempealeau, a French name, 441; Perrot's post at, 231-232; Linctot's, 328-329, 335, 400; picture of, 328.
Trempealeau County, a French name, 441.
Tremper Mound, in Ohio, 341.
Trent River, portage via, 55; on map, 51.
Trottier, Antoine, Lake Superior trader, 115-118.
Turenne, Henri, marshal de, French general, 215.
Tuscarora Indians, band, 196.
Twigtwee Indians, English name for Miami, 413.

ULPIUS Globe, described, 13.
United States Bureau of Ethnology, *Reports*, 23, 29, 69, 72, 344.
United States Executive Documents, 343.
United States Geological Survey, *Monograph*, 32.
United States Senate Documents, 358.
University of Michigan, library at, 349.
Upham, Warren, cited, 108.
Urbana (Ill.), manuscripts at, 362.

Utica (Ill.), fort near, 223.
Utrecht, treaty of, 282, 290.

VALLARD, Nicolas, map, 23.
Vaudreuil, Philippe de Rigaud, marquis de, governor of New France, 279, 282, 305; mining interests, 350-351; rebuke for, 307; letter to, 306; quoted, 301-302; death, 307; successor, 317; sons, 320, 382.
Vaudreuil, Pierre Rigaud de, governor of Louisiana, 372, 382; governor of New France, 373, 431-433; appointees, 382; report, 372, 432; last stand, 436.
Vaugondy, Robert de, map, 372.
Vera Cruz (Mexico), battle of, 39.
Verchères, Jean Jarret de, commandant at La Baye, 378-379.
Verchères, Madeleine de, heroine, 378.
Vérendrye family. See La Vérendrye.
Vermillion River, tributary to Wabash, 372.
Verrazano, Gerolamo, map, 12-13; ship from, 20.
Verrazano, Giovanni, discoveries, 9-14; manuscript, 10, 13-14, 35.
Verrazano's Sea, on maps, 11-13.
Vervins, treaty of, 45.
Vesconte de Maggiolo, map, 12.
Viel, Nicolas, Recollect missionary, 59, 60.
Viele, Arent, Dutch interpreter, 255.
Vieux Desert Lac, on early maps, 275; a French name, 441.
Vignau, Nicolas, French interpreter, 52-53.
Villabon, Charles René Desjordy de, commandant at La Baye, 381.
Villeneuve, Daniel, widow, 316; son, 400.
Villeraye, —— de, messenger, 219.
Villiers, Louis Coulon de, wounded, 332; at Fort Duquesne, 425; death, 434.
Villiers, Nicolas Antoine Coulon de, defeats Foxes, 325-327, 329; at La Baye, 328, 330-331; killed, 332, 425.
Villiers, Nicolas Coulon de Jr., messenger, 327; attacks Fox and Sauk Indians, 332.
Vimont, Barthelmy, Jesuit superior, 67, 82.
Vincennes, François de, attacks Foxes, 326-327; murdered, 338, 340.
Vincennes, Jean Baptiste Bissot de, among Miami, 283; death, 292.
Vincennes (Ind.), part of Louisiana,

313, 372; commandants, 326, 338; revolt at, 419.
Virginia, coast explored, 11; Marquette's letter reaches, 196; fur traders from, 407-408, 410; Indian treaty for, 411; land agent, 417; messenger, 424; advance to West, 425; frontiers raided, 428-430.
Volwiler, Albert T., *George Croghan and the Westward Movement*, 411.

WABASH River, Indians on, 70, 271, 325, 409-410, 418; route via, 284, 340; Indian fort near, 326; posts on, 338, 339, 372; boundary touches, 372, 409.
Wahpeton Sioux, habitat, 211.
Waldseemüller, Martin, maps, 3-6, 10.
Wapsipinicon River, in Iowa, 321; Indian fort on, 333, 334.
Warren, William W., historian, 299.
Warren (Pa.), site, 415.
Washington, Major George, meets French officers, 301, 381, 424; causes death of Jumonville, 425; at Braddock's defeat, 427; defends frontier, 428-429.
Washington Island, Indians on, 95, 125.
Waupaca County, Indians in, 127.
Weimar map, of 1527, 7.
Weiser, Conrad, Pennsylvania interpreter, 410-411, 413.
West, map 1650-1700, 266; map 1700-1760, 364.
West, Post of the Sea of the, location, 313; importance, 381; farthest reach, 424; abandoned, 434.
West Indies, discovered, 1; Spanish territory, 5; raided, 39; Champlain visits, 45; route to, 191; Indian prisoners in, 331; exchanged for Canada, 439.
Westover (Ontario), Indian village near, 133.
Wild rice, habitat, 71, 160, 194; used as food, 74; methods of harvesting, 112.
William III, comes to English throne, 243-244; recognized, 263.
Winnebago County Historical Society, activities, 160.
Winnebago (Puant) Indians, names, 75-76; origins, 71-73, 91, 95, 314; traditions, 324; build mounds, 73-74; customs, 74-75; use of copper, 344; villages, 124-125, 160, 309-310, 319, 339; intertribal relations, 75, 76, 88, 94, 100, 282, 306, 310, 337; Nicolet visits, 79-83, 94-95; mission for, 90, 165, 172; at Sault ceremony, 185, 186; French allies, 247, 253, 297, 322, 340; fur trade with, 377; on war parties, 229, 235, 323, 425-426, 429; at peace treaty, 266, 308; war of 1827 with, 402; marry whites, 357, 402, 435; family of chiefs, 435; village pictured, 74.
Winnebago Lake, missionaries on, 160; taken possession of, 242; village on, 310, 319; on map, 314.
Winnipeg Lake, French fort on, 337.
Winship, G. P., *Journey of Coronado*, cited, 29; *Sailors' Narratives*, 39, 49.
Winsor, Justin, opinion, 35; *Cartier to Frontenac*, 53; *Narrative and Critical History of America*, 5, 14, 24, 92, 199.
Wisconsin Archeological Society, surveys, 74.
Wisconsin Archeologist, 60, 74, 125, 127, 287, 341, 343, 359.
Wisconsin Club Woman, 227, 240, 287.
Wisconsin Historical Collections, 68, 73-76, 78, 81, 88, 124, 126, 135, 148, 153, 161-165, 171, 172, 186, 189, 205, 213, 219, 225-228, 231-233, 245-248, 253, 254, 265, 269, 271, 273-276, 281, 283-285, 288-293, 296-298, 300-306, 308-316, 318, 320, 322-333, 335-341, 344, 348, 350-355, 357-363, 368-370, 372, 373-378, 381-384, 387, 389-391, 393, 395, 398-400, 408, 412-417, 419, 421, 422, 424, 426, 428, 430, 432, 433, 435, 436, 438, 439.
Wisconsin Historical Library, maps, 4, 23, 92, 278; atlas, 36; manuscripts, 147, 151, 164, 167, 169, 368, 383, 402.
Wisconsin Historical Museum, relic in, 171; copper artifacts, 341.
Wisconsin Historical Society, *Proceedings*, 87, 125, 127-129, 154, 159, 163, 193, 194, 200, 205, 232, 281, 282, 287, 310, 317, 324, 329, 391, 392, 400.
Wisconsin Journal of Education, 341.
Wisconsin Magazine of History, 108, 148-150, 195, 218, 232.
Wisconsin River, origin of name, 195; mines on, 194, 359, 360; Jolliet on, 194-195; Duluth, 212-213; described, 240, 311, 321; fort at mouth, 213, 232, 241; taken possession of, 242; Indian villages on, 329; settlers, 387, 404; traders on headwaters, 384; a part of Canada, 303-304, 372.
Wolf River, Indians on, 99; Fox village

127, 160, 164, 320; abandoned, 205, 287.
Wolfe, Gen. James, at siege of Quebec, 435.
Wood, Col. Abraham, Virginia trader, 407-408.
Woods, Lake of the, fort on, 336; massacre, 337.
Wright, Edward, map, 41; reproduced, 42.

Wyandot Indians, origin of, 56, 272. See also Hurons of West.
Wytfliet, Cornelius, *Descriptiones*, 42.

YELLOW River (Chippewa tributary), voyage on, 150.
Yellow River (St. Croix tributary), fur trade on, 369.

ZALTERIUS, Bolognino, map, 29, 35.
Zipancri. See Japan.

www.ingramcontent.com/pod-product-compliance
Lightning Source LLC
Chambersburg PA
CBHW051331230426
43668CB00010B/1229